ADVANCED DIVING

TECHNOLOG... ...UES

John N. He...

NAUI ®

National Association of Underwater Instructors

Mosby Lifeline
Dedicated to Publishing Excellence

A Times Mirror
Company

Publisher: David T. Culverwell
Editor-in-Chief: Richard A. Weimer
Editor: Eric Duchinsky
Senior Developmental Editor: Cecilia F. Reilly
Developmental Editor: Julie Bauer
Assistant Editor: Carla Goldberg
Project Manager: Chris Baumle
Senior Production Editor: Shannon Canty
Electronic Publishing: Peggy Hill, Chris Robinson, Terri Schwaegel
Manufacturing Supervisor: Theresa Fuchs
Design Manager: Nancy McDonald
Cover Design/Interior Openers: Sheriff-Krebs Design

3rd edition

Printed in the United States of America

Composition by: Mosby Electronic Production
Printing/Binding by: W.C. Brown

Mosby-Year Book, Inc.
11830 Westline Industrial Drive
St. Louis, MO 63146

International Standard Book Number 0815162863
95 96 97 98 99/9 8 7 6 5 4 3 2 1

CHAPTER ONE

ADVANCED DIVING

TECHNOLOGY AND TECHNIQUES

The diving environment is defined as the physical, chemical, and biological aspects of the underwater environment in which we dive. The purpose of this section is to increase your knowledge and understanding of the diving environments that you enjoy. As a diver, you must know how to move in and under the water in such a way that you can protect both yourself and the life forms you encounter.

THE DIVING ENVIRONMENT

INTRODUCTION

Advanced Diving: Technology and Techniques is divided into two primary sections. The first section is Advanced Diving Science and Technology, which consists of chapters designed to increase your knowledge of the technical aspects of scuba diving. The second section is Advanced Diving Techniques, which is designed to preview the possible skill areas that may be introduced during the NAUI Advanced Diver Course. Specific learning objectives are stated at the beginning of each chapter. Review these carefully before and after studying each chapter to make sure you meet the educational goals.

If this course is being used as part of a course of instruction, your instructor may schedule the course in any sequence desired as long as the curriculum requirements are met. The chapters in this book should be read in the order assigned by your instructor, not necessarily sequentially. You may not be assigned to read some sections at all, but you are encouraged to read the entire book at your leisure in order to learn as much as you can about the varied aspects of diving.

This book is not intended to teach you advanced diving activities without the guidance and supervision of a qualified NAUI Instructor. Local knowledge, techniques, and regulations for all areas cannot possibly be incorporated into this text. This publication provides only part of your education for advanced diving. The bulk of what you will learn will be provided by the instructor. Do not attempt to participate in any of the activities described in this book without the supervision of a qualified instructor.

Thus far in your diving education you have learned the fundamentals of diving. You know what you should and should not do and you understand some basic theory. You are qualified to dive only under conditions similar to those in which you have received training. The purpose of this book, when used as part of a course instruction, is to increase your understanding of why certain things are done or not done in diving and to expand your skills and qualifications. Upon successful completion of this course you will be qualified to handle new diving circumstances and engage in additional diving activities.

ABOUT THE NAUI ADVANCED COURSE

The NAUI Advanced Scuba Diver course is an intensive program consisting of 16 hours of academic sessions plus the application of the knowledge acquired via a schedule of at least eight open water dives. The knowledge you acquire will help make those experiences safe and enjoyable. A maximum of three dives per day may be credited toward the certification requirements. Open water training activities may include:

- *Skin diving*
- *Basic skills review*
- *Dive rescue techniques*
- *Environmental study or survey*
- *Underwater navigation**
- *Limited visibility or night diving**
- *Search and recovery**
- *Light salvage**
- *Deep/simulated decompression diving**
- *Boat diving*

* Required activities for the NAUI Advanced course

The information presented in the academic sessions of your course will increase your knowledge in the topic areas of equipment, environment, physics, physiology, and decompression.

The skills you will develop during the open water training dives in this course will increase your abilities and confidence as a diver. The dives are also orientations to different special interest areas of diving and will help you decide which specialty subject is of the greatest interest to you. In addition, the training dives will introduce you to new diving locations and environments.

Prerequisites for the NAUI Advanced course include a minimum age of 15 and either NAUI Openwater II certification or equivalent training or experience. You are usually expected to provide your own equipment for the course. This includes full open water scuba gear with instrumentation, an alternate air source, and two dive lights — a primary light and a backup light.

To qualify for certification, you will need to attend all academic sessions, demonstrate the ability to safely participate in all open water training activities, and demonstrate comprehension and retention of the material presented by scoring at least 75% on a comprehensive written examination.

Responsibilities

Both you and your instructor have certain responsibilities during the Advanced Scuba Diver course. Your instructor must determine that you have the necessary background and experience to safely participate in the activities of the course, provide an academic session plus an on-site briefing for each activity, ensure that you are properly equipped for the training dives, and oversee your diving activities.

Since you are already certified to dive with a buddy, you will be responsible for your own safety and for the safety of your assigned dive buddy. It is not the responsibility of your NAUI instructor to accompany you during the dives, although he or she must be present at the dive site, in control of the activities, and ready to lend assistance if needed. You will be instructed what to do, how to do it, and how to avoid potential hazards. It will then be your responsibility to follow the instructions given. You will learn by doing controlled activities at sites selected to safely introduce you to each interest area.

Getting the Most From the Course

To learn as much as possible and to become the best diver you can become, the following actions are recommended:

① *Read and study each assigned section prior to the academic session on the subject matter.*

② *Keep the learning objectives in mind as you study the chapters, then review them after completing the chapter to be sure you have acquired the knowledge.*

③ *As you study the chapters, keep notes on areas that are unclear to you, so you can obtain clarification from the instructor during the academic sessions.*

④ *Become familiar with the terms identified in bold letters. When a term is presented a second time in normal text, refresh your memory of its meaning if it unclear to you. The terms are defined in the glossary if you are unable to locate them quickly in one of the sections.*

⑤ *Obtain a notebook and take it with you to every session, including the open water dives. Take notes on all presentations. Save the notebook for future reference. This notebook will be especially useful if you decide to pursue leadership training.*

⑥ *Log your dives in detail.*

We commend you on your decision to become a NAUI Advanced Scuba Diver. You must do more to require this rating than to obtain an Advanced Diver rating with other diver training organizations, but we feel you will agree that it is worth it! A NAUI Advanced Diver is knowledgeable, skilled, and respected. You will know more, be able to do more, and feel more comfortable and confident as a diver when you have successfully completed this program. You will have met one of the highest standards of diver education.

WARNING

Scuba diving is an adventure activity with inherent risks of serious personal injury or death. Good training and good equipment can minimize those risks, but there are no guarantees that these risks can be completely eliminated. The code of the responsible diver states that:

You must accept responsibility for your own actions and safety during every dive.

You must dive within the limits of your ability and training.

Evaluate the conditions before every dive, assuring that they fit your personal capabilities.

Be familiar with and check all equipment before and during every dive.

Know your buddy's as well as your own ability level.

CONTRIBUTORS

Susan Bangasser
Steven Barsky
Ted Boehler
Dennis Graver
Leonard Greenstone
Tom Griffiths
Eric Hanauer
John Heine
Paul Heinmiller
John Kessler
Peter Lynch
Ella Jean Morgan
Yancy Mebane
Milledge Murphy
Erin O'Neill
John Reseck
Bob Rutledge
Pat Scharr
Bob Weathers

CREDITS

Cover Photography
Stephen Frink-Water House Stock Photography,
Tony Stone Images,
The Bettmann Archive

Interior Photography
Stephen Frink-Water House Stock Photography; pgs. 162,
164, 192, 206, 208, 220, 260.
Index Stock; pg. 96.
Telegraph Colour Library-FPG International;
pgs. 34, 36, 98.
Darryl Torckler-Tony Stone Images; pg. 270.
Norbert Wu-Tony Stone Images; pg. 272.

All other photography courtesy of Bret Gilliam-Ocean
Tech, Steven Barsky, Jeff Bozanic, Al Bruton, Lynn Hendrickson, Amos Nachom, Pete Nawrocky, Lloyd Orr, Tammy Peluso, Doug Perrine, David Sipperly.

Illustration
Ben Clemens-Millennium Design

CONTENTS

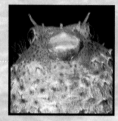

DIVING EQUIPMENT

ou are already familiar with the basic equipment used for diving. As an advanced diver, however, you need to know more about the equipment you use and equipment you might consider purchasing. You should also know about equipment such as dry suits, dive computers, and air compressors. The purpose of this chapter is to increase your knowledge and understanding of diving equipment.

LEARNING OBJECTIVES

By the end of this chapter, you will be able to:

❶ Correctly define the equipment terms presented in **bold letters** in this chapter.

❷ Briefly describe the basic types, theories of operation for, care, and maintenance of the various items of equipment discussed.

❸ Briefly describe the theory of operation for a breathing air compressor; contrast high–pressure, low–volume compressors with low–pressure, high–volume compressors; and explain how compressors are rated.

❹ List the primary components of an air station.

There are three categories of Self–Contained Underwater Breathing Apparatus (SCUBA): open–circuit demand, semiclosed–circuit, and closed–circuit. Only open–circuit demand scuba is used by recreational divers. A scuba system where the breathing gas is inhaled on demand from the breathing apparatus and exhaled directly into the water is called **open–circuit demand scuba**. Closed–circuit scuba units, often referred to as **rebreathers**, are complex systems that remove CO_2 from exhaled breathing gas and add oxygen as needed. They are unique in that they do not give off bubbles underwater. **Semiclosed scuba** recycles part of each exhaled breath while allowing some gas to escape into the water. The use of semiclosed or closed–circuit scuba equipment has in the past been used by specially trained military and scientific divers, but it also is beginning to be used by recreational divers.

SCUBA CYLINDERS

Ⓢcuba cylinders are made of either steel or aluminum, and there are different metal alloys for each type. This results in different physical dimensions, wall thicknesses, and capacities. Table 1–1 lists the specifications for the most popular sizes.

Note on the table that in most cases, the rated capacity of steel cylinders is achieved only when the cylinder is filled to 10% over its rated service pressure. For example, a 71.2 cubic–foot steel cylinder contains only 65 cubic feet at 2250 p.s.i. An increase in pressure of 225 p.s.i. (to a total of 2475 p.s.i.) results in a capacity of 71.55 cubic feet. The 10% overfill pressure was introduced during

World War II and has been in effect ever since. For a cylinder to be charged safely to 10% beyond its service pressure, it must pass a special elastic expansion test. This test is different and more complex than the standard permanent expansion test of **hydrostatic** (i.e., non–moving water) pressure testing of cylinders.

Scuba cylinders that may be safely overfilled by 10% have a + sign stamped on the cylinder following the last test date. Because overfill retesting is not commonly done, you may need to request it when having your cylinder tested. If a cylinder does not qualify for overfilling, it may still pass the permanent expansion test and can continue to be used at its rated working pressure. The elimination of overfilling ratings and their replacement with a higher working pressure is being considered by the regulating agency (Fig. 1-1).

In addition to the optional + sign, there are several codes that must be stamped onto scuba cylinders. These codes provide valuable information to those who use and service them.

DOT stands for the Department of Transportation, which specifies the regulations for all high–pressure vessels. CTC is the Canadian Transport Commission, which is the Canadian equivalent of the DOT. Some older cylinders may have the code ICC, for the Interstate Commerce Commission, which regulated cylinders before 1970.

Following the regulating agency code is the metal alloy code. 3AA or 3A stands for steel alloys, while 3AL stands for aluminum alloy. Some cylinders may have SP6498, which means special permit alloy. Others may have E6498, which stands for exemption.

Following the metal code number is an important four–digit number that is the working pressure of the cylinder. Common pressures are 1800 p.s.i., 2250 p.s.i., and 3000 p.s.i. A few cylinders are rated at over 4000 p.s.i.

On the line beneath the agency code, metal code, and working pressure is the serial number for the cylinder. You should record this in your training record so you will have the information in case your cylinder is ever stolen or lost. The cylinder manufacturer's name or code may be next to or below the serial number. This name is required on all cylinders made after 1982.

Perhaps the most important code is the test date code. This must contain the month, a special hydro facility mark, and the year of the test.

Another important aspect of scuba cylinders is buoyancy. Refer to Table 1-1, and note the change in buoyancy between full and empty cylinders of various sizes. Air weighs approxi-

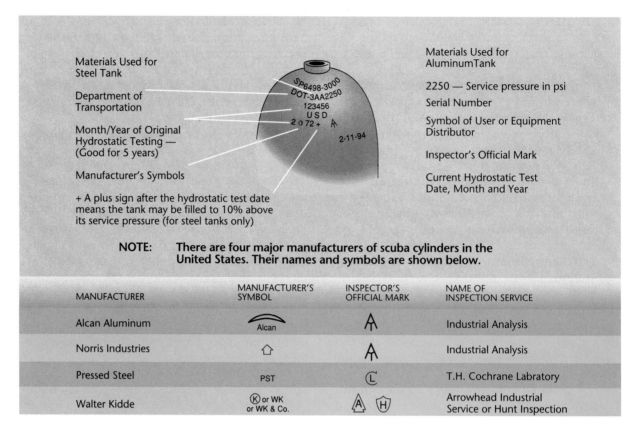

Materials Used for
Steel Tank

Department of
Transportation

Month/Year of Original
Hydrostatic Testing —
(Good for 5 years)

Manufacturer's Symbols

+ A plus sign after the hydrostatic test date
means the tank may be filled to 10% above
its service pressure (for steel tanks only)

Materials Used for
AluminumTank

2250 — Service pressure in psi

Serial Number

Symbol of User or Equipment
Distributor

Inspector's Official Mark

Current Hydrostatic Test
Date, Month and Year

NOTE: There are four major manufacturers of scuba cylinders in the
United States. Their names and symbols are shown below.

MANUFACTURER	MANUFACTURER'S SYMBOL	INSPECTOR'S OFFICIAL MARK	NAME OF INSPECTION SERVICE
Alcan Aluminum	Alcan	A̶	Industrial Analysis
Norris Industries	⌂	A̶	Industrial Analysis
Pressed Steel	PST	ⓒ	T.H. Cochrane Labratory
Walter Kidde	Ⓚ or WK or WK & Co.	A̶ Ⓗ	Arrowhead Industrial Service or Hunt Inspection

Fig. 1-1. Scuba cylinder markings.

mately 0.08 pounds per cubic foot. The weight of the varying amount of air (usually 4 to 6 pounds) combined with external cylinder volume and cylinder weight result in the buoyancy specifications. The less the change in cylinder buoyancy, the better.

Care of Scuba Cylinders

Beyond preventing physical damage to your cylinder from dropping, banging, or overheating, the most important consideration is keeping moisture from entering the cylinder. There are several ways in which moisture can enter. Water will cause corrosion by combining with the high–pressure oxygen inside the cylinder. In a steel cylinder, this corrosion is called **ferrous oxide**, or rust. In an aluminum cylinder, the corrosion is called **aluminum oxide**. Water may enter a scuba cylinder from:
• An improperly operated air compressor.
• Droplets in the cylinder valve or filler attachment during filling.
• Back flow through the regulator when the cylinder is empty.
• Changes in temperature when the cylinder is empty and the valve is left open.
• Rapid bleeding of the cylinder air.

In addition to corrosion, a serious problem can result from the prolonged storage of air in a cylinder containing water. Over time, the oxidation process will consume the oxygen in the air, leaving only nitrogen. An unsuspecting user would then lose consciousness without warning. This is one of the reasons why cylinders should be stored with only a small amount of air in them and filled before use.

To prevent moisture accumulation, always maintain a small amount (e.g., 300 p.s.i.) of air in your cylinder. If a whitish mist is detected when the valve is opened, if sloshing can be heard when the cylinder is tipped back and forth, or if the air has a damp and metallic odor, do not use the cylinder and have it inspected as soon as possible (Fig. 1-2).

All scuba cylinders must be inspected externally and internally by a qualified professional at least once a year. This testing requires special training, procedures, and equipment. NAUI sanctions a special **Visual Cylinder Inspection** (VCI) program and authorizes the issuance of Evidence of Inspection (EOI) stickers by qualified cylinder inspectors.

If internal inspection reveals corrosion in a scuba cylinder, it may need to be cleaned by tum-

TABLE 1.1 SCUBA CYLINDER SPECIFICATIONS

ALLOY	ADVERTISED VOLUME	CAPACITY RATED	(CU. FT.) @10% O.F.	SERVICE PRESSURE	OVERFILL PRESSURE	CUBIC INCHES	LENGTH (INCHES)	DIAMETER (INCHES)	EMPTY WT. (LBS.)	BUOYANCY EMPTY	(SEA WATER) FULL
Steel	15	14.24	15.65	3000	3300	120	13.80	4.00	0.75	-1.300	-2.5
Alum.	14	14.06	-	2015	-	176	16.60	4.40	05.4	3.20	2.1
Alum.	50	50.43	-	3000	-	425	19.00	6.90	21.5	2.25	-1.8
Steel	45	40.99	45.05	2015	2216	513	19.10	6.80	20.0	1.40	-2.2
Steel	38	37.86	-	1000	-	530	19.10	6.80	20.0	1.40	-1.6
Steel	42	38.00	41.77	1800	1980	532	19.10	6.80	20.1	1.40	-1.9
Steel	52.2	47.43	52.14	2250	2475	532	19.37	6.90	22.0	neutral	-4.2
Steel	53	47.43	52.14	2250	2475	532	19.10	6.80	20.5	1.40	-2.8
Alum.	63 or 50	63.13	-	3000	-	532	18.70	7.25	25.1	0.80	-3.04
Steel	71.4	65.15	71.39	3000	3300	549	20.47	6.84	28.6	-4.600	-10.3
Alum.	72	72.39	-	3000	-	610	26.00	6.90	28.5	3.60	-1.8
Steel	55	44.79	49.23	1800	1980	627	22.50	6.80	20.8	2.40	1.4
Alum.	80	79.87	-	3000	-	673	26.40	7.25	33.3	4.00	-1.9
Alum.	80	80.70	-	3000	-	680	27.00	7.25	34.5	4.10	-1.9
Steel	71.2	65.08	71.55	2250	2475	730	25.00	6.80	29.5	3.50	-2
Alum.	71.2	71.55	-	2475	-	730	28.80	6.90	30.6	10.600	5.2
Steel	75.8	69.39	76.29	2400	2640	730	26.18	6.76	29.3	1.50	-4.6
Steel	94.6 or 96	86.63	95.25	3000	3300	730	25.00	7.00	39.0	-6.000	-13.3
Steel	95.1	85.98	95.62	2400	2640	915	23.82	8.02	37.2	1.50	-6.2
Steel	103.5 or 104	96.01	105.550	2400	2640	1010	26.50	7.80	44.0	neutral	-8.2

Fig. 1-2. The internal inspection of a scuba cylinder is performed by a trained technician using a special light.

bling. The tumbling process involves filling the cylinder by approximately 50% with an abrasive material such as carbide or aluminum oxide chips and rotating it for a number of hours. The abrasive materials remove rust and polish the inside surface of the cylinder, which is then rinsed to remove loose material and dehydrated internally to remove all traces of moisture.

At least once every 5 years in the United States, and even more frequently in some other countries, scuba cylinders must be pressure tested (Fig. 1-3). There are several methods of **hydrostatic testing**, including direct expansion, pressure recession, and the water–jacket method, which involves filling the cylinder with water, placing it in a water–filled pressure chamber, raising the pressure inside the cylinder with a hydraulic pump, and measuring the amount of cylinder expansion in terms of water column displacement. The pressure is increased to five thirds of the rated pressure of the cylinder. A permanent expansion of 10% or more of the total expansion indicates that the cylinder is unsafe and must be condemned. The cylinder will not be rated for a lower working pressure.

Fig. 1-3. Scuba cylinder in a hydrostatic test chamber.

Cylinder Care Rules

Cylinder care rules include:

1. Do not exceed the maximum allowable pressure.
2. Do handle cylinders carefully.
3. Do prevent moisture from entering the cylinder.
4. Do not drain a cylinder completely of air except for internal inspections; if it must be drained, do it slowly.
5. Rinse the outside of the cylinder thoroughly with clean, fresh water after diving.
6. Do store cylinders in a cool, dry place and with a small amount of pressure in them.
7. Do have cylinders visually inspected annually, or more frequently if damage is suspected.
8. Do not use a dented, welded, or deeply scarred cylinder.
9. Do remove the cylinder boot periodically and inspect it for corrosion.
10. Do not heat cylinders to high temperatures (e.g., baking, welding, and so on).
11. Do fill cylinders slowly, approximately 300 to 500 p.s.i. per minute.
12. Transporting cylinders requires care to assure that they do not roll around and that the valve is protected from damage.

Cylinder Valve Assemblies and Manifolds

A scuba cylinder valve is a simple, manually operated, on–off valve that controls the flow of high–pressure gas (Fig. 1-4). Features of all scuba valves include a valve snorkel and a burst disc. The purpose of the **valve snorkel**, or "dip tube," is to prevent foreign matter from entering into and perhaps blocking the gas flow through the valve when the cylinder is inverted. The **burst disc** is a

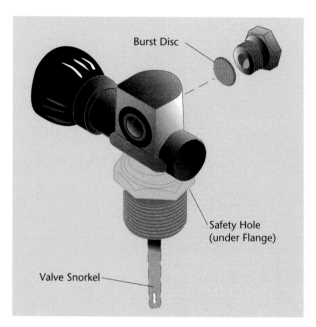

Fig . 1-4. Cylinder valve safety features.

safety feature to prevent the cylinder pressure from reaching dangerously high levels during filling or under conditions of extreme heat (e.g., fire).

Some scuba valves have a safety hole located near the top of the valve threads. The purpose of the hole is to indicate that there is pressure in a cylinder if someone tries to remove the valve when the cylinder is not empty. Air hisses from the valve and warns the worker.

A cylinder valve assembly houses a high–pressure blowout disc as a safety feature. Burst discs are rated at a maximum of five thirds of the working pressure of a cylinder. The rated bursting pressure range of burst discs for 2250–p.s.i. cylinders is from 3375 to 3750 p.s.i.g., and for 3000–p.s.i. cylinders, the bursting pressure range is from 4500 to 5000 p.s.i.g. The thin, metal burst discs are usually both color coded and stamped with their maximum pressure rating.

When a burst disc ruptures, which can occur under normal circumstances, a loud noise and hissing result, but the only danger is to your hearing. The escape of air cannot be stopped, and the burst disc must be replaced by a qualified professional before the cylinder can be used again.

The standard, on–off cylinder valve is known as the **K–valve** (Fig. 1-5). A cylinder valve that incorporates a low–air warning/reserve air mechanism is known as a **J–valve**. The J–valve is a spring–loaded check valve that begins to close as the cylinder pressure approaches a predetermined pressure (usually 300 or 500 p.s.i.). The J–valve permits unrestricted flow of air to the regulator throughout a dive until the valve closing pressure is approached. At the predetermined closing pressure, a spring forces a flow check against the air passage and restricts air flow, causing increased breathing resistance. This is followed by total obstruction of the air flow unless the spring–loaded check valve is manually overridden by turning the external lever. When the reserve lever is manually depressed, a plunger pin forces the flow check valve away from the air passage and the remaining 300 to 500 p.s.i. becomes available for use. J–valves were popular before the advent of submersible pressure gauges (SPGs).

K–valves tend to be more popular than J–valves, especially because SPGs are now considered to be standard equipment. Some additional reasons why include:

1. The reserve pressure of a J–valve may be either 300 p.s.i.g or 300 p.s.i. above the gauge pressure. If the reserve is not depth compensated, the available reserve air is decreased as depth is increased.

2. The J–valve reserve lever must be fully up for the reserve mechanism to function. A diver may forget to put the lever up before diving, it may be turned down by another diver, or it may be accidentally depressed by diving activities. Any of these actions allows the reserve air to be exhausted without warning.

3. The J–valve reserve lever must be depressed when the cylinder is being filled. Failure to do this may damage the reserve mechanism and will prevent a correct fill.

4. J–valves cost more initially than K–valves, and they also are more expensive to have serviced.

5. A J–valve mechanism retains a reserve air supply in only one cylinder of a multiple set of cylinders. When the reserve is activated, the reserve air distributes itself equally among all cylinders and the reserve pressure is reduced by a ratio equal to the number of cylinders. The reserve pressure can be set to a higher pressure to compensate for multiple cylinders.

Galvanic corrosion or electrolysis occurs when dissimilar metals are in contact and moisture is present. This can occur between aluminum cylinders and brass scuba valves. Ions will flow from the aluminum and deposit themselves on the brass. Fortunately, the chrome plating of brass scuba valves and the scuba cylinder coating, combined with a periodic coating of a dielectric compound, negate electrolysis in most instances. If the valve plating is worn away, however, galvanic corrosion can be a problem and will appear as pits or missing threads in the cylinder adjacent to the valve. If this problem develops, it should be corrected by a qualified professional. The valve also should be serviced any time air leakage occurs or the handle becomes difficult to turn.

Excessive force should not be used when turning a scuba valve on or off. Valve seat discs, gaskets, and seals will be damaged. Open valves slowly and gently. Open the valve fully, and then close the valve one–quarter turn (but no more) to relieve pressure on the stem seal. This procedure also provides a clue as to the correct way to turn the valve when you are ready to close it. If it only turns one quarter of a turn, you know that you have just turned it on all the way. Some divers open a cylinder valve only slightly to measure cylinder pressure, then forget to open the valve fully before diving. This produces a restricted opening that limits air flow and causes you to think that you have had an air supply failure. Always open a valve fully (Fig. 1-6).

Cylinder valves can seize to the threads of a scuba cylinder, especially in aluminum cylinders. This is a result of galvanic corrosion. Some older valves have pipe threads and are tightened with a wrench; they may require a lot of force to remove. Having your cylinder valves serviced annually, as is recommended, will prevent valve seizure.

Special Valves and Manifolds

Special scuba valves are available for specialty applications and multiple–cylinder configurations. The activities requiring such valves are considered to be advanced specialties that require special training.

A dual valve for a single cylinder, known as a **Y–valve** or **Slingshot valve** (Fig. 1-7), is available. This allows a diver to mount two regulator systems on a single cylinder. This configuration is useful for deep dives or enclosure dives made with a single cylinder.

Fig. 1-5. A K valve is a simple on-off valve on scuba cylinders.

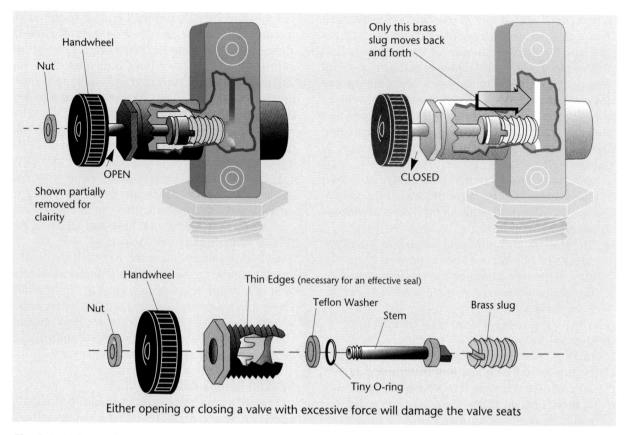

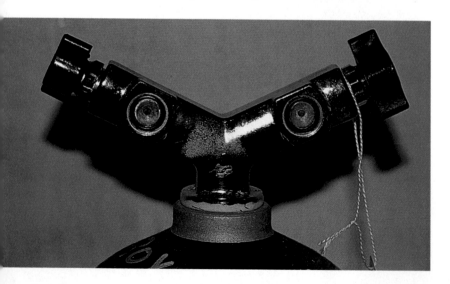

Fig. 1-6. Valve seats.

A high–pressure connection between two or more cylinders is called a **manifold**. This device allows multiple cylinders to be "ganged together" for specialty activities that require a large reserve of air for safety.

Another type of valve that is becoming popular is the **DIN** valve (Fig. 1-8). This allows the firm attachment of a regulator to cylinders using higher working pressures. It has a captured O–ring, which lessens the chance of failure at the regulator–to–valve interface.

Fig. 1-7. A slingshot valve allows the diver to mount two independent regulators to one cylinder.

SCUBA REGULATORS

Your scuba regulator reduces the pressure of air in your scuba cylinder to ambient pressure and delivers the air on demand. It uses the pressure differential created by the respiratory action of your lungs to regulate air flow. Scuba regulators automatically adjust to changes in depth and your respiration rate.

High–pressure air from your scuba cylinder is reduced in **stages** (i.e., pressure–reduction stops) to ambient pressure. Nearly all scuba regulators are two–stage devices. The **first stage** reduces cylinder pressure to an **intermediate pressure** (or **low pressure**) of 90 to 130 p.s.i. The **second stage** reduces the low–pressure air to ambient (i.e., surrounding) pressure.

To understand the operational theory of a regulator, you must be familiar with the types of internal regulating valves used. The fundamental types are downstream and upstream valves. An **upstream valve** is one that is forced closed by high–pressure air, and a **downstream valve** is one that is forced open by high–pressure air. Upstream valves are rare in modern regulators. As the cylinder pressure decreases, less ambient pressure is required to open an upstream valve. The downstream valve is configured with springs that can keep the valve closed at the maximum cylinder pressure; therefore, this type of valve is more resistant to opening as the cylinder pressure decreases.

Types of Regulators

There are three basic types of regulators: two–hose, single–hose, and integrated. The original scuba consisted of a **two–hose regulator** in which both stages were combined into one mechanical assembly that mounted onto a scuba cylinder valve. Two flexible hoses led from either side of the regulator to a mouthpiece containing both inhalation and exhalation, nonreturn valves. The hose that led over the right shoulder carried fresh air to the diver, while the hose over the left shoulder carried exhaled air back to the regulator assembly on the cylinder, where the used air was exhausted into the water.

Regulator design later evolved to **single–hose regulators**, which are the standard type in use today because of their reliability, simplicity, and ease of maintenance (Fig. 1-9). Although many hoses may be attached to a single–hose regulator, only one hose is involved in the operation of the regulator itself. With a single–hose regulator, the first pressure–reduction stage is attached to the scuba cylinder, while the second reduction stage and the exhaust port are included in the mouthpiece portion, which is attached to the first stage via a low–pressure hose.

Integrated regulators are those that are incorporated into other items of equipment. Such equipment can include a buoyancy compensator low–pressure inflator or a small contingency scuba unit.

First–Stage Valves

The internal valves of scuba regulator first stages are available in two types: diaphragm, and piston. Both valves are produced in an unbalanced or a balanced configuration. A **balanced valve** is one in which air pressure does not affect the force needed to operate the valve; in other words, the valve operates the same regardless of the cylinder pressure. The operation of an **unbalanced valve**, however, is affected by cylinder pressure.

The **diaphragm first–stage valve** is an unbalanced, upstream valve. A spring opposes the force of cylinder pressure and acts against a flexible diaphragm. The forces exerted by the spring, ambient pressure, and high–pressure air combine

Fig. 1-8. A DIN valve is used on cylinders with higher working pressures.

Fig. 1-9. Regulator first stage with high pressure hose and low pressure hoses on a swivel.

to activate the valve. During descent, the increasing water pressure in the spring chamber (which is free flooding) causes the diaphragm to bulge, which displaces the diaphragm and opens the valve until pressure equilibrium is restored. When you inhale, the reduced pressure in the **intermediate–pressure chamber** allows the spring to push in on the diaphragm and open the valve until equilibrium is restored (Fig. 1-10).

The **balanced diaphragm first–stage valve** is designed so that the stem of the upstream valve extends completely through the high–pressure chamber. Therefore, the operation of this valve is not affected by cylinder pressure.

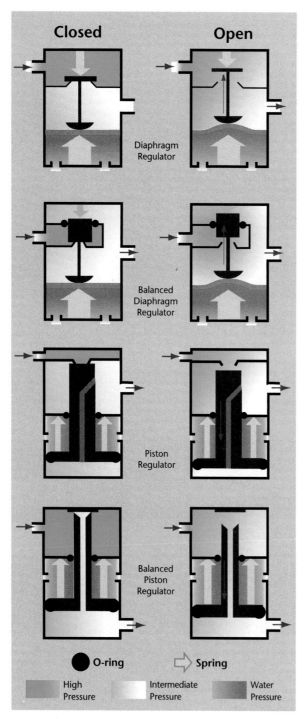

Closed   **Open**

Diaphragm Regulator

Balanced Diaphragm Regulator

Piston Regulator

Balanced Piston Regulator

⬤ O-ring   ⇨ Spring

High Pressure   Intermediate Pressure   Water Pressure

Fig. 1-10. Typical regulator first stages. Arrows represent springs. Black dots represent O rings.

For both types of diaphragm first–stage valves, a failure of the diaphragm causes the valve to close. This is very rare, however.

The **unbalanced piston first–stage valve** is a downstream valve. A bias spring in the free–flooding spring chamber controls the intermediate pressure. A hole in the shaft of the piston allows the dry side of the piston to equalize at the inter-

mediate pressure. During descent, increasing water pressure in the spring chamber displaces the piston and opens the valve until equilibrium is restored. When you inhale, the reduced pressure in the intermediate–pressure chamber displaces the piston, opening the valve until equilibrium is restored. The **balanced piston first–stage valve** is designed so that the piston movement is isolated from the high–pressure chamber by an O–ring; therefore, the operation of the valve is independent of the cylinder pressure. For both types of piston first–stage valves, a failure of the piston seal tends to cause the valve to fail in the open or **free–flow** position.

Second–Stage Valves

Located in the mouthpiece of your regulator, the **downstream second–stage valve** is connected to the first stage by a low–pressure hose. A reduction in pressure in the second–stage chamber causes the second–stage diaphragm to bulge inward and depress a lever, which opens the valve and admits air into the mouthpiece at ambient pressure. As long as you continue to inhale, air will continue to flow. When inhalation ceases, the diaphragm returns to a flat position, releasing pressure on the lever, which closes the valve with spring pressure. On exhalation, pressure in the second–stage chamber unseats the nonreturn exhaust valve, allowing used air to be exhausted into the water. With a downstream second–stage valve, any buildup of pressure in the first stage of the regulator will simply push past the second–stage valve (Figs. 1-11 and 1-12).

An **upstream second–stage valve**, although rarely encountered, should be understood because of its potential hazards and inefficiency. A dangerous feature of this regulator is that if a buildup of pressure in the first stage occurs, the valve will be held tightly against its seat and shut off the flow of air. The low–pressure hose will rupture if its burst pressure is exceeded. Regulators with upstream second–stage valves must be equipped with a pressure–relief valve in the intermediate–pressure chamber of the first stage to relieve any excess pressure. Alternatively, an extra second stage with a downstream valve must be attached to the first stage (Fig. 1-13).

An upstream second–stage valve operates in a manner similar to a downstream second–stage valve, but the diaphragm pushes against a stem instead of a lever. The stem is attached to the valve seat, and the valve is tilted or partially unseated when the stem is depressed by the diaphragm (Fig. 1-14).

Fig. 1-11. Side-exhaust type second stage regulator.

Fig. 1-12. Traditional lower exhaust type second stage regulator.

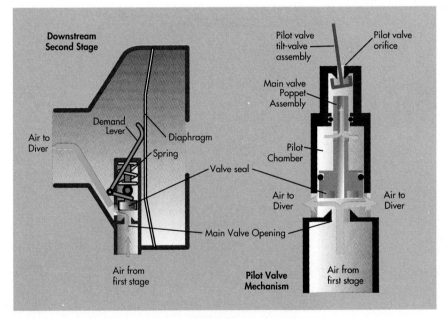

Fig. 1-13. Cross-sectional views of regulator second stages.

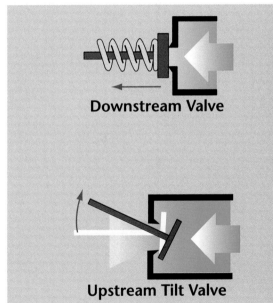

Fig. 1-14. Second stage valves.

The main valve of a **pilot valve regulator** is opened and closed using air pressure rather than mechanical leverage. The valve opening pressure is generated by air flow through a diaphragm–activated, downstream pilot valve. A simple mechanical linkage is used between the diaphragm mechanism and the pilot valve. Because the pilot valve is tiny, only a small spring tension is required to counterbalance the pressure and, therefore, less force is required to open or close it. The pilot valve opens only slightly and operates the air–supply valve by passing a small amount of air into a control chamber.

Because a piston opposite the valve opening exactly counteracts the opening force pressure, the supply valve is balanced and unaffected by variations in the intermediate pressure. The system can be described as a pneumatically amplified second stage—the small pilot valve pneumatically moves the larger air–supply valve.

A pilot valve requires only one fourth of the inhalation effort required for other types of second stages. The operation of the second stage is initiated when the diaphragm is depressed, and the linkage opens the pilot valve. Air flows through the pilot valve faster than it can flow through the hole in the flexible main valve, so a pressure difference occurs in the chamber, causing the main valve to open. This allows air to flow into the second stage until the pilot valve is closed and a buildup of pressure in the air chamber closes the main valve. The pilot valve acts as a safety relief valve in the event of a pressure buildup in the first stage (Fig. 1-15).

Fig. 1-15. Pilot valve regulator second stage.

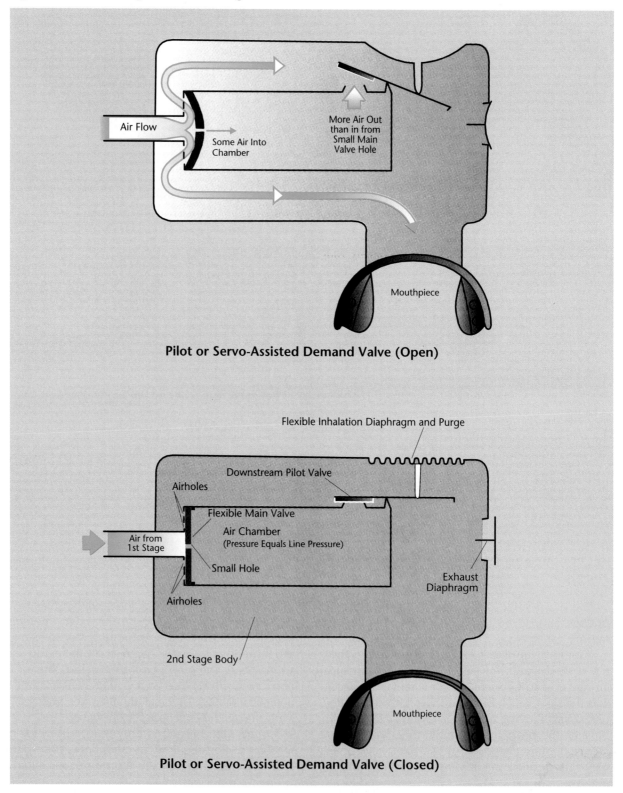

Pilot or Servo-Assisted Demand Valve (Open)

Pilot or Servo-Assisted Demand Valve (Closed)

Regulator Attachments

Although single–hose regulators are used today, they can have many hoses attached to them. The following are regulator attachments:

1. SPG (high pressure).
2. Buoyancy compensator (BC) low pressure inflator hose (low pressure).
3. Extra second stage (octopus; low pressure).
4. Dry–suit inflator hose (low pressure).

A number of regulators have several low–pressure ports in the first stage. If your regulator will not accommodate all of the items you would like to attach, multiple–port adapters are available at dive stores (Figures 1-16 through 1-19).

Regulator Care and Maintenance

Your regulator must be rinsed after each use, and the purge button must not be depressed when there is water in the second stage. Your regulator must also be professionally serviced annually. The first-stage dust cover must be in place any time the regulator is not in use.

In addition, there are other aspects of care that you should know at the advanced level. These include:

1. It is better to soak your regulator in warm water and then rinse it, rather than just rinsing it. Be sure the first–stage dust cover is well secured and sealed.
2. Do *not* lubricate your regulator, and especially avoid the use of silicon spray, which ruins regulator parts and can allow the second–stage diaphragm to be sucked out.
3. Your regulator should be functionally tested every 6 months. This test, which is quick and inexpensive, involves only a simple device known as a **manometer**, which checks the breathing resistance.
4. An extra second stage attached to a regulator also should be functionally tested semiannually and serviced annually.
5. Regulators used frequently in swimming pools require more frequent service than others, because the chlorine used to purify the pool water dispels the lubricant used on internal seals.
6. Coloration of the filter on the first stage of your regulator may provide clues about the condition of the scuba cylinder you are using. A greenish filter indicates corrosion from moisture inside a cylinder or dripped onto the filter; a reddish filter indicates rust from a steel cylinder; and a blackish filter indicates carbon dust in your cylinder from a compressor filter. None of these conditions is good for your regulator. Any such indicator should prompt you to have the problem corrected.

Fig. 1-16. Buoyancy compensator integrated second stage regulator and power inflator mechanism.

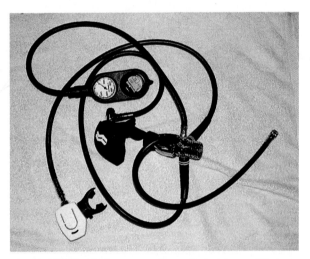

Fig. 1-17. Single-hose regulator first stage, with two second stages, console with pressure and depth gauges, and low-pressure inflator hose.

Fig. 1-18. Hose protectors can extend the life of regulator hoses.

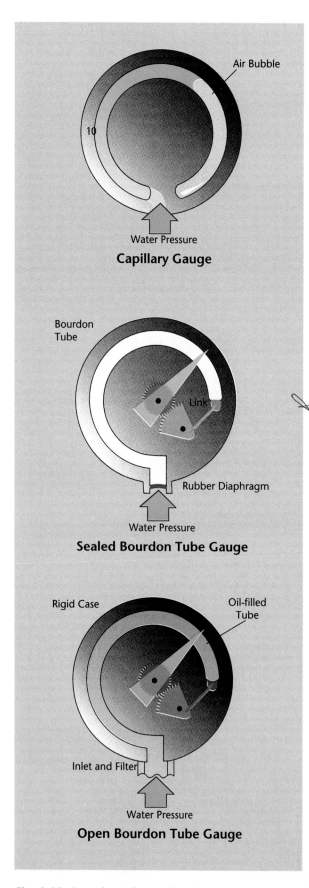

Capillary Gauge

Air Bubble

10

Water Pressure

Bourdon Tube

Link

Rubber Diaphragm

Water Pressure

Sealed Bourdon Tube Gauge

Rigid Case

Oil-filled Tube

Inlet and Filter

Water Pressure

Open Bourdon Tube Gauge

Fig. 1-19. Bourdon tube mechanism.

7. Leaks from parts of your regulator, or tiny bubbles oozing from hoses under water, require prompt repair by a professional before the leakage becomes more serious. It is permissible to finish a dive with a minor air leak, but the problem should be corrected before the next outing.

8. Have strain reliefs (i.e., hose protectors) installed on every hose of your regulator. These sleeves relieve strain on the hoses and prolong their life.

9. Secure all regulator attachments while diving. This helps to prevent damage to the attachments and the diving environment. Pressure gauges and extra second stages that are dangling or dragging easily snag.

Many manufacturers require an annual regulator overhaul to keep the regulator covered under warranty. The first– and second–stage regulators are broken down and cleaned, and new O–rings and seats are replaced. The regulator is then adjusted to be within factory specifications.

Regulator Concerns

There are several aspects of scuba regulators that may be of concern to you from time to time. As an advanced diver, you should be aware of the following:

1. Water can flow through a regulator if your cylinder is empty. Although you are not supposed to use all of the air in your cylinder, you may inadvertently do so. If this occurs, close the cylinder valve to prevent water from reaching your first stage and/or entering your scuba cylinder.

2. Regulators can freeze in very cold water, and air is cooled during pressure reduction. When diving in near–freezing (i.e., 40° F) water, the air flowing through your regulator can further decrease the temperature and cause water in the regulator to freeze. Ice can jam mechanical parts, such as the first–stage bias spring and the second–stage lever return spring inside your regulator, and affect their operation. Some regulators can be "weatherized" to help reduce the possibility of first–stage freezing. Special precautions to exclude moisture in the second stage are necessary to keep it from freezing.

3. Air flow may be limited in some regulators at greater depths. Your regulator may not be capable of delivering high–flow rates at low cylinder pressures when two divers are breathing from it at the same time. Keep this in mind when selecting a regulator, and choose one that can meet high demands when at low pressures at depth.

4. Regulator performance evaluation was traditionally based on breathing resistance or effort. This was expressed in terms of inches or centimeters of water pressure exerted by the diver to inhale and exhale through the regulator. For example, 5 and 7 centimeters of water pressure at the surface was the maximum inhalation and exhalation effort, respectively, that was acceptable by US Navy standards. Modern regulator performance is defined in terms of **maximum respiratory work level**, or **breathing work**. The US Navy defines 0.14 kg–m/L at a depth of 132 feet and a breathing rate of 62.5 RMV (respiratory minute volume in liters per minute) as the maximum acceptable level. Some recreational diving authorities have suggested that this value far exceeds the requirements of the average diver. US Navy regulator test results are available in diving journals.

5. Keep the regulator out of the sand. A single grain can jam the second–stage lever and cause a regulator to free flow. To remedy this problem, connect the regulator to a cylinder and pressurize it, submerge it in water, depress the purge button, and rapidly move it back and forth. This might dislodge any sand inside the second stage.

DIVING INSTRUMENTS

Ⓢeveral gauges are required for diving, such as a SPG, depth gauge, and a timing device. This section describes how these gauges function and how to care for them.

Analog Versus Digital

An **analog** instrument has hands that move on a dial, while **digital** instruments provide a numeric information display. Mechanical instruments give analog data, and electronic instruments give digital information. Analog gauges are reasonably accurate and reliable. Digital gauges are very accurate but are more subject to failure, and they are more expensive than mechanical instruments.

Cylinder Pressure Gauges

One of the most common types of pressure gauges is known as a **bourdon movement gauge**. A bourdon movement is a flattened, helic tube that is sealed at one end. The tube tends to uncurl when pressurized because of pressure differences between the inner arc of the tube and the outer arc. One end of the tube is attached to a linkage that moves an indicator needle. If both ends of a bourdon tube are sealed, the tube may be used to measure external pressure, which tends to curl the tube inward when a pressure greater than the internal pressure of the tube is surrounding it.

There are two types of pressure gauges for determining the amount of air in a scuba cylinder. A **surface cylinder pressure gauge** is used to check the amount of air in a cylinder above water. It attaches to the cylinder valve in the same manner as a regulator to provide a one–time check of cylinder pressure. A bleed valve relieves trapped pressure so that the gauge can be removed when the cylinder valve has been closed.

Submersible pressure gauges are attached to the first stage of your regulator and provide a continual readout of the air pressure in your cylinder. It contains a spiral form of bourdon movement, consisting of numerous coils, with the closed end connected directly to the indicator needle. As pressure uncoils the spiral tubing, the needle moves. This design is commonly used for SPGs.

Some units have a **console** to incorporate other gauges (Figs. 1-20 and 1-21). SPG movements are designed with an accuracy range of ±35 to 100 p.s.i. at a reading of approxmately 500 p.s.i. At full scale, the accuracy is approximately ±5%.

Fig. 1-20. A console is a convenient way to group gauges such as the submersible pressure gauge, depth gauge, and compass.

Fig. 1-21. Console with digital submersible pressure gauge.

Fig. 1-22. First stage regulator with high-pressure port with plug removed. Note the tiny pin hole in HP port. Low-pressure ports are located on the swivel cap.

A SPG is attached to the high–pressure port of your regulator. Some important information you need to know about this attachment point is:

1. The high–pressure regulator port is larger than the low–pressure ports on modern regulators. This prevents attachments with low–pressure hoses from being installed in the high–pressure port, which is dangerous because the hose can rupture. Older regulators that are still in use have ports of equal size for both high and low pressure, so care is required when making first–stage attachments. Adapters are available for connecting old–style attachments to newer regulators.

2. Regulator high–pressure ports have a restricted **orifice** (i.e., opening) to limit the flow of air in case of a rupture of the SPG or its hose. The tiny hole (diameter, 0.005 in) prevents rapid depletion of the air supply. A high–pressure leak does not constitute an emergency situation; should one occur, simply make a normal ascent and close the cylinder valve (Fig. 1-22).

Some new pressure gauges are "hoseless." They receive a signal that is transmitted from a unit mounted on the cylinder valve.

Cylinder pressure gauge types include spiral bourdon movements or digital instrumentation. A digital gauge uses a pressure–sensitive transducer, a battery, some electronic circuitry, and a liquid crystal display to provide information.

Should a leak develop in the bourdon movement, high–pressure air will flow into the gauge housing. This is why you are instructed not to look at your gauge when opening your cylinder valve.

To prevent injury from an explosion of the housing in this instance, a safety plug is incorporated into the housing of most cylinder pressure gauges. Avoid obstructing the area over the plug so that the plug will be free to blow out and release pressure if necessary.

If water is visible inside a cylinder pressure gauge, the gauge should not be used until it has been repaired and tested. Pressure gauges require professional service and repair.

Cylinder pressure gauges should not be subjected to shock and abuse. In addition, they occasionally should be inspected and verified for accuracy.

Depth Gauges

There are several types of depth gauges, including capillary, bourdon tube, diaphragm, and electronic (Figs 1-23 through 1-25). The simplest and least expensive of all is the **capillary gauge**.

In a capillary gauge, air is compressed according to Boyle's Law in a length of clear tubing that is sealed at one end. Water enters the open end when the tube is submerged and compresses the column of air in proportion to the depth. The scale is nonlinear; therefore, the graduations on the scale become difficult to read in deeper water. A well–constructed capillary gauge can be extremely accurate in shallow water. It also is valuable for altitude diving, because it automatically provides equivalent depth readings at higher elevations.

Problems associated with capillary gauges include clogging of the tube, air bubbles in the tube, and difficulty in reading at low light levels.

1 ft for every 100ft +5% gauge reading.

Doesn't read correctly at altitude.

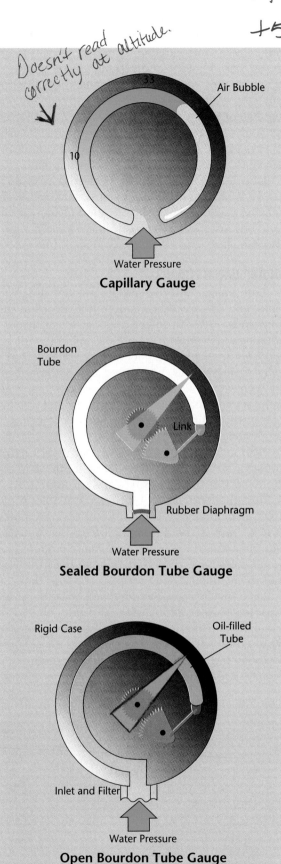

Capillary Gauge

Sealed Bourdon Tube Gauge

Open Bourdon Tube Gauge

Fig. 1-23. Types of depth gauges.

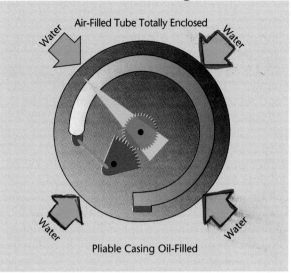

Fig. 1-24. Enclosed Bourdon tube gauge.

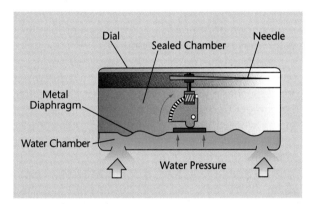

Fig. 1-25. Diaphragm gauge.

For these reasons, a capillary gauge should not be used as your primary depth gauge.

Open bourdon tube depth gauges are the least expensive form of bourdon movement depth gauge. The tube is mounted inside a case with the open end exposed to the water, which enters the tube. This type of gauge is subject to corrosion, silting, and blockage by salt crystals. They no longer are readily available and are unpopular because of maintenance problems.

The **sealed bourdon tube** depth gauge was developed to overcome the problems associated with the open tube design. This gauge is fundamentally the same as the open bourdon tube, except that this tube is fluid–filled and the end sealed with a rubber diaphragm. Water pressure is transmitted through the diaphragm to the oil, which exerts pressure on the tube.

The **oil–filled bourdon tube** gauge consists of a bourdon movement sealed at both ends and enclosed in an oil–filled case. Either a pliable case or a diaphragm transmit pressure through the case and the oil to the bourdon movement.

The **diaphragm depth gauge** is the only mechanical gauge that does not use a bourdon movement, and it is expensive but accurate. A thin, metal diaphragm is mounted in a case that is rigid and hermetically sealed. Most of the air is removed from the case to form a partial vacuum, and water pressure on the diaphragm moves mechanical linkage attached to the indicator needle. Some diaphragm gauges are adjustable for use at altitude.

An electronic depth gauge is frequently called a **digital depth gauge**. This gauge operates in the same way that an electronic cylinder pressure gauge does, but at lower pressures. Digital depth gauges can be sensitive to temperature variations, and they require batteries for operation. A digital depth gauge also can be difficult to read in low light levels unless the instrument has a backlit screen. These gauges are extremely accurate and easy to read without error. Other features, such as a maximum depth indicator or an ascent rate indicator, may be easily incorporated.

Depth gauges measure pressure and are usually marked in feet of sea water, so an adjustment must be made for fresh–water diving. Gauges may be subject to damage if exposed to reduced pressures when flying and should be transported inside pressure–tight containers or a pressurized cabin in aircraft (Fig. 1-26).

A desirable feature of a depth gauge is a **maximum depth indicator**, which retains the maximum depth reached during a dive. This indicator can be mechanical on analog gauges or electronic on digital gauges. The maximum depth indicator resets automatically on digital gauges, but you must remember to manually reset the indicator on mechanical gauges.

Accuracy for mechanical gauges is typically ±1% for the first half of the depth scale and ±2% for the second half. This accuracy is further affected by age, abuse, and reduced ambient pressure exposures. The accuracy of electronic depth gauges is ±6 in (15 cm). All depth gauges must be calibrated annually either by means of a marked line for comparison or with a "pressure pot" (i.e., a small pressure chamber) at your local dive store. Interim checks can be performed by comparing your depth gauge to a capillary gauge at shallow depths.

Depth gauges should be treated with care to prevent shock and low–pressure damage. Avoid leaving gauges, especially oil–filled gauges, in the sun, because heat will expand the oil and can produce leakage.

Underwater Timers

Both analog and digital dive watches are available, and some watches feature both types of displays (Fig. 1-27). An analog dive watch usually has a rotating outer **bezel** (i.e., rotating collar) to indicate elapsed time. A bezel that rotates counterclockwise only is preferred as the elapsed time indicated can only err on the side of safety, by adding to and not subtracting from underwater time. Digital watches can have additional desirable features such as a stopwatch, alarm, timer, and light.

Bottom timers are pressure–activated instruments that automatically record the time spent below a depth of approximately 5 feet (1.5 m). Both digital and analog types are available. A distinct advantage of a bottom timer over an underwater timer is the automatic operation, because you may forget to set a watch. Many modern bottom timers have a memory to keep track of previous dives, which can be recalled at a later time.

Dive watches and bottom timers must be rinsed with fresh water after diving, and both should be cleaned and inspected annually. Avoid wearing your dive watch in a spa, hot tub, or shower, because the combination of high temperature and soap can result in damage.

Fig. 1-26. Depth gauge accuracy.

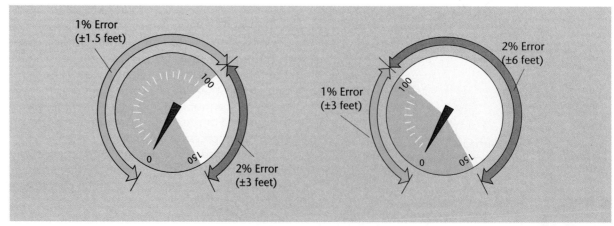

Fig. 1-27. Digital dive watches are relatively inexpensive and offer many features.

Electronic Dive Computers

An **electronic dive computer** (Figs. 1-28 through 1-30) is an instrument that provides a digital display of several or all of the following items:

- Current depth
- Maximum depth
- Elapsed bottom time
- Surface interval
- Temperature
- No–decompression time remaining
- Dive time remaining based on air supply and consumption
- Air pressure
- Repetitive group designation
- Ascent rate
- Dive number
- Dive profile
- Time to fly
- **Scrolling** (displaying in sequence the no–decompression limits for various depths for repetitive dives)
- **Ceiling** (decompression stop depth)
- Battery level

Electronic dive computers are the "ultimate instrument" for diving activities. Some computers merely combine information that usually would require several instruments and present that information in a single digital display. Others are decompression computers that continuously calculate nitrogen pressure in various tissue models. These computers allow longer dive times, because they compensate for the time spent at varying depths throughout a dive compared with "square" dive profiles required when using tables.

You may be encouraged by some to use a computer only as a backup for dives planned according to the NAUI dive tables. This is inconsistent with the purpose of a diving computer, which pro-

Fig. 1-28. Combination submersible pressure gauge and dive computer.

Fig. 1-29. A dive computer can be mounted on a hose.

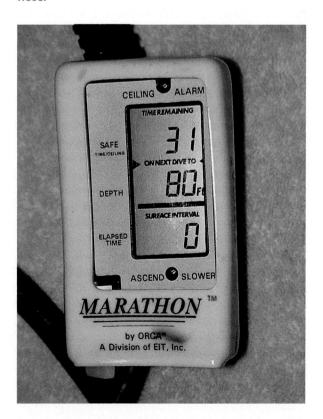

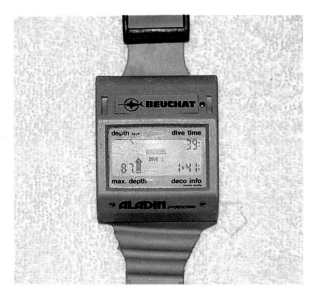

Fig. 1-30. A dive computer can be worn on the wrist.

vides information based on **multilevel diving** (i.e., dives at more than one depth level) computations, not on the "total time at the maximum depth" calculations of the dive tables. Limiting a dive to the dive–table time limits defeats the purpose of the computer. For a particular profile, dive tables might specify that decompression is required, while the dive computer might indicate that no decompression is required because of multilevel calculations. Most dive computers can be used for decompression diving; however, it is recommended that they be used within the computer's no–decompression limits. The devices should be used in such a way that any ceiling is avoided at any time during a dive. This allows a direct ascent to the surface in case of emergency (Fig. 1-31).

Most dive computers have ascent rates that are slower than the traditional ascent rate of 60 ft/min. NAUI recommends ascents of 30 ft/min, which is consistent with many dive computer recommendations. Most models also have indicators that display ascent rate violations to the diver. The ascent rate is an important part of the decompression program and must not be violated (Fig. 1-32).

Another nice feature of many dive computers is the **log mode**. This display shows the essential information from one or more previous dives, and it allows the user to transfer the information to the logbook. Some models store many hours and numbers of dives, which can then be recalled or even downloaded into a personal computer (Fig. 1-33).

Many computer programs have different **time to fly** indicators. These times can vary widely from the traditional 12–hour rule, and users should plan accordingly when planning to fly after diving. Consult your dive computer's owner's manual to

see how long the time to fly after diving can be (Fig. 1-34).

It is not practical to dive according to the tables when using a decompression computer. Therefore, divers using computers must understand the devices and use them properly. The basic design of an electronic decompression computer is presented in Figure 1-35. A pressure transducer in the decompression computer produces a signal that is changed from analog to digital by the Analog–to–Digital (A/D) converter. A microprocessor reads the digital transducer signal, makes calculations, and controls the display. The Read–Only Memory (ROM) contains the program for the microprocessor, and the Random Access Memory (RAM) stores the information resulting from the computations. A clock synchronizes the operations and serves as a timer. A battery supplies power for the operation of the circuitry, and a housing protects all of the components from the environment.

There are two basic types of computers: tissue–based, and table–based. A **tissue–based** computer calculates nitrogen absorption in a number of theoretic body tissues, and it displays a warning or ceiling if the nitrogen level in any tissue approaches or exceeds programmed limits (Fig. 1-36). A **table–based** dive computer compares

Fig. 1-31. Dive computer with ceiling.

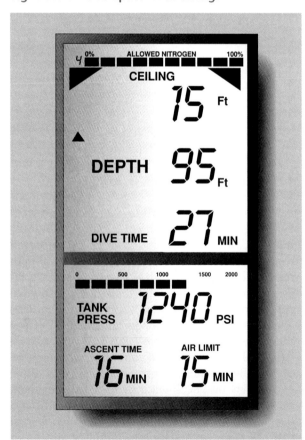

Fig. 1-32. Dive computer with ascent rate violation.

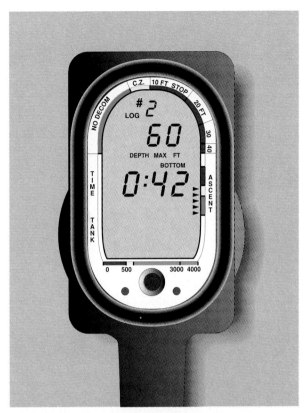

Fig. 1-33. Dive computer display in log mode.

Fig. 1-34. Dive computer with time to fly indicator.

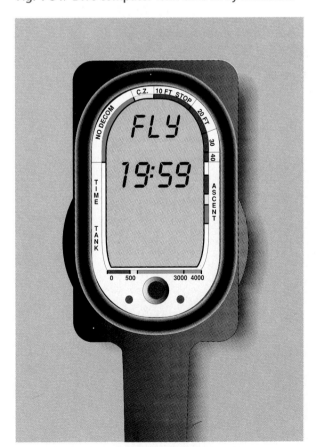

time and depth data with the mathematic model of established dive tables. Warnings are displayed when the no–decompression limits of the tables programmed into the computer are approached or exceeded. A table–based computer does more than simply store a set of dive tables electronically; it continuously compares time and depth input against the tables to credit the diver for multilevel dives. This provides longer dive times than can be obtained using conventional dive tables. A table–based computer also can provide a repetitive group designation following a dive so that the user can revert to using standard dive tables even following multilevel dives.

Most dive computers do not consider all of the factors affecting your body when making no–decompression calculations, so they must be used accordingly. Most make the same computations in cold water as in warm water, for older divers and younger divers, for those who are feeling well and those who are not, and for those who are exerting and those who are not. You therefore must adjust and limit your dive profiles based on such factors; however, there are some models that can be adjusted.

As with any electronic device, there is always the possibility of operational failure. You should carry a backup depth gauge and underwater timer in case your computer fails. The possibility of a computer failure is quite low, but it is not impossi-

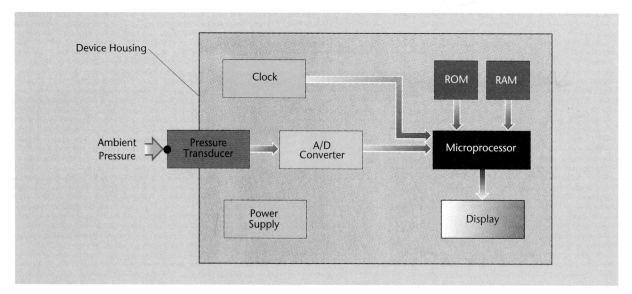

Fig. 1-35. Decompression computer block diagram.

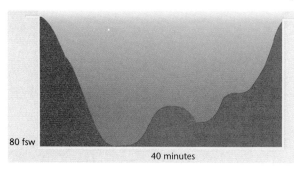

80 fsw

40 minutes

Fig. 1-36. Square wave vs. actual dive profile. Shaded region indicates times during the dive where less inert gas is absorbed than what the tables assume.

Fig. 1-37. Monitor your dive computer often during the dive.

ble. If your computer fails while diving, you should ascend immediately and perform, as a safety precaution, a decompression stop of at least 5 minutes at a depth of 15 feet (Fig. 1-37).

Failure of a computer, or accidentally switching one of these instruments off when it contains information from current diving activities, poses a problem that can be handled only by delaying further diving for the number of hours required by the manufacturer. The delay in diving, which is not necessarily 12 hours, allows the instrument to outgas completely.

Dive buddies may not share a single computer. Each diver relying on a computer for dive planning and no–decompression status must be equipped with a individual dive computer.

Electronic dive computers require considerable care and maintenance. Take care to prevent shock, extreme heat, close proximity of magnetic fields, and so on. Dive computers are not damaged by reduced pressure at higher elevations; in fact, some computers adjust for reduced atmospheric pressure and function correctly for altitude diving. Rinse your

Fig. 1-38. Parts of a diving compass.

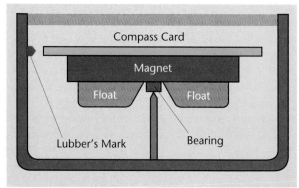

Fig. 1-39. Wrist-worn diving compass.

computer well after every use. Carefully follow battery replacement procedures as well. Your computer will provide ample warning when replacement of batteries is needed. Many models require periodic maintenance and calibration checks.

A computer can make diving easier and allow you to spend more time underwater than with conventional dive tables. You must, however, use your dive computer wisely and properly. Be sure to read the manual provided with your dive computer, and take a course to learn about its operation.

Diving Compasses

A freely suspended magnet tends to align itself with the magnetic field created by the Earth, which acts as a large magnet. This principle is the basis for a valuable reference device called a **compass**. Special compasses designed to withstand the environment are available for diving and are extremely useful reference instruments (Figs. 1-38 through 1-40).

Diving compasses are either dry or liquid–filled. The preferred type of compass for diving is liquid–filled. This type consists of a magnetic disc or arrow, called a **compass card**, that rests on a bearing. Incorporated into the card is a float that minimizes the weight of the card on the bearing. Well–constructed liquid–filled compasses can correctly indicate direction even when considerably tilted from a level position. The liquid also serves to dampen movement of the arrow or the compass card, which makes the instrument easy to use. Because the instrument is full of liquid, it is unaffected by pressures encountered at depth.

A dry compass construction is similar to that of a liquid–filled compass, but in this case, the compass card does not have a float assembly and must

Fig. 1-40. Console-mounted diving compass.

be lighter in weight. This type is less expensive than the liquid–filled compass. It is less accurate, however, and the card tends to oscillate (i.e., swing back and forth) and is subject to the effects of pressure.

A compass merits the same treatment that should be given to all diving instruments. Rinse it well after use, giving particular care to the bezel. Prevent shock and prolonged exposure to sunlight and high temperatures; heat will cause the liquid in a liquid–filled compass to expand and can cause leakage. Recalibration of compasses is not required.

Use of diving compasses is described in the Naviation chapter in the Diving Techniques section.

Buoyancy Compensators

There are many types, designs, and features of BCs. The three basic types are called horsecollar, jacket, or back inflation units. All BCs are equipped with a pressure–relief valve, which prevents overpressurization of the bladder. The valve is held closed by a spring with a tension of approximately 2 p.s.i. (i.e., 0.1406 kg/cm^2). When the internal pressure of the BC exceeds this amount, the spring pressure is overcome and any excess pressure vented (Figs. 1-41 through 1-44).

Some BCs are equipped with a **dump valve** to allow rapid manual deflation of the bladder. A lanyard from a point high on the bladder extends to a location that enables easy operation by the user. The functions of the pressure–relief valve and a dump valve are combined by some manufacturers.

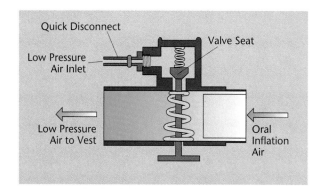

Fig. 1-41. Unbalanced BC power inflator.

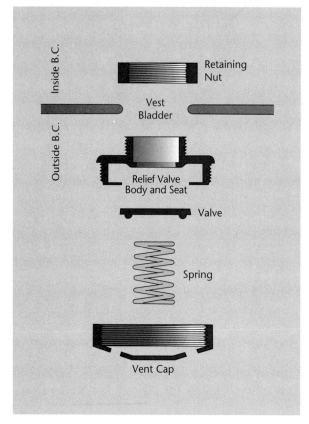

Fig. 1-42. BC overpressure relief valve.

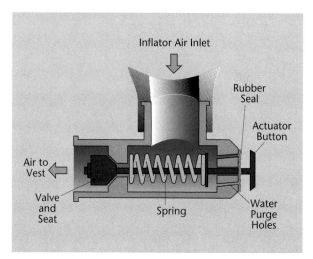

Fig. 1-43. BC oral inflator valve.

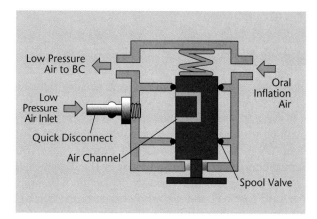

Fig. 1-44. Balanced BC power inflator valve.

Some BCs, particularly older styles, may be equipped with a CO_2–cartridge emergency inflator. The intent of this device is to enable rapid inflation of the BC at the surface. The preferred inflation method is with a low–pressure inflator, which is standard equipment on today's BCs. The CO_2 cartridge requires a high degree of care and maintenance to ensure reliable operation. As a result, they have lost popularity, but some manufacturers still offer CO_2–cartridge inflators as an option.

If a CO_2 inflator is desired or used, its care is important. Following every dive, the mechanism must be carefully rinsed and dried. The cartridge must then be removed and the threads cleaned and lubricated before replacement. Expended cartridges must be replaced promptly, or rust particles will form, which can cause damage to the mechanism and your BC.

A **low–pressure inflator**, which uses low pressure air from your regulator to inflate your BC, is considered to be standard equipment. These inflators are available with either balanced or unbalanced valves. A balanced valve is recommended. Its operation is easier, because it is unaffected by the low–pressure air.

A type of BC that is available in Europe and Canada includes a small air cylinder for emergency inflation of the bladder independent from the primary scuba unit. The unit also has a demand mouthpiece that allows air in the bladder to be inhaled while the exhausted breath passes into the water, just as it does in a scuba regulator. Depressing the manual inflator valve allows rebreathing of exhaled air to prolong the air supply. The use of a BC as a breathing bag is a skill that requires training and that must be reserved for emergency use only.

Buoyancy compensators require more than casual care. Internal rinsing is critical, especially for ocean diving, because sand and dried salt can cause wear. Prevent water from entering the bladder by orienting the mouthpiece of the deflation valve downward when the valve is open. The BC can still be deflated by raising the deflator valve above the BC, but the inverted mouthpiece will act as an air trap to exclude water. Your BC should be inflated for storage. The storage area should be temperature regulated and free from smog and ozone. Many divers store their expensive diving equipment in a garage, which is not a good fume–free environment for the materials used in such equipment.

Dry Suits

Dry suits are the most efficient way for a scuba diver to remain comfortable in cold water. The most popular dry suits on the market today are made from a variety of waterproof materials, including vulcanized rubber, waterproofed nylons, and compressed neoprene (Figs. 1-45 through 1-47). The suits seal at the neck and wrists, and they are equipped with waterproof zippers for entry. Low–pressure inflator mechanisms prevent suit squeeze, and suit exhaust valves allow air to escape on ascent. The theory behind these suits is that they form a waterproof barrier but offer little or no insulation value themselves. To be warm, you must wear some type of thermal insulation underneath the suits. These suits also have no inherent buoyancy.

Compressed neoprene suits possess the ability to stretch, which allows the suit to be tailored well to the individual diver's body. The seams of these suits are glued and stitched. On–site repairs to this material when punctured can be difficult (see Fig. 1-45).

Waterproof, laminated nylons have almost no stretch. Suits made from these materials must be cut quite loosely to allow you to dress in them without difficulty. This creates some added volume in the suit, which may increase your weight requirements. You can do some repairs to these types of suits yourself, but major repairs must be handled by the manufacturer.

Vulcanized rubber dry suits should be manufactured from a combination of natural and synthetic materials to resist ozone. This material has fairly good stretch. Patching this type of dry suit is similar to patching an inner tube or inflatable boat.

All dry suits for active divers should be equipped with attached hard–sole boots and knee pads. Automatic suit exhaust valves, which vent air on ascent without manual operation by the diver, are another important feature. Exhaust valves usually are located on a sleeve of the suit.

Fig. 1-45. Foam neoprene dry suits are made of the same material as wet suits.

Fig. 1-46. Shell dry suits are lightweight and comfortable.

Fig. 1-47. Vulcanized rubber dry suits are strong and durable.

Better dry suit inflator valves and hoses are designed with restricted orifices. This helps to prevent accidental overinflation should the inflator valve stick. Valves with large orifices or high flows may freeze during ice diving. The exhaust valve on the suit should vent the suit faster than the inflator valve can supply air. Inflator valves normally are located on the chest of the suit (Figs. 1-48 and 1-49).

Inflator hoses for dry suits should only be connected to a low–pressure port on your regulator's first stage. The hose should reach the inflator valve without strain. Some inflator valves can be rotated to provide you with a choice of how to route the inflator hose (i.e., under the arm, over the shoulder, and so on). Not all inflator hoses are compatible with all dry–suit inflator valves. The safest hoses for recreational divers will disconnect themselves automatically from the inflator valve if the cylinder is ditched.

The quality of waterproof zippers varies greatly among manufacturers. A careful comparison will assure you of reliable operation. Generally speaking, the larger waterproof zippers are the strongest (Fig. 1-50).

There are many options available on today's dry suits, and one of the most important is a dry hood. More than one half of your body heat is lost through your head. A dry hood with an insulating liner will help to keep you warm, even under the coldest conditions. If a dry hood is used, you must remember to equalize the air space in the hood during descent by exhaling through your nose into your mask and forcing a small amount of air into the hood. Scuba mask purge valves can be mounted in dry hoods to allow excess air to escape during ascent. Ordinary wet suit hoods can also be worn with dry suits, and other dry–suit options include pockets, relief zippers (for men only), and dry gloves.

Dry gloves are recommended for diving in water colder than 40° F. A complete dry glove system is composed of a set of insulating liners, gloves, and rings. The inner rings are designed to fit inside the sleeve of the dry suit at the cuff. The outer rings fit over the sleeve and snap into position when properly aligned with the inner rings. The dry gloves or mittens stretch over the outer rings and are held in place by a compression fit.

Dry suits generally fit quite a bit looser than wet suits, and custom suits are available. The most critical part of a dry suit's fit is the length. The suit should be long enough that you can bend and squat comfortably, but without the suit being too long. If the suit is too short, you will not be able to swim effectively or climb a ladder comfortably.

Fig. 1-48. Dry suit exhaust valve.

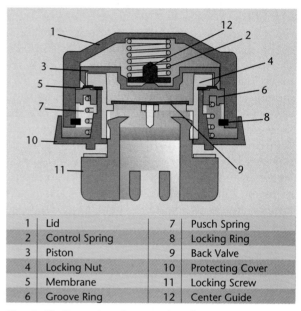

1	Lid	7	Pusch Spring
2	Control Spring	8	Locking Ring
3	Piston	9	Back Valve
4	Locking Nut	10	Protecting Cover
5	Membrane	11	Locking Screw
6	Groove Ring	12	Center Guide

Fig. 1-49. Dry suit exhaust valve that vents automatically.

Fig. 1-50. Some dry suit zippers can be opened and closed by the user.

Once you have purchased a dry suit, be sure to take the time to adjust the neck seal to your individual neck size. Latex neck seals are cone shaped and must be trimmed with sharp scissors. Neoprene neck seals must not be cut; they should only be stretched. As a rule of thumb, the circumference of the neck seal opening should be approximately 10% to 15% less than the circumference of your neck.

Dry suits must be carefully maintained. Latex wrist seals (Fig. 1-51) and neck seals should be periodically washed with mild soap and water to remove body oils, which will attack the rubber. Once the suit is dry, dust the latex seals with pure, unscented talc.

Clean your dry suit zipper periodically using a small nylon brush and soapy water on the teeth. Dry suit zippers should be lubricated with paraffin wax on the outside only. Silicone spray should never be used on dry suits or dry suit zippers. Silicone on your suit will make it impossible to create a strong bond when patches are applied during repairs.

Rinse the outside of your suit after each day of diving, paying particular attention to the valves. If the suit has been flooded in salt water, or if you sweat heavily while wearing the suit, rinse the inside as well. Be sure to allow both the outside and inside of the suit to dry before storage. Many people make the mistake of only feeling inside the upper torso of the suit to check if it is dry; however, sweat accumulates in the lower portions of the suit, creating mold if the interior is not allowed to dry before storage. Turn the suit inside out and be sure that it dries thoroughly before you put it away. Your dry suit should always be stored rolled up in a bag.

Waterproof zippers are especially vulnerable to mishandling. More zippers are broken through improper storage and handling than through actual use. Zippers have a reasonable bend radius when open but less than 50% of the same bend radius when closed. If your suit is stored with the zipper closed and a weight belt is dropped on it, the zipper may break.

Effective dry suit underwear is critical to the optimum performance of your suit in cold water. The function of dry suit underwear is to trap a layer of air inside the suit. The number of layers and type of underwear you will require depend on the water temperature as well as your individual body type and physiology. There are several different types of underwear materials commonly used for diving, including Thinsulate, radiant insulating material, "woolly bears," and polypropylene liners (Fig. 1-52).

Fig. 1-51. The wrist seals must be properly adjusted to function properly.

Fig. 1-52. Dry suit undergarments are available in a variety of types and thicknesses.

Dry suit underwear must not drastically compress when pressure is applied, or it will not work efficiently at depth. Thinsulate™ is one type that maintains most of its original thickness in use. Conversely, woolly bears lose much of their insulating capacity during a dive.

You may not realize it while you are diving, but you frequently will sweat while wearing your dry suit. For this reason, you will want to launder your dry suit underwear occasionally. Woolly bears may be laundered with mild detergents. Radiant insulating material may only be laundered with non-phosphate detergents. Thinsulate can be laundered with bleach or soap; however, improper laundering of Thinsulate garments will destroy their insulating abilities. Consult the manufacturer's directions for proper laundering.

Be especially cautious of undergarments that produce lint. Woolly bears in particular will create lint, which can clog your dry suit exhaust valve. Lint can cause the valve to jam, either open or closed. If the valve jams open, it will leak and you will get wet. If the valve jams closed, you will not be able to vent air from the suit and could experience an uncontrolled ascent.

Thinsulate and radiant insulating material are both efficient insulators even when wet. Open-cell foam maintains good efficiency when damp but will not keep you warm if your suit floods. Woolly bears rapidly lose their heat-trapping capabilities when damp.

The combination of dry suit and insulation that is worn will determine the amount of weight you will need for diving. The more insulation worn, the more air will be trapped in the suit. In general, most dry suit underwear combinations require some additional weight beyond what you might wear with a full one quarter-inch thick (i.e., 7-mm) wet suit.

Polypropylene liners can be worn next to your skin beneath the dry suit undergarments. The purpose of the liner is to wick moisture (i.e., sweat) away from your body to keep you feeling dry. The liner also serves as an extra layer of insulation in colder waters.

Other equipment adaptations also must be made when using a dry suit. Extra large fins are often a necessity with dry suit boots. Back-mounted buoyancy systems work better with many dry suit valve configurations. Low-pressure swivel "Ts" may be needed on some regulators to accommodate the addition of the dry suit inflator hose. Ankle weights may be used to help distribute additional weight. Careful selection of all of the components of your dry suit system will give you the greatest comfort, safety, and productivity for cold water diving.

AIR COMPRESSORS

There are two main types of compressors: high-pressure, low-volume compressors, used to fill scuba cylinders; and low-pressure, high-volume compressors, used for surface-supplied diving (Fig. 1-53). High-pressure, low-volume compressors are similar to other types used for industrial purposes, except that nontoxic oil must be used for lubrication and special attention is required to prevent contamination of the air.

A compressor operates on the principle of Boyle's law: pressure is increased by reducing volume. The air is compressed in stages. The volume of each successive stage in a compressor is smaller to achieve an increase in pressure at that particular stage. Air is prevented from returning to a previous stage by the use of one-way "check valves" located between each stage. To protect the machine from damage, each stage is equipped with an overpressure relief valve.

Compressors may be driven by either internal combustion or electric motors. Fewer toxins are produced by an electric motor (Fig. 1-54).

Air compressors are rated according to how many **cubic feet per minute** (CFM) on the average they can pump. If an empty, 80-cubic foot cylinder were pumped to 3000 p.s.i. in 10 minutes, the rating of the compressor would be 8 CFM.

Fig. 1-53. Scuba high-pressure air compressors come in a range of sizes.

Air is heated when it is compressed, and the compressed air contains moisture, which is undesirable in scuba cylinders. Air from the final stage of a compressor is usually directed into an expansion chamber, where the expansion reduces the temperature and causes the condensation of most of the moisture. Water collects at the bottom of this "moisture trap," which requires periodic draining.

Air from a compressor usually passes through two or more filters in series. These filters remove odors and further reduce the humidity of the air, but they will not remove carbon monoxide. The air then passes through a manifold system into large storage cylinders, each equipped with a separate shut off valve. A storage system, sometimes called an **air bank**, allows high–pressure air pumped over a relatively long period of time to be used to fill scuba cylinders in a comparatively short period of time. The storage cylinders are charged during periods of low demand, and air from both the storage cylinders and the compressors is used during periods of high demand. One or more filler hoses with cylinder connectors, on–off valves, and bleed valves are connected to the storage cylinder bank.

Small, portable compressors are available for filling scuba cylinders at remote locations. Portable compressors are usually rated at approximately 3 to 5 CFM and are similar to larger, fixed–position compressors. An exception is that

Fig. 1-55. Typical filling station for multiple cylinders.

Fig. 1-54. Typical four stage compressor.

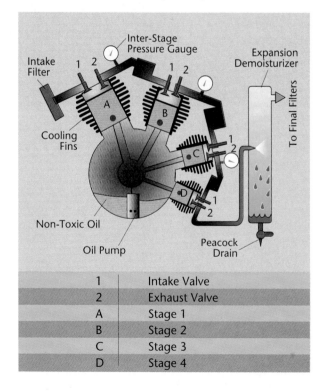

1	Intake Valve
2	Exhaust Valve
A	Stage 1
B	Stage 2
C	Stage 3
D	Stage 4

storage–cylinder banks are not used; cylinders are filled directly from the compressor. Positioning of the air intake and faithful maintenance are extremely important for safety when portable compressors are being used (Fig. 1-55).

Low–pressure, high–volume compressors are available for surface–supplied diving, often referred to as **hookah diving**. A standard regulator second stage is attached to a harness that is attached to an air hose leading to the compressor on the surface. Such a compressor should have a "volume cylinder" on its output to provide a limited emergency supply of air in case the compressor should stop. A backup air supply in the form of scuba cylinders on the surface or a "bailout bottle" (i.e., small scuba cylinder carried by the diver) also should be used for surface–supplied diving operations. Divers should be trained for diving with an umbilical hose before engaging in surface–supplied diving.

SUMMARY

Scuba diving is an equipment–intensive recreational activity. As you broaden your diving skills, you will undoubtedly purchase additional diving equipment. To make an informed decision, you must have a solid educational background concerning the types, methods of operation, care, and maintenance of diving equipment. There are specialty courses available for equipment repair and maintenance that cover these areas in great detail.

SUGGESTED READINGS

- Barsky SM, Long D, Stinton S: *Dry suit diving: a guide to diving dry*, Watersport Publishing, 1992.
- Compressed Gas Association: *Compressed air for human respiration*, Compressed Gas Association, 1980.
- Compressed Gas Association: *Standards for visual inspection of compressed gas cylinders*, Compressed Gas Association, 1985.
- Farley M, Royer C: *Scuba equipment care and maintenance*, Marcor Publishing, 1980.
- High WL: *A guide for visual inspection of scuba and scuba cylinders*, NAUI, 1987.
- Loyst K: *Dive computers: a consumer's guide to history, theory, and performance*, Watersport Publishing, 1991.
- *NOAA diving manual: diving for science and technology*, US Department of Commerce, National Oceanic and Atmospheric Administration, 1991.

LEARNING OBJECTIVES

By the end of this chapter, you will be able to:

1. Correctly define the environmental terms presented in **bold letters**.
2. Identify and explain the following: waves, surge, surf, tides, seiches, currents, thermoclines, haloclines, bottom composition, weather conditions, water conditions, man–made structures, plankton, algae, invertebrates, fishes, birds, mammals, hazardous aquatic animals, predators, and pollution.

WAVES

Waves are a series of undulating energy forms moving through water while the water remains in the same place. Waves generally propagate on the water's surface as a result of wind, and they move in the same direction as the wind. They are secondarily caused by geologic disturbances and the gravitational influences of the sun and moon.

Waves are measured in terms of their height, length, and period. The **height** of a wave is the vertical distance from its crest (i.e., highest point) to its trough (i.e., lowest point). The **wavelength** is the horizontal distance between successive crests (or troughs), and the **period** is the time required for two successive crests to pass a given point (Fig. 2-1).

The volume of water transported by a passing wave is negligible, and it can be disregarded for all practical purposes unless the wave breaks. The water particles within a wave move in an orbital

motion as the waveform moves forward, and they return to nearly their original position as the wave passes. This means that objects do not move horizontally underwater because of wave action. Objects are transported by wind at the surface or by currents underwater. The surface particles move in a circular orbit that equals the wave height. Beneath the surface, these orbits become smaller and smaller, finally diminishing to nothing at a depth equal to approximately one half of the distance between waves. If waves have a wavelength of 50 feet, the influence of those waves will be greatly diminished at a depth of 25 feet or more (Fig. 2-2).

Water waves develop under the influence of newly formed winds. Changes in air pressure on the surface of the water as well as the frictional drag of the air develop ripples on the surface. These ripples evolve into waves whose dimensions increase with the wind velocity, duration, and fetch; **fetch** is the distance over which the wind blows. Energy is transferred directly from the air to the water. Waves pushed by the wind continue to grow until the wind subsides or their steepness increases and they break to form whitecaps. In a steady wind, waves of various dimensions develop, with progressively increasing heights and periods, until a steady state is reached in which the surface is fully developed for the prevailing wind speed. This steady state, known as SEA, is maintained as long as the wind remains constant (Fig. 2-3 and Table 2-1).

When the wind velocity decreases or the waves leave the fetch area, their height decreases and their crests round. Their wavelength also shortens.

Fig. 2-2. Orbital movement of water. As a wave passes, water particles (represented by the circles) do not move with the wave; rather, they complete their orbit by returning to their starting point.

Fig. 2-1. Wave terminology.

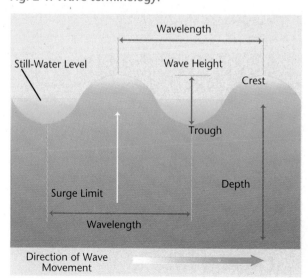

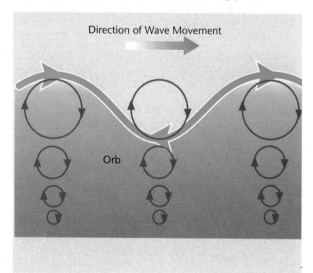

Such waves are called swells. A swell is a wave that is fairly regular in height, period, and direction. In this form, waves can travel thousands of miles while retaining much of their energy.

Extremely large, destructive waves can be generated by earthquakes beneath the seas. These rare occurrences generate waves, once called *tidal waves* or *Tsunamis*. In reality, however, they have nothing to do with the tides and are now more properly called seismic waves. These great waves travel at tremendous speed and build to great heights as they approach land. For this reason, diving must be avoided following major geologic disturbances, even if the seismic event occurs many miles away. Seismic wave predictions are announced on radio and television.

WAVES IN SHALLOW WATER

As a train of waves moves into water shallower than one half of a wavelength, the bottom surface begins to interfere with the orbital motion of the water moving within the waves. The orbits flatten into ellipses, and the net movement of the water becomes a back–and–forth motion known as **surge.** Surge is greatest when the water is shallow, the waves are large, and the wavelength long.

The effect of surge on your diving activities is that it sweeps you back and forth as the waves pass overhead. Diving in strong surge can be hazardous and should be avoided. It is better to drift back and forth with moderate surge than to waste energy fighting it. In light surge, it is possible to secure yourself by holding onto a structure while the surge passes. Generally, the movement of water toward shore is greater than the movement of the water away from the shore, so it is possible to use this tendency to assist you in shallow water when returning to shore. Simply hang on or dig in while the motion is offshore, then move with the motion when it is toward the shore (Figs. 2-4 and 2-5).

As waveforms approach shore and move across shallow bottoms, they are reflected, diffracted (i.e., bent), and refracted. When a wave encounters a vertical wall, such as a seawall or a steep cliff rising from deep water, the wave is reflected back on itself with little loss of energy. The surface chop resulting from such reflected waves can produce

TABLE 2.1 THE BEAUFORT WIND SCALE

		AS USED AT SEA			AS USED ON LAND			
BEAUFORT INTERNATIONAL NUMBER	WIND	NAUTICAL MILES PER HOURS (KNOTS)	FEET PER SECOND	INDICATIONS AT SEA	WIND	STANDARD MPH RECORDED AT 33 FT. ABOVE GROUND LEVEL	INDICATIONS ON LAND	DIVNG OUTLOOK
0	Calm	<1	<2	Sea mirror smooth	Calm	<1	Smoke rises vertically	Excellent
1	Light Air	1-3	2-5	Sm. scale wavelets, no foam crests	Light Air	1-3	Direction shown by smoke but not by wind vanes	Excellent
2	Lt. Breeze	4-6	6-11	Waves short and more pronounced; crests begin to break; foam has glassy look	Lt. Breeze	4-7	Wind felt on face; ordinary vanes move; leaves rustle	Very Good
3	Gentle Breeze	7-10	12-18		Gentle Breeze	8-12	Leaves and small twigs in motion; wind extends flag	Good
4	Mod. Breeze	11-16	19-27	Waves are longer	Mod. Breeze	13-18	Raises dust and waste paper, small branches moved	Care Needed
5	Fresh Breeze	17-21	28-36	Waves pronounced & long white foam crests	Fresh Breeze	19-24	Sm. trees in leaf begin to sway	Great Care Needed
6	Strong Breeze	22-27	37-46	Larger waves; white foam crests more extensive	Strong Breeze	25-31	Lg. branches in motion; whistling heard in telephone wires	No Dive!
7	Strong Wind	28-33	47-56	Sea heaps up, wind blows foam in streaks	Mod. Gale	32-38	Whole trees in motion; difficult to walk against wind	No Dive!
8	Fresh Gale	34-40	57-68	Height of waves& crests increases visibly; foam blown in denser streaks	Fresh Gale	39-46	Breaks twigs off trees, greatly impedes progress	No Dive!
9	Strong Gale	41-47	69-80		Strong Gale	47-54	Slight structural damage	No Dive!
10	Whole Gale	48-55	81-93	High waves with long overhanging crests; great foam crests	Whole Gale	55-63	Seldom experienced inland; trees uproted, considerable structural damage	No Dive!
11	Storm	56-65	94-110	Waves that hide ships within the troughs; sea covered with streaky foam; spray fills air.	Storm	64-75	Very rarely experienced; widespread damage results	No Dive!
12	Hurricane	>65	>110		Hurricane	>75		No Dive!

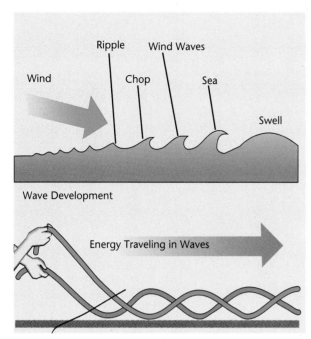

Fig. 2-3. Wave development and movement. Wave movement is a flow of energy similar to that caused by vertically shaking one end of a rope.

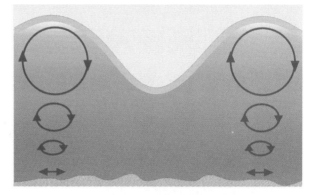

Fig. 2-4. Surge (simple wave). In shallow water there is not sufficient depth for the water particles to complete their circular orbits. The orbits are therefore compressed into oval shapes and, at the very bottom, to horizontal back and forth movements.

uncomfortable situations for divers. Avoid being at the surface in areas of reflected waves (Fig. 2-6).

When waves encounter an obstruction, their motion is diffracted around it. As the waves pass the obstruction, some of their energy propagates sideways because of friction with the obstruction. In other words, the waves bend around into areas that would otherwise be sheltered (Fig. 2-7).

Fig. 2-5. When waves move in shallow water they slow down and crowd together. This shortens their wave lengths and is analogous to automobiles crowding together when they go from a fast speed zone to a slow one. When waves crowd together their wave heights increase.

When a wave front or group of waves approaches a shoreline at an angle, successive portions of the front are slowed as the waves encounter resistance with the bottom. Because different segments of the waves are moving in water of varying depths, the crests and direction of the waves bend until the wave front nearly parallels the contours of the bottom. Thus, waves become parallel to a straight shoreline, concentrated on points of land, and dispersed in coves or bays. Entries and exits by divers on rugged points of land are usually unwise when wave action is significant (Fig. 2-8).

SURF

As the lower portion of a wave slows in shallow water, the top portion moves faster than the bottom, and an unstable condition results. When the depth is approximately twice the wave height, the crest begins to heighten and peak, the wave velocity and wavelength decrease. Finally, at a

Fig. 2-6. Reflected waves.

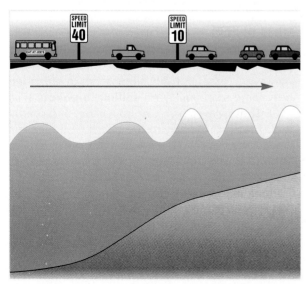

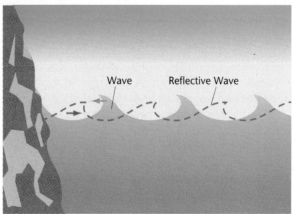

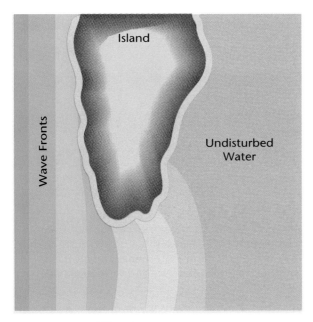

Fig. 2-7. Wave diffraction.

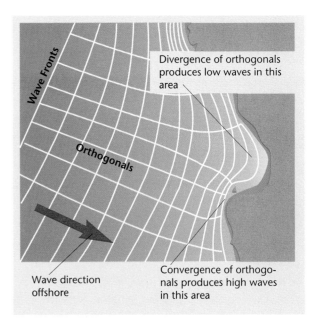

Fig. 2-8. Wave refraction.

depth of approximately 1.3 times the wave height, when the steepest surface of the wave inclines forward more than 60 degrees, the wave becomes unstable and the top portion plunges forward. At this point, water within the wave actually moves with the wave. The broken wave, known as **surf,** forms a "white water" area in which the waves give up their energy and systematic water motion gives way to violent turbulence. This area is known as the surf zone. The white water results from air bubbles trapped in the water; aerated water is less dense and, therefore, provides less buoyancy (Fig. 2-9).

The breaking wave continues landward until the momentum finally carries it into an uprush or swash on the face of the beach. At the uppermost limit, the wave's energy is expended. Water transported landward during the uprush must now return seaward as a backrush or countercurrent flowing back toward the water. This offshore movement of water usually is not evident beyond a depth of 3 feet, and it is *not* to be considered an undertow. An undertow, or a current that flows seaward and pulls swimmers under the surface, is a myth and does not exist. The backrush on a steep beach can be quite strong, however, and it may require you to crawl out of the water to avoid having your feet swept out from beneath you.

If the water deepens again after a wave has broken, such as happens where sandbars or reefs are adjacent to the shore, the wave may reform into systematic orbital motion. This new wave will be smaller than the original, and it will proceed into water approximately equal to 1.3 times its height and may break again. You may use the presence of

waves breaking offshore as an indicator for the location of reefs or sandbars.

One frequent characteristic of breaking waves is variability in their height. Generally, breaking waves approach in **sets** of smaller waves followed by another group of larger waves, each of which is usually higher than its predecessor. These sets result from the arrival of two trains of swells from two different sources. When the crests of two sets of swells coincide, they can reinforce each other and produce waves higher than those of either individual swell train. When the crests of one set coincide with the troughs in the other, a cancellation effect produces smaller waves. A definite cycle or pattern to the sets often results. By studying breaking waves, you can determine the surf beat, or frequency of the sets, and time your entry or exit to coincide with the lull period of minimum wave height.

Types of Surf

The slope of the beach significantly influences the width of the surf zone and the violence of breaking waves. On a gradually sloping beach, a moderately large swell will form **spilling breakers** (Fig. 2-10). These waves break far from shore and continue to break all the way to the beach. The long surf zone allows waves to release their energy gradually. Water is usually turbid in the surf zone because of sediment, which is disturbed over a wide area.

Plunging breakers release their energy quickly. This type of surf is formed by large swells over a moderately steep bottom. As the swell moves toward shore, the waves steepen quickly and break suddenly. These waves break with tremendous force, and they are the most hazardous type.

Large ones (i.e., over 3 ft) can easily knock over a standing diver. The crest of a plunging breaker curls over, forming a "tube" or large air pocket. A spectacular crash of water results, and foam is thrown into the air as that air pocket expands after being compressed by the weight of the wave. Visibility is usually better beyond plunging breakers, because these waves expend their energy in a very narrow area.

Collapsing breakers are formed by swells of medium height over a very steep bottom. As the waves break over their lower half, very little splash or foaming occurs. Thus, the wave breaks rather uneventfully.

Small swells approaching a very steep bottom produce surging breakers. These waves slide up and down the steep incline with little or no foam production.

Effects of Surf on Beaches

During the winter, waves generally break closer together than they do during the summer. These shorter–length winter waves break closer to shore and carry sand offshore, exposing rocks both on the beach and in the surf zone. During the calmer summer months, wave periods are longer and the waves break well offshore, washing sand back onto the beach and covering the rocks again.

Surf Passages

The wave patterns and surf beat must be observed to determine when and if it is desirable to make a passage through the surf zone. On grad-

ually sloping beaches, divers who are completely outfitted (including fins) shuffle into the surf sideways or backward while watching the incoming waves over their shoulders. Knees should be bent to maintain balance when standing in the surf zone. Maintain a wide stance for support and a low center of gravity. If you fall or are knocked down, remain horizontal and swim or crawl rather than trying to regain your footing. As soon as the water is sufficiently deep (i.e., approximately thigh level), you should lie down and begin snorkeling. Swim under the incoming waves. If a float is used, it should be towed behind you through the surf zone.

A high surf on a steeply sloping beach can be dangerous for a fully equipped diver. The surf zone in this case is only a few feet wide, but the waves break violently and directly on the beach. Your feet may be swept from beneath you if you enter while large waves are breaking. The waves also could potentially break directly on top of you. When conditions are severe, it is best to seek a safer, alternate location. If conditions are reasonable, the following procedures are suggested:

1. Have your buoyancy compensator partially inflated for *slight* positive buoyancy.
2. Be fully equipped.
3. Get as close to the water's edge as possible after timing the sets and lulls to match your entry with the smallest waves.
4. Enter the water as quickly as possible immediately after a wave breaks, and get beyond the surf zone quickly, before the next wave breaks. This is an advanced skill.

Fig. 2-9. Surf zone and surf. 1. Surf zone; 2. Translatory waves; 3. Inner line of breakers; 4. Peaked-up wave; 5. Reformed oscillatory wave; 6. Outerline of breakers; 7. Still-water level; 8. Waves flatten again; 9. Waves break-up, but do not break on this bar at high tide; 10. Limit of uprush; 11. Uprush; 12. Backrush; 13. Beach face; 14. Inner bar; 15. Outer bar (inner bar at low tide); 16. Deep bar; 17. Mean lower low water; 18. Breaker depth; 19. Plunge point.

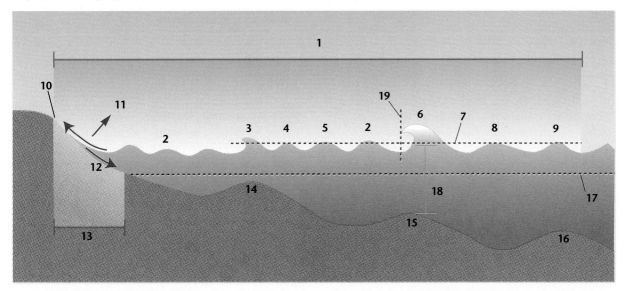

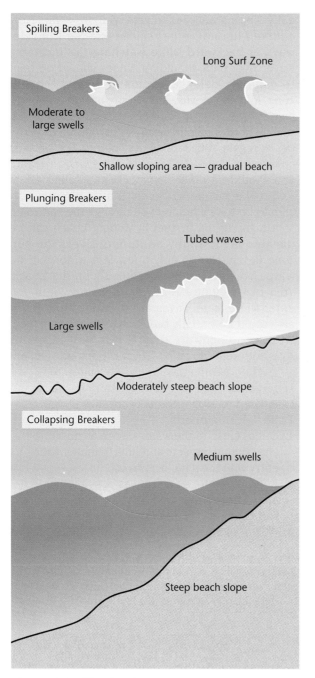

Fig. 2-10. Spilling breakers.

Fig. 2-11. Surf entries should be practiced under the supervision of an instructor.

shore to waist–deep water, then stand, turn your back toward the beach, watch the oncoming waves, lean forward with your knees bent, and shuffle to shore. You should duck beneath any oncoming waves that are higher than chest level.

To exit through plunging breakers, again time the surf beat and ride the back of a wave toward the beach. Beware of being sucked into the wave and "over the falls." Swim hard to pass quickly through the surf zone before the next wave breaks. Remain horizontal and literally crawl clear of the water before standing (Fig. 2-12).

When exiting through surf, keep all equipment in place until you are clear of the water. During such exits, avoid having a float between yourself and oncoming waves, because the float could be pushed into and over you.

TIDES

Tides are the predictable, periodic rising and falling of waters, primarily because of the gravitational attraction of the Moon and, secondarily, of the Sun on the Earth. The Moon, being closer to the earth, influences the tides approximately twice as much as the Sun. On seacoasts, tides are regular and rhythmic, and they are essentially long–period waves with a wavelength equal to one half the circumference of the earth.

The gravitational attraction between the Earth and the Moon results in a tide–producing force on

Surf entries over shallow rocks or coral are potentially hazardous, and they require special training to prevent injuries. Such entries should be avoided until the proper procedures are developed under the supervision of a trained and experienced instructor (Fig. 2-11).

When exiting through surf, stop outside the surf zone and evaluate the surf conditions. Your exit should be timed so that you ride the back of the last large wave of a set. Keep a hand on your mask if waves are breaking on you in the surf zone. To exit through spilling breakers, swim toward the

the Earth's hemisphere nearest the Moon. On the hemisphere opposite the Moon, the tide–producing force is in the opposite direction (i.e., away from the Moon). The resulting effect is two bulges of water on opposite sides of the Earth. Visualize the bulges remaining relatively stationary as the Earth rotates on its axis. Ideally, most points on the Earth should experience semidiurnal (i.e., twice daily) tides. Because of the tilt of the Earth, however, the position of the Moon relative to the equator results in an inequality of tidal patterns in many locations.

The Sun acts similarly on the waters, but with lesser effect. The total tide–producing force exerted on the Earth results from both the Sun and the Moon. Solar tides increase or reduce lunar tides. The two most important situations are when the Earth, Sun, and Moon are aligned (i.e., in phase) and when all three are at right angles to each other (i.e., out of phase). When in phase, the solar tide reinforces and amplifies the lunar tide, causing higher–than–usual spring tides that occur at the new and full moons. Neap tides, or lower–than–usual tidal changes, occur when the Sun and Moon are out of phase.

Tidal range is further influenced by the proximity of the Moon to the Earth. When the Moon is in its orbit nearest to the Earth (i.e., at perigee), tides are higher; when the Moon is farthest from the Earth (i.e., at apogee), tides are lower. When spring tides coincide with a perigee, the highest tides of the year are produced. When neap tides coincide with an apogee, the lowest tides of the year occur (Fig. 2-13).

Although tidal forces exert themselves over the Earth in a regular manner, the configurations of the ocean basins and interference of land masses prevent the tides from assuming a simple, regular pattern. As water flows over land, friction creates drag and slows its movement. Water is funneled between and around land masses. Therefore, tidal variances are formed around our planet. These variations are usually documented, however, and tables are available to assist with dive planning.

A body of water has a natural period of oscillation (i.e., back–and–forth movement, like water sloshing in a basin) that depends on its dimensions. The waters of the Earth comprise numerous oscillating basins rather than a single oscillating body. The response of a basin of water to tide–producing forces determines the type of tide produced in that basin.

Tides are classified in three types:

1. **Diurnal** (i.e., daily): One high and one low tide occurring every 24 hours and 50 minutes (i.e., the time required for the Moon to pass a fixed point on the Earth twice).
2. **Semidiurnal** (i.e., twice daily): Two high and two low tides of approximately equal height every 24 hours and 50 minutes. A tidal change occurs approximately every 6 hours.
3. **Mixed:** A combination of diurnal and semidiurnal. The heights of the tides are unequal.

The height of tides varies considerably (Fig. 2-14) as a result of many factors, including shoreline configuration, time of month and year, and wind conditions. Tidal amplitude on an open shore is usually 2 to 5 feet, but the tidal range in harbors and estuaries can be very great (e.g., 40 feet or more), resulting in extremely strong currents during ebb or flood. Further, the height of tides may vary over 30 feet between two locations only a few hundred miles apart.

Fig. 2-13. Tide cycle. The relationship of the sun and the moon affect the tides.

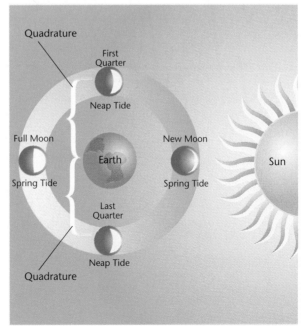

Fig. 2-12. One method of a surf exit is to crawl on hands and knees.

A tidal current is the periodic, horizontal movement of water associated with the tides, reversing the direction of flow as the tide changes. Water flowing toward shore or upstream with a rising tide is called a flood tide, and water flowing offshore or downstream with a falling tide is called an ebb tide. Tidal currents can be very strong, especially when the water is moving through narrow areas. A narrow channel connected to a large body of water concentrates and amplifies the tidal currents. On an open coast, where the direction of flow is not restricted, tidal currents flow continuously, with the direction changing according to the tidal period (Fig. 2-15).

At each reversal of current, a short period of little or no current exists. This period is called slack water. During flow in each direction, the speed will vary from zero at the time of slack water to maximum strength approximately midway between the slack periods (Fig. 2-16).

Divers are encouraged to refer to local tide tables. Personal evaluations of water movement must be made to determine slack–water times, which often present more favorable diving conditions. Tide tables and specific information are contained in various forms in many navigational publications and newspapers. Tidal current tables, issued annually, list daily predictions of tides.

In some channels or straits, you will be limited to only 15 to 20 minutes of easy diving time during slack water. Precautions are essential when diving in such areas. Careful preplanning is necessary to take advantage of this narrow window of diving opportunity. You should not attempt to swim against a strong current. If caught in such a current, inflate your buoyancy compensator and swim perpendicular to the current toward the shore; alternatively, signal and wait to be picked up by a boat.

SEICHES

When the surface of a large, partially enclosed body of water such as one of the Great Lakes or a bay is disturbed, long waves may be established that oscillate rhythmically as they reflect from opposite ends of the basin. These waves, called *seiches* (pronounced "say–chez"), have a period that depends on the size and depth of the basin. Many people are unaware of seiches because of their very low wave height and extremely long wavelength (Fig. 2-17).

In large lakes, seiches may result from differential barometric pressure changes, but they are caused more frequently by winds. For example, a strong wind blowing for several hours along the axis of a large lake will drive the surface water toward the leeward (i.e., downwind) end of the lake, raising the water surface there by as much as 10 feet while lowering the level at the windward end of the lake. This oscillation, which diminishes rapidly in amplitude, has a period that may exceed 12 to 14 hours.

Fig. 2-14. Types of tide curves.

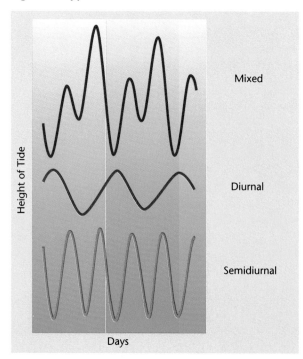

Days

Fig. 2-15. Flood and ebb. Tides have significant effect in narrow waterways on the coast.

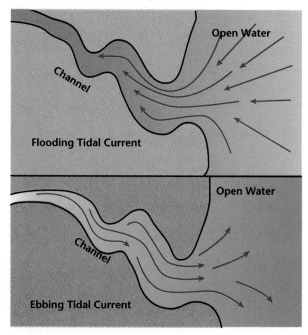

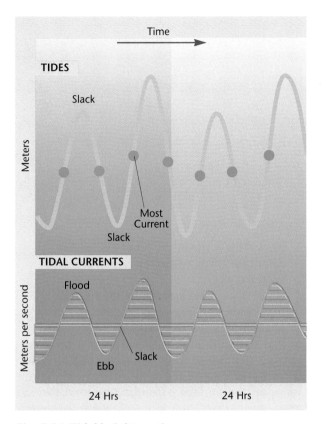

Fig. 2-16. Tidal height vs. time.

In bays that are open to the ocean, seiches nearly always result from a long–period wave train. When the water in the bay is set in motion by the initial wave, seiches continue at the natural period of oscillation for that harbor or bay. Seiches can affect diving by reducing visibility and rapidly changing the water level at the entry and exit points.

CURRENTS

In addition to tidal currents, there are several other types of currents with which you need to be familiar.

Longshore Current

Waves approaching shore at an angle cause a current system that flows parallel to the shore. These currents, which can achieve a velocity too great to swim against when the surf is large, are known as **longshore currents**. The speed of the current is usually less than 1 knot, but this speed increases with wave height, increased angle of waves to the shore, and the steepness of the beach. The intensity of a longshore current is greatest inside the surf zone and diminishes as you move away from shore (Fig. 2-18).

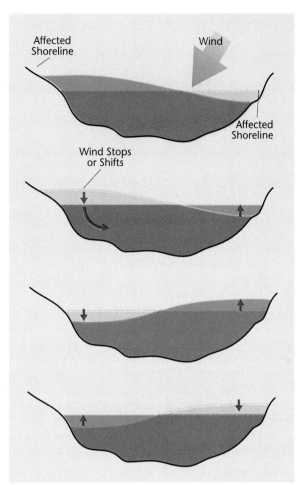

Fig. 2-17. Seiching.

A longshore current can move you down the beach and perhaps to an undesirable exit area. Visibility near shore will be reduced by a longshore current, which transports sediment downcurrent. Items dropped near shore will tend to move in the direction of the longshore current. A strong longshore current tends to form a "cut," "trench," or "inshore hole" in the surf zone, especially on steeply sloping beaches. When wading on what you might consider to be a continuous incline, you may suddenly and unexpectedly find yourself in water over your head. Longshore currents should be evaluated before entering the water so that actions can be taken to compensate for any effects. They often can be detected by watching floating wood, birds, or other debris for movement in the current. If the surf is so large that a strong longshore current is produced, diving is inadvisable.

Rip Current

A **rip current** is formed by water seeking its own level. When a large set of waves approaches a beach, the surge of the water builds the water level on the incline of the beach. Being higher

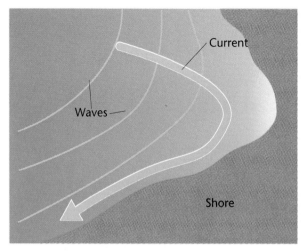

Fig. 2-18. Longshore current.

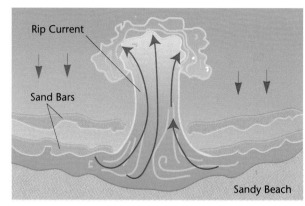

Fig. 2-19. Rip current.

than the average water level, this water seeks to return to that level. If the return occurs through a deeper section of the offshore bottom, then a rip current may form. The distance that a rip current may flow varies in length from 20 yards to one half of a mile or more. These currents are the leading cause of surf rescues of swimmers, and they can pose problems for divers when they are encountered unexpectedly (Fig. 2-19).

The intensity of a rip current is greatest during the lull in a set of waves. There also is a direct relationship between the size of the surf and the intensity of a rip current. Larger surf equates a stronger rip current.

There are four types of rip currents:

1. Permanent: This is formed by a rock channel or subsurface topography that changes very little. Permanent structures such as piers, jetties, pipelines, or outcroppings can also create rips.
2. Fixed: A fixed rip is second in its longevity of location only to a permanent rip current. A hole or gully in the offshore bottom can create a rip current that may last from several hours to several months.
3. Flash: This is temporary in nature for any given location and is caused by a large surf buildup during a short period of time. They appear suddenly and without warning and are relatively short lived.
4. Traveling: A traveling rip current is propelled along a shore frontage by a strong longshore current. This type may travel over large segments of beach before dissipating.

There are three basic parts of a rip current:

1. Mouth: This is the shoremost part, known as a feeder zone. It can be fed by a longshore current and the buildup of water on the incline of a beach.

2. Neck: This is the midpoint of a rip current, where the offshore motion has its greatest velocity.
3. Head: This is the area where the rip current dissipates its energy and ceases to flow offshore.

Rip currents may be recognized by a fan-shaped buildup of water on a beach, a stream of dirty water extending outward from the shore, foam on the surface extending beyond the surf zone, and a distinct lack of surf where the current flows outward. Detection of a rip current is most difficult on windy days when the surf is choppy (Fig. 2-20).

Modest rip currents may be used to aid offshore movement. If you realize that you are in a rip current and wish to get out of it, do so by swimming perpendicular to the current, which is seldom wider than 100 feet. Swim out of the rip on the downcurrent side if a longshore current exists as well. The velocity of a rip current is often greater than 1 knot and should not be fought. Experienced divers sometimes use rip currents to get offshore quickly. They ride the current to its head and then exit on the downcurrent side. If you are not familiar with rip currents, it is best to avoid them entirely.

Wind Currents

Offshore currents in large bodies of water are caused by the wind. They are essentially streams of water moving within a larger body of water. Temperature differences create convection currents in the oceans, although convection currents have very low velocities.

The stress of wind blowing across water causes the surface layer of that water to move. This motion is transmitted to succeeding layers of water beneath the surface. The rate of motion decreases with depth. A wind current does not flow in the direction of the wind because of the force of the rotation of the Earth, or the **Coriolis force.**

Deflection by the Coriolis force is to the right in the northern hemisphere and the left in the southern. Therefore, major ocean currents tend to flow clockwise above and counterclockwise below the equator. The Coriolis force is greater in the higher latitudes and most effective in deep water. Current direction varies from approximately 15° from the wind along shallow coastal areas to a maximum of 45° in deep oceans.

The velocity of a wind–produced current depends on the speed of the wind, its constancy, the length of time that it blows, and other factors. A wind blowing for 12 hours or longer in the same direction will cause a surface current equal to approximately 2% of the wind speed. The **set** and **drift** of a current refer to the current's direction and velocity, respectively. The strength of a current is affected by:

1. Water depth: The speed of a wind–driven current decreases rapidly with depth.
2. Bottom formations: The bottom acts to resist water movement. Therefore, a current is generally weakest at the bottom.
3. Water temperature: Water becomes colder with depth. As the temperature decreases, the density or weight of the water increases, and heavier water impedes wind–driven currents.

If unexpectedly caught downstream from your exit point, the preferred order of options is:

1. Return upstream on the bottom if air is available. Pulling hand over hand is best.
2. Swim perpendicular to the current in an attempt to get clear of it.
3. Exit at a preplanned, alternate exit location.
4. Obtain positive buoyancy, signal for assistance, and wait to be rescued. Useful devices to signal rescuers include a whistle, a mask faceplate that can be used as a reflector, or an inflatable rescue tube. Waving both arms overhead is also a recognized diver–distress signal.

Fig. 2-20. Overhead view of a rip current.

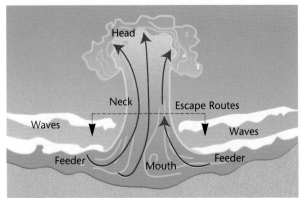

The following procedures are recommended for diving when currents are either anticipated or present (Fig. 2-21):

1. Always begin the dive against a current and not with it unless you are trained, prepared, and equipped to make a drift dive. Stay close to the bottom, pull yourself along, and avoid unnecessary kicking that can lead to overexertion and fatigue. Turn around with at least one half of your air supply remaining, and return with the current.
2. Descents should be made down a weighted descent line or down the anchor line. Free descents in currents should be avoided.
3. A trail line at least 100 feet in length should be extended from the dive boat to assist divers back to the vessel if they surface downstream.
4. A qualified operator should remain on the boat at all times to assist anyone who is swept downstream.

Note that the maximum sustainable swimming speed of a fully equipped, physically fit scuba diver is approximately 1 knot. Swimming against a 1–knot current therefore is unwise, because it will quickly lead to exhaustion.

Also note that diving by drifting with a current is a popular activity in some areas, but training and supervised experience are paramount for safety. An orientation to drift diving is presented later in this book.

River Currents

Currents are also caused by gravity, such as when water flows downhill. Such currents can be extremely strong and hazardous. Sediment and other matter, or bubbles on the surface, can reduce visibility in rivers to zero.

Currents in rivers are strongest in the middle, at the surface, and on the outside edges of bends. The strength of the current decreases with depth and proximity to the shore.

The swift waters of rivers as well as their varying bottom conditions can produce rapids, whirlpools, sucking holes, waterfalls, eddy currents, and other unique and hazardous forms of water movement. Special training, procedures, and equipment are required for diving in swift–flowing rivers.

Fig. 2-21. Procedures for current diving.

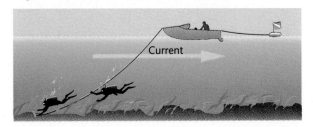

THERMAL CHANGES

Water temperatures can vary with the season, depth, and changing wind and weather conditions. The common thermal changes in both freshwater and saltwater are described here.

Upwelling

During conditions of continuous and strong offshore, sideshore, or side–onshore winds along a coast, warm surface water can be blown offshore and replaced by colder, nutrient–laden water from beneath. This colder water, brought vertically to the surface from the depths, is known as **upwelling.** Certain areas with offshore dropoffs and seasonal winds are prone to upwellings (Fig. 2-22).

An upwelling initially results in colder, clearer water with increased amounts of nutrients, which can lead to plankton blooms. Good diving conditions prevail for a few days, until the excess nutrients begin to foster plankton growth that will reduce water visibility.

Thermal Stratification

During the summer months, the surface waters of lakes and quarries are warmed by the sun and form a layer of water called the **epilimnion.** Beneath this layer, a cold and dense layer of water, termed the **hypolimnion**, remains. The surface may reach a temperature of 70° F or more, but the bottom temperature in a typical deep lake remains approximately 39.2° F, which is the temperature of maximum density for freshwater. Between the two layers is a zone of rapid temperature change called a thermocline (Fig. 2-23).

During the fall months, the surface waters of lakes cool. When the water temperature is approximately 43° F, wind–caused circulation is sufficient

to destroy the thermocline and mix the entire water column, producing condition called an isotherm (i.e., same temperature). This isothermal condition (i.e., **fall turnover**) exists until late winter, when the lake has cooled to approximately 35.6° F. Further cooling then produces sufficiently less–dense surface water, with a temperature of near 32° F. This lighter water forms a stratification sufficient to prevent circulation of the deeper water, and a reverse thermocline is developed (Fig. 2-24).

As the spring sun warms the surface water, the **spring turnover** begins. This mixing continues until the surface water exceeds 39.2° F, producing a less–dense upper layer and initiating the summer stratification period.

Water is one of the few substances whose solid form, ice, is less dense than its liquid form. This is why ice stays on the surface when it forms in water. It is also one of the conditions that allowed life to develop in aquatic systems.

Thermal stratification in lakes affects the amount of oxygen in the water and, therefore, the distribution of fish. The temperature also affects plankton populations, which in turn affect visibility. In many lakes, isothermal conditions present the best times for diving, unless wind action disturbs sediment and reduces the visibility.

A **halocline** is a horizontal boundary between waters of differing salinity. In some situations where freshwater comes into contact with sea water, the waters remain separated in layers because of their different densities. At the bound-

Fig. 2-23. Lake temperature profile.

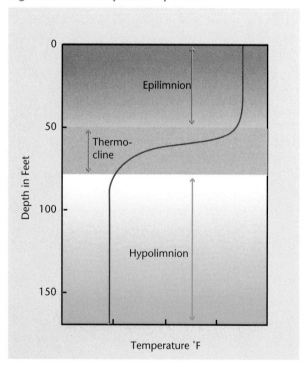

Fig. 2-22. Upwelling.

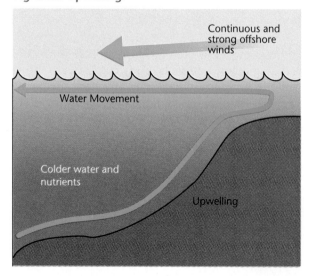

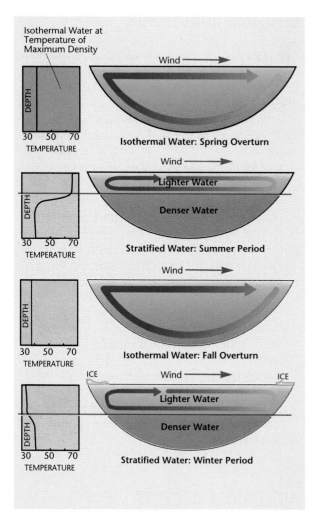

Fig. 2-24. Annual cycle of lakes.

ary where the two layers come into contact, however, a mixing occurs. This boundary, which can be several feet deep, affects your vision as you pass through it, and it can produce a feeling of disorientation. Although it is not physically dangerous, you should avoid lingering in a halocline if one is encountered while diving.

BOTTOM CONDITIONS

The type of bottom in the diving area affects visibility, aquatic life, navigation, dive planning, and the equipment that is necessary. Coral bottoms usually offer good visibility, warm water, abundant fish, and exciting diving. Hazards include coral cuts, marine-life stings, and exceeding your planned depths because of clear water. Wear protective clothing, avoid contact with the corals, and monitor your depth gauge frequently.

Rocky bottoms exist in many colder areas and usually offer many of the benefits of coral reefs.

Visibility varies from area to area and season to season. Hazards include slippery algal growth on rocks at entry and exit areas, surf, currents, and marine plants.

Sandy bottoms are found everywhere and offer varying visibility depending on the amount of water movement. This environment may look like a desert to some divers, but many animals make it their home. Diving on sandy bottoms requires that you maintain neutral buoyancy and minimize fin action near the bottom to avoid raising silt. Avoid dragging your equipment, especially gauges and extra second stages, through the silt as well.

Muddy bottoms vary in consistency from compact, firm clay to a semifluid silt. These types of bottoms are found everywhere, but they are most common in rivers, lakes, and bays. Many animals similar to those found in sand live in the mud. The visibility is generally poor because of the ease with which sediment can be disturbed. Muddy bottoms can significantly affect entries and exits. Beware of slipping and of sinking deeply into the mud.

ENVIRONMENTAL DIVING ACTIVITIES

Divers engage in many specialized activities created by the environment. Natural formations such as caves, caverns, sink holes, and blue holes arouse our curiosity and spark our interest. People dive beneath the ice, in mountain lakes at high elevations, in the blue waters of the open sea, and to depths in excess of 100 feet.

All of these environmental diving activities have something in common: they all require specialized knowledge, equipment, and skills. Specialty training is required for any diving activity that is significantly different from that in which you are currently trained. Special diving techniques to reduce environmental damage can be found in the chapter on Conservation.

MAN-MADE STRUCTURES

Jetties, piers, and wharves can pose dangers from waves, currents, poor visibility, boats, and fishing lines and hooks. Submerged shipwrecks often attract divers, and some are extremely hazardous. Serious dangers include entanglement, entrapment, and becoming lost. Special training and equipment are essential for diving in such areas.

Offshore oil rigs can provide sites for excellent diving (Fig. 2-25). Such rigs are located anywhere

Fig. 2-25. The pilings of oil platforms can be an interesting place for underwater photography.

from just outside the surf line to over 200 miles from shore, in waters of depths that may exceed 300 feet. Spear fishing is often popular in these environments. In addition, the area both under and around a rig is a virtual junkyard of cable, pipe, and so on. Caution must be exercised to avoid entanglement or injury.

Large underwater pipelines are common in some areas as well. Diving in the vicinity of active pipelines is discouraged, because the lines may be discharging large amounts of pollutants that can cause illnesses. Pipelines also may include intakes that can suddenly suck a diver inside.

Diving in the vicinity of dams is also discouraged, because strong currents can literally grab and hold you underwater. You could also be swept through an overflow channel.

WEATHER CONDITIONS

Weather is an important factor affecting diving operations. You must be familiar with local weather conditions and monitor forecasts when planning dives. Different areas may have unique weather conditions. In some areas, offshore operations in small boats are prohibited by weather and surface conditions.

The following are examples of weather–related concerns for divers:
1. Squalls, which are brief, intense rainshowers and can occur on open water quite suddenly.
2. Storms, which produce wind, waves, and runoff that decreases visibility. Lightning, tornadoes, waterspouts, and driving rain also can be dangerous.
3. Low temperatures, which can freeze equipment and cause frostbite and hypothermia.
4. High temperatures and humidity, which can cause hyperthermia, heat exhaustion, and heat stroke.
5. Sunlight, which is more intense near the equator and can cause eye strain and sunburn.
6. Winds, which affect surface conditions, can lower the temperature, and cause currents and seasickness.

BIOLOGICAL ASPECTS

One of the most interesting aspects of the diving environment is the wide variety of living plants and animals that can be seen. Your diving will be more enjoyable if you know more about the aquatic life that you encounter.

Identification

One of the primary divisions of animals and plants is the phylum. Each phylum is divided into a number of classes, which are further divided into orders, which in turn are divided into families. Each family also contains still smaller groups, each of which is called a genus. Finally, the genus is followed by one or more species. An organism's name actually describes the life form, and it consists of the genus and species, which are usually derived from either Latin or Greek. Classifications are keyed externally to such features as color, scales, shape, skeleton, and so.

Ecological Overview

Ecology is the scientific study of organisms in relation to their environments. Animals and plants occupy certain regions within a major environment, such as the sea. The precise "micro–environment" of a species is called its **habitat.** Within any habitat there are different species, each with their own feeding habits and reproductive rates. The position that each species occupies in its habitat is called its **niche.** The niches of various species are determined by physical factors as well as relationships to other species in the same habitat. Thus, the niches of species in a habitat are adjusted to each other, and they form an integrated community. You might notice a number of fish species living in the same kelp forest or coral reef; each has a separate niche based on what they eat (i.e., prey), when they feed, and what type of space they occupy.

Communities react to the nonliving parts of the environment, and vice versa, to form a balanced ecosystem. An example of such an **ecosystem** is a coral reef. Coral polyps secrete carbonates (i.e., limestone), which are bound together by calcareous algae. When man alters a natural environment by fishing, hunting, anchoring, and polluting, this initial disturbance of the animals and plants may eventually disturb the entire ecosystem and eventually destroy it.

Life Zones

There are four basic plant and animal life zones in the ocean:

1. Intertidal or littoral: Plants and animals in the region between high and low tides that are adapted to withstand water loss, temperature extremes, and strong water movement (Fig. 2-26).
2. Planktonic: Drifting and floating forms that are at the mercy of the wind and current. Many animals have planktonic stages in their life cycles. The most common "plants" in the oceans are the phytoplankton, which are algae that use sunlight to produce carbohydrates; they represent the basic food source for all life in the oceans.
3. Nektonic: Free–swimming forms, including fish, which rely on speed and streamlining for their survival. Some live at a constant depth in one area, while others prefer the open seas. Fish may live in schools for a greater chance of survival.
4. Benthic: Bottom–dwelling organisms such as clams, anemones, and seastars. They can live on all types of bottoms, including rocky, sandy, or muddy.

Marine and Freshwater Plants

In contrast to land plants such as grasses, shrubs, and trees, most underwater plants lack a root system, do not require strong and woody limbs for support, and do not need a series of vessels to carry water to the plant from the roots.

Fig. 2-26. The rocky intertidal zone is very rich in marine life, and can be slippery when crossed by divers.

They are called seaweeds, which consist of a group of nonflowering plants that are properly called **algae.** The three most common groups are green algae, brown algae, and red algae. To remain in one place, these plants hold fast to the bottom with a root–like structure called a holdfast. Seaweed–covered rocks can be very slippery, affecting entries and exits. Divers can also become entangled in algae, but this should not pose a serious threat. Panic is the diver's worst foe in this situation. By simply remaining calm and thinking, a diver can usually get free of such an entanglement quickly and easily, or a buddy can assist the entangled diver.

Kelp is the name for the group of large brown algae found in temperate waters. Forests of kelp on the western coast of the United States grow from depths of up to 100 feet, and they abound with life just like the forests on land (Fig. 2-27). Like their terrestrial counterparts, these undersea forests have a beauty that is unique. A tough holdfast anchors the algae to the bottom, while gas bladders called pneumatocysts float groups of stipes (i.e., strands) to the surface, where the kelp spreads out to form a thick, floating canopy. It is much easier to swim under the canopy than through it at the surface, so experienced kelp divers save enough air for a return to their exit point beneath the canopy at the end of a dive (Fig. 2-28).

Surf grass, or eel grass, are flowering plants that are found in the surf zone. Entanglement in these plants is not common. Surge may wash it over you, causing apprehension, but if you remain calm and patient, the grass will clear when the surge reverses direction.

Freshwater plants such as water lilies or hydrilla can grow densely in some inland lakes and streams. You can become entangled in these plants, and surfacing can be difficult. A calm, controlled procedure of freeing yourself is the best solution to an entanglement. In some states, it is illegal to remove and transport certain plants from lakes, so all equipment must be clear of weeds before packing and transporting it.

Invertebrates

Approximately 97% of all animal species are **invertebrates** (i.e., animals without a backbone). These include relatively simple organisms like sponges, jellyfish, and corals up through the worms, molluscs (e.g., snails, clams, and octopus), arthropods (e.g., shrimps, lobster, and crabs,) and echinoderms (e.g., seastars and sea urchins). It is

Fig. 2-27. The kelp forest is a place of special beauty and abundant marine life.

beyond the scope of this book to describe the thousands of species of invertebrates that live in the world's oceans and freshwaters. Only the potentially hazardous types are discussed.

Fishes

The fishes are the oldest and simplest of all living **vertebrates** (i.e., animals with backbones). They are very important economically and provide a vital source of protein for millions of people. They are divided into three major groups: the jawless fishes, bony fishes, and cartilaginous fishes (e.g., sharks, skates, and rays).

Birds and Mammals

Seabirds, birds, and mammals are conspicuous members of the oceans and freshwater regions of the world. You might see birds such as pelicans or cormorants diving into the water, or even see them underwater! Marine mammals include seals, sea lions, walruses, manatees, dugongs, whales, dolphins, and porpoises. Marine mammals are protected in the United States as well as many other areas, and divers should be aware of these laws to avoid problems.

The Food Chain

The **food chain** is a term describing a group of organisms that is linked together primarily by consumption as food items. The first link in the food chain are the one–celled plants. These phytoplankton (also called *diatoms* and *dinoflagellates*) exist in their countless millions in the surface layers of the oceans and are eaten by tiny animals called zooplankton, which in turn are eaten by small invertebrates and small fishes, which in turn are eaten by still bigger fish, and so the process goes. By the time you eat a fish, energy has been transferred through several organisms by a food chain of trophic (i.e., nutritional) levels in the marine community. The higher the trophic level of the organism, the fewer individuals generally will be found. This is because the organism concerned must pay the high energy costs of converting the food to the energy that is needed for respiration, movement, and reproduction. The conversion of one form of energy to another as well as the maintenance of the population becomes more and more expensive as higher trophic levels are considered (Fig. 2-29).

In the warmer waters of the tropics, there is not much plankton because of a lack of nutrients. Plankton thrive in colder, nutrient–rich water. Because of this, the tropical waters are normally clearer than the temperate waters. When conditions are right and plankton do very well, they may rapidly reproduce and form a bloom, causing a drastic decrease in visibility. An extremely heavy bloom is called a **red tide**, because several types of organisms, mainly dinoflagellates, have a red pigment that turns the water brown or reddish.

Some plankton produce a toxin, and if a bloom is heavy, it can kill all of the fish in that area. Some animals such as clams and mussels feed by filtering plankton and concentrate the toxin in their flesh without harm to themselves. If a human eats their flesh, however, the concentrated toxins can cause serious illness. Most of the concentrating organisms are bivalves, such as the cockle clam. It is always wise to ask about the safety of eating local filter feeders.

Many places that do not have red tides have shell fish contaminated from pollution. It is prudent to avoid eating shellfish from a bay where pleasure boaters anchor. The boat toilets empty directly into the water, and this waste settles to the bottom. Many cases of hepatitis and diarrhea have occurred when people have eaten animals from such a bay. Awareness and avoidance are the best safety guidelines.

Hazardous Saltwater Animals

Just how deadly are various species of aquatic animals? How toxic or venomous are they? These are important questions for the modern underwater explorer. The purpose of this section is to familiarize you with some of the more common injuries from aquatic animals without scaring the wits out of you and perpetuating any myths.

Poisonous animals are those creatures whose tissues, either in part or in their entirety, are toxic. In general, marine oral toxins are small molecules that are heat stable or unaffected by cooking. Ichthyosarcotoxism is a term used for a type of poisoning that is identified with eating a specific type of fish.

Venomous animals are those creatures capable of producing a toxin in a highly developed secretory gland (i.e., venom sac) or group of cells and which can deliver this material (i.e., toxin) through a sting or bite. These are the animals with fangs, claws, stingers, spines, or some other mechanism for delivering a toxin. Unlike the oral toxins, venoms are usually large molecules that are detoxified by heat or gastric juices. Toxins delivered by a venom apparatus are often called parenteral toxins.

Oral Toxins

Divers often gather things from the sea to eat, either by spear fishing, crabbing, or picking up shellfish. Paralytic shellfish poisoning is caused by

Fig. 2-28. Divers must be trained to dive in thick kelp.

chemical agents known as saxitoxin and neosaxitoxin. These agents are synthesized in microscopic plants known as fire algae (Pyrrophyta), specifically dinoflagellates (*Gonyaulax tamarensis* or *Gymnodinium breve*) commonly found in marine plankton. These toxic dinoflagellates occasionally increase their numbers tremendously, causing a red tide. Shellfish, such as clams, oysters, and mussels are filter feeders, ingesting large numbers of dinoflagellates and concentrating their toxins in the shellfish tissues. If you collect contaminated shellfish, you could get poisoned. This is a seasonal toxin and only occurs when there has been a dinoflagellate bloom or red tide, usually between May and October.

Paralytic shellfish poisons (i.e., saxitoxins) are neurotoxins, which means that they can cause you to stop breathing (i.e., respiratory arrest). The effective treatment is to keep the victim breathing for the next 24 hours while the toxin is slowly destroyed in the body. Cardiopulmonary resuscitation may be lifesaving for the individual who has been exposed to a large dose of this phytotoxin. Getting the victim to a hospital respirator is essential.

Fig. 2-29. The food chain.

Fish are a high–protein, low–fat source of food for anyone following the American Heart Association guidelines for good nutrition. Most fish contain little or no cholesterol. Some of the more popular fish are becoming difficult to catch, however, and their supply is dwindling. Therefore, we find ourselves eating new species. Fortunately, we are simultaneously becoming more sophisticated in our tastes, but in some cases, the demand for seafood is outgrowing our scientific information about specific species. Fish can be rapidly transported by air to people in areas of the world who have never tried that species before. Along with this improved transport system, we are finding outbreaks of fish poisoning far from the sea, often to the surprise of the local health officials. There is increasing consumption of fish and shellfish worldwide, and technologic improvements have also increased the harvesting of traditional seafoods and new species. All of these factors have contributed to a rise in the occurrence of illness resulting from fish toxins (i.e., ichthyosarcotoxism).

Ciguatera fish poisoning is probably the most common ichthyosarcotoxism. It is a disease with both neurologic and gastrointestinal symptoms. Various reef–dwelling fishes may transmit this poison or group of toxins, known as ciguatoxin. Again, a dinoflagellate (*Gambierdiscus toxicus*) generates the toxins and finds itself as prey in the food chain for many species of fish. The toxin does not seem to affect these fish, who eventually concentrate the material in their tissues and become poisonous to man.

Generally, the larger the fish, the more toxic it can be. Symptoms usually develop 6 to 12 hours after eating the fish, but in some cases, they may show within 1 hour. The first signs are usually gastrointestinal in nature, such as nausea, vomiting, cramps, and diarrhea. These are soon followed by neurologic symptoms, such as tiredness, itching, pain or weakness in the legs, painful joints (i.e., arthralgia), numbness around the mouth, hot and cold reversal of sensation, headache, muscle ache, chills, watery eyes, dizziness, tremors, sweating, and a red rash. Clinical signs vary from minor complaints to coma and death. With proper and prompt diagnosis, the patient can be effectively treated by a physician with drugs. Consumption of fish such as barracuda (sphyraeniadae), grouper (serranidae), red snapper (*Lutjanus bohor*), amberjack (*Seriola dumerili*) and surgeonfish (acanthuridae) can transmit ciguatoxin. Eating any affected fish, whether it is cooked or raw, may result in poisoning.

Another ichthyosarcotoxism is scombroid poisoning, which the Hawaiians refer to as **mahi mahi** (i.e., dolphinfish) **flushing syndrome** or **saurine poisoning.** Scombrotoxic poisoning generally results from eating fish from the families Scomberesocidae, Scombridae, and Pomatomae, which include tuna, bonito, mackerel, and bluefish. Scombroid poisoning occurs when individuals eat fish that are partially decomposed and contain high levels of histamine. Bacteria cause the breakdown of the tissue histidine into histamine and saurine at temperatures above 37° C. The spoiled fish frequently has a peppery or sharp taste, which to some people is not unpleasant.

Signs and symptoms of scombroid poisoning usually occur within the first hour. Symptoms include diarrhea, hot and flushed skin, bright red rash (face and trunk), sweating, nausea, headache (sometimes severe), stomach pain, vomiting, mouth–throat burning sensation, fever, dizziness, tight chest, swollen face, and respiratory distress. Cooking does not destroy the toxic substance in the fish flesh. Cimetidine (Tagamet®) has proved more useful therapeutically than antihistamines for treatment. Always eat fresh fish that has been well refrigerated; if you catch or spear fish, keep them well refrigerated until you can eat or freeze your catch.

The most dangerous of all food poisonings is without doubt those produced by tetrodotoxin, which is a very potent material found in the flesh of pufferfish, globefish, blowfish, or swellfish—what the Japanese refer to as **fugu.** Many people worldwide risk death by eating species from the Tetradontiadae family. Some describe this as playing "Russian roulette" with chopsticks. Eating these fish often produces a strange, warming sensation or a tingling over the entire body. In high concentrations, the tetrodotoxin can cause death in a few minutes by blocking the sodium channels of the muscles and nerves. In other words, this is a potent neurotoxin that stops nerve functions, stops breathing, and causes death. The toxicity varies from species to species and from organ to organ (Fig. 2-30).

The liver and gonads are usually the most toxic parts of pufferfish. Pufferfish raised in aquaculture (i.e., an artificial environment) do not produce tetrodotoxin. In their natural environment, however, pufferfish feed on algae that are covered with a bacteria of the genus *Alteromonas*, which we know produces tetrodotoxin. The northern puffer, *Spheroides maculatus*, which is caught along the east coast of the United States is consumed in large quantities during some years, and it appears to be safe to eat. This is probably because the levels of toxin are so low in their tissues.

The symptoms of "fugu" or tetrodotoxin poisoning include: weakness, dizziness, pallor, tingling around the mouth, lips, tongue and throat, increased salivation, low blood pressure (i.e., hypotension), vomiting (severe and frequent), cyanosis, slow heart beat (i.e., bradycardia), difficulty breathing (i.e., dyspnea). This is followed by shock symptoms. The onset of symptoms is rapid, from 5 to 45 minutes, and death may occur sudden-

Fig. 2-30. Pufferfish can "inflate" to show their numerous spines.

ly and without warning. Treatment includes cardiopulmonary resuscitation (CPR), oxygen, intravenous fluids, atropine, and saline stomach washes. Avoid eating boxfish, cowfish, puffer fish, and any fish that you are unfamiliar with unless it is purchased in a reliable restaurant or seafood center.

Parenteral Toxins

It really is quite easy to reduce your chances of being stung by most creatures in the ocean. The first rule is always to wear protective clothing (e.g., wet, dry, or Lycra suit) whether you are diving in tropical or temperate waters. Australian divers have found that wearing "panty hose" is an effective protection from their dreaded sea wasp, *Chironex fleckeri*. A second rule is to make sure that you always wear gloves and boots, protecting your hands and feet. Finally, look at the bottom before putting your feet down. In this way, you will avoid a surprising confrontation with an electric ray, stingray, or scorpionfish.

There are many animals that sting or have some method of introducing venom. From the most primitive of species to the more complex, venomous marine animals have developed some form of protective apparatus or a unique form of food gathering, and most can be easily avoided. In some cases, you would need to go out of your way to be harmed by these creatures.

For example, no member of the phyla Porifera (i.e., sponges) is going to jump off a rock or coralhead to attack a diver underwater. On the other hand, if a diver should be stupid enough to squeeze a sponge without gloves on, he or she may be in trouble. Sponges have spicules or internal spines, made of silica or calcium carbonate, embedded in the fleshy body (Fig. 2-31). Only a few sponges are harmful to divers, and then only if they come into contact with your skin. The red–beard sponge (*Microciona prolifera*), fire or dread–red sponge (*Tedania ignis*), and the poison–bun sponge (*Fibulila* sp.) can produce a stinging sensation. Other symptoms include a local sensation of severe burning, swelling (i.e., edema), red rash, muscle aches, and joint stiffness (i.e., arthralgia). Physicians have treated these conditions with local hydrocortisones, systemic corticosteroids, aspirin, and soothing skin creams. Take pictures of sponges; do not squeeze them.

Moving up the phylogenetic scale, the next group to be discussed is the Cnidarians (Coelenterates), which contain some of the most venomous animals that are known, even if the vast majority are harmless. These animals are mostly marine, including true corals (Madreporia), soft corals (Alcyonaria), fire coral (Hydrozoan), jellyfish

Fig. 2-31. Sponges can have sharp spicules and should not be handled.

Fig. 2-32. Many corals are sharp and delicate and should not be handled.

(Scyphozoans), and sea anemones (Anthozoans). These carnivorous animals are characterized by radial symmetry, a gut with one opening, and tentacles with stinging cells called **nematocysts**. It is these nematocysts or stinging cells that deliver the venom. Some can penetrate human skin; others cannot. The amount of venom delivered by different species varies considerably. Consequently, some are harmless and others extremely dangerous. Fortunately, the more dangerous ones can be avoided with proper precautions such as full–body suits, a hood, gloves, and boots (Fig. 2-32).

Three members are particularly known for their ability to sting: fire coral (M*illipora* sp.), the Portuguese man–of–war (P*hysalia* sp.), and stinging hydroids. Many members of this group of carnivorous animals look like innocent plants. The hydrozoans produce symptoms that range from a mild, itching sensation to a severe, painful sting. They produce a redness of the skin, urticarial rash (appearing similar to hives), blistering vesicles, and pustule formation. This may be followed by itching and skin eruptions. Victims of P*hysalia* stings report an "electroshock–like" sensation, followed by severe pain. In turn, this can be followed by systemic symptoms such as chills, fever, fatigue, headache, muscle cramps, nausea, and vomiting.

Scyphozoans, or true jellyfish, are classified into three groups according to their ability to sting:
1. Relatively mild (A*urelia*, P*elagia*, and C*arybdea*),
2. Moderate to severe (C*assiopea* and C*yanea*), and

3. Severe to highly dangerous (T*amoya*, C*hiropsalmus*, and C*hironex*).

Symptoms range from a mild prickly sensation and itching to burning, throbbing, and shooting pain. The skin becomes red, swollen (i.e., edema), has a rash, and may blister, hemorrhage (petechial), and experience tissue death (i.e., necrosis) through its full thickness. In more severe cases, one may find muscle cramps, difficulty in breathing, lung congestion (i.e., pulmonary edema), loss of consciousness, or even death. Treatment of jellyfish stings includes the use of household white vinegar, which prevents the nematocysts of most species from firing. Removing tentacles from the victim's skin may be dangerous, so always wear gloves and wash them afterward thoroughly. Pain relief may be obtained by giving aspirin. More severe cases may require CPR, morphine, and eventually, a hospital respirator. The four aims of treatment are to relieve the pain, deactivate the toxins, keep the victim breathing, and control any shock–like symptoms.

The third group of Cnidarians that cause trouble for the unprepared diver are the Anthozoans, which include the stony corals, gorgonians, and sea anemones. With a few exceptions, this is generally a colorful and harmless group of animals. Every diver should know that he or she may be cut by shallow–water corals such as elkhorn (A*cropora palmata*) or staghorn (A*cropora cervicornis*). If you do receive a coral cut, wash it with warm, soapy water and apply some antiseptic cream to the area.

Most people consider shellfish as something to eat (e.g., clams, oysters, scallops, and so on) or as something to collect, but few realize that there are venomous molluscs. The phylum Mollusca contains a genus of gastropod known as *Conus* that contains a venom sac as well as a small, poisonous dart capable of penetrating an ungloved human hand. These creatures feed on other gastropod molluscs, polychaete worms, and fish. Consequently, they have developed a highly effective venom apparatus. If stung, the victim usually experiences immediate, intense pain or a sharp stinging sensation, which is followed by a burning and then a numbness around the wound site. This may eventually spread over the entire body, producing a muscle paralysis. CPR, a respirator, and the treatment for primary shock are usually effective. This envenomation is easily avoided by picking up any unknown shellfish with wetsuit gloves, or more simply by avoiding the handling these creatures completely.

Another mollusc that is known to have killed an individual through envenomation is the blue-ringed octopus (*Octopus maculosus*) (Fig. 2-33). This species contains tetrodotoxin in its salivary glands, which it probably acquires through its prey. Symptoms following the bite of this octopus are similar to those after eating fugu, because this is a potent neurotoxin. In general, all members of the octopus family (Cephalopods) are shy, and they are not inclined to bite. The only time that people have been bitten is when they handle these gentle creatures. Look, take pictures, but do not touch.

The last invertebrate group of animals to consider are the echinoderms (Echinodermata), which include seastars, sea urchins, and sea cucumbers (Fig. 2-34). These are a group of exclusively marine bottom–dwellers with external skeletons, protruding spines, radial symmetry, and a gut with two openings. Sea urchins have spines, some of which are hollow and brittle. These spines can penetrate the skin, break off, and become irritating. Crushing those of some fine–spined species when in the skin may fragment them and lead to the eventual absorption process; this practice should be avoided with thick–spined urchins. In addition, some spines may need to be removed surgically. Learn the best treatment for each type in each new area where you dive, and always keep the affected area of skin clean to prevent wound infection. Some sea urchins have a special venom apparatus called a *pedicellaria*, which can inject a venom that causes some pain, swelling, and joint stiffening. It is best to avoid handling sea urchins, but if you do, always wear gloves. One species of starfish, the

Fig. 2-33. Blue-ringed octopus. (From Auerbach: A Medical Guide to Hazardous Marine Life, ed 2, St Louis, 1991, Mosby.)

Fig. 2-34. Sea urchin spines are sharp and brittle.

Crown of Thorns (*Acanthaster planci*), also has stout, poisonous spines. Wounds from these spines are extremely painful, but this Pacific species is the only poisonous seastar.

There are many venomous fish, such as the lion fish, stingrays, scorpionfish, and stonefish (Figs. 2-35 and 2-36), and all have some general characteristics in common. First, as soon as the spines from these animals enter the skin, there is an immediate, intense pain that may become excruciating over the next hour. The pain may persist for

Fig. 2-35. Lion fish.

6 to 10 hours before diminishing. There will also be a swelling (i.e., edema) and "redness" around the injury site. The victim may experience dizziness, weakness, cardiac arrhythmias, anxiety, sweating, muscle weakness, cramps, nausea, and vomiting. This may be followed by primary shock, coma, and death, although death is rare. To treat victims of fish envenomation, first remove them from the water and immobilize the affected limbs. The victim may be in great pain, so reassure them. Place a wounded limb into hot, but not boiling, water; the ideal temperature is somewhere around 50° C or 122° F. As stated previously, all marine venoms are heat–labile, high–molecular–weight proteins. Relieve the pain, and transfer the patient to a hospital for further management.

Another group of venomous marine animals are the sea snakes of the family Hydrophiidae, all of which are poisonous. Aquatic inhabitants of the tropical Pacific and Indian Oceans, these reptiles have bodies that are more or less compressed posteriorly and paddle–shaped tails. Sea–snake bites are often inconspicuous, sometimes painless, and without swelling. Symptoms usually begin mildly and become progressively worse. The victim may experience a mild anxiety, drowsiness, or even euphoria. Swallowing may become difficult as the patient's tongue swells, and muscle weakness may progress to a frank paralysis. Fortunately, there are antivenoms, but they may not be readily available. Many consider the sea snake to be a docile animal and reluctant to bite, but one must remember that all are poisonous and potentially lethal. Divers should always give them full and thorough respect. In other words, keep clear of them.

Predators

This section deals with those animals that bite and are aggressive specifically against man. Fortunately, this is an extremely small group, and these are animals that generally can be avoided. We cannot include everything that is known about predators in this chapter. Read more in this area, however, and become an informed diver.

Essentially, there are six principle predators found in the marine environment: barracuda, moray eels, large grouper, killer whales, sharks, and poisonous sea snakes (Figs. 2-37 through 2-39). All have two things in common: humans are not their normal prey, and they rarely bite humans. This should be comforting, but if these creatures do bite, the consequences can be devastating.

Some of the things that we can do to prevent problems include:

1. Do not swim or dive in areas with great concentrations of predators. If you can see a killer whale underwater, you are too close. Marine mammals are protected in the United States and other countries; learn the laws about approaching and interacting with them.

Fig. 2-36. Stingrays should not be handled as some species can inflict a serious wound.

Fig. 2-37. Moray eels are often found in cracks and crevices but sometimes are out free swimming.

2. Do not spear fish. Wounded fish and fish blood are great attractions to sharks and barracuda. In particular, do not spear large predators.
3. Do not feed wild predators such as barracuda, moray eels, sharks, groupers, or killer whales.
4. Do not harass or handle predators.
5. Do not swim or dive alone.
6. Some sharks feed on sea lions and seals. If you look like one either on the surface or underwater, you may be mistaken as prey.

These suggestions may appear to be just common sense, but many divers break all of these rules. If left alone, barracuda, moray eels, and large groupers probably represent little threat to the diver. If molested, however, all of these animals are effective in biting and producing serious wounds.

The bite from a shark or a killer whale could be severe and fatal. When these animals are spotted underwater, there is usually time to swim purposefully and slowly in retreat. Most shark attacks have occurred in murky, shallow water. In general, the surface appears to be the most dangerous location for a diver. Few authenticated shark attacks to a diver on the ocean floor have occurred. Do not set yourself up for a problem by provoking a shark or other predator. It is not known for certain just what provokes and bothers large sharks, so it is wise to be cautious. Some areas of the world are riskier than others, so know your diving site.

Whether severe or very moderate, bites from sea creatures should be handled with great care. First, control the bleeding by using large, gauze, pressure bandages. The wound or wounds should be filled with gauze and the material held in place with a flexible bandage and, occasionally, a splint to immobilize the limb. Once the bleeding is controlled, treat the victim for shock, then transport

Fig. 2-38. Large sharks should not be provoked by divers.

Fig. 2-39. Barracuda can look menacing but in fact they are relatively harmless.

the individual as rapidly as possible to the nearest medical facility. The wounds should be cleaned as soon as possible and any necessary surgical procedures completed. Transfusions and skin grafting are needed in many of these cases. In addition, these wounds can easily become sites for severe infections.

Freshwater Life Hazards

Compared to the oceans, freshwater streams, ponds, and lakes have relatively few forms of animal life that present a specific danger to divers. Even so, the diver must be aware of those few species that can inflict considerable harm.

Reptiles

The venomous cottonmouth water snake is found in lakes and rivers south of 38° north latitude. This snake is probably the diver's most serious freshwater hazard. It predominantly inhabits stagnant or sluggish water, but it also has been observed in clear and moving water.

There has been a persistent notion that the cottonmouth will not bite underwater; however, two fatalities caused by such cottonmouth bites have been documented. The cottonmouth is considered to be pugnacious, adamant, and vindictive when disturbed, and it will attack unprovoked. It does not show fear toward humans as most other aquatic snakes do. Its behavior is unpredictable, but attack is more likely to occur in the evening.

Recognition of the cottonmouth is difficult, because its color varies from jet black to green, with markings absent or vaguely similar to the copperhead. Consequently, in areas where the cottonmouth is known to exist, the diver should regard any snake that does not swim away when encountered as a cottonmouth. The best defense is a noiseless, deliberate retreat. Wet suits afford reasonably good protection, but they can be penetrated by larger specimens. Bare hands should be tucked under the armpits. The diver should never attempt to fight, because this will probably only result in multiple bites. Although evidence is inconclusive, it appears that this snake will not dive deeper than approximately 6 feet.

The timber rattlesnake is an excellent swimmer on the surface. Skin divers should be alert and avoid contact.

First aid for venomous snake bites include:
1. Keep the victim quiet, and take measures to combat shock.
2. Wash the wound, and immobilize the injured area, keeping it lower than the heart if possible.
3. Find medical attention immediately.
Antivenom treatment may be required.

Turtles

Three species of aquatic turtles may be hazardous to the diver if provoked and mishandled, especially if the turtles are large specimens. Although not venomous, they may inflict a serious, dirty wound. The alligator snapping turtle, which is found throughout the watershed of the Mississippi River, is vicious and aggressive when provoked. It has powerful jaws and sharp claws. The alligator snapper is recognized by three distinct, keel–like lines running longitudinally along the full length of the upper shell. There are also wart–like projections about the head and forelimbs. The neck of the alligator snapper is extremely long and muscular, and it can strike rapidly by extending the neck.

The common snapper turtle is smaller and similar in appearance to the alligator snapper. This species is considered by some authorities to be more vicious when provoked than the alligator snapper.

The softshell turtle also may inflict a serious wound. Contact with these turtles should be avoided, or special precautions should be taken in handling.

Standard first aid for laceration–type wounds is recommended. Tetanus immunization is also recommended.

Alligators and Crocodiles

The American alligator has been encountered by divers, and it has shown aggressive behavior and caused injury to swimmers. The potential for injury is present, especially with nesting animals, and divers should be cautious. In Central and South America, the crocodile may certainly constitute a hazard to divers, and in Africa, it is responsible for many human deaths each year. The saltwater crocodile of the coast of Queensland, Australia, is very large (e.g., up to 30 ft) and is reported to be a vicious aggressor.

Mammals

The common muskrat may be one of the few warm–blooded animals that might attack a freshwater diver in the United States. It attacks only in defense, however, and the wound is usually minor. Even so, the possibility of rabies is present and serious. It is important for the diver to seek medical advice if bitten and for the animal to be captured, or killed, for laboratory examination. If encountered while diving, the muskrat should not be provoked. If it is provoked into attacking, escape for the diver is virtually impossible.

Fishes

The only freshwater fishes posing a noted hazard to divers are the freshwater sharks of Lake Nicaragua in Central America and the piranha fish of the Orient and South America. In US waters, the only fish capable of inflicting serious injury are those of the catfish family and the gar. The gar fish commonly weighs in excess of 100 pounds and, if provoked by spear fishermen, has the capability of inflicting wounds with needle–sharp teeth.

The previous discussion has concentrated on the hazards of freshwater life in the United States. Certainly, it is only common sense for the diver to consult with local authorities before he or she commences diving operations when working in other parts of the world.

SUMMARY

Ⓣhis section has briefly described some of the problems one can encounter in the underwater environment. It also has discussed how to avoid most of these problems with some simple rules for each. For oral toxins, avoid eating unknown species (i.e., fish or shellfish), check with local authorities about the safety of their species, and do not eat shellfish collected from an area that recently suffered a "red tide." For parenteral toxins (i.e., the "stingers"), always wear protective clothing while diving, wear gloves even in the tropics, and watch where you place both your feet and hands while underwater. For predators, do not enter the water where sharks or other predators are known to frequent. If you find yourself in the presence of predators, leave the water; do not feed or molest predators. Finally, know your diving area.

SUGGESTED READINGS

- Alevizon WS: *Caribbean reef ecology*, Pisces Books, 1994.
- Bascom W: *Waves and beaches: the dynamics of the ocean structure*, Anchor Books, 1980.
- *Diving and snorkeling guides*, Pisces Books.
- Eschmeyer WN, Herald ES, Hammann H: *A field guide to Pacific coast fishes of North America*, Peterson Field Guide Series, Houghton Mifflin, 1983.
- Gotshall D: *Fishwatchers' guide to the inshore fishes of the Pacific coast*, Sea Challengers Publications, 1979.
- Gotshall D, Laurent LL: *Pacific coast subtidal marine invertebrates*, Sea Challengers Publications, 1979.
- Halstead BW: *Dangerous marine animals that bite, sting, shock, and are non–edible*, Cornell Maritime, 1980.
- Housby T: *The concise illustrated book of freshwater fish.*
- Marx RF: *The underwater dig: introduction to marine archaeology*, Available at Best Publishing.
- McPeak R, Glantz D, Shaw C: *The amber forest: beauty and biology of California's submarine forests*, Watersport Publishing, 1988.
- NOAA Diving Manual: *Diving for science and technology*, US Department of Commerce, National Oceanic and Atmospheric Administration, 1991.
- *Sefton N, Webster SK:* Caribbean reef invertebrates, Sea Challengers Publications, 1986.
- Wilson R, Wilson JQ: *Watching fishes: understanding coral reef fish behaviour*, Pisces Books.

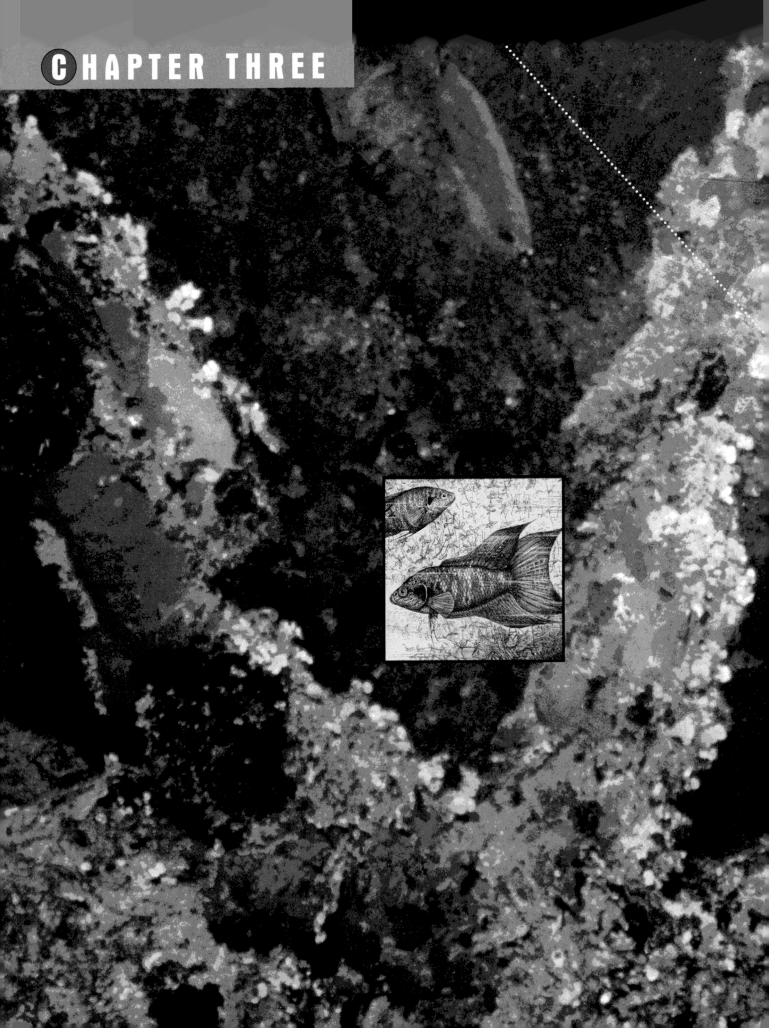

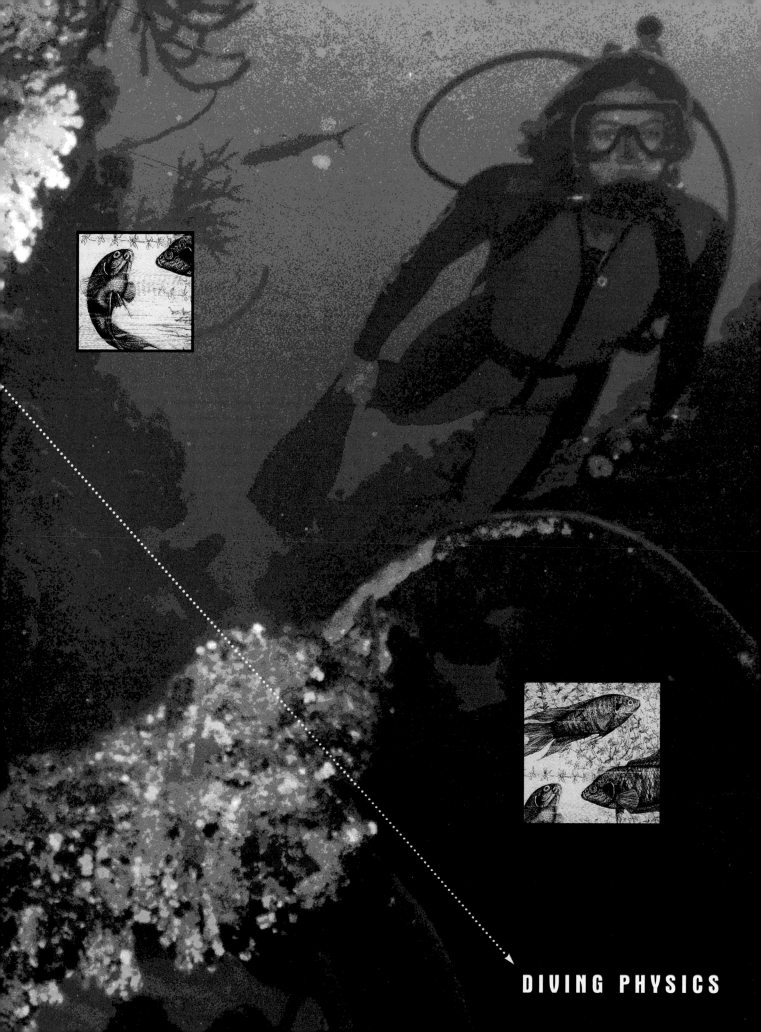

CHAPTER THREE

DIVING PHYSICS

A s land-dwelling, air-breathing creatures, we have evolved perceptions, behaviors, practices, and procedures for living in an air atmosphere. Because we now choose to venture into the underwater world, where we cannot breathe, it is necessary to understand some aspects of that realm. A number of important physical principles pertain to this underwater world and are important to us as divers. Understanding these principles will minimize our risk while increasing our enjoyment of diving. This chapter defines concepts and presents methods of problem solving that will help you to better apply the principles that govern many of your actions underwater.

LEARNING OBJECTIVES

By the end of this chapter, you will be able to:

1. Correctly define the terms presented in **bold letters**.
2. State the constituent gases and their percentage volumes in air.
3. Define the English and metric systems and their common measurement units.
4. Define Archimedes' Principle and apply it to buoyancy problems.
5. Explain the ways that a diver loses heat.
6. State the types of temperature scales and how they are used in diving physics calculations.
7. Discuss how light and sound are altered underwater.
8. Calculate gauge and absolute pressure at any depth in freshwater or saltwater.
9. Discuss how altitude affects pressure- and depth-gauge readings.
10. Work problems associated with the various laws of gases and air consumption.

BASIC DEFINITIONS

Before we can use the language of science to help us understand the physical principles affecting a diver, we must first learn the vocabulary. The study of the physical world has traditionally been divided into a number of interrelated disciplines. **Physics** is the broad name given to the study of our physical world. **Chemistry** is the investigation of chemical substances that compose that world. These disciplines share a common philosophy, vocabulary, and methodology with only minor variations. Once the "vocabulary" and "methodology" of these disciplines are understood, their principles can be applied.

Matter is defined as anything that occupies space (i.e., possesses a measurable volume) and has mass (i.e., weight). Matter can exist in one of three common states: solid, liquid, and gas.

Solids are characterized by rigidity and a definite form: **Liquids** flow; and **gases** diffuse and will uniformly fill any container in which they are placed. Using water as an example, ice is a solid, water a liquid, and steam a gas. The physical state (i.e., solid, liquid, or gas) of a substance depends on the surrounding pressure and temperature. Conversion from one form of matter to another, like the melting of ice, is termed a *change of state*.

According to accepted scientific theory, matter is composed of **atoms** (Fig. 3-1). An atom is the smallest possible entity into which a material can be divided and still retain its identity. For example, if we take a piece of pure iron and cut it into smaller and smaller pieces, we will eventually reach something that can no longer be cut apart and still be iron. This "something" is an atom. (from the Greek word *uncut*.)

Materials that are composed of only one kind of atom are termed **elements**, and these elements are the fundamental "building blocks" used by nature to assemble all that we observe as the universe. There are more than 100 elements, all with different respective characteristics. Each has been assigned a unique symbol, an atomic number, and atomic mass (i.e., weight). Chemists have arranged the elements in a chart termed the *periodic table*. This table allows chemists to understand certain aspects of the way elements react with each other. Divers interested in advanced gas-law calculations can use the chart to obtain molecular weights. These molecular weights can be used to estimate gas densities and are also part of more complex equations used in preparing nonair breathing-gas mixtures.

GASES IN DIVING

Recreational divers primarily breathe **compressed air**, which is comprised of a variety of gases. In certain types of technical, commercial, military, or scientific diving, special gas mixtures may be blended and used.

Air is a mixture of gases that includes primarily nitrogen and oxygen. It also contains water vapor, small amounts of trace gases (e.g., argon, neon,

Fig. 3-1. Atoms combine to form molecules.

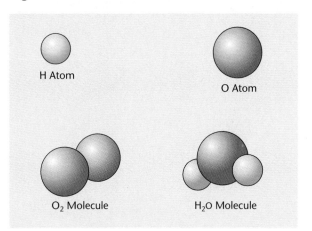

H Atom

O Atom

O_2 Molecule

H_2O Molecule

and so on), carbon dioxide, and various hydrocarbons from pollution, engine exhaust, and so forth. The typical constituents of dry air are illustrated in Figure 3-2. For most diving applications, divers may assume that air is 78% nitrogen, 21% oxygen, and 1% other gases.

Nitrogen

Nitrogen is a colorless, odorless, and tasteless gas. It is the major component in the Earth's atmosphere. Our body does not use nitrogen physiologically, but this gas does pose some potential problems for divers when breathed under pressure. These problems include nitrogen narcosis and decompression sickness, which are covered in detail in the physiology and decompression sections.

There are mixtures of nitrogen and oxygen called **nitrox**, or **oxygen enriched air**, that have different concentrations of nitrogen and oxygen than are found in compressed air. The use of these mixtures by recreational divers requires special training in the theory, equipment, handling, and usage of these gases (see the *Technical Diving* chapter).

Oxygen

Oxygen is one of the most abundant chemical elements on earth. Like most gases, oxygen is colorless, odorless, and tasteless. By itself, oxygen is not combustible, but the ease with which it reacts with other materials can lead to fires and explosions if it is handled improperly.

Oxygen is essential for life. The body uses chemical reactions based on oxygen to generate heat and chemical energy; this is a process called **metabolism**. Oxygen in the breathing gas must be maintained within certain limits. Too much or too little can cause serious problems for the diver. These topics are covered more thoroughly in the physiology section of this book.

Carbon Dioxide

Carbon dioxide is a compound that is also colorless, odorless, and tasteless. It reacts with water to form a potentially lethal acid called **carbonic acid**. Carbon dioxide is noncombustible, and is often used in fire extinguishers.

Carbon dioxide is a waste product of human respiration. Its concentration within the body is a trigger that signals the brain it is time to breathe. Excess carbon dioxide is potentially dangerous and is discussed in detail in the physiology section.

Carbon Monoxide

Carbon monoxide is a colorless, odorless, and tasteless poisonous gas. It is produced by incomplete combustion of hydrocarbons, which can occur in internal combustion engines. This gas seriously interferes with the blood's ability to carry oxygen, and it can be extremely dangerous to divers. It is covered in detail in the physiology section.

MEASUREMENT SYSTEMS

Much of our comprehension of our surroundings comes from the interactions of five fundamental concepts. These are:
1. Length (i.e., the distance between two points).
2. Time (i.e., a measurement of duration).
3. Mass (i.e., an intrinsic property of matter which is best understood as that which resists a change in movement).
4. Force (i.e., a push or pull that tends to produce a change in movement).
5. Energy (i.e., the ability to do work).

Measurement systems allow us to quantify (i.e., ask or answer the question "how much of?") our surroundings. This in turn leads to understanding. There are two primary systems of measurement: the **English** and the **metric**. The English system has a series of units based on human anatomy. The metric system was specifically developed to make conversions between units simple. In the metric system, all units are related by factors of 10, so conversion within the system is simple. The

Fig. 3-2. Components of dry air.

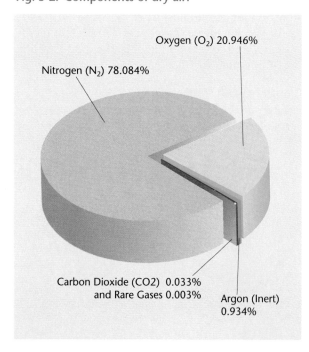

Oxygen (O_2) 20.946%

Nitrogen (N_2) 78.084%

Carbon Dioxide ($CO2$) 0.033%
and Rare Gases 0.003%

Argon (Inert) 0.934%

English system is still used in the United States; the metric system is used nearly everywhere else. Eventually, the United States will probably officially adopt the metric system (Table 3-1).

Length

The standard unit of **length** in the English system is the *foot*. The unit of length in the metric system is the *meter*.

Units of length include:

English

12 inches	= 1 foot
36 inches	= 1 yard
3 feet	= 1 yard
6 feet	= 1 fathom
5280 feet	= 1 statute mile
6076 feet	= 1 nautical mile

Metric

1 millimeter	= 0.001 meter
1 centimeter	= 0.01 meter
1 decimeter	= 0.1 meter
1 kilometer	= 1000 meters

Conversions

1.0 inch	= 2.54 centimeters
39.37 inches	= 1 meter
3.28 feet	= 1 meter

Units of "weight" include:

English

16 ounces	= 1 pound
14 pounds	= 1 stone

Metric

1 kilogram	= 1000 grams

Conversions

1 kilogram	= 2.2 pounds
453.5924 grams	= 1 pound

Note that for most diving applications, the conversion of 454 grams to 1 pound is sufficient.

Volume

Volume is the term used to describe capacity. It is measured in cubed units of length: length x width x height.

Units of volume include:

English

2 pints	= 1 quart
4 quarts	= 1 gallon
1 gallon	= 0.134 ft^3

Metric

1 cubic centimeter	= 1 milliliter
1000 milliliters	= 1 liter

Conversions

1 ft^3	= 28.316 liters
1 liter	= 1.06 quarts
1 liter	= 0.0353 ft^3

Note that cc = cubic centimeters = cm^3 and that ft^3 = cubic feet.

Density

Density is a measurement of the "molecular packing" of a particular substance. The heavier the molecule and the more molecules per unit of volume, the more dense a substance will be. Density is defined as the mass per unit volume. Expressed as a formula, this is:

$$\text{Density} = \frac{\text{Mass}}{\text{Volume}}$$

Density can be used to calculate the mass of an object by rearranging the previous equation to:

$$\text{Mass of object} = \text{Density} \times \text{Volume}$$

English Problem: Determine the mass (in pounds; remember that divers do not use the rigorous scientific definition and routinely do not distinguish between mass and weight) of 1 ft^3 of water given that pure freshwater has a density of 1.0 g/cc. *Note that because the scientific community uses the metric system, tables of density values for many materials are often listed in reference books in the metric units of g/cc. American divers who wish to use English units for their buoyancy calculations will need to know how to make this conversion.*

Answer: Using the previous equation:

$$\text{Mass} = \frac{1.0 \text{ g}}{1 \text{ cc}} \times \frac{1 \text{ lb}}{453.39 \text{ g}} \times \frac{1000 \text{ cc}}{1 \text{ L}} \times \frac{28.316 \text{ L}}{1 \text{ ft}^3}$$

$$= \frac{62.4 \text{ lbs}}{1 \text{ ft}^3}$$

Thus, 1 ft^3 of freshwater weighs 62.4 pounds.

TABLE 3.1 CONVERSION TABLE FOR BAROMETRIC PRESSURE UNITS

	atm	N/M²	bars	mb	kg/cm²	gm/cm²	mm Hg	in Hg	lb/in²
1 Atmosphere	1	1.013x10⁵	1.013	1013	1.033	1033	760	29.92	14.70
1 Newton/M²	.9869x10⁻⁵	1	10⁻⁵	.01	1.02x10⁻⁵	.0102	.0075	.2953x10⁻³	.1451x10⁻³
1 bar	.9869	10⁵	1	.1000	1.02	1020	750.1	29.53	14.51
1 millibar	.9869x10⁻³	100	.001	1	.00102	1.02	.7501	.02953	.01451
1 kg/cm²	.9681	.9807x10⁵	.9807	980.7	1	1000	735	28.94	14.22
1gm/cm²	968.1	98.07	.9807x10⁻³	.9807	.001	1	.735	.02894	.01422
1 mmHg	.001316	133.3	.00133	1.333	.00136	1.36	1	.03937	.01934
1 in Hg	.0334	3386	.03386	33.86	.03453	34.53	25.4	1	.4910
1 lb/in²	.06804	6895	.06895	68.95	.0703	70.3	51.70	2.035	1

English Problem: Determine the mass of 1 ft^3 of seawater given that seawater has a density of 1.0256 g/cc.

Answer: Using the previous equation:

$$\text{Mass} = \frac{1.0256 \text{ g}}{1 \text{ cc}} \times \frac{1 \text{ lb}}{453.39 \text{ g}} \times \frac{1000 \text{ cc}}{1 \text{ L}} \times$$

$$\frac{28.316 \text{ L}}{1 \text{ ft}^3} = \frac{64.0 \text{ lbs}}{1 \text{ ft}^3}$$

Metric Problem: Calculate the mass (in kilograms) of 1 liter of freshwater given that the density of freshwater is 1.0 g/cc.

Answer: Using the previous equation:

$$\text{Mass} = \frac{1.0 \text{ g}}{1 \text{ cc}} \times \frac{1 \text{ kg}}{1,000 \text{ cc}} \times \frac{1,000 \text{ cc}}{1 \text{ L}} = \frac{1.0 \text{ kg}}{1 \text{ L}}$$

Freshwater (density, 62.4 lbs/ft^3; 1.0 g/cc) is less dense than seawater (density, 64 lbs/ft^3; 1.0256 g/cc). Pure freshwater theoretically contains only water molecules. Because seawater also contains a variety of dissolved materials, an equal volume of seawater has more mass than a corresponding volume of freshwater.

Problem: If a layer of freshwater is slowly added to a body of seawater so that no mixing occurs, the layers will remain separated. Which layer will be on top?

Answer: Freshwater (density, 62.4 lbs/ft^3 or 1.0 g/cc) is less dense than saltwater (density, 64 lbs/ft^3 or 1.0256 g/cc). Therefore, if layers do not mix, the less dense material, freshwater, will be on top.

Note that this phenomenon does exist in nature, such as near the mouths of rivers, because of the density differences caused by solution of salts. The sharp area dividing the regions of such different densities is termed a **halocline**. Divers swimming near a halocline will observe a "shimmering" as light moves through the area where mixing occurs when the diver's movement disturbs the sharp boundary between the two layers. Water changes because of nonsaline solutes should not be referred to as haloclines.

Substances may expand or contract (i.e., change volume) as temperature changes. This means that density, particularly that of liquids and gases, will change with temperature. Divers may be familiar with a **thermocline**, which is a zone of rapidly changing temperature that often appears as a sharp interface between colder, more dense water and warmer water. Thermoclines are quite common in freshwater lakes, where the colder, more dense water sinks relative to the warmer water.

BUOYANCY

While in the public baths of ancient Syracuse (on the island that is now Sicily), Archimedes, a renowned Greek natural philosopher, noted that the level of water rose in the tub when he entered the bath. From this phenomenon, he then produced what has become known as **Archimedes' Principle**: An object partially or wholly immersed in a fluid is buoyed up by a force equal to the weight of the fluid displaced by that object. This means that objects more dense than water (e.g., lead) will sink and objects less dense (e.g., cork) will float. Objects of the same density will remain at the same level (hover) and neither sink nor float. Objects that sink are frequently termed **negatively buoyant**. Objects that float are termed **positively buoyant**. Objects that remain stationary at depth are termed **neutrally buoyant**.

Buoyancy is easiest to understand by the application of "force arrow" principles. Weight is a downward force (i.e., gravity acting on mass), and buoyancy is an upward force. If these two forces are balanced, then so-called neutral buoyancy (i.e., object hovers) is achieved. If they are not balanced, the object immersed will either sink (i.e., weight greater than upward buoyant force) or float (i.e., weight less than upward buoyant force) (Fig. 3-3).

Buoyancy-type problems involve three factors: the weight of the object being submerged, the volume of the object being submerged, and the density of the liquid involved in the problem. Any two of these factors can be used to determine the third. Some representative numeric examples will help to clarify these concepts.

English Problem: What is the weight or buoyancy in seawater of a piece of wood that weighs 2000 pounds and measures 6 ft × 2 ft × 3 ft?

Answer: Determine the forces involved:

a. The weight of wood = 2,000 pounds
b. The volume of wood = 6 ft × 2 ft × 3 ft = 36 ft^3
c. The corresponding weight of an equal volume of seawater therefore is:

$$36 \text{ ft}^3 \times \frac{64 \text{ lbs}}{\text{ft}^3} = 2304 \text{ lbs}$$

Fig. 3-3. Buoyancy. A, Water is displaced by the weight of an object. B, More water is displaced when a buoyant object is submerged.

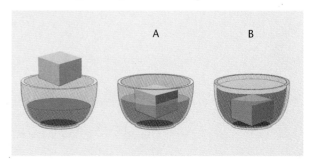

At this point, we know that the wood object weighs less than the corresponding volume of water (i.e., the volume of seawater that would be displaced if the entire object were to be submerged). Thus, it will float. Applying "force arrows," we see that:

Weight of wood = downward force = 2000 lbs ↓
Weight of displaced water = upward force = 2304 lbs ↑
Net force = upward = 304 lbs ↑

The object will float with a buoyant force of 304 pounds. To sink, the object would have to weigh more than an additional 304 pounds (without changing volume). This is the amount of "push" you would have to exert on this log for it to sink. Although the object is buoyant (i.e., there is a net force of 304 pounds pushing up on this log), it will not be completely out of the water. The density of the log can then be used to determine how much of the log will be submerged:

$$\text{Density of log} = \frac{2{,}000 \text{ lbs}}{36 \text{ ft}^3} = \frac{55.6 \text{ lbs}}{1 \text{ ft}^3}$$

Because this log is less dense than seawater, it will float. The amount of the volume that is submerged will be determined by the ratio between the density of the log and the density of the seawater. In general, this is expressed as:

$$\text{Volume submerged} = \frac{\text{Density of object}}{\text{Density of liquid}}$$

Substituting the value of this log and seawater, we find:

$$\text{Ratio} = \frac{55.6 \text{ lb/ft}^3}{64 \text{ lb/ft}^3} = 0.869$$

So, approximately 87% of the log's volume will be submerged.

English Problem: A fully suited diver weighs 200 pounds. This diver displaces a volume of 3.0 cubic feet of seawater. Will the diver float or sink?

Answer: Determine the forces involved:
a. Weight of an equal volume of seawater:

$$3.0 \text{ ft}^3 \times \frac{64 \text{ lbs}}{1 \text{ ft}^3} = 192 \text{ lbs}$$

b. Applying force arrows:

Weight of diver = 200 lbs ↓
Displaced weight = 192 lbs ↑
Net force = 8 lbs ↓

The diver will sink. This diver weighs 8 pounds in the water and is severely overweighted. Removal of 8 pounds will allow the diver to hover, which means the diver will have to do less work while diving (see the trim discussion). Because the object of recreational diving is to enjoy the environment, less work translates into more bottom time and more fun!

English Problem: A fully geared diver in a wet suit weighs 210 pounds. In freshwater, this diver with a scuba cylinder containing 500 p.s.i.g. needs 18 pounds of lead to hover. How much lead will this diver need when diving in a wet suit in seawater?

Answer: Using force arrows:

Weight of diver = 210 lbs ↓
Weight of lead = 18 lbs ↓
Total weight acting on the water = 228 lbs ↓

For the diver to hover, the volume of water that he or she displaces must exert a buoyant force upward equal to the total weight of the diver plus gear (i.e., downward force). This is the buoyant force exerted by a volume of freshwater (density, 62.4 lbs/ft^3) that weighs 228 pounds. Determine volume of diver:

$$\text{Density} = \frac{\text{Mass}}{\text{Volume}}$$

Rearranging:

$$\text{Volume} = \frac{\text{Mass}}{\text{Density}}$$

Then, substituting:

$$\text{Volume} = \frac{228 \text{ lbs}}{62.4 \text{ lbs/ft}^3} = 3.65 \text{ ft}^3$$

Now that we know the volume of the diver, we can determine (with the assumption that the volume of the weight belt is negligible) the buoyant force from the seawater (density, 64 lbs/ft^3) that the diver would displace:

$$3.65 \text{ ft}^3 \times \frac{64 \text{ lbs}}{1 \text{ ft}^3} = 233.6 \text{ lbs}$$

Applying force arrows:

Buoyant force of seawater = 234 lbs ↑
Weight of the diver and gear = 210 lbs ↓
Net force = 24 lbs ↑

So, the diver who was comfortable with 18 pounds of lead on the weight belt in freshwater, must add 6 more pounds (for a total of 24 lbs) on the weight belt to dive in seawater.

English Problem: A fully geared diver in a wet suit weighs 210 pounds. In seawater, this diver needs 18 pounds of lead to hover. How much lead will this diver need when diving in a wet suit in freshwater?

Answer: Using force arrows:

Weight of the diver = 210 lbs ↓
Weight of the lead = 18 lbs ↓
Total weight acting on the water = 228 lbs ↓

For the diver to hover, the volume of water that he or she displaces must exert an upward buoyant force equal to the total weight of the diver plus gear (i.e., downward force). This is the upward buoyant force exerted by the displaced volume of seawater (density = 64 lbs/ft^3) that weighs 228 pounds. Determine the volume of the diver remembering that divers use weight and mass as equivalent terms.

$$\text{Density} = \frac{\text{Weight}}{\text{Volume}}$$

Rearranging:

$$\text{Volume} = \frac{\text{Weight}}{\text{Density}}$$

Then, substituting:

$$\text{Volume} = \frac{228 \text{ lbs}}{64 \text{ lbs/ft}^3} = 3.56 \text{ ft}^3$$

Now that we know the volume of the diver, we can determine the buoyant force from the freshwater (density, 62.4 lbs/ft³) that the diver would displace:

$$3.56 \text{ ft}^3 \times \frac{64 \text{ lbs}}{1 \text{ ft}^3} = 222.1 \text{ lbs}$$

Applying force arrows:

Buoyant force of seawater = 222 lbs ↑
Weight of diver and gear = 210 lbs ↓
Net force =   12 lbs ↑

So, the diver who was comfortable with 18 pounds of lead on the weight belt in seawater must remove 6 pounds (for a total of 12 lbs) from the weight belt to dive in freshwater. The difference in density between freshwater and seawater is why different amounts of weight must be used when diving in different environments. When moving from freshwater to seawater (with the same equipment configuration), divers must add weight. When moving from seawater to less dense freshwater, divers must remove weight.

Metric Problem: A log weighing 6000 kg measures 1 m × 3 m × 2 m. Will this object sink or float in seawater (density, 1.0256 k g/L)?

Answer: Determine the volume of the object:

$$\text{Volume} = 1 \text{ m} \times 3 \text{ m} \times 2 \text{ m} = 6 \text{ m}^3$$

Convert cubic meters to liters:

$$6 \text{ m}^3 \times \frac{(100 \text{cm})^3}{(1\text{m})^3} \times \frac{1 \text{L}}{1000 \text{ cm}^3} = 6000 \text{ L}$$

Determine weight of the displaced water:

$$6000 \text{ L} \times \frac{1.0256 \text{ kg}}{1 \text{ L}} = 6154 \text{ kg}$$

Using force arrows:

Weight of the object = 6000 kg ↓
Weight of the displaced water = 6154 kg ↑
Net force =   154 kg ↑

Now we know that this object will float.

Metric Problem: A wet-suited diver weighs 74 kg with gear. The diver has a volume of 80 L. How much lead should the diver wear for diving in seawater (density, 1.026 kg/L)? Answer: Determine the weight of the displaced seawater:

$$80 \text{ L} \times \frac{1.026 \text{ kg}}{1 \text{ L}} = 82.1 \text{ kg}$$

Using force arrows:

Weight of the diver = 74 kg ↓
Weight of water displaced = 82 kg ↑
Net force =   8 kg ↑

Because there is a resultant buoyant force of 8 kg, the diver will have to wear 8 kg to compensate.

Divers wearing wet or dry suits have an additional factor to consider. Within the wet suit are trapped bubbles of gas. A dry-suit diver has air spaces between the diver and the suit. This gas (in fact, all air spaces) is subject to changes in volume because of changes in pressure (see Boyle's Law). This means that as the diver moves up or down in the water column, the volume of these gas spaces changes, and this change in gas volume affects the diver's buoyancy. As a diver descends, the volume of the gas decreases. Thus, less water is displaced, and the diver is less buoyant and sinks. On ascent, the pressure on the diver decreases. The gas then expands and occupies a larger volume, displacing more water and increasing the buoyant (i.e., upward) force.

Archimedes' Principle points out that if we are not hovering, we *must* be either floating (i.e., moving up) or sinking. So, unless our buoyancy and weight are equal, we must expend energy to hover in the water column. If the buoyant force exactly matches the downward force contributed by the weight of the submerged object, however, then a "weightless" state is achieved. This is why NASA uses underwater training for its astronauts. By finely tuning the buoyancy of a space-suited astronaut underwater, the weightless environment of space can be simulated.

Lifting

The lift associated with air spaces can be used to raise objects from the bottom. Because air weighs very little compared with the weight of the displaced water, it can be assumed that the lifting capacity is equal to the weight of the volume of water that is displaced by the air volume of the lifting device.

English Problem: You wish to lift a 300-pound anchor from the bottom of a lake bed. (The bottom is hard and flat, so no excess lift will be needed to overcome the suction associated with bottom muck). You have access to 55-gallon drums, weighing 20 pounds each, that have been fitted with overexpansion vents. How many 55-gallon drums will it take to lift the anchor?

Answer: Determine the forces involved. First, determine the weight of the water displaced:

$$\text{Weight} = \text{Density} \times \text{Volume}$$

A lake bed implies freshwater so:

$$\text{Density} = \frac{62.4 \text{ lbs}}{\text{ft}^3}$$

Therefore:

$$\text{Weight} = 55 \text{ gal} \times \frac{0.134 \text{ ft}^3}{1 \text{ gal}} \times \frac{62.4 \text{ lbs}}{1 \text{ ft}^3} = 459.9 \text{ lbs}$$

Applying force arrows:

Weight of displaced water = 460 lbs ↑
Weight of drum =   20 lbs ↓
Net force = 440 lbs ↑

Because the object to be lifted weighs less than the 440-pound lifting capacity of a 55-gallon drum, a single drum should be sufficient to lift the 300-pound anchor. In practice, large lifting objects (like a 55-gallon drum) have a large surface area and will generate considerable drag, which decreases lifting capacity. Without getting mathematically rigorous and calculating drag coefficients, a safe rule of thumb is to assume approximately 75% of the calculated lifting capacity for the lifting device in an actual operation.

Problem: Which weighs more underwater, 1 pound of lead or 1 pound of concrete?

Answer: Although both weigh the same on the surface, lead will weigh more when totally submerged. Lead is more dense than concrete, thus an equal weight will displace less water. Therefore, lead will have less buoyancy counteracting its weight; thus, its underwater weight will be greater.

Trim

A diver moving in the water column is subject to a number of forces. In the vertical plane, gravity (i.e., weight) tends to make the diver descend, and buoyancy (from too little weight or too much air in the BC). BC makes the diver ascend. In the horizontal plane, the diver moves forward propelled by the force of the kick. The thrust (or forward motion) must over come **drag** (or friction) that the diver and equipment present to the water. A good diver tries to adjustdiving styles to balance the forces involved (Fig. 3-4).

Part of the unique exhilaration of diving is the ability to glide, weightless, under the surface of the water. It is the most efficient and enjoy-able way to dive. If the diver is overweighted (a too common occurrence), then he or she must continually expend energy to overcome gravity and remain at a constant depth. If underweighted, the diver must also continually expend energy in an attempt to overcome buoyancy with leg power. (In battles with the forces of buoyancy and weight, these forces always overcome leg power and fatigue is certain.) The way to maximize efficiency, that is, to decrease workload and thus increase enjoyment in the water, is to balance weight and buoyancy so that the thrust from the fins can be

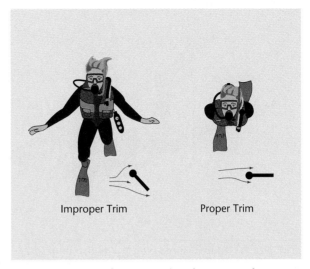

Fig. 3-4. Increased cross-sectional area equals increased resistance equals increased energy requirement.

directed toward forward movement, not toward overcoming buoyancy errors (Fig. 3-5).

Drag can be reduced by assuming a horizontal position in the water. A more horizontal position presents a smaller area to the path of movement and thus lessens resistance. The more horizontal the diver, the smaller the frontal area and the less drag (i.e., resistance to movement caused by friction between the diver and the dense water environment) will occur. Thus, the easier underwater swimming will be! In general, a diver cutting the cross-sectional frontal area by a factor of two requires four times less energy to go the same distance (Fig. 3-6).

Fig. 3-5. A positive angle of attack. Ideally the diver should be level.

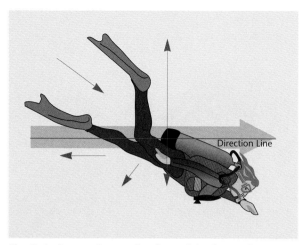

Fig. 3-6. A negative angle of attack is also undesirable.

ENERGY

Energy is the ability to do work. Energy that can be derived by a future change in position is termed **potential energy**, and energy that results from moving mass is called **kinetic energy**. Consider a pile driver. This giant hammer device uses the kinetic energy of a large mass to drive supports into the earth. Energy is used to lift the "driver" to the top of the device. Here, while motionless, it possesses only potential energy. As the mass falls toward its target, the potential energy is transformed into kinetic energy. During the entire movement, the large falling mass will possess different portions of potential and kinetic energy, but the sum of these two types of energy will remain constant. There are several types of energy:

1. Mechanical: The sum of potential and kinetic energies derived from the movement of a body.
2. Heat: Energy derived from molecular motion.
3. Radiant: Energy in the form of electromagnetic waves, such as light, x-rays, or radio waves.
4. Chemical: Energy released from chemical reactions.
5. Electrical: Energy derived from moving electrons.
6. Nuclear: Energy derived from atomic forces within the atom.

Under ordinary conditions, energy can be neither created nor destroyed. This is known as the principle of **Conservation of Energy**. Energy can, however, be changed in form. For example, the potential energy of water at a high level is converted to kinetic energy as it falls through a pipe to a lower level within a hydroelectric dam. The kinetic energy of the falling water turns a turbine (i.e., mechanical energy) that drives a generator producing electricity (i.e., electric energy). The electricity lights a light bulb (i.e., radiant energy) and heats a small space heater (i.e., heat energy). During this entire process, energy is not created; it is simply transformed from one form to another.

Force

Force is a push or a pull. It has a magnitude (i.e., how much push) and direction (i.e., from which direction is the push coming).

Work

Work is the movement of mass over a distance. Work requires energy. If no movement occurs, no work is accomplished. (This means that if you push against a stone wall, no matter how much sweat is generated in your exertion, no work is done if the wall does not move.) Work is expressed as length multiplied by a constant force. Examples include foot-pounds (i.e., work done when a constant force of 1 lb moves an object 1 ft), newton-meter (i.e., work done when 1 N of force moves an object 1 m) and the erg (i.e., work done by a constant force of 1 dyn moving an object 1 cm). Consider two divers of the same size in the water, where both are hovering (i.e., "weightless"). One has achieved this state by properly balancing the forces of weight and buoyancy. The other, much overweighted, has compensated for this extra weight by inflating the BC (matching the negative weight with a positive buoyancy). Even though "weightless," the overweighted diver with the inflated BC will do more work (i.e., the movement of mass through a distance) because more mass (i.e., the extra weight) will need to be moved. In addition, overweighted divers generally are not horizontal in the water. This means they have a larger cross-sectional area, creating more drag. More drag means that more work is necessary for forward movement.

Heat

Heat is thermal energy, or the sum of the kinetic energies for all the random movements of all molecules contained within a substance. It is convenient to measure the amount of heat as if heat were independent of the particular substance whose molecular motion determines the magnitude of heat energy present. The amount of heat necessary to raise 1 g of pure water from 14.5° to 15.5° C is defined as 1 **calorie**. One thousand calories is a kilocalorie (kcal). The corresponding English measurement is the amount of heat necessary to raise 1 pound of pure water from 63.0° to 64.0° F. This unit is called the British Thermal Unit (BTU). One BTU is equivalent to 252 calories.

Matter may be thought of as a heat reservoir. Because of their molecular make-up, different substances will be capable of holding different amounts of heat. The amount of heat required to raise 1 g of a substance 1° C is called the **specific heat**. This corresponds to the definition of a calorie and thus water has a specific heat of 1.0 cal/g° C. The heat capacity of a particular substance is defined as the specific heat of the material multiplied by its mass. The higher the heat capacity, the more heat a substance is capable of absorbing and storing. Substances like water or helium have high specific heats compared with air, and thus divers in contact with water or helium will lose more heat than they would in air. Heat capacities of gases are commonly listed at a specific temperature and pressure (usually 25° C at 1 atm). Because adding heat to a system can affect either the volume or pressure of a gas (depending on the nature of the container), it is customary to measure thermal properties of a gas at constant pressure (C_p) or constant volume (C_v) (Table 3-2).

Heat capacity is the amount of heat required to raise the temperature of the substance by 1° C. Thus:

Heat capacity = Mass of body $\times$ Specific heat of body

The amount of heat necessary to change the temperature of a body is:

Heat Required = Mass $\times$ Specific heat $\times$ Change in temperature.

Divers in a helium environment (e.g., in a commercial diving bell or habitat) will lose large amounts of heat from their bodies. A small part of this heat loss will occur in the respiratory system as cold, dry, inhaled gas is warmed and humidified by the body. The major loss will come from the conduction, convection, and radiation heat loss from the diver's skin into the surrounding atmosphere. Thermal (heat) capacity is not the entire problem. In addition, one must consider the thermal conductivity of the breathing gas and environment in which the diver is operating. **Thermal conductivity** is the rate at which heat is transferred away from warmer objects to a cooler surrounding. It is expressed as the amount of heat that can be transmitted from a fixed area across a known distance in a fixed amount of time. The higher the thermal conductivity, the quicker a warm object will cool. As a corollary, the lower the thermal conductivity, the better the material will be a heat retainer or insulator. Thermal conductivity of an object will vary with the pressure and temperature of the surroundings. For example, some thermal conductivity values expressed as heat conducted (kcal/h) through a 1 cm thick slab of 1 m^2 material evaluated per degree of temperature gradient would be:

Air	=	2.3
Foam neoprene	=	4.6
Wool	=	8.0
Helium	=	12.2
Seawater	=	52.0

The increased heat loss because of the high specific heat and thermal conductivity of helium (and water) compared with air is responsible for heat loss problems associated with working in either an aqueous or heliox environment. This heat loss can be life threatening.

A large mass (e.g., a physically large diver) will possess more heat capacity (i.e., more heat stored in the body) than a smaller diver. Thus, in general, the smaller diver, regardless of sex, will be at higher risk to hypothermia. Physical size, however, is not the only factor. Variables such as age, physiologic condition (particularly if affected by drugs or alcohol), physical fitness, amount of in-water exercise, the thermal protection system employed, temperature of the water, duration of immersion, and so on can also influence the severity of hypothermia (Fig. 3-7).

Temperature is a measurement of the intensity of heat energy. When two materials possessing different heat energies (i.e., different temperatures) come together, heat will always move from the warmer to the cooler. Heat will continue to be transferred until the two bodies possess the same energy (i.e., have same temperature). This means that any time a diver is in water cooler than body temperature, the diver will lose heat. Water has approximately 2800 times the heat capacity of air (i.e., water has the capacity to "store" enormous quantities of heat) and approximately 25 times the thermal conductivity of dry, still air at the same temperature (divers lose heat faster in water than in air!). For example, if a diver enters Lake Superior at 34° F (1.1° C), the diver will lose heat in an effort to warm the entire mass of Lake Superior to the temperature of the diver. Because the mass of Lake Superior is enormous (i.e., incredible heat capacity) compared with the mass of the diver, the diver will lose a lot of body heat.

TABLE 3.2 EXAMPLES OF GAS HEAT CAPACITIES AT 25° C AND ONE ATM PRESSURE		
SUBSTANCE	C_p (cal/g° C)	C_v (cal/g° C)
Air	0.3439	0.2943
Argon	0.1252	0.0750
Helium	1.2420	0.7620
Nitrogen	0.2477	0.1765
Oxygen	0.2200	0.1554

HEAT LOSS

Fig. 3-7. Heat loss in water can be reduced with insulation; however, as the insulation is compressed under pressure, heat loss increases.

The temperature decrease to the diver will be significant, but the temperature increase to Lake Superior will be infinitesimal.

It is not necessary that the water be frigid (medically, the definition of "cold water" is water less than 70° F) for hypothermia to occur. Any time water is cooler than body temperature, the diver will lose heat. Repeated exposure, even in tropical water (so-called "silent hypothermia") can create a hypothermia situation.

The diver loses heat in several ways:

1. **Conduction** is the primary heat loss mechanism in diving. This is the loss of thermal energy by direct contact between substances. Heat moves from the warm diver to the cooler water. Water is more dense than air, and thus more molecular collisions per unit of volume occur, resulting in more heat transfer. Water will remove heat from a diver 25 times faster than will dry, still air of the same temperature. If the diver is breathing gas at a temperature below body temperature, the diver will lose heat as the breathing gas is warmed by body heat. The more dense the breathing gas mixture (i.e., the deeper the dive), the greater the heat loss from respiration.

2. **Convection** is associated with conduction. As a volume of cooler fluid in contact with a warm body is heated, that fluid expands and circulates away from the contact point. The area vacated by the warmer fluid is filled with cooler fluid, and more heat transfer occurs. Convection increases the conductive heat loss. A wet suit functions in part by limiting the conductive and convective heat loss as it restricts the flow of the volume of water immediately surrounding the diver.

3. **Evaporation** is the loss of heat associated with a change in the state of liquid water to water vapor. A significant amount of energy is required to change liquid water to water vapor. Divers breathe a very dry gas, but the lungs need a humidified gas. As the diver breathes, water is evaporated along the respiratory tract to humidify the breathing mixture. This can result in significant heat loss from the diver. Additionally, much heat can be lost from the evaporation of water on a diver's clothing (e.g., a wet suit) on a breezy day.

4. **Radiation** is the loss of heat energy by direct emission of heat energy (e.g., infrared radiation). Although this means of losing heat is critically important in the vacuum of outer space, (which lacks air molecules for the process of conduction and convection to occur) heat loss to the submerged recreational diver is small.

The loss of heat from a diver immersed in cold water *cannot be prevented*. It can, however, be slowed. The purpose of insulation, generally gas trapped in some physical matrix (like nitrogen bubbles in a wet suit or air in the dry-suit underwear), is to slow the loss of heat from the diver to the water by imposing a physical barrier. Thus, heat must move through the insulation on its way from the diver to the water. The better the insulation, the longer it will take the body heat of the diver to move into the water.

Wet suit compression associated with the increased pressure of descent not only decreases buoyancy, it reduces the volume of the protective insulation (i.e., gas trapped in the rubber material of the wet suit). This is why wet suits offer less thermal protection in deeper water. Dry suit volume is compensated for by adding air to the suit on descent.

Adiabatic Expansion

An **adiabatic system** is one in which no heat is added or removed. This relationship explains many diver observations. In an adiabatic system, as the volume increases, temperature decreases to hold the product of the temperature and the volume term constant. Thus, the scuba cylinder gets hot when filled. The air has been compressed, has less volume, and so temperature goes up. This increase in temperature can be substantial. In the presence of hydrocarbon contaminants (e.g., greases and most lubricants), this heat can serve as an energy source for fire and/or explosion in an oxygen-enriched atmosphere. When air is rapidly released from a scuba cylinder, either from directly opening the valve to release its contents before inspection or by using the purge valve, the volume of the gas increases, and so the temperature must go down. Likewise, as offshore wind moves up a mountain slope, it expands from the decrease in pressure, and cools. Eventually, the cooling will result in the temperature falling below the dew point, and clouds or fog then form. The formation of clouds or fog by adiabatic cooling is common along the western coast of the United States and many tropical Pacific islands with high mountains.

Temperature

Temperature is measured by a variety of scales. Historically, the first reliable calibration of temperature was introduced by Daniel Fahrenheit in 1724. He picked the lowest temperature he could obtain (a mixture of ice, salt, and water) and called that his zero point. He next picked the temperature of a healthy man's blood and arbitrarily gave it a value of 96. (There must have been some cooling of the blood between the time of collecting the blood and measuring the temperature, because human body temperature is 98.6 on the Fahrenheit scale.) Using mercury as the expanding fluid that would mark his temperature-sensing gauge, called a *thermometer*, he found that water would freeze at a temperature of 32 and boil at a temperature of 212 on his scale. His system, the **Fahrenheit temperature scale**, is still used in the United States.

Some 12 years later, Anders Celsius proposed a scale that would be based on 100 units between the freezing and boiling points of water. Originally, he called the boiling point 0 and the freezing point 100, but this has been inverted to give a scale of 0 for the freezing point of water and 100 for the boiling point.

The two systems of measurement can be converted using the following expressions:

$$°F = (1.8 × °C) + 32 \quad or \quad °F = 9/5 °C + 32$$
$$°C = (°F − 32) / 1.8 \quad °C = 5/9 (°F − 32)$$

There are two other temperature scales of importance to divers. They are the **Rankine** (i.e., absolute Fahrenheit) and the **Kelvin** (i.e, absolute Celsius). The significance of these absolute temperature scales is discussed in the section on Charles' Law. The definition of absolute temperature is in degrees Kelvin; thus, no degree symbol is used for Kelvin temperatures.

$$°R \text{ (Rankine)} = °F + 460$$
$$K \text{ (Kelvin)} = °C + 273$$

Although it is possible to use these above formulas to convert one temperature scale to another, this is rarely done in diving. Divers accustomed to Fahrenheit will use ° Rankine (i.e., ° F + 460) and divers familiar with Celsius will use Kelvin (i. e., ° C + 273) for doing problems that require the use of absolute temperature scales (Fig. 3-8).

Fig. 3-8. Equal temperature measured by four different methods.

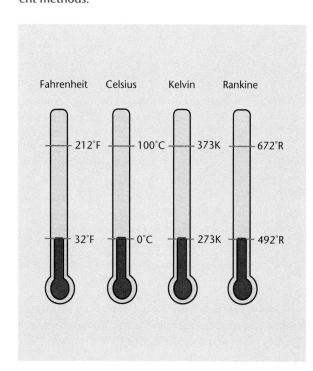

Temperature Conversions

Problem: The normal human body temperature is 98.6° F. What is the corresponding Centigrade (Celsius) temperature?

Answer: Using the previous conversion formula:
$$°C = 5/9 (°F − 32)$$
$$°C = 5/9 (98.6 − 32)$$
$$°C = 37.0$$

Problem: Historically, room temperature has been considered to be 25° C. What is the Fahrenheit equivalent?

Answer: Using the previous conversion formula:
$$°F = 9/5 °C + 32$$
$$°F = 9/5 (25) + 32$$
$$°F = 77$$

Problem: What is the Kelvin equivalent of freezing point of water (i.e., 32° F)?

Answer: a. First determine ° C:
$$°C = 5/9 (°F − 32)$$
$$°C = 5/9 (32 − 32)$$
$$°C = 0$$
b. Determine Kelvin from C:
$$K = °C + 273$$
$$K = 0 + 273$$
$$K = 273$$

Problem: What is the Rankine equivalent of 32° F, the freezing point of water?

Answer:
$$°R = °F + 460$$
$$°R = 32 + 460$$
$$°R = 492$$

LIGHT

Ⓛ**ight** is a form of energy. It provides the illumination that we use to visually perceive and characterize our surroundings. White light, first discussed by Isaac Newton, is comprised of a number of components, each perceived as a different color. If white light passes through an optical device known as a *prism*, then these colors, known as the *light spectrum*, can be seen. This separation of colors in nature is called a rainbow! The colors in the rainbow always have the same order, remembered by the mnemonic "ROY G. BIV" for red, orange, yellow, green, blue, indigo, and violet (Fig. 3-9).

The color that we see depends on which components of the light have been reflected or absorbed by the object we are observing. If an object reflects all the colors, it is observed to be white; if no colors are reflected, the object is observed to be black. Black is really the absence of color. White is considered a "cool" summer color—it reflects light energy. In contrast, black objects absorb rather

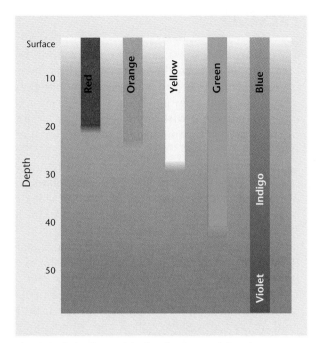

Fig. 3-9. Color loss with depth. General for clear, oceanic water.

than reflect light energy. So, divers wearing all black wet or dry suits absorb radiant radiation. This could contribute to potential diver overheating problems at the surface on hot days, but it would lower heat loss from the diver at the surface on cold days. Other colors result from combinations of reflection and absorption of the various light components. The propagation of light is influenced by a number of factors. These are:

1. **Absorption**. Each color in the light spectrum possesses a different energy. One measure of that energy is the **wavelength** of the light. The longer the wavelength, the less the energy. Red is the least energetic color, while blue is the most energetic form of visible light. As light moves through the water, the components of light are absorbed by the water. Because red is the least energetic, it is absorbed (i.e., lost) first. Each of the colors in turn is absorbed as light passes through any appreciable distance in water. The diver observes that colors "disappear." In shallow water, only the reds may disappear, but as depth increases (i.e., light reaching diver has had to pass through more water) the underwater realm takes on a bluish cast. Eventually, everything visible becomes deep blue, then black. Application of artificial white light (i.e., all the colors present) from a dive light or camera strobe allows the diver to observe (or photograph) nature in its true color (Fig. 3-9).

2. **Diffusion**. As light moves through water, it interacts at the molecular level with all substances present in the water. The result is that light is

scattered and moves in random directions. Some is further absorbed. This process is referred to as diffusion. Divers see less light at depth, because the total amount of light available at the surface has been scattered or absorbed (Fig. 3-10).

3. **Turbidity** refers to the water quality resulting from particulate material suspended in the water. If turbidity is high, the abundance of suspended material will increase the amount of diffusion and absorption that occur. The diver sees less light in turbid water.

4. **Refraction**. Light travels at different speeds in different substances. Light slows by approximately 25% when it enters water from air. This change in velocity results in a bending of the light path as it changes from air to water, as if it had moved through an optical lens. This alteration in the path of light because of changing media is termed refraction. The diver's mask is an air/ water interface, thus the mask also acts as a lens. One reason why a diver needs a mask is that our eyes have evolved to focus in air. The reason objects appear fuzzy underwater is that our eyes cannot adjust enough to bring these objects into focus underwater. Our eyes are such that without a mask, we would need them to be approximately 1 foot long to focus the light that we perceive underwater. So, one reason for the mask is to provide an air/eye interface so that our eyes can focus the light and allow us to see clearly. The result of the air/water interface of the mask is that divers (and camera lenses) will perceive objects to be larger (by four-thirds) and closer (by one quarter) than they really are. In other words, a fish 4 feet away from the diver will appear as if it were only 3 feet away.

5. **Reflection**. This is the phenomenon observed when one looks in a mirror. When light waves strike a smooth, polished surface, they bounce off the surface much like a ball bounces off the side cushions of a billiard table. The angle formed by the light leaving the polished surface is the same angle as the light striking the surface when measured (i.e., compared) to a line perpendicular to the surface. In the same fashion, a portion of the light striking water will be reflected away from the surface. Near sunrise or sundown, this effect can significantly reduce the amount of ambient light at depth. Divers can observe this phenomenon during a night dive. If the water is very smooth, the surface of the water will act as a reflecting surface. While submerged near the surface, shine your light in front of you at an angle directly toward the surface; a significant portion of the light beam will be reflected from the surface back into the water.

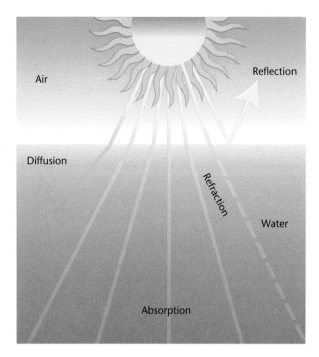

Fig. 3-10. Light in water. Reflection, refraction, diffusion and absorption all affect light in water.

SOUND

Ⓢound is a longitudinal wave that moves through a fluid. In other words, sound energy is produced by mechanical vibrations. For example, as the propeller from an outboard motor turns, it presses against the water. This produces a series of pressure waves that move through the water. Our ears, through a vibrating membrane (i.e., the eardrum), convert the vibrations to electrical pulses that the brain interprets as sound. In essence, we hear with our brains, and the ears are merely vibration collectors.

In air, we can perceive the direction of a sound source. Our brain does this by measuring the time delay between the sound energy striking one ear and then the other. The time delay is then processed by the brain to give a direction. Underwater, the velocity of sound is approximately four times faster than in air; this means the time delay between sound energy striking each ear is approximately four times less in water than in air. Localization by sound underwater is possible by humans, particularly with low-frequency signals, but it is extremely difficult. For humans to determine direction underwater in the same manner as on the surface, our ears would have to be approximately 3 feet apart! So, although a loud noise can be used to attract attention, recreational divers should consider sound to be an unreliable directional cue.

PRESSURE

Ⓟressure is defined as a force acting on a unit area. The force most often encountered by divers is weight. Thus, pressure is measured in terms of a weight (not mass) per unit area. The pressure that divers must cope with results from the weight of the water and atmosphere above the diver (Fig. 3-11).

An early Italian scientist showed that the height of the mercury (760 mm) in a tube was defined as **atmospheric pressure**. This is why pressure is often expressed in mm Hg. (Hg is the chemical symbol for mercury; a pressure reading given in mm Hg means that the observed pressure equals the weight, or force, necessary to hold a column of mercury at the height given in the measurement.) The diameter of the tube or surface area of the dish is immaterial, as the mercury in the tube is held up by the weight of the entire atmosphere. Equivalent measurements of pressure can be made with different fluids; mercury was originally chosen because of its high density (specific gravity, 13.6). Thus, measurements of atmospheric pressure could be made with a reasonably sized instrument. An equivalent instrument using water (specific gravity, 1.00) would be over 30 feet high.

Defined values for a pressure of 1 atm are:
760 mm Hg
760 torr
29.92 in Hg
10.1 meters seawater (msw)
10.3 meters freshwater (mfw)
33 feet seawater (fsw)
34 feet freshwater (ffw)
14.7. pounds per square inch (p.s.i.)
1.01 bar

Problem: What is the pressure expressed in p.s.i., mm Hg, atm, and bars exerted by 4 feet (1.2 m) of seawater?

Answer: This is just another example of the ease of getting desired answers by multiplying appropriate conversion factors:

$$\frac{14.7 \text{ psi}}{1 \text{ atm}} \times \frac{1 \text{ atm}}{33 \text{ fsw}} \times 4\text{fsw} = 1.78 \text{ psi}$$

$$\frac{760 \text{ mm Hg}}{1 \text{ atm}} \times \frac{1 \text{ atm}}{33\text{fsw}} \times 4\text{fsw} = 92.1 \text{ mm Hg}$$

$$\frac{1 \text{ atm}}{33 \text{ fsw}} \times 4\text{fsw} = 0.12 \text{ atm}$$

$$\frac{1.01 \text{ bar}}{\text{atm}} \times \frac{1 \text{ atm}}{33 \text{ fsw}} \times 4\text{fsw} = 0.12 \text{ bar}$$

Problem: Determine the hydrostatic and absolute (i.e., ambient) pressure at a depth of 78 fsw (23.8 msw).

Answer: Using the definition of hydrostatic pressure, we find:

$$\text{Hydrostatic pressure} = \frac{\text{Depth of water}}{\text{Definition of atm}}$$

Note that water depth is in units of length, atm should be in the same units. So, if depth is in fsw, 1 atm equals 33 fsw. If depth is in ffw, 1 atm equals 34 ffw. If depth is in msw, 1 atm equals 1 m/bar or 1 m/atm, and so on.

Substituting:	(English)	(Metric)	
Hydrostatic pressure =	$\dfrac{78\ \text{fsw}}{33\ \text{fsw / atm}}$	$\dfrac{23.8\ \text{msw}}{10.1\ \text{m / atm}}$	$\dfrac{23.8\ \text{msw}}{10\ \text{m / bar}}$
Hydrostatic pressure =	2.36 atm	2.36 atm	2.38 bar
Absolute pressure =	hydrostatic pressure + atmospheric pressure		
	= 2.36 atm + 1 atm		
	= 3.36 ata		

where *ata* is absolute atmospheres. Alternatively:

Absolute pressure = 2.38 bar + 1.01 bar

= 3.39 bar

The validity of the solution can be checked by comparing answers. Converting metric pressure (in bar) to atmospheres, we find:

$$3.39\ \text{bar} \times \frac{1\ \text{ata}}{1.01\ \text{bar}} = 3.36\ \text{ata}$$

The procedures used to solve diving physics problems are the same using English or metric units. Physical principles are independent of the units employed. Because the numeric values will differ (English units are *not* exactly identical to metric units), however, it is important to pay attention to the units and use the *same units* for temperature, pressure, volume, and so on during the entire calculation. For example, if using depth in fsw, atmospheric pressure *must be* defined in terms of fsw. Ignoring units can lead to problems. For example, there is a classic formula in the United States:

$$\text{Absolute pressure} = \frac{\text{Depth}}{33} + 1$$

This formula is only valid when diving in seawater at sea level, with depth measured in feet of seawater (fsw). Because this text assumes that some divers will dive in other conditions or with gauges calibrated to units other than fsw (e.g., one American manufacturer offers depth gauges calibrated in ffw) or in locations other than sea level, a more general approach with an emphasis on understanding hydrostatic and absolute pressure in all environments will be used. *If the units are wrong, the numeric answer is wrong!* Get in the habit of using units. The solutions make more sense, and they are easier to obtain!

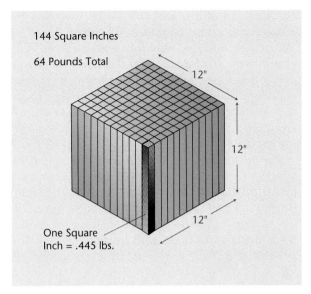

144 Square Inches

64 Pounds Total

12"

12"

12"

One Square Inch = .445 lbs.

Fig. 3-11. One cubic foot of salt water (64 pounds) exerts .445 pounds per square inch (64/144 = .445). This pressure multiplied by 33 feet of salt water equals 1 atm. of pressure (14.7 p.s.i.).

Remember that if you only memorize formulas and apply formulas without understanding them, then the potential for disaster exists! Gases in cylinders are measured in gauge pressure; however, gauge pressure reads zero at 1 atm. To find the absolute pressure, 1 atm (in the same units as the gauge) must be added to the gauge pressure.

English Problem: An 80 ft^3 cylinder contains gas at a pressure of 3000 p.s.i.g. (pounds per square inch gauge). Determine the absolute pressure.

Answer: Using the formula:

Absolute pressure = Gauge pressure + Atmospheric pressure

yields:

3000 psi + 14.7 psi = 3014.7 psia

where *p.s.i.a.* stands for absolute pounds per square inch.

Metric Problem: A scuba cylinder contains 2400 L at a gauge pressure of 200 bar. Determine absolute pressure.

Answer: This corresponds to an absolute pressure of:

200 bar + 1.01 bar = 201.01 bar

Depth Gauges

Depth gauges do not measure water depth! Rather, they measure pressure. Inside the device, a mechanical mechanism coupled with a printed scale on the face of the instrument converts a measured pressure into an equivalent scale reading for water depth. The gauge will be accurate only if it is used in the environment for which it has been calibrated. When the device is taken to a different environment, such as high altitude, the reading of water depth on the gauge may be substantially different from the actual measured water depth. This is most often a problem when depth gauges calibrated at sea level are taken to altitude, as illustrated by the following example.

Problem: You are diving in a high-altitude mountain lake. The barometer reads 24.61 in (625 mm) Hg. Thus, at this altitude, 24.61 in (625 mm) Hg and not 29.92 in (760 mm) Hg is the atmospheric pressure! Consider also that high mountain lakes usually are filled with freshwater (density, approximately 62.4 lbs/ft^3 or 1.00 g/cc), not saltwater (density, 64 lbs/ft^3 or 1.03 g/cc). What will the depth gauge read at an actual depth of 60 ffw (18.29 m) in this lake?

English Answer: First calculate the depth (x) of water that corresponds to 1 atm at the observed barometric pressure. Remember that atmospheric equivalent height is inversely proportional to the density of the fluid being used to measure pressure:

$$\frac{24.61 \text{ in Hg}}{x \text{ in H}_2\text{O}} = \frac{1.0 \text{ g / cc}}{13.6 \text{ g / cc}}$$

$$x = 334.7 \text{ in of water}$$

This means that 1 atm of pressure at this altitude corresponds to a water column depth of approximately 334 inches of water. In feet, this is:

$$334.7 \text{ in} \times \frac{1 \text{ ft}}{12 \text{ in}} = 27.9 \text{ ft}$$

Thus, every 27.9 feet of freshwater (not 33 fsw) at this altitude corresponds to 1 atm of pressure at this altitude, where a depth measured by a lead line (not gauge) of 60 feet would be:

$$\frac{60 \text{ ffw}}{27.9 \text{ ffw / atm}} = 2.15 \text{ atm}$$

In terms of "at-altitude" atmospheres, the absolute pressure would be:

$$2.2 \text{ atm} + 1 \text{ atm} = 3.2 \text{ ata}$$

This corresponds to a pressure of:

$$\frac{24.61 \text{ in Hg}}{1 \text{ ata}} \times 3.2 \text{ ata} = 78.75 \text{ in Hg}$$

The depth gauge "senses" a pressure corresponding to 78.75 in Hg. The mechanism inside the device converts this pressure to:

$$\frac{78.75 \text{ in Hg}}{29.92 \text{ in Hg / sea level ata}} = 2.63 \text{ sea level ata}$$

This would then correspond to a hydrostatic sea-level pressure of:

$$2.6 \text{ ata} - 1 \text{ atm} = 1.6 \text{ atm}$$

This in turn would be read on the sea level–calibrated scale as:

$$1.6 \text{ atm} \times \frac{33 \text{ fsw}}{1 \text{ atm}} = 52.8 = 53 \text{ fsw}$$

So, for a measured depth of 60 feet at this altitude, the sea level–calibrated gauge reads 53 feet.

Metric Solution: Determine the water equivalent of 1 atm at this altitude:

$$\frac{625 \text{ mm Hg}}{x \text{ mm H}_2\text{O}} = \frac{1.00 \text{ g / cc}}{13.6 \text{ g / cc}}$$

$$x = 8500 \text{ mm H}_2\text{O}$$

This converts to:

$$8500 \text{ mm} \times \frac{1 \text{ m}}{1000 \text{ mm}} = 8.5 \text{ m}$$

Thus, at this altitude, 8.5 m corresponds to 1 ata. At a depth of 18.29 mfw, the hydrostatic pressure is:

$$\frac{18.29 \text{ m}}{8.5 \text{m/atm}} = 2.15 \text{ atm}$$

This is an absolute "at altitude" pressure of:

$$2.2 \text{ atm} + 1 \text{ atm} = 3.2 \text{ ata}$$

This means the gauge at this altitude is responding to a pressure of:

$$3.2 \text{ atm} \times \frac{624 \text{ mm Hg}}{1 \text{ atm}} = 1996.8 \text{ mm Hg}$$

This corresponds to a sea-level pressure of:

$$\frac{1996.8 \text{ mm Hg}}{760 \text{ mm Hg / sea level atm}} = 2.63 \text{ sea level ata}$$

This would then correspond to a hydrostatic sea-level pressure of:

$$2.6 \text{ ata} - 1 \text{ atm} = 1.6 \text{ atm}$$

This in turn would be read on the sea level–calibrated scale as:

$$1.6 \text{ atm} \times \frac{10.1 \text{ m}}{1 \text{ atm}} = 16.2 \text{ m}$$

So, the measured depth was 18.29 meters, and the sea-level depth gauge at this altitude would read 16.2 m.

If the sea level–calibrated gauge were to be used for extended diving, a series of corrections (generally at 10-ft [3-m] increments) could be calculated to be added to the in-water depth readings for use at this altitude. True depth could then be determined by adding this "correction factor" to the observed sea level–calibrated depth gauge reading. Tables of these correction factors are available (e.g., *Altitude Procedures for the Diver* by CL Smith.)

Remember that depth gauges measure pressure, not depth! The water depth indicated on the gauge dial reflects the actual depth only if used in the environment for which the gauge was calibrated.

Ocean Equivalent Depth (for Decompression Obligation)

The following is a physics discussion on the method used to obtain ocean equivalent depth for use with sea–level based tables. Such conversions are not as desirable as using tables or computers specifically designed for use at altitude.

Decompression obligation (i.e., dive table) calculations are based on pressure ratios, not actual measured in-water depths. Thus, when a diver changes altitude, the diver must be careful about the decompression tables and procedures used. Unless the dive table/computer specifically provides procedures for varying altitudes, divers should assume that the table/computer is only valid at sea level.

Decompression procedures are based on a theoretic maximum pressure ratio that can be tolerated within the tissue compartments without injury to the diver. This amount of pressure may vary with the depth of the diver and the particular mathematic simulation being used. The important consideration is that the **pressure difference** (i.e., ratio between the current pressure and the pressure at some shallower depth reached on ascent) and not the actual water depth, controls the decompression obligation. This is best illustrated with a numeric example.

Problem: At the altitude used in the previous example, 1 atm of pressure corresponds to 27.9 feet (8.5 m) of freshwater. Thus, the pressure at this altitude would increase by 1 at-altitude atm every 27.9 feet (8.5 m) of descent/ascent (as opposed to every 33 feet [10.1 m] of seawater) at sea level. This means that every 27.9 feet (8.5 m) at this altitude would correspond to a pressure (in terms of atmospheres) equivalent of 33 feet (10.1 m) of seawater at sea level. So, to maintain approximately the same pressure ratios as in the US Navy tables (or equivalent sea level–derived tables) for determining decompression obligations, one must determine the actual number of "atmospheres pressure" at altitude and convert this to a sea-level saltwater depth. For the high-altitude dive at 60 feet (18.29 m, or 2.16 "altitude" atmospheres) example used previously:

English: $2.16 \text{ atm} \times \dfrac{33 \text{ fsw}}{1 \text{ atm}} = 71.3 \text{ fsw}$

Metric: $2.16 \text{ atm} \times \dfrac{10.1 \text{ msw}}{1 \text{ atm}} = 21.8 \text{ msw}$

Note that in this high-altitude example, our actual in-water depth was 60 feet (18.3 m). The depth gauge indicated a depth of 53 fsw (16.2 msw). The equivalent sea-level depth to maintain the same pressure differential as in the US Navy table between bottom depth and safe ascent depth was 71.3 fsw (21.7 msw). Thus, using gauge pressure–measured depth at altitude to enter the sea level–computed decompression tables would allow the diver far more bottom time (increase risk to DCS) at depth, because the diver would be entering the table at too shallow a depth.

Equivalent Ascent Rates

Finally, ascent rates are also part of the decompression calculations. Previous US Navy sea-level tables *assume* a rate of 60 fsw/min. (The newer tables about to be published at press time specify an ascent rate of 30 fsw/min.) The BSAC tables recommend an ascent rate of 15 m/min. This ascent rate is part of the calculations used to derive the decompression schedules. Because at altitude the actual amount of water column that "defines" 1 at-altitude atm is less than 33 feet (10.1 m) of seawater, an ascent in a high-altitude mountain lake must be slower than an ascent from the corresponding depth at sea level to maintain the same rate of pressure change with time. Again, this is best illustrated with numbers. For the previous example: the recommended ascent rate at sea level is:

English: $\dfrac{60 \text{ fsw}}{1 \text{ min}} \times \dfrac{1 \text{ atm}}{33 \text{ fsw}} = \dfrac{1.82 \text{ atm}}{1 \text{ min}}$

Metric: $\dfrac{15 \text{ m}}{1 \text{ min}} \times \dfrac{1 \text{ atm}}{10.1 \text{ m}} = \dfrac{1.49 \text{ atm}}{1 \text{ min}}$

At this altitude, the corresponding at-altitude ascent rate is:

English: $\dfrac{1.82 \text{ atm}}{1 \text{ min}} \times \dfrac{27.9 \text{ ffw}}{\text{atm}} = \dfrac{50.8 \text{ ffw}}{1 \text{ min}}$

Metric: $\dfrac{1.49 \text{ atm}}{1 \text{ min}} \times \dfrac{8.5 \text{ m}}{\text{atm}} = \dfrac{12.7 \text{ m}}{1 \text{ min}}$

Thus, while diving to a measured depth of 60 feet (18.29 m) in this high altitude mountain lake, your depth gauge would read 53 fsw (16.2 msw). Your No-Stop decompression obligation would be determined by the 80 foot (24 m) sea-level schedule using a recommended ascent rate of either 50.8 ffw/min or 12.7 mfw/min.

Remember that sea level–based dive procedures (tables or calculators) are inadequate for determining decompression obligations at high-altitude dive sites. Divers at high altitudes (i.e., above 1000 ft or 300 m) should consider high-altitude conversion tables (The Cross Tables) based on the above technique, dive tables with variable altitude entries (Swiss, DCIEM, or BSAC air tables), or altitude-compensating dive computers. Also, there is a high-altitude ocean depth calculator available from NAUI for determining ocean equivalent depths to use sea-level tables at altitude. In general, these methods are considered theoretic and without extensive experimental validation. There is more discussion in the altitude diving section of this textbook; however, those who wish to dive at altitude should obtain specialty training in high-altitude diving procedures.

KINETIC THEORY OF GASES

Regardless of their chemical composition, all gases demonstrate similar behavior in response to physical changes of composition, temperature, and pressure. This uniformity of physical behavior greatly interested early scientists. It is one of the dogmas of science that the behavior of a material is a reflection of the particles that compose the substance. Differences between a solid, liquid, and gas reflect the movement of the small particles (i.e., atoms) that compose all matter. This assumption is part of the **Kinetic Theory Of Gases** (*kinetic* is from the Greek word for motion).

Charles' Law

The relationship between temperature, pressure, and volume has been extensively studied. In 1787, the French scientist Jacques Charles studied the relationship between temperature and volume at constant pressure. This study was prompted by an attempt to understand how hot-air balloons worked. He noted that in the vicinity of 0° C, the volume of a gas decreased by a factor of 1/273 for each decrease of 1° C. If one theoretically continued this decrease in temperature, a gas would have zero volume at -273° C. This value is termed **Absolute Zero** (if a gas has zero volume, there will be no molecular motion and thus no kinetic energy). Measurements of temperature based on this absolute zero point are termed **Absolute Temperature**. (Because gases will liquefy before absolute zero is reached, the "zero volume" state is not obtainable.) Because this 1/273 change in volume corresponds to a 1° change on the absolute temperature scale, absolute temperatures are used when using "the gas laws" described later to predict variations in pressure, temperature, and volume. Charles' observations have been formalized into **Charles' Law**, which states that the volume of a gas at constant pressure is directly proportional to the absolute temperature. Expressed mathematically this is:

$$\frac{V_1}{T_1} = \frac{V_2}{T_2}$$

where:

V_1 = the volume at first measurement
V_2 = the volume at second measurement
T_1 = the absolute temperature at first measurement
T_2 = the absolute temperature at second measurement

English Problem: If a scuba cylinder is capable of delivering 40 ft³ of air to a diver at 78° F, how much air is available at 55° F?

Answer: Using Charles' Law (with absolute temperature), we find:

$$T_1 = 78° F + 460 = 538° R$$
$$T_2 = 55° F + 460 = 515° R$$

Charles' Law states that:

$$\frac{V_1}{T_1} = \frac{V_2}{T_2}$$

So, substituting:

$$\frac{40 \text{ ft}^3}{538° R} = \frac{V_2}{515° R}$$

This produces: $V_2 = 38.3$ ft³

Metric Problem: A scuba cylinder is capable of delivering 1000 L of air at 25° C. If this cylinder is used at 18° C, how much air will be available to the diver?

Answer: Charles' Law states that:

$$\frac{V_1}{T_1} = \frac{V_2}{T_2}$$

We then determine absolute temperature:

$$T_1 = 25° C + 273 = 298 K$$
$$T_2 = 18° C + 273 = 291 K$$

Substituting:

$$\frac{1000 \text{ L}}{298 \text{ K}} = \frac{V_2}{291 \text{ K}}$$

This produces:

$$V_2 = 976.5 \text{ L}$$

This demonstrates a reduction in the air available to the diver if the gas in the cylinder is cooled.

Guy-Lussac's Law

Near the turn of the nineteenth century, Guy-Lussac investigated the relationship between pressure and temperature while the volume was held constant. He did his measurements using a fixed-volume, gas-filled sphere. He measured the temperature and pressure of the gas in the sphere while ascending in a hot-air balloon. His published observation (known as **Guy-Lussac's Law**) states that the pressure of a gas at constant volume is directly proportional to the absolute temperature. Stated mathematically this is:

$$\frac{P_1}{T_1} = \frac{P_2}{T_2}$$

where P and T are absolute measurements of pressure and temperature at conditions 1 and 2. It makes no difference if the units of pressure are expressed in p.s.i., mm Hg, cm H_2O, bars, kilopascals, g/cm², kg/m², and so on. It is necessary to use absolute measurements, however, and to keep the units consistent. It also makes no difference whether the "unknown" (i.e., initial vs. final) is P_1, P_2, T_1, or T_2.

English Problem: A scuba cylinder contains 3000 p.s.i.g. (3014.7 p.s.i.a.) at 78° F. It is left in the trunk of a car on a hot summer day. If the temperature of the trunk is 115° F, what will be the gauge pressure of the cylinder?

Answer: Using Guy-Lussac's Law (remember absolute temperature and pressure), we find:

$$T_1 = 78° F + 46 = 538° R$$
$$T_2 = 115° F + 460 = 575° R$$

Substituting into Guy-Lussac's Law:

$$\frac{3014.7 \text{ psia}}{538° R} = \frac{P_2}{575° R}$$

Solving, we find:

$$P_2 = 3222 \text{ psia}$$

Then, converting to gauge pressure yields:

$$3222 \text{ psia} - 14.7 \text{ psi} = 3207.3 \text{ psig}$$

Metric Problem: A cylinder at 25° C (298 K) contains gas at a gauge pressure of 200 bar (201.01 bar absolute). Predict the pressure at 42° C (315 K).

Answer: Guy-Lussac's Law (remember absolute temperature and pressure) states:

$$\frac{P_1}{T_1} = \frac{P_2}{T_2}$$

Substituting, we find:

$$\frac{201 \text{ bar}}{298 \text{ K}} = \frac{P_2}{315 \text{ K}}$$

Solving, we find:

$$P_2 = 212.5 \text{ bar}$$

Then, converting to gauge pressure:

$$P_2 = 212.5 \text{ bar} - 1.01 \text{ bar}$$
$$P_2 = 211.5 \text{ bar}$$

Thus, a scuba cylinder with a gauge pressure of 200 bar at 25° C that is heated to 42° C will show a gauge pressure of approximately 212 bar.

Note that a scuba cylinder is a constant-volume device. As kinetic energy increases with temperature, the molecules travel faster. They hit the vessel walls harder and more often. This means pressure within the cylinder increases as the temperature is raised, and there is an increase in pressure associated with heating a scuba cylinder. To prevent this increase in pressure (and possible rupture of the safety disc), it is especially important to store full scuba cylinders in a cool place.

Boyle's Law

In 1662, Sir Robert Boyle published the classic "The Spring of Air and Its Effects" in which he measured the relationship between pressure and volume at constant temperature. He mea-sured the volume of air trapped at the small end of a J-shaped tube filled with mercury. Adding mercury (i.e., increasing the height of the mercury in the J-tube) decreased the volume of air trapped at the small end of the tube. Boyle noted that the product of the pressure (as determined by the height of the mercury column) and the volume was constant. Expressed mathematically, this is:

$$PV = k$$

where P is the pressure (i.e., height of mercury in tube), V the volume (of air space in tube), and k a constant.

This relationship, PV = k, held for a variety of P and V combinations. In mathematics, products equal to the same value can be set equal to each other. This gives us Boyle's Law:

$$P_1V_1 = P_2V_2$$

where P is the absolute pressure and V the volume measured at set of conditions 1 and 2.

Boyle's Law states that at constant temperature, volume varies inversely with pressure. A corollary to this law states that density (i.e., mass/volume) increases directly with pressure. These principles are best illustrated by numeric examples:

English Problem: What is the physical volume (in ft³) of an aluminum "80" scuba cylinder?

Answer: An aluminum 80 delivers 80 cubic feet of air at 1 atm (14.7 p.s.i.a.) when filled to a pressure of 3000 p.s.i.g. (3014.7 p.s.i.a.). Thus, the physical volume of the tank will be the volume of 80 cubic feet of air at 3000 p.s.i.g. (3014.7 p.s.i.a.). Substituting into Boyle's Law, we find:

$$(14.7 \text{ psia}) (80 \text{ ft}^3) = (3014.7 \text{ psia}) V_2$$

Solving for V_2, we find:

$$V_2 = 0.39 \text{ ft}^3$$

This physical volume also represents how much water the cylinder would hold if the valve were removed and the cylinder filled with water. This is the value that Europeans refer to as the *water capacity* of a scuba cylinder.

Metric Problem: A scuba cylinder is rated at 2400 L with a pressure of 200 bar. What is the physical volume (i.e., water capacity) of the cylinder?

Answer: The cylinder delivers 2400 L if all of the air is released at 1 bar. The physical volume (i.e., water capacity) of the cylinder is the volume of gas compressed to 200 bar. The volume can be found by using Boyle's Law:

$$P_1V_1 = P_2V_2$$

Then determine absolute pressure (i.e., gauge + atmospheric):

$$200 \text{ bar} + 1 \text{ bar} = 201 \text{ bar}$$

Substituting into Boyle's Law we find:

$$(1 \text{ bar}) \times (2400 \text{ L}) = (201 \text{ bar}) V_2$$

Solving, we find:

$$V_2 = 11.9 \text{ L}$$

English Problem: A scuba cylinder has a rated capacity of 80 cubic feet on the surface. Determine the amount of air the cylinder will deliver at 33, 66, 99, and 132 fsw.

Answer: Boyle's Law allows the calculation of decreasing volume of air with increasing depth. First, determine the absolute pressure (i.e., hydrostatic pressure + atmospheric pressure). For 33 feet:

$$\frac{33 \text{ fsw}}{33 \text{ fsw/atm}} = 1 \text{ atm} + 1 \text{ atm} = 2 \text{ ata}$$

For 66 feet:

$$\frac{66 \text{ fsw}}{33 \text{ fsw/atm}} = 2 \text{ atm} + 1 \text{ atm} = 3 \text{ ata}$$

For 99 feet:

$$\frac{99 \text{ fsw}}{33 \text{ fsw/atm}} = 3 \text{ atm} + 1 \text{ atm} = 4 \text{ ata}$$

For 132 feet:

$$\frac{132 \text{ fsw}}{33 \text{ fsw/atm}} = 4 \text{ atm} + 1 \text{ atm} = 5 \text{ ata}$$

Substituting into Boyle's Law, which states:

$$P_1 V_1 = P_2 V_2$$

We find that for 33 fsw:

$$(1 \text{ ata}) (80 \text{ ft}^3) = (2 \text{ ata}) V_2$$
$$V_2 = 40 \text{ ft}^3$$

For 66 fsw:

$$(1 \text{ ata}) (80 \text{ ft}^3) = (3 \text{ ata}) V_2$$
$$V_2 = 26.7 \text{ ft}^3$$

For 99 fsw:

$$(1 \text{ ata}) (80 \text{ ft}^3) = (4 \text{ ata}) V_2$$
$$V_2 = 20 \text{ ft}^3$$

For 132 feet:

$$(1 \text{ ata}) (80 \text{ ft}^3) = (5 \text{ ata}) V_2$$
$$V_2 = 16 \text{ ft}^3$$

The answers can be summarized as:

Depth (fsw)	Absolute Pressure (ata)	Volume (ft³)	Fraction	Change (%)
0	1	80	1/1	0
33	2	40	1/2	50
66	3	27	1/3	33
99	4	20	1/4	25
132	5	16	1/5	20

The volume shown is the volume calculated for an 80-cubic-foot cylinder. The fraction represents the proportional amount of the surface volume at that absolute pressure available from *any* size scuba cylinder. The percentage change represents the difference in volume between each successive 1 ata pressure change.

Metric Problem: The corresponding metric table for a 2000-L cylinder is:

Depth (msw)	Absolute Pressure (bar)	Volume(L)	Fraction	Change (%)
0	1	2000	1/1	0
10	2	1000	1/2	50
20	3	666	1/3	33
30	4	500	1/4	25
40	5	400	1/5	20

The volume shown is the volume calculated for a 2000 L cylinder. The fraction represents the proportional amount of the surface volume at that absolute pressure available from *any* size scuba cylinder. The percentage change represents the difference in volume between each successive 1 bar change in pressure.

Remember, that as pressure increases, volume decreases. Breathing is basically a constant volume operation, so this is the same as saying that the deeper you go, the less air will be available to you. Thus, the sooner you will consume the air contained in your scuba cylinder (see the Estimation of Air Consumption section) (Figs. 3-12 and 3-13).

Fig. 3-12. Divers lifting a port-hole with a lift bag.

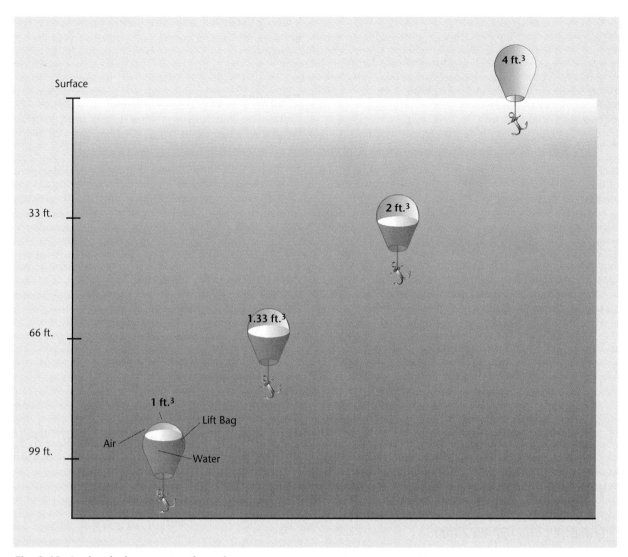

Surface

33 ft.

66 ft.

99 ft.

4 ft.³

2 ft.³

1.33 ft.³

1 ft.³

Lift Bag

Air

Water

Fig. 3-13. As depth decreases, volume increases.

Likewise, as pressure decreases (as on ascent), the volume of gas in the lungs and other air spaces increases. The physical size of the body cavity containing the air (i.e., lungs, ears, sinus, and so on) is limited, so the volume of expanding gas either properly vents through open, unobstructed passages or increases by damaging or rupturing tissue. This is analogous to increasing the size of a chewing gum bubble by exhaling into it until it bursts. The greatest volume change per unit of pressure is in the vicinity of the surface, which means the most risk of a pressure–volume type of injury (i.e., air embolism) is near the surface.

General Gas Law

Any two of the three gas laws of Boyle, Charles, or Guy-Lussac can be combined into a relationship termed the **General or Combined Gas Law**. Expressed mathematically, this is:

$$\frac{P_1 V_1}{T_1} = \frac{P_2 V_2}{T_2}$$

where P, V, and T are as previously defined. This relationship can be used to predict pressure, volume, and temperature relationships where any five of the six variables are known.

English Problem: The gas in a scuba cylinder occupies a volume of 72 cubic feet at 78° F on the surface. What volume of gas is available to the diver at a depth of 126 ffw and a temperature of 40°F?

Answer: First, determine the pressure. On the surface, this is:

$$P_1 = 1 \text{ ata}$$

At 126 ffw:

$$P_2 = 126 \text{ ffw} \times \frac{1 \text{ atm}}{34 \text{ ffw}} = 3.7 \text{ atm}$$

Remember, pressure must be absolute. Therefore, at 126 ffw:

$$P_2 = 3.7 \text{ atm} + 1 \text{ atm} = 4.7 \text{ ata}$$

Next, determine the absolute temperature:

$$T_1 = 78° \text{ F} + 460 = 538° \text{ R}$$
$$T_2 = 40° \text{ F} + 460 = 500° \text{ R}$$

The General Gas Law states:

$$\frac{P_1 V_1}{T_1} = \frac{P_2 V_2}{T_2}$$

So, substituting:

$$\frac{1 (ata)(72 \text{ ft}^3)}{538° \text{ R}} = \frac{(4.7 \text{ ata})V_2}{500° \text{ R}}$$

And solving, we find:

$$V_2 = 14.2 \text{ ft}^3$$

This demonstrates the decrease in available breathing gas volume associated with descent to deep, cold freshwater that might be encountered in the Great Lakes of the United States.

Metric Problem: Calculate the volume of gas available to a diver when a cylinder having a volume of 2000 liters with a gauge pressure reading of 200 bar at 25° C (298 K) is used at a depth of 20 msw (3 bar) and a temperature of 30° C (303 K).

Answer: Substituting into the General Gas Law, we find:

$$\frac{(1 \text{ bar})(2000 \text{ L})}{298 \text{ K}} = \frac{(3 \text{ bar})V_2}{303 \text{ K}}$$

Solving, we find:

$$V_2 = 678 \text{ liters}$$

Because both the temperature and resultant pressure most likely will vary between the filling of a scuba cylinder and its use, the General Gas Law will give a slightly more realistic evaluation of the volume available at depth than will a relationship that only examines two of the three pressure-temperature-volume variables.

Estimating Gas Consumption

Less air is available to the diver as that diver descends in the water column. The actual volume of gas within a scuba cylinder does not decrease (i.e., all of the gas molecules have not been confined to the bottom of the tank) on descent. The tank physically does not shrink under pressure; however, air being delivered to the diver is at the ambient pressure. This increased ambient pressure means there are more gas molecules present in each unit volume (i.e., the gas is more dense). Because the diver consumes more molecules per breath (i.e., constant volume breathing), the gas in the scuba cylinder will last a shorter amount of time. Although gas consumption can be affected by numerous factors (e.g., physical size, workload, water temperature, general physical and emotional condition), it can be approximated.

The best approximation comes from personal experience (i.e., knowledge of individual gas consumption rates). It has been stated that the "average" diver consumes air at a surface consumption rate of 1 cubic foot (28.3 L) per minute. Each diver's air consumption rate will change based on personal comfort, physical fitness, and experience, so individual surface consumption rates will vary with time and *must* be determined from periodic personal observation.

Pressure-based Calculations

The air consumption rates in this unit, for purposes of illustration, have intentionally been made excessive, but similar to those of an anxious, inefficient, or beginning diver. This is to magnify the decrease in available time at deeper depths.

If the average rate of consumption is already known, this value can be used to determine the duration of any cylinder. This is best demonstrated by numeric example.

Problem: Determine the "average" duration of an 80-cubic-foot (2266-L) cylinder at 99 fsw (30.2 msw) for that "average diver" (i.e., 1 ft³/min, or 28.3 L/min).

Answer: Estimate the surface duration time:

$$\text{Surface duration} = \frac{\text{Volume of cylinder}}{\text{Consumption rate}}$$

Surface duration at 1 ata yields:

(English)	(Metric)
$\dfrac{80 \text{ ft}^3}{1 \text{ ft}^3/\text{min}}$	$\dfrac{2{,}266 \text{ L}}{28.3 \text{ L/min}}$

English and Metric Problem: If surface duration equals 80 minutes on the surface (1 ata), convert the surface duration to estimate at depth.

Answer: For our "average diver" at 99 fsw (30.2 msw), the hydrostatic pressure at depth is:

$$\frac{99 \text{ fsw}}{33 \text{ fsw/atm}} = 3 \text{ atm}$$

English: Absolute pressure at depth is:

$$3 \text{ atm} + 1 \text{ atm} = 4 \text{ ata}$$

Metric: Absolute pressure at depth is 4 bar.

Note that to avoid confusion as to whether *bar* refers to cylinder or water pressure, we use ata for water pressure and bar for cylinder pressure in the metric air-consumption examples.

$$\text{Depth duration} = \frac{\text{Surface duration}}{\text{Pressure (ata) at depth}}$$

$$\text{Depth duration} = \frac{80 \text{ minutes at 1 ata}}{4 \text{ ata}}$$

$$\text{Depth duration} = 20 \text{ minutes at 4 ata}$$

Breathing 80 cubic feet (2266 L) from an 80-cubic-foot (2266 L) scuba cylinder would consume the entire contents of the cylinder. This is most unwise at any depth! Regardless of any calculated numbers, divers must remember to monitor their air supply gauges and to begin their ascent with adequate air for the ascent and a reserve for contingencies plus safety stop.

Problem: A diver's air supply lasts 60 minutes at 33 (10.1 m) feet. Assuming the same air consumption rate as before, how long will the gas supply last the diver at 99 fsw (30.2 msw)? Remember that absolute pressure *must* be used.

Hydrostatic pressures at depth are:

$$\frac{33 \text{ fsw}}{33 \text{fsw/atm}} = 1 \text{ atm}$$

$$\frac{99 \text{ fsw}}{33 \text{ fsw/atm}} = 3 \text{ atm}$$

Absolute (i.e., hydrostatic plus atmospheric) pressures at depth are:

$$1 \text{ atm} + 1 \text{ atm} = 2 \text{ ata}$$
$$3 \text{ atm} + 1 \text{ atm} = 4 \text{ ata}$$

This is because:

$$(\text{Duration 1}) \, P_1 = (\text{Duration 2}) \, P_2$$

Substituting, we find:

$$(60 \text{ min}) \, (2 \text{ ata}) = (\text{Duration 2}) \, (4 \text{ ata})$$

Solving, we find:

$$\text{Duration 2} = 30 \text{ min}$$

At deeper depths, a wise diver would plan less bottom time than in this prediction, because a larger safety reserve would be appropriate. The diver would begin ascent at a higher air supply pressure.

These calculations assume that the diver either consumed air at an "average" rate *or* that some estimation of duration had already been determined. However, air consumption is individual. Thus, to use air consumption values in personal dive planning, each diver must determine individual rates of air consumption.

Individual air consumption can be determined as follows. The diver descends to a known depth (measured by a marked, weighted line). At a recorded depth, the diver remains stationary while recording p.s.i.g. (bar) consumed over a measured time. (The longer the time period, the more representative of the diver the consumption rate will be in terms of pressure consumed per minute.) This represents a "resting" rate (i.e., pressure consumed/min) of air consumption. Because swimming (physical labor or any stressor) will increase air consumption, the rate of air consumption should also be determined under workload. One method uses a marked line (approximately 100 ft, or 30 m) rigged at a constant depth. The diver swims lengths along the line. The diver monitors number of "kick cycles" (a "cycle" is each time a diver kicks with both legs and is routinely measured as each time one particular leg goes

below the plane of the body) and the air consumed (in terms of p.s.i. or bar per 100 ft or 30 m of line). The dive buddy measures the time it takes to swim the length of the line. At the end of each length, the diver records "kicks" and p.s.i.g. (bar) consumed; the buddy records the time. After swimming several lengths of the line, the divers switch roles. At the end of this exercise, both divers will know the average number of kicks, amount of time, and air consumed to travel 100 feet. If the diver wishes to estimate a more realistic "working" consumption rate, he or she swims the length of line while towing a float that has a 10-pound anchor attached.

Problem: After swimming several lengths of a 100-foot line at a depth of 33 fsw (2 ata), a diver has consumed an average of 50 p.s.i.g. (3.4 bar) per length. The diver took 1 minute on average to swim this length. What is the surface consumption rate?

Answer: At depth, this diver consumed 50 p.s.i.g./min (3.4 bar/min). On the surface, where absolute pressure is less, the density of the available breathing gas will be less (Boyle's Law), so the diver has more volume to consume the same 50 p.s.i.g. So, the diver will consume less p.s.i.g. (bar) per minute at the surface. The amount of increase will be representative of this change in density described by Boyle's Law:

$$\frac{(\text{Surface consumption})}{\text{At-depth air consumption}} = \frac{\text{Surface absolute pressure}}{\text{At-depth absolute pressure}}$$

Substituting for this particular diver, we find:

English: $\dfrac{\text{Surface air consumption}}{50 \text{ psig/min}} = \dfrac{1 \text{ ata}}{2 \text{ ata}}$

$$\text{Surface Air Consumption} = 25 \text{ psig/min}$$

Metric: $\dfrac{\text{Surface air consumption}}{3.4 \text{ bar/min}} = \dfrac{1 \text{ ata}}{2 \text{ ata}}$

$$\text{Surface Air Consumption} = 1.7 \text{ bar/min}$$

The value that we have just determined, the **Surface Air Consumption Rate**, or SAC Rate, can be used in a variety of ways to assist the diver when planning dives.

Surface Air Consumption Calculations

If the diver monitors air consumption (in terms of p.s.i.g. or bar consumed), monitors the duration of the dive, and holds a constant monitored depth, an average rate of air consumption at depth in terms of p.s.i.g./ata-min or bar/ata-min (analogous to miles per gallon or kilometers per liter in a car) can be calculated. This rate of consumption (i.e., p.s.i.g./min or bar/min) can be converted to a surface p.s.i.g./min (bar/min) value based on the assumptions of Boyle's Law. This value is called the SAC Rate.

Problem: A diver consumes 200 p.s.i.g./min (13.7 bar/min) at 99 fsw (10.2 msw, 4 ata). What is this diver's SAC rate?

Answer: The SAC rate is expressed in terms of p.s.i.g. per minute (bar/min) at some measurement of pressure. Conversion to surface (or any other depth) consumption is then merely a function of determining absolute pressure at the depth desired. In this case, the absolute pressure–based air-consumption rate is:

$$\textbf{English: } \frac{200 \text{ psig}}{4 \text{ ata} \cdot \text{min}} = \frac{50 \text{ psig}}{1 \text{ ata} \cdot \text{min}}$$

$$\textbf{Metric: } \frac{13.7 \text{ bar}}{4 \text{ ata} \cdot \text{min}} = \frac{3.4 \text{ bar}}{1 \text{ ata} \cdot \text{min}}$$

Because there is 1 ata pressure at the surface, the English SAC value is:

$$\frac{50 \text{ psig}}{1 \text{ ata} \cdot \text{min}} \times 1 \text{ ata} = \frac{50 \text{ psig}}{1 \text{ min}}$$

The metric SAC equivalent in this example is 3.4 bar/min. The individual diver's absolute pressure–based air consumption can then be used to estimate the air consumption at any other depth.

Problem: Calculate the air consumption at 132 fsw (40.5 msw, 5 ata) using the previous diver's absolute pressure–based air-consumption rate.

Answer: Convert the absolute pressure–based consumption rate to an at-depth consumption rate. In this case:

$$\textbf{English: } \frac{50 \text{ psig}}{1 \text{ ata} \cdot \text{min}} \times 5 \text{ ata} = \frac{250 \text{ psig}}{1 \text{ min}}$$

$$\textbf{Metric: } \frac{3.4 \text{ bar}}{1 \text{ ata} \cdot \text{min}} \times 5 \text{ ata} = \frac{17 \text{ bar}}{1 \text{ min}}$$

The absolute pressure–based air-consumption rate can be used to estimate duration of the dive as limited by gas consumption.

English Problem: A diver who has an absolute pressure–based air consumption of 50 p.s.i.g./ata-min wishes to begin ascent at 1000 p.s.i.g. Assuming the diver reaches the desired depth with 2800 p.s.i.g., determine the duration of a dive at 33 fsw and at 99 fsw.

Answer: The diver has allowed 2800 p.s.i.g.– 1000 p.s.i.g. = 1800 p.s.i.g. for the dive. Convert the cylinder pressure reading to duration using absolute SAC. For 33 fsw (2 ata) this is:

$$1800 \text{ psig} \times \frac{1 \text{ ata} \cdot \text{min}}{50 \text{ psig}} \times \frac{1}{2 \text{ ata}} = 18 \text{ min}$$

For 99 fsw (4 ata):

$$1800 \text{ psig} \times \frac{1 \text{ ata} \cdot \text{min}}{50 \text{ psig}} \times \frac{1}{4 \text{ ata}} = 9 \text{ min}$$

Metric Problem: A diver has an absolute pressure–based SAC rate of 3.4 bar/ata-min. Assume the diver begins a dive with a gauge reading of 200 bar and wishes to begin ascent at 70 bar. How long will the diver be able to dive at 10 msw (2 ata) and 20 msw (3 ata)?

Answer: The diver has allowed 200 bar − 70 bar = 130 bar for the dive. Convert the cylinder pressure reading to duration at depth using absolute SAC. For 10 msw, this is:

$$130 \text{ bar} \times \frac{1 \text{ ata} \cdot \text{min}}{3.4 \text{ bar}} \times \frac{1}{2 \text{ ata}} = 19 \text{ min}$$

For 20 msw:

$$130 \text{ bar} \times \frac{1 \text{ ata} \cdot \text{min}}{3.4 \text{ bar}} \times \frac{1}{3 \text{ ata}} = 13 \text{ min}$$

Calculations based on cylinder pressure changes will vary when different scuba cylinder sizes are used. For example, a 1500 p.s.i.g. (102-bar) change in a 14-cubic-foot (396-L) pony bottle is *not* the same volume of air as a 1500-p.s.i.g. (102-bar) change in an 80-cubic-foot (2266-L) aluminum cylinder. Therefore, divers must ensure that their absolute air-consumption factor (based on p.s.i.g. or bar consumed) is used *only* with the cylinder size for which the SAC value was determined. This difference is best illustrated by numeric example.

Problem: Determine the volume of air represented by a 1500-p.s.i.g. (102-bar) change in the following full scuba cylinders: an aluminum "80" (2266 L) at 3000 p.s.i.g., a steel "71.2" (2016 L) at 2475 p.s.i.g. and an aluminum "14" (396 L) at 2015 p.s.i.g.

Answer: The volume of gas available from a fixed-volume cylinder will be directly proportional to the absolute pressure. Converting gauge pressure to absolute, we find:

$$1500 \text{ psig} = 1514.7 \text{ psia (104 bar)}$$
$$3000 \text{ psig} = 3014.7 \text{ psia (207 bar)}$$
$$2475 \text{ psig} = 2489.7 \text{ psia (171 bar)}$$
$$2015 \text{ psig} = 2029.7 \text{ psia (139 bar)}$$

For the aluminum "80" (i.e., 80 cubic feet of gas at 3014.7 p.s.i.a.), we find:

$$\frac{3014.7 \text{ psia}}{80 \text{ ft}^3} = \frac{1514.7 \text{ psia}}{V_2}$$

Solving, we find:

$$V_2 = 40.2 \text{ ft}^3 \text{ (1138 L)}$$

For the steel "72" (i.e., 71.55 cubic feet of gas at 2489.7 p.s.i.a.), we find:

$$\frac{2489.7 \text{ psia}}{71.55 \text{ ft}^3} = \frac{1514.7 \text{ psia}}{V_2}$$

Solving produces:

$$V_2 = 43.5 \text{ ft}^3 \text{ (1232 L)}$$

For the aluminum "14" pony bottle (i.e., 14.06 cubic feet at 2029.7 p.s.i.a.), the equation is:

$$\frac{2029.7 \text{ psia}}{14.06 \text{ ft}^3} = \frac{1514.7 \text{ psia}}{V_2}$$

Solving, we find:

$$V_2 = 10.5 \text{ ft}^3 \text{ (297 L)}$$

So, a diver using 1500 p.s.i.g. (103 bar) would consume 40.2 cubic feet (1138 L) with an aluminum "80," 43.5 cubic feet (1232 L) with a steel "72" and 10.5 cubic feet (297 L) with an aluminum "14" pony. This is why the same pressure-based (p.s.i.g. or bar) consumption factors cannot be used for scuba cylinders of different volumes.

Volume-based Calculations

The SAC method, in essence, uses p.s.i.g. or bar as a measurement of the volume consumed. The numeric value of the absolute pressure–based air-consumption factor (in terms of p.s.i.g. consumed/min or bar/min) will vary with the size of the cylinder used. If the volume of the cylinder for which this p.s.i.g./min (bar/min) determination is known, however, this absolute pressure–based air-consumption value may be converted to an absolute volume–consumption factor. The advantage of this is that volume consumed is independent of the size of the breathing gas supply. Thus, the same factor can be used in dive planning for a variety of different sources of breathing gas.

Note however, that the precise volume of standard "72" and "80" cylinders has varied with time and manufacturer. Divers should check the manufacturer's specifications to determine the volume of a particular cylinder.

English Problem: When using an aluminum "80," as decribed previously, a diver had an absolute pressure–based air consumption of 50 p.s.i.g./ata-min. Convert this to a volume measurement, knowing that an "80" contains 79.87 cubic feet of air at a pressure of 3000 p.s.i.g.

Answer: Convert the pressure factor to volume factor by appropriate multiplication. Examination of the units of the pressure factor indicates the arrangement of the cylinder volume and pressure to obtain the appropriate volume factor:

$$\frac{50 \text{ psig}}{1 \text{ ata} \cdot \text{min}} \times \frac{79.87 \text{ ft}^3}{3000 \text{ psig}} = \frac{1.33 \text{ ft}^3}{1 \text{ ata} \cdot \text{min}}$$

Metric Problem: A diver's scuba cylinder with a water capacity of 12 L is filled with air at 200 bar. Using the metric absolute SAC value from the previous example (i.e., 3.4 bar/ata-min), determine the absolute volume value.

Answer: Convert the pressure factor to a volume factor using the cylinder values. First, determine the air available:

$$\text{Air available} = \text{Water capacity of cylinder} \times \text{Pressure reading}$$

$$\text{Air available} = \frac{12 \text{ L}}{1 \text{ bar}} \times 200 \text{ bar} = 2400 \text{ L}$$

Next, cancel the units to obtain the volume-based conversion factor:

$$\frac{3.4 \text{ bar}}{1 \text{ ata} \cdot \text{min}} \times \frac{2400 \text{ L}}{200 \text{ bar}} = \frac{40.8 \text{ L}}{1 \text{ ata} \cdot \text{min}}$$

This volume measurement can then be used to determine either the duration of a dive (knowing the volume of gas available) or the volume of gas needed to conduct a particular dive.

English Problem: How much gas is required to allow a diver with the previous absolute volume–consumption factor (i.e., 1.33 ft³/ata · min) to dive to an ocean depth of 66 feet (3 ata) for 45 minutes?

Answer: Use the volume factor and multiply the values to obtain a volume:

$$\frac{1.33 \text{ ft}^3}{1 \text{ ata} \cdot \text{min}} \times 3 \text{ ata} \times 45 \text{ min} = 179.6 \text{ ft}^3$$

Obviously, this diver is *not* able to make this dive with a typical single scuba cylinder!

Metric Problem: How much gas is required for a diver with the previous absolute volume–consumption factor (i.e., 40.8 L/ata · min) to dive to an ocean depth of 30 meters (4 ata) for 15 minutes?

Answer: Use the volume factor and multiply the conditions given in the problem to obtain a volume:

$$\frac{40.8 \text{ L}}{1 \text{ ata} \cdot \text{min}} \times 4 \text{ ata} \times 15 \text{ min} = 2448 \text{ L}$$

Examination of the air consumption for this diver should indicate that making this dive on a single 12-L cylinder filled at 200 bar (2400 L of available air) would be most unwise!

English Problem: How long will a diver with an absolute volume–consumption factor of 1.33 ft³/ata · min take to consume 60 cubic feet of air at an ocean depth of 33 feet (2 ata)?

Answer: Use absolute volume factor and set up conditions given so that the units cancel to give a duration:

$$60 \text{ ft}^3 \times \frac{1 \text{ ata} \cdot \text{mon}}{1.33 \text{ ft}^3} \times \frac{1}{2 \text{ ata}} = 22.6 \text{ min}$$

Metric Problem: How long will it take a diver with the absolute volume–consumption factor of 40.8 L/ata · min to consume 1200 L at an ocean depth of 30 meters (4 ata)?

Answer: Use the volume factor and conditions desired to obtain a duration:

$$1,200 \text{ L} \times \frac{1 \text{ ata} \cdot \text{min}}{40.8 \text{ L}} \times \frac{1}{4 \text{ ata}} = 7.35 \text{ min}$$

Remember, the absolute volume–consumption factor is independent of the scuba cylinder volume. It can also be used to calculate an absolute pressure-consumption (in terms of p.s.i.g. or bar/min) for any size of cylinder. Again, this is best illustrated by numeric example.

English Problem: A diver has an absolute-volume consumption of 1.33 ft³/ata · min. Determine this diver's absolute-pressure consumption factor for an aluminum "80" (i.e., 80.70 ft³ at 3000 p.s.i.g.), a steel "72" (i.e., 71.55 ft³ at 2475 p.s.i.g.), and a steel "50" (52.14 ft³ at 2475 p.s.i.g.).

Answer: Start with absolute volume–consumption rate, then convert to units of pressure consumed based on individual tank characteristics.

For the "80" cylinder:

$$\frac{1.33 \text{ ft}^3}{1 \text{ ata} \cdot \text{min}} \times \frac{3000 \text{ psig}}{80.7 \text{ ft}^3} = \frac{49.4 \text{ psig}}{1 \text{ ata} \cdot \text{min}}$$

For the "72" cylinder:

$$\frac{1.33 \text{ ft}^3}{1 \text{ ata} \cdot \text{min}} \times \frac{2475 \text{ psig}}{71.55 \text{ ft}^3} = \frac{46.0 \text{ psig}}{1 \text{ ata} \cdot \text{min}}$$

For the "50" cylinder:

$$\frac{1.33 \text{ ft}^3}{1 \text{ ata} \cdot \text{min}} \times \frac{2475 \text{ psig}}{52.15 \text{ ft}^3} = \frac{63.1 \text{ psig}}{1 \text{ ata} \cdot \text{min}}$$

Again, when estimating consumption based on pressure, it is imperative that the pressure factor calculated is based on the size of the cylinder used. The smaller the cylinder, the higher the p.s.i.g. consumption per minute.

Metric Problem: A diver has an absolute-volume consumption of 40.8 L/ata · min. Determine the absolute-pressure consumption for this diver when using a cylinder with 3105 L of available air (i.e., 15-L water capacity at 207 bar) and a cylinder with 1000 L of available air (i.e., 5-L water capacity at 200 bar).

Answer: Start with the absolute-volume consumption, and use the individual cylinder characteristics to determine an absolute-pressure consumption for that sized cylinder. For the "3105-L" cylinder, this is:

$$\frac{40.8 \text{ L}}{1 \text{ ata} \cdot \text{min}} \times \frac{207 \text{ bar}}{3105 \text{ L}} = \frac{2.72 \text{ bar}}{1 \text{ ata} \cdot \text{min}}$$

For the "1,000-L" cylinder:

$$\frac{40.8 \text{ L}}{1 \text{ ata} \cdot \text{min}} \times \frac{207 \text{ bar}}{3105 \text{ L}} = \frac{2.72 \text{ bar}}{1 \text{ ata} \cdot \text{min}}$$

Note that divers must learn to think in terms of volume (i.e., cubic feet or liters) of air consumed at an absolute pressure! Remember that calculations are used primarily for planning dives. Divers should remember to include additional time (i.e., volume) for ascent and safety stops. Finally, regardless of what the calculations have determined, there is no substitute for monitoring the actual air consumption at depth using a submersible pressure gauge.

Dalton's Law

The English chemist John Dalton, with collaborator William Henry (of Henry's Law) observed in 1810 the pressure obtained when gases were mixed. He concluded that when gases are mixed in a container, each gas behaved as if it is the only gas present. Thus, the total pressure in a closed system can be obtained by summing the pressures of each individual component. The pressure of each individual component is termed the **partial pressure**. Expressed mathematically, this is:

$$p_{(total)} = p_1 + p_2 + p_3 + \dots p_n$$

where n is the maximum number of components in the gas mixture.

Problem: A 1-cubic-foot (28.3-L) container contains 500 p.s.i.g. (34 bar) of nitrogen gas. Into the container, an additional 346 p.s.i.g. (23.8 bar) of oxygen gas is introduced. Determine the final pressure.

Answer: Using Dalton's Law:

$$p_{(total)} = p_1 + p_2$$

Substituting, we find:

English: $p_{(total)} = 500 \text{ psi} + 346 \text{ psi}$

Metric: $p_{(total)} = 34 \text{ bar} + 23.8 \text{ bar}$

Solving, we find:

English: $p_{(total)} = 846 \text{ psi}$

Metric: $p_{(total)} = 57.8 \text{ bar}$

Another way of viewing Dalton's Law is:

$$p_n = P_{(total)} \times \text{Fraction of gas}_{(n)} \text{ by volume}$$

Problem: Determine the partial pressure of oxygen in compressed air at a depth of 88 fsw (26.8 msw).

Answer: Using Dalton's Law:

$$p_n = P_{(total)} \times \text{Fraction of gas by volume (Air = 21\% O}_2\text{)}$$

English: $P(\text{hydrostatic}) = 88 \text{ fsw} \times \dfrac{1 \text{ atm}}{33 \text{ fsw}} = 2.7 \text{ atm}$

Metric: $P(\text{hydrostatic}) = 26.8 \text{ msw} \times \dfrac{1 \text{ atm}}{10.1 \text{ msw}} = 2.7 \text{ atm}$

$$P(\text{absolute}) = 2.7 \text{ atm} + 1 \text{ atm} = 3.7 \text{ ata}$$

Substituting, we find:

$$p\,O_2 = 3.7 \text{ ata} \times 0.21$$

$$p\,O_2 = 0.77 \text{ ata}$$

Problem: Determine the partial pressure of nitrogen (78% of air) at the same depth.

$$p\,N_2 = 3.7 \text{ ata} \times 0.78$$

$$p\,N_2 = 2.89 \text{ ata}$$

The increased partial pressure of nitrogen at depth is one reason for the accumulation of nitrogen within the diver. Nitrogen is physiologically inert (i.e., not consumed by metabolism), so this nitrogen accumulation can be detrimental to the diver. The consequences of this absorption are discussed in the Physiology and Decompression chapters.

Henry's Law

Whenever a gas is in contact with a liquid, the gas will dissolve in the liquid. There is a continual movement of gas molecules, which are simultaneously moving out of solution into the gas phase and moving from the gas phase into solution within the liquid phase. Although it is impossible to predict the behavior of an individual gas molecule, the net movement of gas will equilibrate so that the partial pressure of the gas going into the solution is the same as the partial pressure of the gas coming out of the solution. When the gas reaches the state where the amount of gas going into solution is the same as the amount of gas molecules coming out, the solution is said to be **saturated** with gas. This state is termed **equilibrium**. At this point, individual gas molecules will move at random into and out of solution, but there will be no net change in gas concentration within the solution.

Henry's Law states that the amount of gas that will dissolve into a solution is directly proportional to the partial pressure of that gas and inversely proportional to the absolute temperature. The greater the partial pressure of the gas, the greater the driving force for solution and the greater the amount of gas that will dissolve. As the temperature decreases, more gas will dissolve into solution. It is very important to realize that Henry's Law is concerned with the **amount** of gas in solution when equilibrium is reached. It specifically does *not* address how rapidly that state is reached (Fig. 3-14).

The dissolution of nitrogen within body tissues is approximated by Henry's Law. The deeper one dives, the greater the partial pressure of nitrogen (and any gas in the gas mix), and the greater the gas load that each tissue must bear. On ascent, the partial pressure in the gas phase decreases. Gas in solution will then escape from solution in an attempt to obtain equilibrium. If this escape from a tissue is too rapid for the body to handle, decompression sickness results. This is discussed in more detail in the Physiology and Decompression chapters.

Estimating Gas Density

The change in density because of a change in the chemical composition of a gas mix can be determined using established chemical principles.

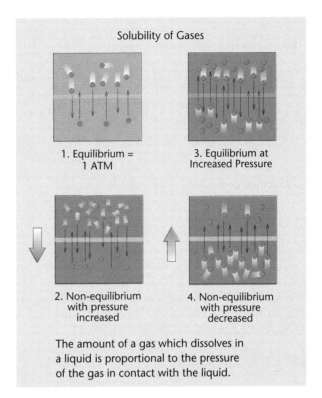

Solubility of Gases

1. Equilibrium = 1 ATM

2. Non-equilibrium with pressure increased

3. Equilibrium at Increased Pressure

4. Non-equilibrium with pressure decreased

The amount of a gas which dissolves in a liquid is proportional to the pressure of the gas in contact with the liquid.

Fig. 3-14. Henry's Law.

One mole of any gas occupies 22.4 liters at standard temperature and pressure (STP) (0° C; 1 ata). This fact, with the molecular weight of the gas (found either from the periodic table or a table of molecular weights) and Dalton's Law, can be used to estimate the density of a breathing gas. Because a breathing gas becomes more dense at depth, it is more difficult to breathe. The relative breathing difficulty of a gas mixture at different depths, or different gas mixtures at similar depths, can be estimated. For example, a table of molecular weights gives the following:

Molecular mass of O_2: 31.998 atomic mass units (amu)
Molecular mass of N_2: 28.014 amu

Density is defined as mass/volume. Because 1 mole of dry gas at STP occupies 22.4 L, the density of a pure substance is easily determined. For example:

Density of O_2 = 31.998 g/mole $\times$ 1 mole/22.4 L = 1.428 g/L
Density of N_2 = 28.014 g/mole $\times$ 1 mole/22.4 L = 1.251 g/L

Problem: Determine the density of a binary mixture of 68% nitrogen and 32% oxygen. This mixture is known as Nitrox-32, or NOAA I.

Answer: The mass for the mixture can be determined simply by summing the masses of the individual components. By choosing a volume of 1 L, the density at STP is merely the mass of the mixture. For the oxygen mass in 1 L of mix:

0.32 L (1.428 g/L) = 0.4570 g

For nitrogen mass:

$$0.68 \text{ L } (1.251 \text{ g/L}) = 0.8507 \text{ g}$$

For density (i.e., mass of NOAA I occupying 1 L) at STP, the sum is: 1.3077 g/L.

Problem: Determine the density at STP of a 36% oxygen, 64% nitrogen mix (Nitrox-36, or NOAA II).

Answer: The oxygen mass in 1 L of mix:

$$0.36 \text{ L } (1.428 \text{ g/L}) = 0.5141 \text{ g}$$

The nitrogen mass:

$$0.64 \text{ L } (1.251 \text{ g/L}) = 0.8006 \text{ g}$$

For density (i.e., mass of NOAA II occupying 1 L) at STP, the sum is: 1.3147 g/L. This method, as long as the components are known, can be applied to any mixture of gases. The values obtained for these Nitrox blends can then be compared with the value of dry air at STP listed in the CRC *Handbook of Chemistry and Physics* of 1.296 g/L.

Gas Density at Depth

Because the pressure changes associated with scuba diving are relatively small, we may assume ideal gas behavior. With this assumption, the gases will behave according to Boyle's Law and density will be directly proportional to the absolute pressure.

Problem: Determine the gas density for Nitrox I, Nitrox II, and air at 100 fsw.

Answer: First, determine the absolute pressure at 100 fsw:

100 fsw/ 33 fsw/atm = 3.03 atm water pressure = 4.03 ata

Density is directly proportional to absolute pressure, so the density of dry air at 100 FSW is:

$$1.296 \text{ g/L} \times 4.03 = 5.22 \text{ g/L}$$

The density of NOAA I is:

$$1.308 \text{ g/L} \times 4.03 = 5.27 \text{ g/L}$$

And the density of NOAA II is:

$$1.315 \text{ g/L} \times 4.03 = 5.30 \text{ g/L}$$

Dalton's Law and Mixing

Dalton's Law assumes that each component in a gas mixture behaves individually as an ideal gas. Although useful at low pressures, this assumption fails at scuba cylinder pressures. Thus, calculations of partial pressures for mixing gases at scuba cylinder pressures based on ideal gas behavior will be in error. Sometimes this error can be potentially lifethreatening. This is best illustrated by a numeric example.

Problem: Assume a deep-diving adventurer wishes to dive on the wreck of the Edmund Fitzgerald. Further assume that the wreck lies at 510 feet (155 m) of very cold freshwater in Lake Superior. (This ultradeep example was chosen to magnify the consequence of error in a real versus ideal situation.) This situation corresponds to an absolute pressure of:

$$\frac{510 \text{ ffw}}{34 \text{ ffw/atm}} = 15.0 \text{ atm hydrostatic}$$

which is

15.0 atm + 1 atm = 16.0 atm absolute (16.0 ata, 16.16 bar)

The diver wishes to keep the oxygen partial pressure at a maximum 1.6 ata, because pO_2 levels higher than 1.6 have been involved in oxygen toxicity problems. So, the diver decides to prepare a diving mix of 1.6-ata oxygen for diving at this depth. Ideally, the concentration of oxygen in the gas mix should be varied at depth to keep the partial pressure of oxygen high enough to maintain consciousness, yet not high enough to cause a toxicity overdose! problem. The ability to vary oxygen concentration with depth is not currently an available option in recreational diving equipment.

Currently, 1.6 ata is the *maximum* recommended pO_2 for oxygen (to avoid oxygen toxicity and to maximize the physiologic/decompression advantage of high O_2 concentrations). Under stress (e.g., workload, cold, depth, and so on) it is currently recommended that the pO_2 not exceed 1.4 ata, with some advising that a pO_2 of 1.2 ata is more appropriate. Because this is an example to maximize the differences between real and ideal, we will use, *for purposes of illustration*, a pO_2 of 1.6 ata.

Answer Using Ideal Relationships:

To estimate pO_2 for a 10% mix, calculate the change in partial pressure of oxygen:

$$(P_2 - P_1) f_g$$

where P_2 is the absolute pressure desired at the end of mixing, P_1 the absolute pressure at the start of operation, and f_g the oxygen fraction desired.

Assume the diver will be filling "empty" cylinders (i.e., gauge pressure = zero) to 3000 p.s.i.g. (206 bar). Further assume the gas previously in the cylinder was 10% Heliox. Substituting for P_1 and P_2, we find:

English: (3014.7 psia − 14.7 psi) (0.10) = 300.0 psia

Metric: (206 bar − 1 bar) (0.10) = 20.6 bar

This yields an absolute final oxygen pressure of

$$P_1 + 300.0 \text{ psia}$$

This yields:

> **English:** 14.7 psia + 300.0 psia = 314.7 psia
>
> **Metric:** 1 bar + 20.6 bar = 21.6 bar

Converting to gauge pressure, we find:

> **English:** 314.7 psia − 14.7 psi = 300.0 psig
>
> **Metric**: 21.6 bar − 1 bar = 20.6 bar

Because this is a discussion of physics, we ignore the practical problems with "plumbing" to measure gas to that tolerance. We also ignore, for the sake of this discussion, the hazards associated with handling pure oxygen. Although often ignored by recreational divers, an analysis of the diving gas mix is an accepted and prudent practice. The mix perfectly prepared to the previous calculations would analyze between 11% and 12% oxygen. In other words, the mix contains too much oxygen and increases the diver's risk of oxygen toxicity. (A 12% O_2 mix at 16.0 ata corresponds to a pO_2 of 1.92 ata.) Confident that the simple, ideal calculations provided a margin of safety, the diver would be diving with a breathing mixture that is most likely too oxygen rich for the depth. A too-rich oxygen mixture increases the probability of an oxygen-toxicity seizure. An oxygen-toxicity seizure is not considered to be a survivable event while wearing "recreational" diving equipment.

Using Real Relationships

There is a distinct difference between the composition of a mix calculated by the simple Dalton's Law equation and the percentage of gas present. Mixing gases to typical scuba cylinder pressures requires consideration of "real" gas law equations to arrive at a calculated value that more closely resembles reality. In the field, this can be done by consulting tables of empiric values (i.e., "worksheets") that have been determined by experience with a particular mix. Some physical measurement, such as mass (based on "mole fraction") or density, is often used to arrive at the proper pressure for mixing. Additionally, there are computer programs available that use real equations to derive the appropriate proportions for any contemplated breathing mix. For this example, we use the 10% Heliox Gas Density Tables from the US *Navy Diving Gas Manual*.

In this table, the extrapolated pressure of the pure oxygen added is 283.5 p.s.i.g. (19.5 bar). When the cylinder is first filled, there may be some layering, because Helium is much less dense than oxygen. Tanks should be rolled or allowed to sit for several hours before analysis or use. Once the gas has been mixed to uniformity, it will remain mixed and will not settle into layers.

The "real" method using tables derived from empiric observations gives a pO_2 that is significantly different from the value obtained from "ideal" simple proportions (i.e., 300 p.s.i.g. [20.6 bar] vs. 283 p.s.i.g. [19.5 bar]). It turns out that mixes of Heliox at scuba cylinder pressures calculated from simple Dalton's Law percentages will always contain more oxygen than calculated. Thus, diving at mixtures derived from simple relationships will increase diver susceptibility to oxygen toxicity, because the diver will be diving with a much higher pO_2 than anticipated.

Remember that no matter what method is used to calculate the gas mixture concentrations, the only way to know what the cylinder contains is by obtaining a detailed chemical analysis. There are oxygen electrodes that will determine the percentage of oxygen in a gas mixture. As long as there are only two components in the mix, this is sufficient information (inert gas = 100 % - % O_2).

SUMMARY

While you may not consciously use actual physical principles on every dive, they are present nonetheless. Changes in the partial pressures of gases, the volume of air spaces, heat gain and loss, light, and sound are present on every dive. Advanced divers should understand how these physical principles apply to diving. The following chapter applies these physical principles to human physiology to help you understand the effects of diving on your body.

SUGGESTED READINGS

- Adamson A: *Understanding physical chemistry*, WA Benjamin, 1964.
- Asimov I: *Asimov's chronology of science and discovery*, Harper and Row, 1989.
- Asimov I: *Understanding physics, 3 vols.*, Dorset Press, 1988.
- Battelle Memorial Institute; *US Navy diving gas manual*, Battelle Memorial Institute, 1969.
- Bennett C: *Physics*, Barnes & Noble College Outline Series, Barnes & Noble, 1952.
- Butler G: "Getting your Fill," *Technical Diver*, Summer 1991.
- Carlucci P, Pletzke T, Pengler R: *Gas mixtures—facts and fables*, Matheson Gas Products, 1991.
- Calhoun F: *Physics For Divers*, NAUI, 1978.
- Dickens R: *The physics of diving*, DLS Enterprises, 1981.
- Himmelblau D, editor: *Introduction and computations for gases*, American Institute of Chemical Engineers, 1981.
- Hodgman C, et al, editors: *Handbook of chemistry and physics*, Chemical Rubber Publishing Co., 1962.
- Nelson G: *Gas mixtures: preparation and control*, Lewis Publishers, 1992.
- Smith C: *Altitude procedures for the ocean diver*, NAUI, 1975.
- Taylor L: "Some physical principles," In Mount T, Gilliam B, editors: *Mixed gas diving*, Watersport Publications, 1992.
- Tucker W: *Diver's handbook of underwater calculations*, Cornell Maritime Press, 1982.

he previous chapter explained the physical laws that relate to diving. This chapter applies those physical laws to human physiology, which is defined as the function of the body systems. As a diver, you must understand the effects that diving will have on your body processes and organs. This section provides you with information on a variety of topics that relate to diving physiology.

LEARNING OBJECTIVES

By the end of this chapter, you will be able to:

➊ Correctly define the terms presented in **bold letters**.

➋ Generally explain and roughly diagram the processes of human respiration and circulation, and give examples of the ways in which these processes are affected by diving.

➌ State the causes, signs, symptoms, effects, and general first aid for:
- Respiratory distress
- Carbon dioxide excess
- Carbon monoxide toxicity
- Oxygen toxicity
- Near drowning
- Nitrogen narcosis
- Decompression sickness
- Circulatory distress
- Barotrauma
- Thermal stress
- Seasickness
- Disorientation
- Dehydration
- Infections

➍ Explain the physical fitness requirements for diving, and list at least five ways to achieve and maintain fitness for diving.

➎ Explain the causes, signs, symptoms, remedies, and prevention of diver stress.

➏ State the proper recommendations for diving when pregnant.

RESPIRATION AND CIRCULATION

Ⓡespiration is the process that transports oxygen from the atmosphere to the cells for use in metabolism and removes carbon dioxide from the cells and transports it to the atmosphere. Respiration involves many activities, including breathing, the uptake of oxygen by the blood at the lungs, the transport of oxygen to the cells by the circulatory system, the uptake of oxygen by the cells from the blood, and the reverse process involving carbon dioxide. The act of breathing is frequently termed **external respiration**, while the other aspects are identified as **internal respiration**.

External Respiration

The process of breathing is automatic. Respiratory centers in the brain control the rate of respiration based on the level of carbon dioxide in

the bloodstream. Air is drawn through the nose or mouth and down to a junction of two tubes: the esophagus for food, and the trachea for air. The epiglottis prevents food from passing into the trachea. The trachea passes into the chest, where it divides into two tubes called **bronchi** (one tube is called a bronchus). The bronchi continue to divide into smaller tubes called bronchioles, which continue to divide into still smaller tubes until they terminate into microscopic air sacs (i.e., alveoli). One air sac is known as an **alveolus**. These sacs number some 300 million in an average person. Each alveolus is surrounded by a network of very fine capillary blood vessels, which act as transfer sites for the exchange of gases (Fig. 4-1).

The lungs are surrounded by two layers of very thin membrane called the pleura. One layer covers the lungs, and the other lines the chest wall. The closed space between the two layers (i.e., the pleural cavity) contains only a thin layer of lubricant to facilitate movement. Damage to the pleura may result in air entering the pleural cavity. If this occurs, the lungs may collapse.

Ventilation of the lungs (i.e., movement of air in and out) is achieved by changing the pressure within the lungs. During inhalation, the diaphragm muscle contracts and flattens while the rib cage muscles lift the ribs up and out. This action enlarges the volume of the lungs, creating a negative pressure within the lungs in relation to the atmosphere. Air flows into the lungs until a pressure equilibrium is achieved. Exhalation occurs when the diaphragm and the muscles around the

Fig. 4-1. Respiratory anatomy.

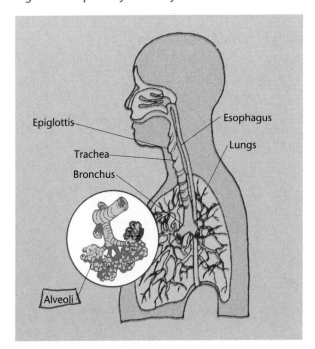

rib cage relax and return to their resting position, raising the air pressure within the lungs in relation to the atmosphere because of the elastic recoil of the lungs. The greater pressure within the lungs at this point causes the air to exit, again equalizing the pressure in the lungs with the atmospheric pressure (Fig. 4-2).

The degree of ventilation of the lungs is controlled by the muscular action of the diaphragm and the chest wall, both of which respond to impulses emitted by the nervous system. The normal respiratory rate at rest is approximately 12 to 16 breaths per minute. During and after heavy exertion, however, the rate may be several times the resting rate.

Following a normal expiration, the lungs contain approximately 2.5 quarts (or liters) of air. Even when one forcefully expels all of the air possible, approximately 1.5 quarts (liters) remain. This remaining amount is called the **residual volume**, which keeps the lungs from collapsing. The volume of air that is inspired and expired during rest is called the **tidal volume**, which averages approximately 0.5 quarts (liters) per cycle. The additional air that can be inhaled after a normal inspiration, or the inspiratory reserve, varies greatly from person to person, but it averages approximately 4.5 quarts (liters). The total volume of breathable air is called the **vital capacity**. Its actual volume depends on the size, development, and physical condition of the individual. Residual volume usually is approximately 25% of the total lung volume, and vital capacity usually is approximately 75%. The term **respiratory minute volume** represents the amount of air breathed in 1 minute; the average is approximately 25 to 30 quarts (liters) per minute for moderate work (Fig. 4-3).

Internal Respiration

Oxygen drawn into the alveoli is absorbed into the blood by the process of diffusion. **Hemoglobin**, which is a protein in red blood cells that makes the blood red, has the ability to combine with oxygen to form oxyhemoglobin, and it can also combine with carbon dioxide and carbon monoxide. The oxygen-carrying capability of blood is increased nearly 50 times by virtue of its hemoglobin content, which carries approximately 98% of the oxygen in our blood.

The exchange of oxygen and carbon dioxide between the blood and body cells occurs in opposite directions. Because oxygen is used continuously in the tissues, its partial pressure is lower there than in the blood. As carbon dioxide is produced in the cells, its concentration is high relative to that in the blood reaching the tissues. Therefore, blood gives up oxygen and receives carbon dioxide during its transit through the tissue capillaries (Fig. 4-4).

When tissues are more active, the need for oxygen is greater. The additional oxygen required is supplied not from an increase in the oxygen content of the blood, however, but rather by a larger volume of blood flow through the tissues and a more complete extraction of oxygen from a given volume of blood. There can be a ninefold increase in the rate of oxygen supplied to active tissues.

The body controls respiration by responding to levels of oxygen and carbon dioxide in the blood. The control center of the brain is sensitive to the level of carbon dioxide, and also of acid, in the blood; this center controls the rate and volume of respiration. Peripheral chemoreceptors monitor the level of oxygen and carbon dioxide in the

Fig. 4-2. Mechanics of breathing.

Fig. 4-3. Lung capacities.

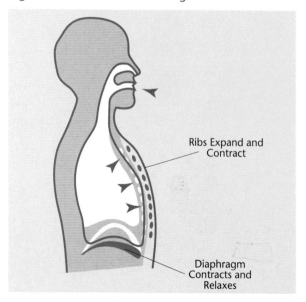

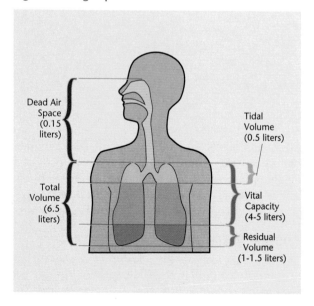

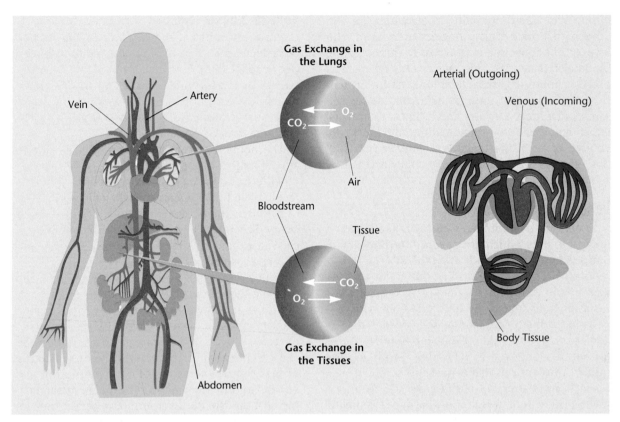

Gas Exchange in the Lungs

Arterial (Outgoing)

Venous (Incoming)

Vein

Artery

$CO_2 \longrightarrow$ $\longleftarrow O_2$

Air

Bloodstream

Tissue

$\longleftarrow CO_2$

$O_2 \longrightarrow$

Body Tissue

Gas Exchange in the Tissues

Abdomen

Fig. 4-4. Circulation and respiration. Gas exchange in the blood occurs between the lungs and the bloodstream and between the bloodstream and body tissues.

blood leaving the lungs. These sensors respond primarily to hypoxia (i.e., low oxygen level). A high level of carbon dioxide in the blood provides the stimulus to breathe, while hypoxia is a relatively minor stimulus.

The respiratory system is very complex. The respiratory rate is affected not only by high levels of carbon dioxide but also by oxygen partial pressure, increased gas density, emotional states (e.g., anxiety), and muscle activity. The respiratory cycle is completed when carbon dioxide–laden blood arrives at the lungs and gives up the carbon dioxide to the atmosphere. Taking up oxygen favors unloading carbon dioxide through the lungs.

Immersion Effects on Respiration and Circulation

Breathing in many positions in the water requires more effort than breathing on land. The range of movement for the diaphragm is shortened by the increased ambient (i.e., surrounding) pressure. Lung volume is slightly less than normal, because the lungs cannot be fully expanded while diving.

During immersion, blood floats into the chest area because of buoyancy. Although a relatively minor effect when compared with buoyancy, the ambient pressure is greater on the lower parts of

the body. When a diver stands upright in air, the column of blood bearing down on the legs causes blood to collect in the lower body. In water, however, the pressure of the blood column is exceeded by the pressure of the water column, and blood shifts from the legs to the chest (Fig. 4-5).

Blood pooling in the chest area causes the right side of your heart to fill with a larger volume of

Fig. 4-5. A normal breathing pattern is essential for diving.

blood than would normally occur. When the volume of blood being pumped increases, the amount of energy that is required to discharge the blood also increases. This can result in as much as a 30% increase in discharge volume and a proportionally increased energy requirement for the same pulse rate. Because more blood than usual is being pumped from the heart into the lungs, the volume of air in the lungs is slightly reduced by this effect as well. Vital capacity can decrease by as much as 6% to 12%.

Respiratory Distress

Divers can suffer from a variety of breathing and lung problems, which are covered here in detail. **Suffocation** is a term indicating the interruption of respiration by some reason other than holding your breath. **Asphyxia** is a state of unconsciousness resulting from suffocation or interference with oxygenation of the blood, leading to hypoxia (i.e., oxygen shortage). Asphyxia results if breathing ceases for any reason, such as drowning. **Strangulation** means prevention of the passage of air. It may result from obstruction of the airway, lodging of a foreign body in the windpipe, spasm or swelling of the larynx, or the inhalation of water or vomitus. A victim will struggle violently and try to breathe despite the obstruction before losing consciousness. Artificial respiration produces little movement of air unless the obstruction is removed.

Breathing Resistance

Problems of breathing resistance have been implicated in some diving accidents. In the human body, rapid air flow in large airways is turbulent and inversely proportional to the square root of gas density. If the air flow is reduced with slow, deep breathing, less turbulence occurs. If the gas density increases fourfold, breathing resistance doubles and flow is approximately 50% of normal. Most individuals only use 50% to 60% of their maximum ventilation capabilities at sea level, however. So at a pressure of 4 atm absolute, there should be no ventilation-imposed limitation for divers unless the air flows rise markedly during excessive stress. As gas density increases with depth, breathing resistance increases.

Some improperly tuned regulators can impose a considerable workload on the respiratory system. A few regulators have unsatisfactory flow characteristics at depths in excess of 100 feet (30 m) during periods of increased ventilatory requirements. Snorkels with a small bore (i.e., diameter) or corrugated inside walls can increase breathing resistance and lead to problems that are described later.

Carbon Dioxide Excess

Production of carbon dioxide in the human body increases when the metabolic rate increases because of factors such as physical exertion, stress, or inadequate ventilation of the lungs. Examples are when there is water in the lungs from near drowning or a decreased alveolar surface area from barotrauma.

The normal concentration of carbon dioxide in atmospheric air is approximately 0.04%. As carbon dioxide buildup occurs, a progression of effects results. The initial response is an increased rate of respiration. Higher concentrations produce respiratory discomfort, and a very high concentration of carbon dioxide causes dizziness, stupor, and unconsciousness.

Ventilation is the process of inhaling oxygen and exhaling carbon dioxide. Inadequate ventilation of the lungs (i.e., hypoventilation) produces insufficient elimination of carbon dioxide. This results in excessive levels of carbon dioxide in the blood (i.e., hypercapnia). The term **carbon dioxide excess** applies to forms of hypoventilation and hypercapnia in which a diver is capable of eliminating carbon dioxide in a normal manner but, for some reason, fails to do so. The usual cause for a scuba diver is an alteration to a shallow, inefficient breathing pattern resulting from anxiety, apprehension, or skip breathing (described later). Panic on the surface in diving situations often results in hypoventilation, which is sometimes aggravated by restrictions caused by equipment.

The amount of carbon dioxide retained in the body during exertion varies from person to person. Some individuals retain more than others and are more prone to carbon dioxide excess. Loss of consciousness from carbon dioxide excess because of scuba equipment is not a common problem; however, inadequate respiratory response to exertion combined with a tendency to retain carbon dioxide can cause unconsciousness. Shallow, rapid breathing during exertion must be avoided. A normal breathing pattern must be established. This situation will occur even more rapidly when poor, or poorly maintained, breathing equipment with high breathing resistance is used.

The level of carbon dioxide in the body is maintained by breathing a sufficient quantity of air to exhale the carbon dioxide that is produced in the body and carried to the lungs. This is easily accomplished while scuba diving if severe exertion is avoided and a proper breathing pattern maintained.

Deliberate reduction of breathing frequency (i.e., skip breathing) causes carbon dioxide excess. **Skip breathing** involves holding each inhalation for a period of time after normal exhalation would occur. It may be practiced by scuba divers who believe erroneously that it will extend the time that their air supply will last. This practice is extremely dangerous, because excess levels of carbon dioxide can lead to panic. Symptoms of carbon dioxide excess give little or no warning. The habit of breath-holding can lead to a lung-expansion injury during ascent; in addition, if you have been skip breathing, your breath-holding ability is limited in the event of an air loss. Skip breathing should not be practiced.

If carbon dioxide excess does occur, quick action to aid the diver is very important. A diver who is unconscious because of carbon dioxide excess revives quickly when the lungs are ventilated with fresh air. After effects include headache, nausea, dizziness, and sore chest muscles.

Hyperventilation and Shallow-Water Blackout

Rapid, unusually deep breathing in excess of the necessary rate for the level of activity is called **hyperventilation**. This is a form of deliberate interference with the normal operation of respiratory control mechanisms. Hyperventilation lowers the carbon dioxide level in the body to below normal, producing a condition known as **hypocapnia.** Mild hypocapnia results in a feeling of lightheadedness. Hyperventilation can occur during high-stress situations and cause symptoms of tingling fingers that may be confused with decompression sickness or arterial gas embolism symptoms. Also, weakness, faintness, and blurring of vision can result. Excessive hyperventilation can prevent the carbon dioxide level from reaching the threshold required for the respiratory control mechanism to respond. When this happens, the oxygen level in the body can fall to below that needed to maintain consciousness (Fig. 4-6).

Extended hyperventilation before free diving as well as extended breath-holding while free diving is hazardous. During long breath-hold periods, your oxygen level can fall to a low level before you realize that you must return to the surface and resume breathing. The oxygen level is lowered because exertion not only causes oxygen to be used faster but decreases the sensitivity of the carbon dioxide breakpoint mechanism. This allows the oxygen level to go even lower than it otherwise would. When you ascend, the drop in the partial pressure of oxygen in the lungs may be sufficient to stop further uptake of oxygen completely. Simultaneously, the partial pressure of carbon dioxide in the lungs also drops, giving the false impression that you do not need to breathe.

Shallow water blackout (i.e., loss of consciousness) may occur and is so-named because it happens in shallow water on ascent at the end of a free dive. To prevent this from occurring, do not hyperventilate before free diving. Just inhale and exhale normally a few times before diving, and do not extend free diving to great depths for extended periods of time.

Involuntary hyperventilation may be initiated by anxiety or physical stress, and it may result in unconsciousness or muscle spasms. You may not be aware of the impending problem. Some individuals are more susceptible to hypocapnia than others, but anyone will lose consciousness with sufficiently prolonged hyperventilation.

Be aware of the hazards associated with hyperventilation. If you notice that you are involuntarily hyperventilating, take immediate steps to slow your breathing. Also, avoid excessive hyperventilation before prolonged breath-holding.

Overexertion

It is possible to exceed your respiratory capabilities before sensing that you may be getting into trouble breathing. There is a delay between exertion and the increased respiratory demands that are imposed by exercise. On land, this would simply necessitate a recovery period. Underwater, however, it can create a sensation of suffocation and anxiety, leading to a deteriorating spiral of cause and effect. Labored breathing might require air at a higher rate than some regulators can provide, producing a tendency in the diver to panic. Prevention is best. Pace your efforts to avoid

Fig. 4-6. Hyperventilation and shallow-water blackout. Blackout results from prolonged breath holding following excessive hyperventilation.

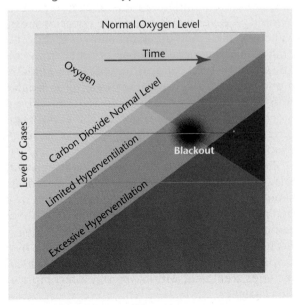

overexertion. At the onset of any feeling of air starvation or labored breathing, stop all activity, rest, and allow you breathing to return gradually to normal. Besides prolonged heavy exertion, factors contributing to overexertion include being out of shape physically, using a poorly maintained and/or designed regulator, wasted effort, and excessive cold. It also is important to have your regulator serviced according to the manufacturer's specifications.

Carbon Monoxide Toxicity

Carbon monoxide is a serious breathing-gas contaminant. It readily combines with blood hemoglobin, forming carboxyhemoglobin and rendering the hemoglobin incapable of transporting sufficient oxygen to the body tissues. Hemoglobin combines with carbon monoxide approximately 200 times as readily as with oxygen. Because of the decreased oxygen-carrying capability of carbon monoxide–poisoned blood, hypoxia develops even though the supply of oxygen to the lungs is adequate.

The reconversion of carboxyhemoglobin to oxyhemoglobin takes hours. A diver affected by **carbon monoxide poisoning** will likely develop symptoms of carbon monoxide toxicity during ascent. Using Dalton's Law, a relatively safe level of carbon monoxide at the surface can become deadly when breathed under pressure at depth. Consequently, contamination of scuba air with even small amounts of carbon monoxide is very dangerous.

The wide spectrum of symptoms associated with carbon monoxide toxicity include headache, dizziness, nausea, weakness, and confusion. Signs include failure to respond, clumsiness, and bad judgment. Frequently, no signs or symptoms are evident. A diver may simply lose consciousness without warning, and breathing may cease. In general, symptoms parallel those of other forms of anoxia with one exception. Because carbon monoxide combined with hemoglobin is bright red, a victim who becomes anoxic from carbon monoxide toxicity may exhibit an unnatural redness of the lips or nail beds. This is variable, however, and is not a reliable sign.

First aid for carbon monoxide toxicity is fresh air and oxygen, which should be administered as soon as possible. Pure oxygen will replace the carbon monoxide on the hemoglobin molecule as the carbon monoxide is eliminated through the lungs. Artificial respiration is required if breathing has stopped. A victim requires medical care, which includes treatment with oxygen in a recompression chamber.

Contamination from carbon monoxide can result from the fumes of an internal combustion engine being drawn into the air intake of a compressor. It also can result from the partial combustion of lubricating oil within a compressor that is not properly operated or maintained. Purity standards for breathing air allow a maximum of 0.001% carbon monoxide. You can only be certain that your air supply meets that recommended purity standards if it is acquired from reliable sources where periodic air analyses are obtained.

Smoking cigarettes also creates high levels of carboxyhemoglobin in the blood and reduced exercise tolerance. Increased partial pressures of carbon monoxide at depth can exacerbate the problem.

Oxygen Toxicity

Prolonged exposure to higher-than-normal oxygen partial pressures causes a variety of toxic effects that are known as **oxygen poisoning.** Pulmonary oxygen poisoning will occur from prolonged exposure to any oxygen partial pressure above 0.5 atm. When oxygen is breathed in long-term, low-dose exposures, such as in a saturation exposure or long-term oxygen therapy, mild symptoms on the order of chest pain and coughing occur. The higher the partial pressure of the oxygen, the shorter the time before symptoms develop. Susceptibility is further increased by exercise.

Central nervous system oxygen poisoning can occur by breathing oxygen at higher partial pressures. This type of oxygen poisoning can occur while breathing pure oxygen at a depth of only 20 fsw (see the Technical Diving chapter). There are established guidelines and time-exposure limits based on the partial pressure of oxygen in the breathing gas. The partial pressure of oxygen cannot exceed 1.6 ata for a maximum of 45 minutes on any dive, and the total dive time is limited to 150 minutes in any 24-hour period. This varies with conditions and individuals, however, and may be reduced for extreme cold-water conditions.

Symptoms include muscular twitching in the face, lips, or hands, and this may progress to convulsions. Tolerance to high partial pressures of oxygen varies with individual divers and may also vary within individuals from day to day.

The warning symptoms of oxygen toxicity are muscular twitching, nausea, abnormal vision and hearing, breathing difficulty, anxiety and confusion, fatigue, lack of coordination, and convulsions. These symptoms are reversible. Convulsions can appear without warning and are self-terminating. They are dangerous underwater, however, because they can lead to air embolism and drowning.

Traditional recreational divers who breathe compressed air should never experience problems with oxygen toxicity if they abide by the recommended depth limit of 130 feet. Attempts by untrained divers to use rebreathers, cryogenic scuba units, oxygen-enriched gas mixtures, or oxygen-filled scuba cylinders can, however, result in oxygen toxicity. Training courses are available for learning how to dive with enriched-air nitrox.

Near Drowning

Near drowning is the term for a clinical condition that follows suffocation by submersion in liquid after which there are at least 24 hours of survival. The term **drowning** indicates death because of asphyxia (i.e., lack of oxygen) that occurs within 24 hours of suffocation by submersion.

In severe cases, signs of near drowning include unconsciousness, cyanosis (i.e., blue skin), cessation of breathing, and froth in the mouth. In mild cases, however, early signs may consist only of labored breathing and confusion.

Brain tissues suffer permanent damage after 4 to 5 minutes of hypoxia, but this time may be lengthened under extremely cold conditions. Additionally, the degree of hypoxia initially suffered by a near-drowning victim is difficult to determine. Such victims have recovered after more than 40 minutes of immersion in cold water. Attempts should be made to revive the victim in all cases.

Near drownings have been categorized as either "wet" or "dry." The dry type results from asphyxiation because of spasm of the larynx, which is caused by water striking it (like "choking" on a bit of food "going the wrong way"). This occurs in all cases where the victim is conscious enough to have reflexes. The wet type can occur initially or result from the dry-drowning victim taking a breath as consciousness is lost. In the wet type, some volume of the immersion liquid enters the lungs. When this happens, various physiologic events occur depending on the volume of fluid aspirated and the nature of that fluid. Neither seawater nor freshwater have the same concentration of salts as the human body. As a result, both seawater, which is hypertonic (i.e., more concentrated than blood), and freshwater, which is hypotonic (i.e., less concentrated than blood), cause damage to alveolar tissue. This damage allows body fluids from the bloodstream to "weep" into the alveolar spaces in a process termed **secondary drowning** (Fig. 4-7). As alveolar spaces fill with these secondary fluids, hypoxia becomes worse and froth formed by the fluids as well as proteins washed out of the lungs may be seen in the mouth and

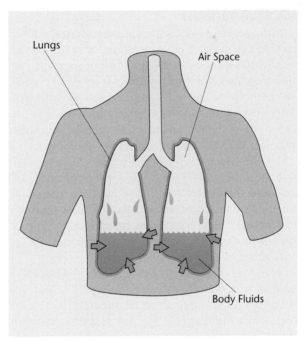

Fig. 4-7. Body fluids from the bloodstream can weep into the alveolar spaces in a process termed secondary drowning.

nose. Secondary drowning can occur hours after the initial incident. Continued medical observation of apparently stable near-drowning victims is necessary.

If a near-drowning victim is unconscious and not breathing, immediate artificial respiration is imperative. Full ventilations are important so that the airway is fully open. Care should be taken not to inflate the stomach by overventilation, because this can lead to vomiting. The acidic nature of the vomitus can cause further injury if it is inhaled. Oxygen should be administered as soon as possible, and it should be continued even if the victim begins to breathe. The pulse on a cold, unconscious diver is difficult to detect, so check very carefully before beginning chest compressions. Near drowning can progress from mild to very severe distress, so all near-drowning victims should be administered oxygen and transported immediately to a medical facility for observation and care.

Hospital tests following near drowning can include chest radiography, sampling of arterial blood gases, blood tests, and electrocardiograms (ECGs). Intravenous fluids and drugs may be given. Prolonged mechanical ventilation with supplemental oxygen may also be required. The lungs are the prime target of both injury and treatment in near drowning, but associated hypoxia affects other sensitive organs, such as the kidneys, heart, and brain. Recovery may not be complete.

Nitrogen Narcosis

Nitrogen is physiologically inert under normal conditions, but it can induce signs and symptoms of narcosis or anesthesia at sufficiently raised partial pressures. The exact cause of **inert gas narcosis** is not known. The most often cited reason, the *Meyer-Overton Hypothesis*, is that nitrogen dissolves in the protein sheath covering the conductive paths, possibly "short circuiting" the nerve impulses.

Divers can become impaired by the effects of nitrogen narcosis as they exceed depths of 100 fsw, and the severity of impairment inceases with depth. There is considerable individual variability in narcosis. Some divers may be seriously compromised at depths of 100 to 130 fsw; while others may show little effect.

Narcosis is usually characterized by symptoms similar to alcoholic intoxication, such as impairment of thought, judgment, and the ability to perfom tasks that require mental or motor skills. A diver under the influence of narcosis may experience lightheadedness, increasing self-confidence, and loss of fine discrimination. This can make it difficult to monitor time, depth, air supply, and the location of the diving buddy. These skills become more reflexive with experience, so novice divers should not dive deeper than 60 feet.

The onset of narcosis is rapid, but recovery is equally rapid and accomplished by ascending to a shallower depth, which reduces the effect of the inert gas. Information learned before a dive (i.e., dive plan information) may not be recalled during a dive. Amnesia regarding events occurring at depth also may occur.

Carbon dioxide excess increases the severity of narcosis. A diver doing work or exercising experiences narcosis more rapidly than a resting diver. Other factors that increase susceptibility include alcohol, hangovers, fatigue, anxiety, cold, and the effects of medications. Novices tend to be affected more readily than experienced divers, so acclimatization or adaptation may be a factor as well. The hazards of narcosis are one reason why recreational diving depths are limited to a maximum of 130 feet.

DECOMPRESSION SICKNESS

Decompression sickness (DCS) is an illness caused by a reduction in the surrounding pressure, which causes dissolved blood and tissue gases to come out of solution and form bubbles within the diver. The physiology of nitrogen absorption and elimination as well as the different types of DCS are covered here in detail.

Nitrogen Absorption and Elimination

Upon exposure to altitude or depth, the partial pressure of nitrogen in the air within the lungs changes. Body tissues either lose or gain nitrogen to reach a new equilibrium with the nitrogen pressure inside the lungs. Taking up nitrogen in tissues is called **absorption** (or **ingassing**), while the release of nitrogen is termed **elimination** (or **outgassing**).

Absorption consists of several steps, including the transfer of inert gas from the lungs to the blood and then from the blood to the various tissues through which it flows. The gradient (i.e., driving force) for gas transfer is the partial pressure difference of the gas between the lungs and blood and the blood and tissues. The volume of blood flowing through tissues is usually small compared with the mass of the tissue. Over a period of time, however, the tissue will become equilibrated with the blood, and both will become equilibrated with the ambient pressure. This state is called **saturation**. Some tissues (e.g., bone marrow) take much longer to reach a state of saturation, while others (e.g., blood) saturate very quickly.

To develop mathematic models of gas solubility in tissues, a series of **tissue compartments** have been theorized. Each tissue compartment represents a different type (i.e., speed) of body tissue. The **half-time** of a tissue is the time in minutes that is needed for the tissue to become 50% saturated with nitrogen. The range of half-times for various tissue compartments in modern models is from 5 to over 500 minutes. The 5-minute tissue is considered to be 50% saturated in 5 minutes; the unsaturated portion becomes 50% saturated in an additional 5 minutes, making the tissue 75% saturated. The tissue becomes 99% saturated during a period of six half-times (i.e., 30 minutes). A 120-minute tissue attains 50% saturation in 2 hours and 99% saturation in 12 hours (Fig. 4-8).

The process of elimination is the reverse of absorption. During ascent and after surfacing, the tissues lose excess inert gas to the circulating blood by diffusion. The diffusion gradient is the difference between the inert gas partial pressure in each tissue and that in the lungs. The amount of inert gas that can be taken into the blood is limited, so the inert gas tension of the tissue falls gradually. As in absorption, the rate of blood flow, difference in partial pressures, and amount of inert gas dissolved in the tissues determine the rate of elimination.

During outgassing, the blood and tissues theoretically can hold gas in a supersaturated solution without bubbles being formed (Fig. 4-9). Some researchers, however, believe that bubbles are

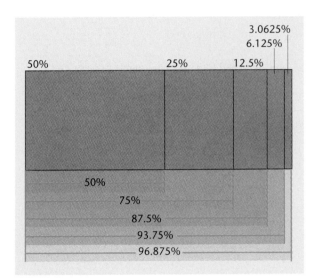

Fig. 4-8. The box represents the way nitrogen fills a compartment. During a time interval of one half-time, one half of the remaining unfilled space is filled with nitrogen. After 5 half-times, the compartment is 96.875% filled to its capacity.

probable beyond any supersaturation. A supersaturated solution is one holding more gas than is possible at equilibrium for a particular temperature and pressure. Because of the ability of compartments to become supersaturated for short periods of time, ascent can be faster than would be predicted from half-time considerations only. Dive tables and dive computers are structured to account for all of these considerations. If heeded, they allow ascent with minimal risk. The diver's body will still contain inert gas in some tissues, but this is normally safe if further pressure reduction (e.g., ascending to a higher altitude) does not occur.

The English physiologist Haldane theorized that bubbling occurs when the gas pressure in the tissue is twice that of the external pressure of nitrogen. His work formed the basis for a decompression model developed by the US Navy, which led to the development of the US Navy Dive Tables.

Types of Decompression Sickness

If the elimination rate of gas is not fast enough to match a diver's ascent, the excessive supersaturation of gas in tissues may cause that gas to come out of solution in the form of bubbles. The formation of bubbles causes a condition known as DCS, or the bends. This condition is caused by too rapid a reduction in the external pressure. The primary constituent of DCS bubbles is nitrogen.

If bubbles are formed in the bloodstream, they block circulation. Bubbles in tissues distort the tissues as the bubbles expand. Symptoms depend on the location of the bubbles.

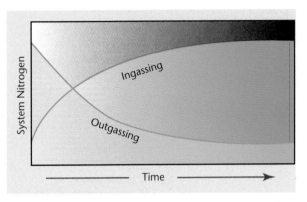

Fig. 4-9. Ingassing and outgassing.

The possible manifestations of DCS are skin bends, limb bends, central nervous system "hits," and chokes, in which bubbles actually block the circulation to the lungs. In severe cases, death can result.

With skin bends, the skin itches, burns, and is mottled. The rash disappears spontaneously over a period of time from a few hours to a few days. In some cases when skin mottling occurs, more severe DCS may develop in the central nervous system or elsewhere.

Limb bends are the most common form of DCS, and shoulder and elbow joints are the most frequent sites. The pain is usually steady but occasionally may be throbbing. It reaches a peak in minutes to hours and often subsides spontaneously within several hours. The limb usually looks completely normal, although there is tenderness. Treatment by recompression helps to relieve the pain and may decrease subsequent tissue damage. Prompt treatment involving the administration of oxygen and recompression also averts the chance of progression to more serious types of DCS (Fig. 4-10).

Central nervous system hits, which are in the spinal cord or brain, are especially serious cases that can cause permanent nerve damage, paralysis, or death. It is important to recognize the early manifestations of this type, because prompt treatment in a recompression chamber may result in at least a partial recovery. Delay, however, significantly decreases the chances of a favorable outcome. Soon after surfacing, the diver's first symptom may be back pain that extends to the abdomen, which may be attributed mistakenly to lifting or a pulled muscle, so the first symptom to catch the diver's attention may be paraesthesia, or a feeling of "pins and needles" in the legs. The legs may become weak or unsteady, urination may become difficult or impossible (even though the bladder may be distended), and there may be a loss of bowel and sexual function. Paralysis below

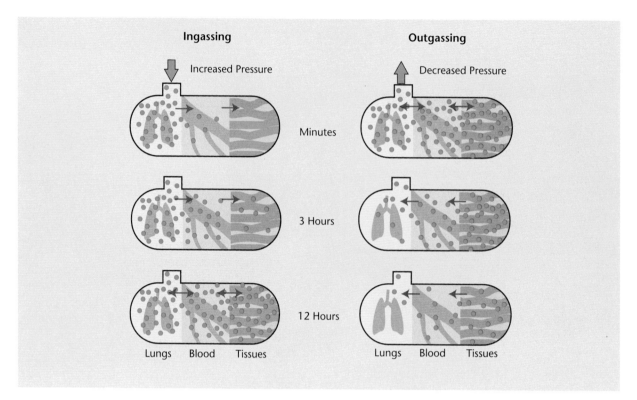

Ingassing

Increased Pressure

Minutes

3 Hours

12 Hours

Lungs   Blood   Tissues

Outgassing

Decreased Pressure

Minutes

3 Hours

12 Hours

Lungs   Blood   Tissues

Fig. 4-10. It takes time for gas to move from the lungs to the blood to the tissues and for the reverse to occur.

the waist or neck also may ensue. This condition is similar to that of a broken back with spinal cord injury. A diver is more fortunate, however, because recovery is likely with prompt treatment.

Injury to the central nervous system is often associated with an unusually rapid rate of ascent during an emergency situation. Symptoms may appear immediately and progress to paralysis within minutes or hours.

Rarer forms of DCS include brain damage, inner ear bends, and the "chokes." Symptoms of brain damage include visual disturbances or weakness on one side of the body. Vertigo (i.e., dizziness) may result from damage to the inner ear; this condition is sometimes called "the staggers." The chokes is a severe but rare form of the disease, characterized by shortness of breath, chest pain, and a cough. Without recompression therapy, circulatory collapse and death may result from the chokes.

Emergency first aid for DCS consists of having the victim breathe 100% O_2, preferably via a demand system, and initiating transport to a staffed hyperbaric chamber capable of reaching at least 5 atm of pressure. Full treatment consists of taking the victim to a pressure sufficient to cause the bubbles to return to solution (i.e., relief of symptoms). The victim is then slowly decompressed with a controlled administration of oxygen to hasten nitrogen outgassing.

Susceptibility to DCS varies with individuals. Predisposing factors include obesity, age, fatigue, cigarette smoking, alcohol consumption before a dive, and impaired circulation to an area of the body. Environmental factors that increase risk include carbon dioxide retention, cold water and/or arduous work during the dive, and postdive exercise. Divers must understand that they are still susceptible to DCS even if they follow acceptable dive procedures and use dive tables or computers (Fig. 4-11).

CIRCULATORY DISTRESS

A number of conditions can develop in divers that are related to the circulatory system.

Cramps

A **cramp** is a muscle spasm producing pain and temporary disability. It occurs when a muscle outworks its supply of blood. Cramps usually develop in untrained muscles or from overexertion (e.g., swimming with oversized fins). Other predisposing factors include circulatory restrictions, cold, sudden exertion, sweating and dehydration, fatigue, poor nutrition, and poor health. Although the most common sites are the calf of the leg and the sole of the foot, other muscles can also cramp.

Decompression Theory

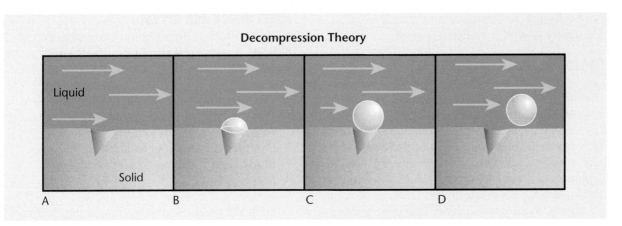

Liquid

Solid

A   B   C   D

Fig. 4-11. According to Haldane, bubbles will not form in a supersaturated solution unless the pressure is halved. Modern studies using electronic instruments known as ultrasonic Doppler detectors have identified the presence of nonsymptom producing bubbles. These bubbles may be present even though the no-decompression limits have not been exceeded. These intravascular bubbles have been termed "silent bubbles." Silent bubbles are microscopic in size and are believed to originate from tiny gas pockets in the walls of tissues. Excess nitrogen during decompression dissolves into the microscopic pockets, causing them to enlarge and extend into the circulatory path until they finally break free and become tiny bubbles, which by themselves cause no harm. These bubbles can join together, however, to form larger bubbles that can produce symptoms of decompression sickness. The theory of microscopic gas separation within tissues helps explain why bubbles are formed in the body when they are not formed in a pure liquid subjected to the same change in pressures. If your body contained a pure liquid, you could dive to a depth of over six miles and then ascend directly to the surface with no bubble formation! During an ascent, the volume of a microscopic bubble increases due to Boyle's Law. This lowers the gas pressure inside the bubble which attracts more gas into the bubble. Therefore, bubbles grow not only because of the laws of physics, but also because of the inward diffusion of gas. Recompression, on the other hand, compresses bubbles and increases their internal pressure. Gas then diffuses out of the bubbles.

An early warning symptom is a twinge of the affected muscle. An alert diver who recognizes this signal and stops to stretch and rest the muscle can prevent a full locking contraction from occurring (Fig. 4-12).

First aid includes slowing the kicking activity, stretching the cramped muscle, and massaging. An alternate kicking style also will help to avoid immediate recurrence. Prevention includes the maintenance of adequate physical fitness, regular diving, properly fitting equipment, good nutrition and health, and adequate thermal protection.

Carotid Sinus Reflex

The principal arteries supplying blood to your brain, known as the **carotid arteries**, have a sinus (i.e., small bulge) at a bifurcation (i.e., fork) of the artery in the neck. The carotid sinus controls your heart rate according to your blood pressure. A tight hood or neck seal can apply pressure over the carotid bifurcation, and as your blood pressure rises, a signal is sent to slow the heart rate. Thus, pressure applied over the carotid sinuses produces bradycardia and concurrent low blood pressure leading to fainting or dizziness, especially when exertion is involved. Be aware of this reflex, its symptoms, and the hazards that it

Fig. 4-12. A diver can stretch her own muscles to relieve a cramp.

poses. Select an exposure suit that does not fit too tightly around the neck (Fig. 4-13).

Sudden Death Syndrome

Diving fatalities can result from heart attacks or cardiac irregularities. These problems do not always stem from cardiac disease, however, because diving increases the workload of the heart. This muscle's ability to receive or provide an adequate supply of blood can be altered, so fatal problems can result for an individual with a marginal or unknown heart condition. These victims are commonly male, over 30 years of age, in poor condition, and smokers. A sound heart and physical fitness are very important for diving fitness.

The Diving Reflex

Cold water in contact with your face and body slows the heart rate. This is called **bradycardia.** Concurrently, blood circulation to the limbs is decreased, and this effect is known as the **diving reflex.** This reflex is very pronounced in marine mammals, but it is sometimes dramatic and sometimes minimal in adult humans. There is high individual variability. The diving reflex does not reduce the oxygen demand in humans as it does in marine mammals.

Cardiac irregularities that probably pose no threat to a healthy person can be associated with this bradycardia, and they can be a problem to those with underlying cardiac irregularities. Cold water may have some protective value in the drowning situation, and it may explain why some victims have been revived after prolonged submersion in cold water. This phenomenon is not caused by the diving reflex, however.

Fig. 4-13. Carotid sinus reflex. Pressure on your neck can slow your heart rate and lead to unconsciousness.

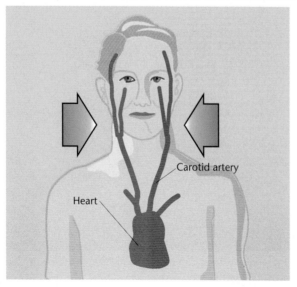

Carotid artery

Heart

Heart Attack and Arrest

Heart attack is possible in divers who are experiencing heavy exertion. Of particular concern are people who are older, overweight, out of shape, and smokers.

The signs and symptoms of a heart attack are:
1. Chest pain that may radiate to one or both shoulders or arms or to the neck.
2. Shortness of breath or exhaustion.
3. Bluish discoloration of the lips and skin.
4. Shock.
5. Indigestion, nausea, and vomiting.

First aid involves placing the victim in a comfortable, sitting position; administering oxygen; summoning help; and waiting for medical assistance before transporting the victim. Signs and symptoms of cardiac arrest (i.e., heart stoppage) include unconsciousness, no respiration, no pulse, cyanosis, and dilated (i.e., expanded) pupils. First aid for a heart attack requires cardiopulmonary resuscitation (CPR) and urgently summoning, or transporting the victim to, medical aid.

BAROTRAUMA

Your body contains several semirigid air spaces that are subject to mechanical damage when a pressure differential exists between the air space and the ambient pressure. This pressure differential usually occurs because blocked openings to the air spaces prevent equalization. The structures involved include the middle-ear spaces, the paranasal sinuses, the lungs and airways, air spaces behind dental fillings, and the gastrointestinal tract. With the exception of these spaces, the entire body consists of fluids and solids, which for all practical purposes are incompressible.

The middle ear and sinuses are lined with membranes that contain tiny blood vessels called capillaries. When the ambient pressure increases without a corresponding increase in the pressure within an air space, the external pressure is transmitted through the body to the blood vessels in the membranes lining these spaces. An unequal pressure is created between the air space and the surrounding tissues. Unless equalization of pressure occurs promptly, edema (i.e., tissue swelling) and damage will occur. Physical damage to the body as a direct result of pressure changes is known as **barotrauma.**

Ear Barotrauma

The anatomy of the ear is shown in Figure 4-14, and this will help to illustrate the basics of mid-

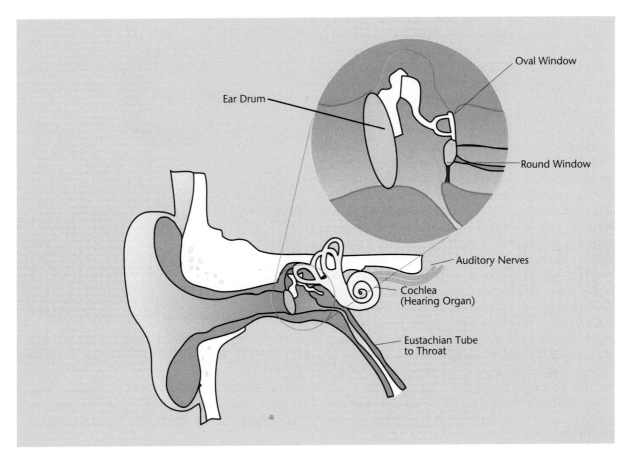

Fig. 4-14. Anatomy of the ear.

dle-ear squeezes. The **Valsalva maneuver** for ear clearing also should be well known to you. This section addresses more advanced aspects of potential middle-ear problems and how they can be avoided.

The middle ear is connected to the throat by the **eustachian tube**, which drains and ventilates the middle ear. The throat-end of this tube is normally closed and is located in very soft tissue. A delay in ear clearing during descent results in the ambient pressure sealing the eustachian tube opening tightly closed, thus preventing equalization. This condition is termed the trapdoor effect. Some divers attempt to overcome a trapdoor effect by a forceful Valsalva maneuver. This is ineffective, however, because the increased pressure in the throat caused by the maneuver only serves to seal the tube opening more tightly.

There are also several hazards associated with this practice. Increased lung pressure caused by a prolonged Valsalva maneuver can produce heart irregularities and fainting. In addition, increased pressure in the body from a Valsalva maneuver is transmitted to the inner ear. With a closed eustachian tube and the middle ear at reduced pressure, the pressure differentials can damage or rupture the round window of the inner ear. If this occurs,

fluid from the inner ear will leak into the middle ear, resulting in hearing loss, tinnitus (i.e., ear ringing), and vertigo (i.e., dizziness). This condition is serious, can result in permanent hearing loss, and must be prevented. Also, too vigorous a Valsalva maneuver can damage the inner ear because of too rapid a pressure change. Forceful, prolonged attempts to clear your ears must be avoided. Descend slowly and feet first, and equalize gently and frequently. Ascend (completely if necessary) to relieve any discomfort or abnormal sensation, clear your ears, and resume your descent.

There are alternative ear-clearing technique that you should develop the ability to use. The **Frenzel maneuver** involves sealing the nose and mouth, contracting various muscles in the mouth to open the eustachian tubes, and using the tongue as a piston to push air up the tubes. The **Toynbee maneuver** involves swallowing with the mouth and nose closed. Jaw movements, tilting the head to the side, and yawning with the mouth closed also may be helpful, as may be a combination of various maneuvers.

Failure to equalize pressure in the middle ear creates a pressure differential across the **tympanic membrane** (i.e., ear drum), which can cause it to rupture with a pressure difference of as little as

3 psi. If this occurs underwater, cold water rushing into the middle ear can produce vertigo by stimulating the inner ear and semicircular canals, which control your equilibrium. This dizziness can be hazardous and must be avoided. The effect will subside when the water within the ear has warmed to body temperature; holding onto a secure object may help to combat the dizziness until you can regain equilibrium (Fig. 4-15).

A painful **reverse block** or reverse ear squeeze occurs when pressure builds in the middle ear during ascent because air cannot escape through the eustachian tube. Standard ear-clearing techniques only worsen the situation. The correct action is to descend several feet and then slowly reascend. Yawning or wiggling the jaw sometimes helps to relieve pressure. Because you will eventually need to ascend, you may have to surface and tolerate the pain until you can receive medical care. The ear drum may rupture, but it is more likely that the pressure will be relieved through the eustachian tube than by tearing the ear drum. Reverse blocks usually occur when you dive with a sinus infection or cold (Fig. 4-16).

Decompression sickness involving the inner ear also can produce vertigo and hearing loss. Ear bends are rare, however, and tend to result from rapid ascents when no-decompression limits have been reached or exceeded. Recreational divers should never experience this malady.

Signs and symptoms of middle-ear barotrauma include ear pain, vertigo, hearing loss, ear ringing, a feeling of "fullness" in the ear, and the spitting of blood, which may drain into the throat through the

Fig. 4-15. The rupture of an ear drum is a serious and avoidable injury.

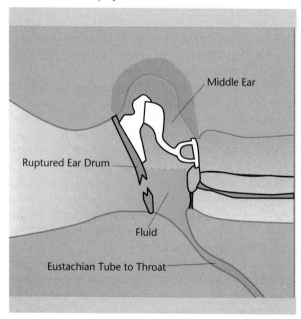

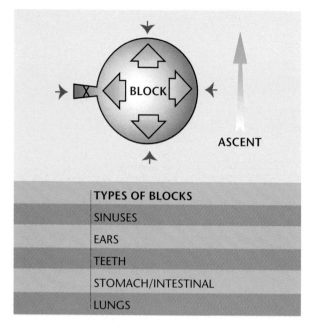

Fig. 4-16. A reverse block exists when the pressure within an air space is greater than the surrounding pressure.

eustachian tube. Diving should be terminated and prompt treatment sought from an ear, nose, and throat doctor who understands diving injuries.

Sinus Barotrauma

Blockage of the air passages to a paranasal sinus can result in a **sinus squeeze** with painful edema (i.e., tissue swelling) and hemorrhage (i.e., bleeding) within the sinus cavity. These cavities are located within the skull and are lined with mucous membrane. When the ambient pressure exceeds that within the sinus, pressure is transmitted to the sinus membrane lining via the blood, and a vacuum effect is created within the cavity. Without prompt equalization, the capillaries within the mucous membrane may swell and rupture, causing severe pain and injury (Fig. 4-17).

Signs and symptoms of sinus squeeze include intense localized pain, blood and mucous discharge from the nose, and headache. Diving activities should be terminated, and medical attention is generally required.

Sinus squeeze can be avoided by refraining from diving when you are experiencing nasal congestion resulting from allergy, cold, or infection. Some people attempt to dive with these conditions by using various medications designed to open the air passages to the sinuses. This is unwise, however, because any decrease in the effect of the medication could lead to a situation where the sinuses become closed spaces containing high-pressure air. This can lead to a serious reverse block condition during ascent. Dive only when in good health.

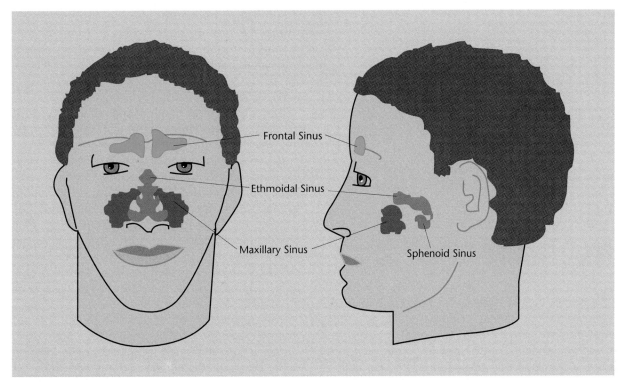

Fig. 4-17. Paranasal sinuses.

Nasal deformities, masses, cysts or polyps can block sinus openings. Many such abnormalities can be corrected medically (Fig. 4-18).

Dental Barotrauma

Tooth decay and incomplete fillings can create air spaces in the teeth. When such cavities are exposed to pressure differentials, a **tooth squeeze** results. This produces pain because of tissue swelling and bleeding into the air space. During ascent, increasing pressure in the tooth will cause increased pain and bleeding, and it may even break the tooth.

Diving should be terminated if dental discomfort is experienced. Regular visits to your dentist can prevent dental barotrauma, and divers with a tooth squeeze should be referred to a dentist for repair of the affected tooth (Fig. 4-19).

Pain in a tooth also can be attributed to sinus barotrauma. This is because the roots of some upper teeth extend into the sinus cavities.

Lung Barotrauma

During breath-hold dives, the lungs become compressed with increasing depth. Pressure equalization in the lungs results from decreased chest volume (i.e., Boyle's Law); however, the chest cannot be infinitely compressed without causing damage. At some point, tissue damage and hemorrhaging will occur. This condition is known as a **thoracic squeeze,** which is not as common or as dangerous as overexpansion.

For years, it was believed that lung damage would result from breath-hold dives in excess of 5 atm, because a diver's lung capacity would be compressed below the residual volume. It has been discovered, however, that compression during descent shifts blood from the extremities and abdomen into the blood vessels of the chest. This effectively reduces the lung volume and aids in the equalization problem without lung barotrauma.

Fig. 4-18. Sinus block. Blocked sinuses lead to swelling, bleeding, pain and injury. Diving requires healthy sinuses.

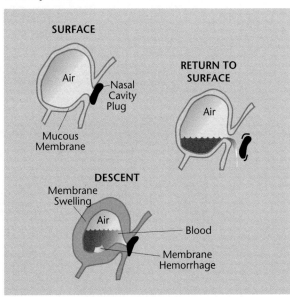

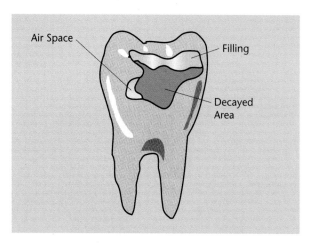

Fig. 4-19. Tooth barotrauma. High pressure air beneath an improperly filled tooth can cause pain and discomfort.

This allows lung volume to fall below the residual volume without damage. Depths in excess of 300 feet can and have been achieved. Therefore, breath-hold diving with lungs full of air does not pose a problem, but descending with less than a full inspiration can produce a lung squeeze. Also, a diver who loses consciousness may exhale involuntarily and suffer lung squeeze from an unintentional descent. Thoracic squeeze can be fatal. It is a rare malady, but it does exist as a diving hazard.

Failure of a diver breathing compressed gas to permit expanding air in the lungs to escape during ascent can produce several forms of **lung barotrauma.** This section addresses the potential injuries of overexpansion in detail (Fig. 4-20). Failure to exhale during an ascent results in lung overexpansion, expansion of the alveoli, and

finally, ruptures of the alveoli. Depending on where the rupture occurs, several forms of pulmonary barotrauma may occur, either separately or in combination.

Air Embolism

The most serious result of pulmonary overpressurization is the dispersion of alveolar air directly into the pulmonary venous system. This air is carried to the heart and then into the arterial circulation, and air emboli can block the coronary, cerebral, or other arteries. The gas bubbles continue to expand with further decrease in pressure until they become too large to pass through an artery, thus obstructing circulation. An **arterial gas embolism (AGE)**, also called an air embolism, is a blockage of the arterial bloodstream by a gas bubble. This injury can result with a pressure change as small as 0.1 ata (i.e., 4 ft, or slightly over 1 m).

The signs and symptoms of an air embolism are dramatic, and they usually occur within seconds of surfacing. Specifics are determined by the location of the blockage. Circulation to the heart can be cut off, producing symptoms similar to those of a heart attack. Frequently, however, the blockage arrests blood flow to the brain. When this occurs, dizziness, incoordination, paralysis, convulsions, unconsciousness, and even death may result. Other organs that may be affected include the liver, spleen, or kidneys. Also, many cases occur with no symptoms before the diver loses consciousness.

First aid involves placing the victim in a prone position, administering oxygen, and arranging his or her immediate evacuation to a staffed hyperbaric chamber. Recompression is the only effec-

Fig. 4-20. Possible consequences of lung overpressurization.

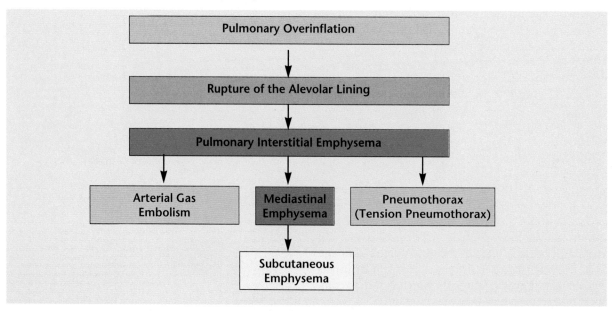

tive treatment for this disease; no attempt should be made to recompress the victim in the water. Artificial respiration or CPR also may be required.

Many divers are under the impression that lung overpressurization cannot occur during an ascent involving continuous exhalation. This is incorrect. Lung ailments, deformities, contaminants, and so on can cause airway blockage in a portion of the lung that is sufficient to rupture alveoli in that area. Forced, continuous exhalation can lead to the collapse of small airways in the lungs. Air in alveoli beyond the collapsed airways will expand as the ambient pressure decreases, which can lead to ruptures (Fig. 4-21).

Fig. 4-21. Lung injuries.

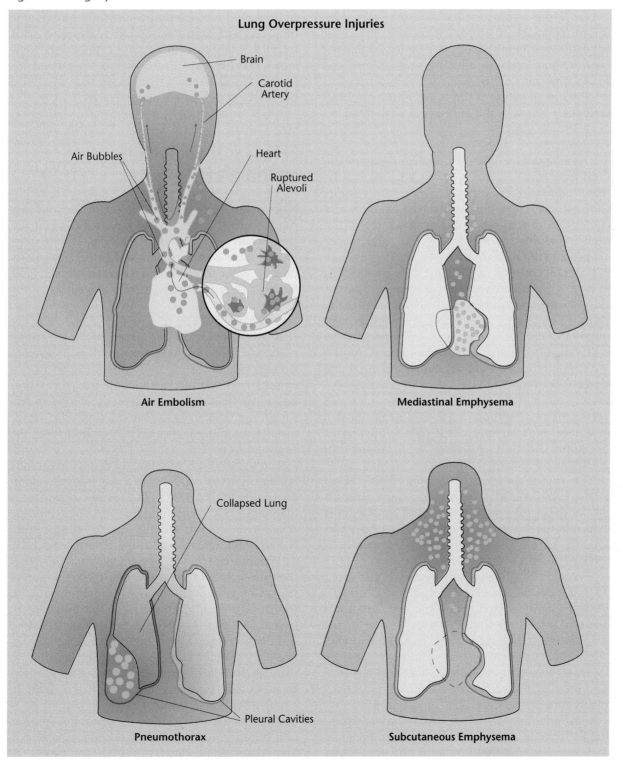

Lung Overpressure Injuries

Brain

Carotid Artery

Air Bubbles

Heart

Ruptured Alevoli

Air Embolism

Mediastinal Emphysema

Collapsed Lung

Pleural Cavities

Pneumothorax

Subcutaneous Emphysema

Emphysemas

From a rupture in the lungs, gas may enter the space in the chest between the lungs and behind the sternum, called the mediastinum. Gas in this space is called **mediastinal emphysema.** Emphysema refers to air in tissues. A diver with this malady may experience substernal pain, breathing difficulties, and even collapse because of direct pressure on the heart and great vessels.

Gas in the mediastinum may rise to the neck, where it "crackles." Here, it becomes known as **subcutaneous emphysema.** The prefix *sub-* means "under," and *cutaneous* means "skin." Signs and symptoms may include breathing difficulty, swelling in the area of the lower neck, crackling skin, voice changes, and difficulty in swallowing.

Pneumothorax

The area between the pair of pleura surrounding each lung is called the pleural cavity. Normally, there is no space between the pleura, which simply slide against each other as the lung expands and contracts with respiration. If alveoli rupture at the pleura, a tear in the lining may occur, and air can escape into the pleural space and result in the partial or total collapse of the lung. This condition is known as **pneumothorax,** which means air in the chest. P*neumo-* pertains to air, and *thorax* refers to the chest. This malady is an infrequent but serious complication of diving and recompression treatment.

If a pneumothorax occurs during ascent, further reduction in pressure causes the air in the pleural space to expand. This interferes with the diver's respiration and circulation, and it can lead to a very serious condition. Signs and symptoms of pneumothorax include chest pain, difficulty in breathing difficulty, reduced chest movement, leaning to the injured side, shock, and cyanosis.

The recommended breathing cycle for an ascent is a continuous breathing cycle. If no air is available for inhalation, attempted inhalation is sufficient to reopen any airways that may have collapsed. Good health, including no smoking, reduces the risk of lung overpressurization.

First aid for all pulmonary injuries is the same as for air embolism, which should always be suspected whenever pertinent signs and symptoms appear in the victim. If no evidence of air embolism is found, recompression treatment usually is not needed. All victims of lung overpressure injuries, however, should be transported to a recompression chamber for evaluation and possible treatment by a hyperbaric physician.

Prevention of pulmonary barotrauma is essential and simple. The diver only needs to maintain a continuous breathing cycle at all times when breathing compressed air.

Gastrointestinal Barotrauma

Foods that produce gas during the digestive process can lead to diver discomfort when that gas expands during ascent. The situation is essentially a reverse block in the stomach or intestines. It can cause belching and abdominal pain, and in severe instances, fainting, shock, and even tissue tearing may result. This condition can be avoided by refraining from gas-producing food before diving.

If you experience gastrointestinal barotrauma during ascent, stop your ascent or descend again to relieve any discomfort, and then slowly reascend. Medical attention may be required for severe cases where a diver is forced to surface before the pressure can be relieved.

EFFECTS OF THE DIVING ENVIRONMENT

The water in which we dive can be cold and rough, and this can cause rapid chilling of the diver, which can lead to hypothermia. Conversely, a diver also can become overheated on a warm day. As water tends to move around, motion sickness can be a problem for divers as well.

Thermal Stress

A diver expects to encounter challenges to the body as a result of the water pressure involved in diving, but he or she may not be alert to the extremely important effects of temperature. Water has a high heat capacity. It is an excellent conductor of heat, and it causes a submerged body to lose heat rapidly if that body is warmer than the surrounding water.

The human body attempts to maintain a steady state despite its exposure to a wide range of ambient temperatures. This stable-temperature state is maintained by controlling heat loss and production. Any downward variation of body temperature is frequently referred to in the diving community as **hypothermia** and an upward variation as **hyperthermia.** It should be noted that the definition of true clinical hypothermia is a reduction of core temperature only, and of that temperature to below 95°F (35° C). People can readily become incapacitated by cold without ever reaching this true hypothermic state, however, and incapacitation in the water can lead to adverse consequences (e.g., drowning) because of an inability to handle diving gear (Table 4-1).

The human body can be considered to consist of a central core containing the brain, spinal cord, and organs of the chest, abdomen, and pelvis, all surrounded by a peripheral shell consisting of the

TABLE 4.1 WIND-CHILL INDEX

WIND MPH	(Equivalent Temperature) — Equivalent in cooling power on exposed flesh under calm conditions																
Calm	35	30	25	20	15	10	5	0	−5	−10	−15	−20	−25	−30	−35	−40	−45
5	33	27	21	16	12	7	1	−6	−11	−15	−20	−26	−31	−35	−41	−47	−54
10	21	16	9	2	−2	−9	−15	−22	−27	−31	−38	−45	−52	−58	−64	−70	−77
15	16	11	1	−6	−11	−18	−25	−33	−40	−45	−51	−60	−65	−70	−78	−85	−90
20	12	3	−4	−9	−17	−24	−32	−40	−46	−52	−60	−68	−76	−81	−88	−96	−103
25	7	0	−7	−15	−22	−29	−37	−45	−52	−58	−67	−75	−83	−89	−96	−104	−112
30	5	−2	−11	−18	−26	−33	−41	−49	−56	−63	−70	−78	−87	−94	−101	−109	−117
35	3	−4	−13	−20	−27	−35	−43	−52	−60	−67	−72	−83	−90	−98	−105	−113	−123
40	1	−4	−15	−22	−29	−36	−45	−54	−62	−69	−76	−87	−94	−101	−107	−116	−128
45	1	−6	−17	−24	−31	−38	−46	−54	−63	−70	−78	−87	−94	−101	−108	−118	−128
50	0	−7	−17	−24	−31	−38	−47	−56	−63	−70	−79	−88	−96	−103	−110	−120	−128

limbs, muscles, and skin. The temperature of the core is controlled within very narrow limits, while the peripheral shell temperature is subject to variation. Normally, the core is warmer than the periphery. The heat that the body uses to maintain the core temperature results from resting metabolism plus the heat produced by exercise. Heat also is produced through shivering and nonshivering.

Heat transfer occurs by physical means whenever there is a temperature gradient. Heat moves from the object or area with the higher temperature to that with the lower temperature.

Heat Loss and Chilling

Exposure to cold results in body chilling at a rate that depends on many factors. The rate of heat loss in water will depend on the efficiency of any protective suit or clothing as well as the body shape. The head, groin, and chest wall beneath the armpits are the areas of greatest potential heat loss. The rate of loss in air also depends on whether the individual is wet or dry as well as protected or unprotected. To allow chilling beyond the level of feeling cold is obviously unsound, and the diver should seek warmth or additional thermal protection before such a condition is reached. Excessive heat loss can be prevented with an appropriate exposure suit for diving, proper nutrition to meet heat production needs, avoidance of alcohol, and avoidance of currents.

Features of Chilling

An individual who is suddenly exposed to very cold water with no thermal protection will often experience immediate disabling effects (Fig. 4-22). As immersion occurs, there is a sudden and involuntary inspiration or gasping response, which may lead to the inhalation of water. This response continues for 1 to 2 minutes with an extremely rapid

breathing rate that the victim cannot control. As time progresses, muscle strength decreases and is accompanied by pain and mental disorganization, with fear and panic reaction developing.

If the individual has some thermal protection, the immediate effects on exposure to cold water will not be as severe; however, heat loss will still

Fig. 4-22. Temperature protection charts.

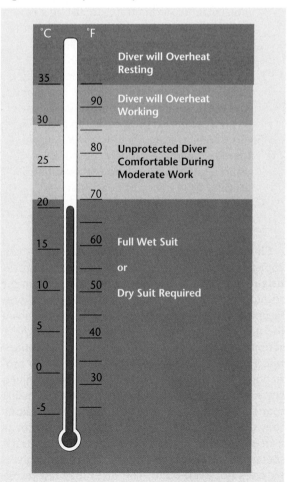

occur. Exercise or shivering will increase heat production, but the agitation of water by such activity increases heat loss. Exercise increases the heat loss much more at low than at high water temperatures, and it always increases the rate of body heat loss. It is not necessarily futile to try to stay warm with exercise, however. Exercise in the water will cause heat loss to the water, but contrary to popular belief, you will not always get colder by exercising in the water. You can overheat as well, because heat production also increases during exercise in water. Whichever prevails, however, and at what time, depends on a great number of factors that should be considered in attempts at self-rescue by swimming.

As chilling progresses and the core temperature falls, the individual will show predictable effects that loosely correspond to the core temperature. These include:

1. Mild to Moderate Chilling
   A. Core temperature of 95° to 98.6° F: Sensation of cold, shivering, increased heart rate, urge to urinate, slight incoordination in hand movements.
2. Severe Chilling (True Hypothermia)
   A. Core temperature of 90° to 95° F: Increasing muscular incoordination, stumbling gait, shivering slows or stops, weakness, apathy, drowsiness, confusion, slurred speech.
3. Severe Hypothermia
   A. Core temperature of 85° to 90° F: Shivering stops, inability to walk or follow commands, paradoxic undressing, complaints of loss of vision, confusion progressing to coma.
   B. Core temperature of 65° to 85° F: Muscle rigidity, decreased blood pressure, lowered heart and respiration rates, dilated pupils, appearance of death.
   C. Core temperature below 65° F: Victim begins to take on the temperature of the environment.

Chilling also can occur in relatively warm or even tropical waters. Scientific divers have experienced fatigue with impaired awareness and judgment because of slow body cooling while they were preoccupied with the task at hand. Very little is known about the effects of long, slow body cooling and the potential for development of undetected hypothermia. This may occur in individuals wearing no protection in water of 82° to 91° F or in those wearing a wet suit in cooler water. Skin temperature remains near the comfort zone at 91° F, and the insidious heat drain from the body by the cooler water is scarcely noticed until the core temperature drops enough to induce shivering. In some cases, shivering does not even occur. The diver may not recognize the problem, but it is usually expressed as a reluctance to dive. Recreational divers may encounter this phenomenon during repeated vacation dives with no thermal protection in warm water; they suddenly find themselves very tired and with no desire to continue their vacation diving plans.

Management of Heat Loss Victims

Suspecting the existence of hypothermia is the first step in its management. Chilling may be mild, with little risk to the individual, or severe, with death a possibility. The mildly chilled individual will be awake, complaining of cold, possibly shivering, and able to converse intelligently. The moderately chilled individual will be awake but may be confused, apathetic or uncooperative, and may have difficulty with speech. If severely chilled or hypothermic, the victim may be unconscious, have slow heart and respiration rates, or even appear dead and with no detectable heart beat. The victim who is moderately or severely hypothermic may be made worse or placed in cardiac arrest by careless attempts at rewarming. Hypothermia is an emergency in slow motion; improper handling may create a fatal outcome. The cold heart is especially sensitive, and victims who are alive when found may develop cardiac arrest if they are handled roughly during the initial evaluation and transport. The rescuer must transport and rewarm the victim without precipitating cardiac arrest.

Rewarming is extremely important, of course, but it should not be attempted unless it can be done properly. It sometimes becomes necessary to rewarm a chilling victim in an area that is far from medical care, however. The first attempts should use passive methods, including protection against further heat loss by removing wet clothing and covering the victim in layers. Do not forget to provide layers between the victim and the ground or deck and to cover the head, which is a major source of heat loss. The fully alert and cooperative victim may be given warm liquids to drink. This will deliver negligible amounts of heat, but it will help to correct the dehydration. Coffee, tea, caffeine drinks, and alcohol should be strictly avoided. Oral fluids may include balanced electrolyte solutions such as Gatorade, Gastriolyte, or Infalyte, which are available in powder form. If the victim is awake, he or she should not be exercised, because muscular activity will bring cold blood from the body periphery into the core. The mildly or moderately chilled victim will soon return to a near-normal temperature.

Immersion of the victim in a hot bath was thought to be risky unless limited to the trunk only, with the extremities left out. Similarly, body-to-body contact has been limited to bare skin in the trunk area only. Current research indicates that the victim will not have increased cooling of the heart on immersion, limbs and all, in a hot bath.

The severely hypothermic victim may be unconscious or appear dead. Look very carefully for signs of life, such as breathing, movement, or a pulse at the groin or in the neck over the carotid artery. If breathing or movement is present, the heart is beating and CPR is not needed. If the breathing rate is six or less respirations per minute, very gentle mouth-to-mouth breathing at a slow rate may be started while being extremely careful to avoid rough handling of the victim.

If there are no signs of life, CPR and arrangements for emergency transport to the nearest medical facility should be started. Rewarming of the severely hypothermic victim cannot be accomplished in the field. If possible, CPR should be continued until emergency assistance is obtained. There have been successful resuscitations after prolonged CPR, in part because of the protective effect of hypothermia.

To prevent chilling requires training, judgment, and experience. The diver must understand the use of external insulation to conserve body heat and be able to control heat loss. Recreational divers sometimes encounter very cold conditions in ice diving or winter diving in deep quarries and lakes. All ocean dives are in water that is below body temperature. Wet suits provide some degree of thermal protection depending on the style, material, and thickness, but they become compressed with increasing depth and lose much of their insulating properties. The "woolly bear" or open-cell undergarment worn under a dry suit is effective, but this also compresses and loses some insulation value. If wet, the woolly bear loses practically all of its insulating value. Type-B marine thinsulate is an alternative that retains its insulation value when wet.

Prevention of chilling also includes preparation for an unexpected immersion. Divers traveling by boat to the dive site should have a floatation device available other than their diving equipment. Personal flotation devices are designed to keep the wearer afloat with no effort on his or her part, to keep the head out of water, and to be self-righting. The diver should practice using the personal floatation device ahead of time to become familiar with its use. Seat cushions or flotation devices that require the victim to hold on are not satisfactory in cold water, because chilling will cause the loss of muscle power. The victim will lose his or her grip.

The diver should be prepared for the actions to be taken once in the water, which include efforts to minimize heat loss such as remaining still and assuming the "**HELP**" position (i.e., Heat Escape Lessening Position). This position is assumed by drawing the knees up to the chest and holding on to them with crossed arms. This position is unstable and not easy to achieve without practice, however, as one tends to roll forward or backward. Consequently, it is good to practice the position from time to time. The huddle position with other persons also is surprisingly effective in conserving heat; everyone wraps arms around one another and pulls into a tight circle, remaining as still as possible (Fig. 4-23). The psychologic preparedness of knowing what to expect if suddenly immersed in cold water, how to use flotation, and how to stay put and wait for rescue will significantly increase your chances for survival.

Hyperthermia

Just as chilling is dangerous, so is an increase in body heat over the normal limits. Divers insulate their bodies to minimize heat loss, but this can lead to the retention of body heat unless the diver is wet or immersed.

The body produces heat as a result of metabolism. If the heat is transferred to the environment, the body temperature remains unchanged. Heat from the body core is brought to the body surface by blood circulation and eliminated primarily through the skin by physical means (i.e., radiation, evaporation, conduction, or convection). If there is interference with this process, heat accumulates within the body and the core temperature rises. When air temperature is equal to or above body temperature and the air is humid with little or no breeze, the normal heat transfer process is blocked. Such conditions lead to a rising body temperature, or hyperthermia.

High environmental temperatures are capable of producing illness in an otherwise healthy person. The diver is not likely to develop a problem because of high environmental temperatures while diving; however, conditions at the dive site may produce a heat-related illness. A diver working at a high energy output while in water that is near or above body temperature is at risk. There have been injuries and deaths in recompression chambers when divers were subjected to high temperatures because of inadequate environmental control. The diver wearing a full wet suit on a hot, humid, or sunny day is also at risk (Fig. 4-24).

Features of Hyperthermia

As the heat-control mechanisms fail and heat overloading increases, a number of problems may appear. During the early stages, most are

NO H.E.L.P.   H.E.L.P.   HUDDLING

Fig. 4-23. H.E.L.P. position. Cover the high heat loss areas to preserve body heat.

related to water loss, because the body has attempted to eliminate heat by sweating. The mildest heat-related illness is heat cramp, which results from muscle spasm following exercise. A more severe problem is **heat exhaustion**, which may be a mild form of shock that is brought on by dehydration and the dilation of blood vessels in the skin. The most severe problem is **heat stroke** (sometimes called sun stroke), which develops as the temperature-regulating mechanisms fail completely. Body temperature may rise to 105° F or higher, and there is damage to vital organs, which may progress to coma followed by death. Survivors also may have permanent brain damage.

The symptoms of heat-related illness usually begin with profuse sweating and painful muscle spasms. As the problem increases to heat exhaustion, the victim becomes weak, pale, and has a weak pulse and rapid respiration. Dizziness and unconsciousness may occur. The next level, heat stroke, may occur suddenly, with cessation of perspiration, hot and dry skin, dilated pupils, and unconsciousness.

Emergency care for heat-related illness requires protecting the victim from further injury, replacement of the water loss, and reduction of body temperature. An individual with mild symptoms can

be removed to a cool place and his or her water deficit corrected by drinking water or a balanced electrolyte solution. When symptoms are more severe, the victim should be transported to a medical facility. During transportation, the conscious victim can be given fluids by mouth and kept flat (or nearly so) to prevent shock. The victim who has become semiconscious or unconscious is a true emergency. Transportation to a medical facility should not be delayed, and measures to reduce body temperature should be started immediately at the scene. The victim should have his clothing removed and then may be wrapped in a sheet, soaked with cold water, and fanned vigorously to reduce body temperature. Ice can be applied to the groin, armpits, and neck. Do not give a semiconscious or unconscious person anything by mouth. In addition, monitor the airway at all times.

Prevention

Heat-related stress can be avoided by giving proper attention to water intake and protection from environmental heat. Sweat contains salt; however, the major threat is the loss of water. A normal individual will obtain enough salt in the diet so that a salt supplement is rarely necessary. If heat exposure is to occur for many hours, commercial elec-

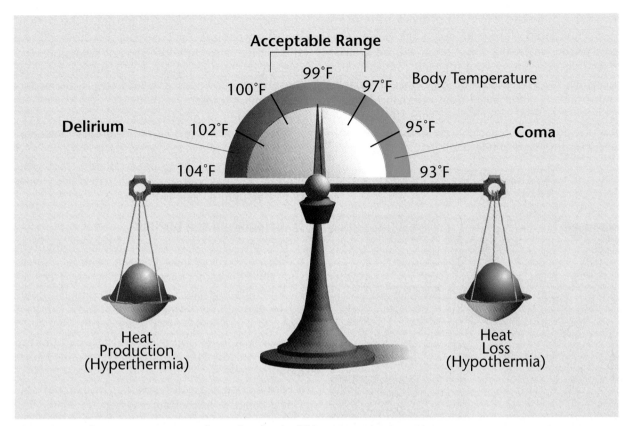

Fig. 4-24. Body temperature must be maintained within a narrow range.

trolyte solutions provide adequate salt; salt tablets are too concentrated and may irritate the stomach, causing vomiting. The normal kidney is very efficient in conserving salt. The risk of salt depletion in heat-related illness has been overstated.

The human body can tolerate extreme temperatures when provided with adequate water. Great quantities of fluid are needed to replace that which is lost through the sweating mechanism. Water intake should be approximately 6 to 10 fluid ounces every 20 minutes during heavy exertion under excessively warm conditions. The very young, very old, or those who are impaired by alcohol or recreational drug usage are at increased risk. Repeated exposure to heat causes a gradual adjustment, resulting in the ability to tolerate heat stress much better than when first exposed. The physically fit person tolerates heat exposure better than one who is in poor physical condition.

Prolonged wearing of an exposure suit out of the water on a hot day can lead to heat exhaustion. First aid involves lying the victim down, cooling the victim, and administering fluids.

Motion Sickness

Sea sickness can ruin diving trips, vacations, and travel. It prevents many divers from even attempting adventures involving travel by boat. Unfortunately, susceptibility to motion sickness is universal, although the amount of motion that is required to produce this problem varies among individuals. No one is immune. It is believed that the cause is "mixed signals" (i.e., one motion-sensing system senses motion while another does not). Fortunately, there are ways to avoid motion sickness by controlling the factors that produce it.

Motion sickness is primarily nausea that results from the brain's inability to resolve conflicting signals that it receives from the ears, eyes, and body. The balance organs of the ears are stimulated by the repeated angular acceleration of the vessel, while the signal from the eyes is that of no motion if visual contact has been lost with the outside horizon. The sensors of the body position are sending still another signal, and the brain is unable to resolve the conflict. Anxiety, confusion, and dismay result, leading to the first symptoms of yawning, pallor, and headache, which are followed by nausea and vomiting, a fear response, and palpitations.

The prevention of motion sickness is more successful than treatment after the onset of symptoms. Your position in the vessel is very important. A susceptible individual should remain on deck at the point of least motion (usually the center) and maintain visual contact with the moving water, thereby allowing the eyes and inner ears to sense the same movement and resolving the conflict. A position near the bow will allow a person to remain oriented with the motion of the vessel relative to the water, but the motion will be greater than that near the center. If visual contact is not possible, the eyes should be kept closed. It also is important to move away from other individuals who are experiencing motion sickness. Psychologic support from companions is helpful for the individual and the group (Fig. 4-25).

Fig. 4-25.   A seasick diver should go up near the bow of the boat to get fresh air. It also helps to stare somewhere far away, such as at the horizon.

A diver may develop motion sickness during a dive because of interference with spatial orientation. A common cause is the motion from a surge encountered during an entry from shore accompanied by the loss of visual clues in poor visibility. Neutral buoyancy distorts the clues provided by gravity, and the brain is unable to reconcile the abnormal sensory input. Motion sickness develops and may result in the necessity of vomiting through a regulator. The safety of the diver under these conditions is seriously impaired; a panic reaction could easily occur. The experienced diver will recognize clues that provide spatial orientation. Entering and exiting along a line is important if visibility is poor and the bottom cannot be seen. Exhaust bubbles move toward the

surface, and weight belts drag toward the bottom in response to gravity. Likewise, the chest will rise and the feet sink if the diver is not swimming. The inadequately trained diver will not be aware of these clues, however, and may ignore them during a panic situation.

Prevention of motion sickness requires adequate rest before a trip, avoiding greasy foods and alcohol, and following the guidelines discussed here. A variety of drugs are available to combat motion sickness, but you should consult a diving physician before using any of these.

Disorientation and Vertigo

On land, you have several means to maintain equilibrium. These include visual reference, pressure differences on joints, and the center of balance in the inner ear. Your ability to remain oriented to your surroundings is much more limited when you are weightless underwater, however, especially when visibility is restricted by turbidity or low levels of light. Your principal means of orientation while diving is the reference provided by a series of semicircular canals in your inner ear. This is called your vestibular system.

The semicircular ear canals are oriented along different planes. They contain fluid and sensors to sense the orientation of the fluid. The relationship of the fluid to the sensors provides information that your brain uses as points of reference for equilibrium.

Signals of equilibrium to your brain can be distorted by body positioning, visual contradictions, lack of reference, pressure changes, and caloric stimulation. The effect of each is a feeling of vertigo (i.e., dizziness) that results in disorientation. You literally do not know which way is up. Obviously, this hazard must be prevented. The following information explains how equilibrium can be affected by diving and the risk of disorientation minimized.

Vertigo can result from unequal stimulation of your ears. These stimuli can be differences in temperature or pressure. If cold water enters one ear and not the other, as may be the case if a hood is worn or there is an accumulation of wax in one ear canal, vertigo may result. This condition is intensified if the diver is in a head-down position, so feet-first descents are advised.

If one ear equalizes with the ambient pressure and the other does not, the unequal stimulation can produce vertigo. This is more pronounced if the pressure change is sudden. A pressure buildup in an ear during ascent (i.e., reverse block) can produce dizziness. This condition is known as **alternobaric vertigo**.

Excessive force used for ear clearing can cause vestibular damage and also produce vertigo. Failure to equalize the middle-ear spaces can result in perforation of the ear drum, and this allows cold water to rush into the middle ear and stimulate the vestibular system, thereby producing sudden and intense vertigo (Fig. 4-26).

Diving when deprived of a reference at night or in very turbid water can result in disorientation. These situations are compounded in the presence of surge.

Should vertigo be experienced while diving, you should stop, grasp a stationary object for reference, and wait for the dizziness to pass. If the problem persists, terminate diving and seek medical assistance. If vertigo occurs in midwater where there is nothing to grasp, hugging yourself may provide some assistance. The value of a nearby diving buddy in such instances is apparent.

Dehydration

Water comprises the greater part of the blood. An abnormal loss of fluid from the body is termed **dehydration**, which occurs when you take in less fluid than you lose in urine, exhaled moisture, and perspiration. Problems of dehydration that are compounded by diving can predispose divers to other diving ailments, especially DCS.

Overheating during diving preparations can cause profuse sweating and fluid loss. This should be avoided by working in shaded areas and wetting down to remain cool.

The effects of cold on the body, combined with the effort required to draw air from a regulator (i.e., negative-pressure breathing) and a relative volume overload from the decrease of gravity, stimulate divers to urinate more frequently than normal. Blood pooling in the body core because of water pressure or cold water temperatures also may stimulate increased urine production. This response is called diuresis. Substances that increase the output of urine by the kidneys are diuretics and include coffee, tea, alcohol, and so on. Divers should avoid diuretics before and during a dive, and they should drink fluids before and between dives to offset the diuretic effects of diving.

Scuba air is dehydrated. Each time you inhale through your regulator, you increase the humidity of inspired air to 100%. This moisture (along with heat to warm the incoming air) is drawn from your body. This is another reason why replacing body fluids during diving activities is required.

Infections

Infections from injuries, inhaled water, or water in body cavities can occur. Illnesses can and

Fig. 4-26. It is sometimes easier to clear the ears when descending on a line.

should be prevented with immunizations and preventive measures. Inoculations for waterborne diseases such as typhoid should be kept current.

Tetanus prevention should be considered if a diver is wounded. Infections of the external ear canal (i.e., "swimmer's ear") should be prevented by irrigating the ear with an appropriate solution after diving. Cuts, abrasions, and punctures should be cleaned well and disinfected.

PHYSICAL FITNESS FOR SCUBA DIVING

Physical fitness can be defined as the ability to perform physical activity. Diving fitness is the ability to perform diving-related tasks. Physical fitness has many interrelated components, such as medical and nutritional status, strength, endurance, flexibility, and skill. A high level of physical fitness reduces your vulnerability to the potential hazards of diving, and it allows you to enjoy effortlessly a variety of diving experiences with minimized risk.

This section considers some of the factors that can significantly affect your ability to meet the physical demands commonly imposed by scuba diving. It identifies medical conditions that make diving unsafe, discusses the effects of drugs and foods, and presents guidelines for improving selected components of physical fitness.

Health Requirements

Physical contraindications to diving are those physical characteristics that make it impossible or unwise to engage in the sport. Conditions are generally considered to be absolute contraindications if they create a risk for loss of consciousness, significantly restrict physical exertion, or prevent the lungs, middle ears, or sinuses from equalizing pressure. Most authorities also place pregnancy in the category of conditions that absolutely rule out diving.

Determination of medical fitness for diving typically begins with an examination of a diver's medical history form. In young, apparently healthy candidates for instruction, this review is usually performed by a diving instructor. Complete medical examinations and physician approval are required for all applicants with questionable histories. The medical examination is desirable for all prospective divers and particularly for those over 35 years of age and with family histories including conditions of concern in diving safety. Common tests include resting and exercise ECGs to screen for cardiovascular disease and exercise tolerance, chest radiography and pulmonary function tests to determine lung health, blood and urine tests for infectious and metabolic disorders, and examination of the eyes, ears, nose, and throat.

Cardiovascular Disorders

Despite encouraging improvements in the past few years, more than 50% of all deaths in the United States result from heart and blood-vessel diseases. Many disorders are in this category. Some are congenital (i.e., present at birth), and some are acquired over a period of time. The two most common causes of death are acquired cardiovascular diseases: heart attack, and stroke. Both typically result from the process of arteriosclerosis, which gradually narrows arteries to the point that blood flow is stopped. When this occurs in the coronary arteries serving the heart muscle, it is called *coronary artery disease* (CAD), and the result is a heart attack. When blood flow to the brain is stopped by plugging of the cerebral arteries, the condition is called *cerebrovascular disease* and a stroke occurs.

Both of these conditions are rare in individuals below 40 years of age. They have become of increasing concern as the diving population has aged, however. Family history, age, and sex seem to play significant roles in determining the risk for arteriosclerosis; you obviously have no choice in these matters. There are many other significant risk factors, however, over which you do have control. The three major ones are high blood cholesterol, high blood pressure (i.e., hypertension), and smoking.

The arteriosclerotic process typically begins in childhood and is significantly advanced when symptoms occur. For approximately 50% of the people who have CAD, the first known symptom is

a heart attack, and sudden death is the result in approximately 50% of these cases. If you have suffered a heart attack and have undergone corrective procedures, it may be possible to initiate or resume diving activities, but as in most cases, there is not unanimous agreement among physicians. Even so, some feel that diving is perfectly safe if you can perform at a moderately high level on a stress test without pain, abnormal ECG, or irregular blood pressure response.

Similarly, there are several types of heart murmurs and ECG abnormalities that show up during routine medical examinations but do not rule out diving. A history of rheumatic fever is of some concern, but the resulting cardiovascular effects may not prevent diving. Your physician will make the judgment based on whether there is a risk for dangerous heart rhythm or a limitation of exercise tolerance.

Screening for latent (i.e., asymptomatic) heart disease is obviously of great importance in determining the medical fitness of males in the coronary-prone years (i.e., over 40 years of age) and of women over 50 years of age. Resting ECGs are of some value in this regard, but they often fail to reveal abnormalities that will show up on an exercise stress test. An annual stress test may be recommended by your doctor even if you do not have several known risk factors.

Pulmonary Disorders

With the exception of cancer and emphysema, disorders of the lungs are not particularly common causes of death among the normal population. Diving, however, creates concern over any condition that even temporarily blocks the escape of air from the lungs. Chest radiogaphs, pulmonary function tests, and listening to the chest with a stethoscope all shed some light on the condition of your lungs—but only at the time of the examination. There is debate in the medical community regarding the frequency with which these tests should be administered to divers. Also, small areas of abnormal lung may not be detectable yet cause lung overpressure injuries.

Some people are born with, but are never aware of, lung abnormalities that are incompatible with scuba diving. Many other people acquire disorders because of infection, environmental pollution, smoking, and other circumstances. These disorders prohibit diving only if they prevent normal ventilation of the lungs or limit exercise tolerance. Asthma, chronic bronchitis, emphysema, and other obstructive lung diseases are among the most common contraindications. The effects of childhood asthma are frequently outgrown, so adults with a history of asthma sometimes may receive medical clearance to dive.

Temporary conditions such as bronchitis, colds, and flu may not be present at the time of a diving medical examination; however, they may restrict the airways enough to prevent expanding air from being vented during a scuba diving ascent. Even though you breathe normally, ascend slowly, and have normally healthy lungs, these conditions could result in fatal lung overexpansion injuries (Table 4-2).

TABLE 4.2   DEFINITIONS OF DIVING MEDICAL TERMS

1. Alveolus	A small membranous sac which is the end portion of the respiratory system in the lung wherein the gaseous exchange takes place.
2. Anoxia	Absence of oxygen.
3. Apnea	The cessation of breathing for short intervals of time.
4. Asphyxia	The existence of both hypoxia and hypercapnia in the body.
5. Barodontalgia	Pain in teeth associated with changes in barometric pressure.
6. Barotrauma	Physical damage to the body as a direct result of pressure changes.
7. Bradycardia	Slowness of the heartbeat.
8. Bronchi	Fibromuscular tubes connecting the trachea to the smaller portions of the respiratory tract.
9. Carotid Sinus	A small dilation in the carotid artery just below its bifurcation that is surrounded by an extensive nerve network, and which is sensitive to pressure changes within the carotid artery, ensuring that arterial pressure is maintained at a suitable level.
10. Chemoreceptor	Carotid and aortic bodies sensitive to changes in partial pressures of oxygen and carbon dioxide in the blood which play an important part in the regulation of respiration.
11. Cyanosis	A bluish discoloration of the skin from insufficient oxygenation of the blood.
12. Dysbarism	A general term applied to any clinical condition caused by a difference between the surrounding atmospheric pressure and the total gas pressure in the various tissues, fluids, and body cavities.
13. Diuresis	Excessive excretion of urine.
14. Dyspnea	Difficulty in breathing.
15. Edema	Swelling caused by excessive amounts of fluid in tissues.
16. Embolus	A plug brought by the blood from one vessel and forced into a smaller one so as to obstruct the circulation.
17. Emphysema	A swelling or inflation caused by the presence of air or other gas in body tissues.
18. Eustachian Tube	The canal, partly bony and partly cartilaginous, connecting the throat (pharynx) with the middle ear (tympanic cavity), serving as an air channel by which air pressure within the middle ear is equalized with that outside.
19. Exhalation	Expelling air from the lungs.
20. Expiratory Reserve	The amount of air that can be exhaled from the lungs after normal expiration.
21. External Ear	That portion of the ear from the outermost portion to the tympanic membrane, encompassing the external canal.
22. Hemoglobin	A component of red blood cells that combines with oxygen, carbon dioxide or carbon monoxide.
23. Hemorrhage	The loss of blood from the vascular system.
24. Hypercapnia	Undue amount of carbon dioxide in the blood, causing over-activity in the respiratory center.
25. Hyperventilation	Breathing excessively fast.
26. Hypothermia	The lowering of the body's core temperature below normal.
27. Hypoventilation	Inadequate ventilation of the lungs.
28. Hypoxia	Failure of the tissues to receive enough oxygen.
29. Inner Ear	That portion of the ear located within the bony confines of the temporal bone, containing the organs of equilibrium and hearing.
30. Inhalation	Drawing air into the lungs.

Table 4-2 continues on next page

TABLE 4.2   DEFINITIONS OF DIVING MEDICAL TERMS (CONTINUED)

31. Inspiratory Reserve	The maximum amount of air that can be breathed in after normal inspiration.
32. Mediastinum	That portion of the chest cavity located between the right and left lungs, containing the heart, the major vessels and some of the major nerves traversing from the neck to the abdomen.
33. Middle Ear	That portion of the ear between the tympanic membrane and the bony enclosure of the semi-circular canals. This portion contains the three bony ossicles for the transmission of the movement of the tympanic membrane and also contains the opening of the Eustachian canal.
34. Normoxic	A breathing gas mixture that supplies the diver with a "normal" partial pressure of oxygen, about 0.21 ATA, at any specific depth.
35. pH	A symbol representing hydrogen ion concentration in a fluid, thus indicating acidity or alkalinity. A pH of 7 is neutral. Less than 7 is acidic, and more than 7 is basic or alkaline.
36. Pleura	Two layers of thin membrane surrounding the lungs.
37. Pneumothorax	The presence of air or gas in the pleural cavity resulting from a rupture of an alveolus, which allows the pleural space to come into equilibrium with the external pressure.
38. Residual Volume	The amount of air left in the lungs after a maximal expiratory effort.
39. Sinuses	Cavities within the bones of the skull lined by epithelium and connected by small openings to the nasal passageways.
40. Tachycardia	Excessive rapidity of heart beat.
41. Thrombus	A plug or clot in a blood vessel or in one of the cavities of the heart.
42. Tidal Volume	The amount of air breathed in and out of the lungs during normal respiration.
43. Tinnitus	Ringing in the ear.
44. Trachea	That portion of the breathing apparatus that extends from the posterior oropharynx or the posterior portion of the mouth to the chest cavity.
45. Tympanic Membrane	A thin membranous partition (eardrum) separating the external ear from the middle ear.
46. Vital Capacity	Maximum volume of air which can be expired after maximal inhalation.

Nervous System Disorders

Abnormal conditions of the nervous system may show up on a diver's medical history or examination. Several are potentially dangerous in diving, but epilepsy is the most common disorder of major concern. Epileptic seizures are an obvious threat to diving safety and cause for exclusion from diving. Loss of consciousness or control underwater are deadly.

Metabolic Disorders

Many diseases of the kidneys, liver, and endocrine glands may temporarily or permanently prevent you from diving. Diabetes mellitus is a relatively common disorder that generally is considered to be an absolute contraindication for diving. The diabetic who is insulin-dependent or has a history of hypoglycemic episodes is at significant risk because of the threat of losing consciousness or the ability to act effectively.

Ear and Sinus Disorders

Some individuals are born with abnormal passages to the middle ears and/or sinuses, and these may make it difficult or impossible for the diver to equalize pressure on descent. Attempting to dive with these conditions may result in severe pain, damage to related tissue, complications from secondary infection, and/or hearing loss. Similar hazards more commonly result from temporary or chronic inflammation of the ear and sinus passages. Suffering from chronic inflammation may rule out diving altogether; however, seasonal inflammations such as hay fever and head colds require that you avoid diving only during the time you are affected.

Smoking and the Diver

It is well established that cigarette smoking increases the risk of bronchitis, emphysema, lung cancer, CAD, and other conditions that reduce the quality and length of life. The effects of pressure changes and exposure to cold temperatures make these diseases more hazardous for divers than for the general population (Table 4-3).

Years of heavy cigarette smoking are usually required for these disorders to develop, but there are also immediate effects of smoking that should be of special concern to divers. Smoking even one cigarette typically irritates the airways, leading to excess mucous secretion, airway spasm, and increased resistance to airflow. This could result in

Contaminant	Maximum Allowance for Surface Air	Maximum Allowance for Air for Diving	Cigarette Smoke
Carbon Monoxide	100 ppm	10 ppm	42,000 ppm
Saturated Hydrocarbon	500 ppm	50 ppm	87,000 ppm
Unsaturated Hydrocarbon	5,000 ppm	50 ppm	31,000 ppm
Acetone	200 ppm	No Detectable Trace	1,100 ppm
Formaldehyde	5 ppm	No Detectable Trace	30 ppm

TABLE 4.3   HAZARDS OF SMOKING

air trapping and lung overexpansion injuries. Smoking also can elevate blood levels of carbon monoxide to the point of limiting oxygen delivery and exercise tolerance. When combined with the coronary artery–narrowing effects of nicotine, this also increases the risk for heart attack. The risk is particularly real during conditions of cold exposure, which are so common in diving.

If you do not smoke, do not start. If you do smoke, consider cutting back or stopping, or at least refrain from smoking for several hours before diving.

Drugs and the Diver

Divers take a variety of drugs for a variety of reasons. Any drug that should not be used when driving a motor vehicle or operating machinery also should not be used when diving. The added effects of cold and pressure often make diving even more dangerous after taking drugs. The physiologic and psychologic changes produced by diving may cause a drug to have a dangerously different effect than the one that is intended.

Alcohol impairs alertness, coordination, and judgment, and it is associated with an increased risk for accidents. The effects of cold, nitrogen narcosis, and other diving factors magnify the negative effects of alcohol on a diver's judgment and performance. Alcohol also constricts the arteries that serve the heart and dilates vessels to the skin. The results are potential heart problems and excessive heat loss, which increases the risk for hypothermia. Drinking before diving is obviously unwise, but it also is potentially hazardous following a dive. If you drink heavily after diving, you may not recognize DCS or other symptoms that sometimes develop during the afterdive hours. Alcohol increases urine output and can potentiate the dehydration of diving.

Amphetamines such as speed and other stimulants are dangerous enough on land, and they have been found to reduce coordination, judgment, and problem-solving ability under hyperbaric conditions. They also can dangerously alter heart rhythm and mask the symptoms of fatigue.

Antihistamines are found in many commonly used medications. Because of their negative effects on alertness and performance, however, they carry warnings against their use before or during demanding activities. Blurred vision and an excessively dry mouth can be observed as effects of antihistamines that affect diving.

Coffee, tea, and several soft drinks contain the stimulant caffeine. This stimulant increases alertness, but it also may cause anxiousness, trembling, heartburn, irregular heart rhythm, and slight elevation of blood pressure and heart rate. Like alcohol, caffeine is a diuretic (i.e., it causes fluid loss by increasing urination). For this reason, there have been some warnings of increased risk for DCS with caffeine use.

Cocaine would be dangerous enough for divers if it just caused alterations in mental function, but it also is known to elevate blood pressure and heart rate, increase sensitivity of the brain and heart, and accelerate the development of arteriosclerosis. There are medical reports of heart attacks suffered by individuals in their twenties and thirties following the use of cocaine.

Marijuana has many of the combined effects of alcohol and tobacco smoking. Some of these effects seem to be more pronounced with increased diving depth.

Divers suffer from most of the ailments common to the general population, and they sometimes desire relief from their symptoms to dive. The first thing to consider in this situation is whether you should be diving in your present condition. Diving under the influence of medication may make a bad situation even worse. There are a host of medicines that may be used to deal with diarrhea, ear and sinus congestion, seasickness, and other maladies. Some are clearly dangerous to use when diving; others are relatively safe for most individuals. Consult with your diving physician about any side effects or interactions that might occur with the medication that you take (or plan to take). Remember, sport diving should be engaged in only when your personal condition is appropriate to the demands of the planned dive! Ask yourself if you should really be diving when you feel like you need medication.

Nutrition and the Diver

Some divers are particularly sensitive to spicy or gas-forming foods and beverages such as pizza, beans, and carbonated drinks. If you are in this category, you should avoid them before diving, because discomfort or significant pain during ascents can occur because of expanding abdominal gases. Eating a great deal of any food immediately before diving also may cause discomfort and be genuinely dangerous if it leads to vomiting while submerged.

General nutritional advice for divers is similar to that offered for good health and risk reduction in disorders such as CAD, cancer, diabetes, hypertension, and obesity. A prudent diet is one that is high in complex carbohydrates (e.g., cereals and cereal products, fruits, and vegetables) and has limited amounts of alcohol, caffeine, salt, saturated fats (primarily animal fats), and sugar.

Developing and Maintaining Fitness for Diving

Because diving fitness is the ability to perform diving-related activities and a great variety of activities relate to diving, diving fitness is a complex matter. Clearly, you may be in great shape for one task while being unable to perform another. This specificity in fitness is sometimes very obvious. Consider the demands of mounting a regulator on your tank, and compare them with the demands of walking one-quarter mile in soft sand with that tank on your back. These two diving-related activities have quite different energy and neuromuscular requirements. You may be fit for one and not the other. The differences between fitness requirements for casual underwater swimming and making a scuba rescue are not quite as obvious, but they are just as real.

Diving opportunities are limited, in part, by the number of diving tasks you can perform. Increasing your ability to perform these activities will broaden your comfort zone; you will be able to execute each task with less sense of stress, making the experience more enjoyable. Dives that are made easy by good planning and conditioning also are less likely to lead to exhaustion, panic, errors in judgment, or accidents. You need to possess the ability to meet all demands that are normally imposed by your type of diving, plus be reasonably prepared to meet any unusual demands when the unexpected occurs. Our considerations here are limited to aerobic fitness, muscular strength, and endurance, although there are many other important components of physical fitness.

The basic principle of conditioning is the **Law of Use and Disuse**. The principle is that within certain limits, the more that you use your body in a particular way, the better it gets at meeting the demands of that activity. If your body is not required to meet particular demands often enough, it will lose its ability to meet them. Imposing demands on your body is known as *overload*, and it may be accomplished by increasing the frequency, intensity, or time of exercise (i.e., the so-called FIT *principle*).

Aerobic Fitness

Aerobic fitness is the ability of your heart and lungs to deliver oxygen as well as the ability of your muscles to use it. This type of fitness is required for cycling, jogging, rowing, and swimming—and for long fin swims or hikes along the beach to the dive site. Because roughly the same muscles are used in approximately the same way as during a hike down the beach, jogging may be just as effective as any other activity to improve your aerobic fitness for this type of diving-related activity. None of the mentioned activities does a very good job of approximating the muscle demands involved in swimming with fins, however. It appears that the best way to condition yourself for performance in the water is with regular fin swimming combined with common tasks such as entries, surface dives, and gear handling (to keep your skills sharp as well). Although significant aerobic demands may not occur frequently in the water, they are probably the most critical there, because the consequences of exhaustion are much greater (Fig. 4-27).

There are a variety of recommended aerobic training guidelines. In general, you should exercise at approximately 70% to 85% of your maximum heart rate, at least three times per week, for at least 20 to 30 minutes a session. This is appropriate if you have nearly average resting and maximum heart rates for your age group. Maximum heart rate (in beats per minute) is estimated by subtracting your age from 220, but this is subject to considerable individual variability (as is the resting heart rate). You should use the exercise heart rate as a general guide, while being very attentive to how you feel. Train, do not strain, in a range of exertion from moderately hard to hard. The effort should not be extremely

Fig. 4-27. Swimming with fins in a pool or open-water is a good way to stay in shape for diving.

hard or exhausting. Be patient. Run the risk of doing too little rather than too much as you begin an exercise program.

These guidelines are based primarily on research with people exercising on land. The recommended exercise heart rates are chosen because they occur at the desired percentage of maximal aerobic power (i.e., oxygen consumption). Some authorities recommend that exercise heart rates be lowered approximately 10 beats per minute when establishing an appropriate intensity of training in the water.

Good aerobic fitness reduces your risk for coronary heart disease in a variety of ways, including reducing blood cholesterol and hypertension. A good aerobic exercise program is one of the best things you can do to improve your diving safety and enjoyment.

Muscular Strength and Endurance

Diving equipment is heavy, and you should be able to handle your own gear. This takes strength and muscle endurance. These qualities are best developed by repeatedly contracting muscles against some resistance (e.g., weights). For maximum benefit, the muscles should be exercised by mimicking the movements involved in diving-related tasks, but you should take care to exercise all of the major muscle groups for general well-being. For a good balance of strength and muscle endurance, resistance should be such that each exercise can be repeated a maximum of 10 to 20 times without rest. That is called *one set*. You should do approximately three sets of 10 to 20 repetitions maximum, 3 days each week, with a day off between exercise days.

PSYCHOLOGICAL FITNESS

Scuba diving involves not only your brains and muscles but also your attitudes, expectations, and personality. You must understand that athletic ability does not predict success as a scuba diver; rather, your attitude does. This chapter should provide an understanding of why some divers become nervous while diving, how excessive anxiety affects underwater performance, and the causes, symptoms, treatment, and prevention of excessive diver stress.

Good breath control and relaxation also are keys to safe and enjoyable diving. Too often, scuba divers are unable to relax sufficiently to control their breathing. Any changes involving tension, anxiety, or stress result in changes of your breathing pattern and rate.

Stress and Anxiety

Stress and anxiety are two very ambiguous and interrelated terms. Although they have extremely similar meanings, there are subtle yet important differences between them.

Stress is a state that evokes effort on the part of the individual to maintain or restore equilibrium. The agents producing such a state are called stressors and may be physical or psychologic. The response to stress may include many physiologic and psychologic reactions that attempt to restore the organism to a balanced state. This response is often referred to as the *fight or flight* reaction, because the individual responds by either attacking or retreating from the stressor.

Anxiety refers to that fear or apprehension that you experience in the face of a real or imagined danger. Some sports psychologists make a further distinction by describing that state of fear or apprehension experienced by an individual just before engaging in a risky or threatening activity as *state anxiety*.

Most scuba-diving literature uses the term *stress* when discussing the psychologic aspects of the sport. The term *anxiety* is often associated only with personality traits and is thought by many to be a phobic response. Thus, the term usually carries a negative connotation.

It is important to note that stress reactivity is perfectly normal and healthy. If the stress becomes extreme and continues unchecked, however, it may lead to panic, which can be dangerous. **Panic** is an emotional and volatile human reaction that occurs in the presence of a real or imagined danger. It is characterized by a total loss of logic and mental control. Panic has been suggested as the leading cause for both diver death and dropout.

Stress and Underwater Performance

Different individuals respond to identical stressors in different ways. Some enter rapidly into a stress state. Others show increased alertness and apparently improved performance. Still others appear to be immune to the stress-producing qualities of the environmental conditions.

While vulnerability to stress varies from individual to individual, so does the cause of diver stress. As a diver, you may be stressed because of physical risks, social risks, or both. Too often, divers are motivated by the fear of looking foolish rather than the fear of being harmed. In other words, you may be tempted to do a dive that you are not capable of completing safely rather than look foolish to your peers.

Human performance underwater is influenced by varying levels of psychologic stress. Stress before a dive can make the diver more aware of the problems and procedures of the dive, while overwhelming stress during a dive can disable the diver. A diver in the panic state becomes all action and movement, but he or she is not capable of thinking clearly. Panicked divers are almost impossible to assist and incapable of helping themselves.

Excessive stress, which can lead to a loss of control underwater, usually begins well before the diver enters the water. By being able to detect the telltale signs of extreme apprehension, divers may be able to help themselves avoid panic. Other divers also may be able to help them, either before the dive begins or in the water.

Psychologic Responses

Psychologic stress is accompanied by several physiologic responses, including increased heart rate, respiration, muscle tension, and perspiration. These increased energy expenditures lead to additional stress problems of hypoxia, hyperventilation, fatigue, and exhaustion, which in turn pave the road for panic. Changes in voice as well as shaking hands also indicate heightened levels of stress.

A stressed diver breathes more often and exhales more forcefully while underwater, so the frequency and intensity of exhaled air bubbles can alert other divers to a problem. Another easy symptom of high stress levels for an alert diving buddy to detect underwater is the "wide-eyed look." When divers are overly stressed while underwater, they will often open their eyes extremely wide and stare at a person or object.

In general, moderate amounts of stress actually may enhance performance. Optimum performance for complex tasks usually occurs when stress is neither extremely high nor extremely low. In some situations, high states of arousal enhance performance, but in others, the same levels of stress can be detrimental.

Relaxation techniques (particularly slow, rhythmic breathing exercises) can be effective in significantly reducing stress levels and thus improving performance. It is important to note that stress must be controlled, but not necessarily eliminated completely, to promote safe diving.

Causes of Stress

Stress can be caused by a number of factors, some of which can be controlled or minimized by the diver.

Physical Stressors

The physical stressors in the diving environment include cold water, limited visibility, strong currents, and rough waves. The physical state of the diver also may present stressors, including fatigue, cramps, rapid respiration, overloading (i.e., performing too many tasks at one time), and time pressure (i.e., racing against the clock). Lack of physical fitness and poor swimming ability are major contributors to these forms of stress. Additionally, the equipment used in scuba diving is generally cumbersome and can create its own stressors, including confinement or restriction of movement, negative buoyancy, fatigue, and discomfort.

Any one of these physical stressors may increase the stress level of the diver. When several physical stressors occur simultaneously, the diver may feel threatened, resulting in dangerously high levels of psychologic stress.

Psychologic Stressors

Peer pressure (i.e., the pressure placed by peers on fellow divers) keeps stress levels relatively high. Humans are very social beings, and peer approval is extremely important to most individuals. Pride in oneself and the respect of others is a goal that most people attempt to achieve. This self-imposed peer pressure can be significant, and when colleagues make statements such as "If I can do it, so can you," additional pressure is created. Failure in the face of peers is a definite ego threat. Any possibility of failure in the face of peers is also an ego threat. A damaging blow to your pride may be inflicted if you fail at a task or refuse to attempt or complete it. The combination of peer pressure and ego threat increases stress levels among scuba divers. Research findings at the University of Maryland have shown consistently that peer pressure, ego threat, concern about receiving a good grade and receiving the certification card—in short, pride—are the most significant stressors for college students in dive courses.

The possibility of underwater dangers also causes stress, although this takes a back seat to peer pressure. Humans know they are not fish, but they adapt very well to the underwater world with the aid of sophisticated equipment. Subconsciously, some divers fear drowning, because they are entirely immersed in the water for an extended period of time. They realize that if equipment problems arise, they do not possess the ability to breathe in the water without a mechanical device.

Psychologic stress produces a stress reaction in the body that in itself is often the cause of additional stress. This stress reaction is part of a feedback loop, perpetuating and augmenting the stress response (Fig. 4-28).

The physiologic symptoms of panic are similar to those of excessive stress. These symptoms include involuntary hyperventilation, the wide-eyed look, dilated pupils, excessive muscle tension, and increased heart and respiration rates. These responses lead to breathing difficulties, fatigue, exhaustion, and muscle cramps that add to the existing panic state and can easily cause drowning. Scuba experts refer to this progression as the panic syndrome, and it is the most significant threat to any diver in the water (Fig. 4-29).

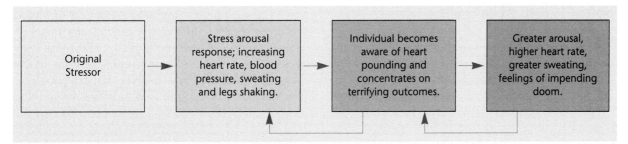

Fig. 4-28. Stress feedback loop.

Fig. 4-29. Panic progression chart.

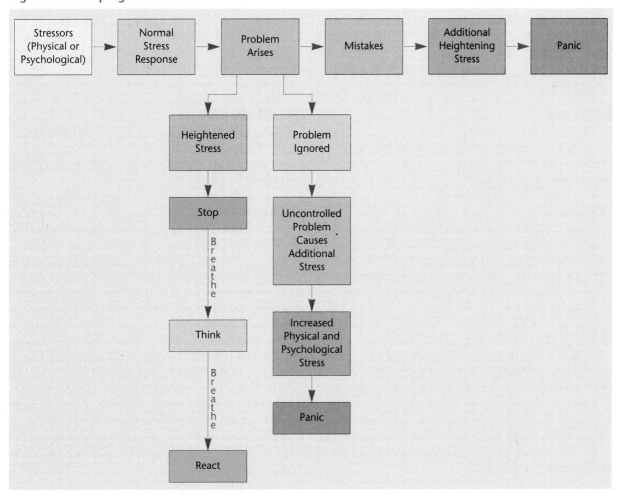

A Special Note on Breathing

Breath control and relaxation go hand in hand when it comes to diving safety. Breathing, which is perhaps the most critical stressor in diving, also is a major indicator of stress. Overbreathing while underwater clearly signals that you are being stressed. When you realize that your breathing rate or pattern has changed, this will cause increased stress, thus producing a deteriorating breath-control cycle. To control excessive diver stress and panic, good breath control is required.

BEHAVIORAL RESPONSES

Many dive masters and instructors rely on certain behavioral cues to detect nervous divers. You should learn to spot these signs of stress in yourself and dive buddy. These signs include procrastination, introversion, tardiness, errors, forgetfulness, and so on.

Before the Dive

Most behavioral patterns seen before a dive are forms of procrastination, which are defense mechanisms used to delay entering an uncertain or a threatening situation. Subconsciously, these nervous divers are seeking help. Examples of such behavioral patterns follow. You should be able to recognize these signs of predive stress.

Introversion

The diver who withdraws from the rest of the group and remains continually quiet throughout the day might be dwelling on the possible negative aspects of the dive.

Tardiness

Some divers will continually be late for several meetings convened the day of the dive. A diver who misses a ride to the dive site or the dive orientation meeting, is late picking up equipment, or is the last one to suit up might be procrastinating because of fear.

Mental Errors

Divers who are excessively nervous will often make simple mistakes before entering the water. Placing the regulator on the tank backward, putting the fins on upside down, and getting hair under the mask are just a few of the many mistakes that can occur. Some of these are innocent enough, but some divers may subconsciously make these mistakes to delay the dive.

Forgetfulness

There is much to remember for a scuba dive, and it therefore is easy to overlook something. When divers forget several items (e.g., bathing suit, mask, wet suit, money), however, this may indicate another type of defense mechanism being used by the nervous diver.

Extreme Cockiness

Many very competent divers are ashamed and embarrassed when they experience excessive apprehension before a dive. To mask this fear, they will often brag about how easy the dive will be or make a big joke about the entire experience. These people probably possess more anxiety than they would like to admit. Many "macho" divers, whether male or female, actually do not possess supreme self-confidence and are really nervous. The "true" macho diver is also a problem, because he or she often fails to follow safe diving practices.

Irritability

Some scuba students display a loss of patience and quick temper on the day of the open-water dive. Any slight change in plans or delay propels these divers into a mild tantrum. This sudden irritability is quite possibly a manifestation of stress that has built up in them, which they cannot mentally accommodate and therefore must impose on others.

During the Dive

Once in the water, a stressed diver may display other behavioral patterns. These include inefficient swimming, equipment rejection, fixation, and mistakes.

Inefficient Swimming

Rather than moving through the water smoothly and slowly to conserve air and energy, a highly stressed diver will swim erratically. Usually, the arms and legs will move wildly underwater as the diver becomes overly dependent on the muscles and fins to make progress. Inefficient swimming manifests itself in many ways. On the surface, a highly stressed diver may tread water extremely high out of the water, without the aid of buoyancy compensation. If an anchor or trail line is being used, the diver becoming panicky often can be found "clinging and clambering" on it. A diver in this state is simply too nervous to swim smoothly through the water. Swimming inefficiently leads to excessive fatigue, which often leads to panic.

Equipment Rejection

Highly stressed divers tend to lose faith in the scuba equipment. While on the surface, the diver may quickly and abruptly remove the mask and/or regulator. Underwater, the diver may continually readjust one piece of equipment (e.g., the weight belt) or frequently fuss with almost every item of equipment being used.

Fixation

Some highly stressed divers will not be attentive to or aware of what is going on around them and instead may concentrate or stare at one person or object. Also, a diver who appears to be listless or apathetic underwater may be a victim of excessive stress. Some experts refer to this concept as narrowing, which may be either mental or perceptual.

Human Error

When making procedural mistakes and judgment errors while underwater, a diver may become overly stressed and unable to function properly. A key contributing factor to panic is a mistake, either mental or physical, that is made by the diver while attempting to correct a small problem. After divers become overly stressed, they typically make mistakes that ultimately lead to a total loss of control. For example, the mistake that a diver might make in dealing with the problem of too much lead is either not removing lead from the weight belt or not using the buoyancy compensator. Failure to compensate for the excessive lead might lead to fatigue, cramps, and ultimately, panic.

Perhaps the most critical factor in the progression of panic after stress increases is whether a problem arises. If a problem does occur, it is usually accompanied by another increase in stress. Potential problems are many, and they may include being overweighted, losing one's diving buddy, becoming entangled, or running out of air. Fortunately, quite often no problems occur even though the diver is highly stressed. If a problem does not arise, no threat is posed to the diver. If a problem does develop, it must be confronted by the diver regardless of how insignificant it appears to be.

TREATMENT OF STRESS

You need not be a psychologist or counselor to treat and prevent diver stress. The techniques described here have been used and tested by scuba instructors and sports psychologists. Do not be afraid to give them a try!

Excessive stress displayed by divers is a problem largely because the stress reaction distracts them from the specifics of the dive.

If a diver displays the physiologic and/or behavioral symptoms described before a dive begins, the dive should be delayed or canceled. The stressed diver should be counseled with the aim of decreasing stress and increasing concentration on the task at hand. Several methods may be used to help a highly stressed diver.

Talk

Taking the time to explain all of the dive procedures in detail is perhaps the easiest and most efficient way to help the diver. While doing this, however, attention should not be drawn to the diver's nervousness. Discussions with the diver should be friendly, informative, and full of encouragement.

Accentuate the Positive

Highly stressed divers find themselves in a poor mental state because they dwell on the negative aspects of the dive. To combat this, focus verbally on all of the positive aspects of the dive (e.g., good weather, unusually good visibility, warm water temperature) while de-emphasizing the negative aspects.

Fight Distraction with Distractions

Excessive stress distracts the diver from functioning properly while underwater. One way to eliminate this distraction is to give the divers something to do while diving that will keep them occupied and distracted from their nervousness. Some examples are helping to collect samples, identifying certain forms of marine life, and keeping track of depth and time. The diver must not be overburdened with too many tasks, however.

Buddy-up Weak with Strong

Every attempt should be made to pair a stressed diver with a strong, confident diver, preferably a talkative and responsible person who will go out of his or her way to be helpful. As diver training continues, however, the weaker diver must be given progressively more responsibility to prevent him or her from becoming a dependent diver and, therefore, a liability. Eventually, diving buddies should share similar skills and abilities.

Use a Buddy Line

Even in clear water, a buddy line can help to reduce stress by increasing contact and communication with the dive partner. Actually holding the hand of the nervous diver also may be beneficial.

Offer Praise and Encouragement

The extremely stressed diver may be helped by you continually offering praise and encouragement, even when the diver makes mistakes. Accentuate the positive aspect of the diver's performance, and to build confidence in training, assign tasks that you know the diver can accomplish.

Remember that you should have a friendly and encouraging manner while attempting to help an extremely nervous diver. Above all, if you are unable to help a diver cope with excessive stress before the dive, you must have enough courage to tell that diver not to dive.

Perhaps the most efficient way to combat excessive stress while the diver is in the water is to remove the victim slowly and carefully from the situation. Another method of treating a stressed diver underwater is to have the diver stop, breathe deeply, and then think about the situation. (The diver can do this even if he or she is alone.) Gaining control during a stressful situation is extremely important. To stop the chain of events which may lead to panic, the following progression is recommended:

Stop • Breathe • Think • Breathe • React

Conscious breath control should permeate each of the three states.

Once on the surface, the victim should be made positively buoyant as discreetly as possible to avoid additional stress. This may be done by dropping the weight belt and/or inflating the bouyancy compensator. At this time, the victim may be treated for stress in the same fashion as during the predive state. Verbal reassurance, encouragement, and accentuating the positive while minimizing the negative aspects of the dive all aid in reducing stress.

Stress Reduction Methods

Because stress is caused by environmental, social, mental, and physical factors and it occurs in many different and varying situations, no single technique can be recommended to prevent, reduce, and control excessive stress. Divers faced with high levels of stress must develop a program of various techniques to learn to relax, to control stress, and ultimately, to improve diving performance. Once again, scuba divers should not attempt to eliminate all stress, which actually can enhance the dive by making it more exciting, challenging, and safer. This is because a moderately stressed diver tends to focus more on particular aspects of a dive than will a totally relaxed diver. Conversely, excessive stress will impair performance, thus making the dive more dangerous.

PSYCHOLOGIC EVALUATION

It is essential that every scuba diving candidate evaluate certain key personality traits before getting involved in the sport, and especially before attempting more advanced dives. When conducting medical examinations of potential scuba divers, physicians also should attend to the emotional and psychologic wellness of the diver. Some of the more important traits are discussed here.

Positive Self-Esteem

Positive self-esteem is a prerequisite for successful scuba diving. The ability to see oneself in a positive light and feel good about oneself is a must for scuba diving candidates. Individuals who downgrade themselves or are experiencing emotional problems should refrain from diving. While it is true that scuba diving can and does build confidence in divers, students with emotional problems tend to focus on the negative aspects of their lives, and the physical and psychologic demands of the sport only add to their problems.

Confidence

Confidence is closely associated with positive self-esteem, and it means believing in oneself to get the job done. Students who lack confidence repeatedly underrate themselves during scuba training, which erodes their ability to perform scuba tasks correctly. These students often program themselves for failure; poor self-expectation leads repeatedly to poor performance. All initial scuba certification courses require a simple prerequisite swim test. Scuba candidates should realize that anyone passing the initial swim test possesses enough skill to pass the course.

Anxious Reactive Personality

A few divers may be described as having *anxious reactive* personalities. These individuals exaggerate the existing stress and actually perpetuate it after the stress is gone. People prone to this reaction can become mentally and physically incapacitated in the face of even the mildest stressor. Needless to say, anxious reactive personalities probably should not engage in scuba diving.

The anxiety feedback loop that anxious reactive personalities often experience, can be related to "narrow spaces." The diving mask eliminates peripheral vision, the wet suit constrains and confines, and dives often occur in close quarters. Therefore, those who cannot deal with their claustrophobia should not dive.

Agoraphobia

Agoraphobia is an abnormal fear of crossing large expanses of land or water and fear of open spaces. This is also a contraindication to diving, because much of dive travel and hovering includes these factors.

Thalassophobia

Thalassophobia is an abnormal fear of the sea and deep water. Unless an individual can overcome this fear, diving is not recommended.

WOMEN AND DIVING

Scuba diving began as a sport by young, daring, mostly male adventure-seekers who somehow managed to survive homemade gear and lack of information. Since those days, diving has evolved into a recreational sport suitable for almost anyone with a love of the water and a quest to explore. Along with the new diver came the development of equipment to fit all sizes and sexes as well as to help ensure safer and more pleasurable diving.

One of the changes in the diving industry is the increasing number of female divers. Most certification agencies report that at least 25% of entry-level certifications are earned by women. As this population of divers grew, questions evolved that had never been asked by the male diving population, and data began to accumulate (Fig. 4-30).

Many topics in this section address questions that women may have had but were reluctant to ask in class. The information is suitable reading not just for women divers but for their male diving buddies as well. By addressing many of the questions that women divers have, both women and their diving partners can dive with more confidence and understanding.

There are some obvious physical differences between men and women, such as increased muscle mass in men when comparing men and women who are in good physical condition. This difference is because the male hormone testosterone, which is needed to produce large muscle mass, is only present in minute levels among women. Muscle mass is not the only determinant of strength, however. Women and older men increase strength more through neural adaptations than size increments. The biceps of a woman or older man may be larger or smaller than that of a comparably strong young male. All divers, male and female, will benefit from an exercise program designed to build strength and aerobic capacity.

One anatomic difference between men and women that is not so obvious is found in the cardiovascular system (i.e., heart, lungs, circulation). Because a woman's heart and lungs are smaller than a man's, the woman diver tends to breathe less air; however, her breathing is just as efficient. One nice consequence is that a woman's air supply may last longer than her male diving buddy's, and she may be able to use a smaller, lighter tank.

Menstruation and Diving

A common question asked by women divers is, "Can I dive during my period?" As with many questions in diving, if you feel well, go ahead and dive. If you feel ill during the first day or two of your period, however, you may want to postpone diving for several days. If you would participate in exercise and swimming activities, you also can dive.

If you dive during your period, you may wonder, "Will I attract sharks?" This question usually is not addressed in scuba classes, yet it is a concern for many ocean-diving women. According to Australian research, there is no evidence that sharks are attracted to menstruating females. Also, based on the results of questionnaires and surveys, sharks have posed no problems to the female respondents who dive during their period. So relax, concentrate on your dive and not the sharks (real or imagined), and enjoy yourself.

Fig. 4-30. Women tend to chill more rapidly than men and should wear appropriate thermal protection.

Birth Control and Diving

In the past, some speculated that because early forms of birth control pills impaired some women's circulation, these pills might pose a risk to divers. This theory has never been shown to be valid. Also, the birth control pills used now have much lower hormone levels than those previously held in suspicion. So, the common consensus is that women using birth control pills do not have any increase in their susceptibility to DCS.

Pregnancy and Diving

The Undersea Medical Society and major diving organizations currently recommend that a woman avoid scuba diving during pregnancy. This, however, is not necessarily based on the known facts but rather on what is not known about the issue. The statement is also a legal necessity. Lack of information has led to this absolute rule.

SUMMARY

A number of physiologic conditions are related to or caused directly by diving. It obviously is important that you understand these physiologic conditions so that you can prevent injury and harm both to yourself and to others. It also is beneficial to have a good working knowledge of diving physiology in case of a diving problem or incident.

The field of diving physiology is fascinating, and we are learning more every day. The ultimate goal is to minimize the risk of injury to recreational divers. You can help in this by learning all that you can.

SUGGESTED READINGS

- Bachrach AJ, Egstrom G: *Stress and performance in diving,* Best Publishing.
- Bennett PB, Elliot DH, editors: *Physiology and medicine of diving,* Best Publishing, 1982.
- Davis JC, editor: *Hyperbaric and undersea medicine,* Medical Seminars.
- Dueker CW: *Medical aspects of sport diving,* AS Barnes, 1970.
- Kindwall EP, editor: *Hyperbaric medicine practice,* Best Publishing.
- Lippmann J: *Oxygen first aid for divers,* JL Publications, 1992.
- NOAA Diving Manual: *Diving for science and technology,* US Department of Commerce, National Oceanic and Atmospheric Administration, 1991.
- Roydhouse N: *Underwater ear and nose care,* Best Bookbinders, 1981.

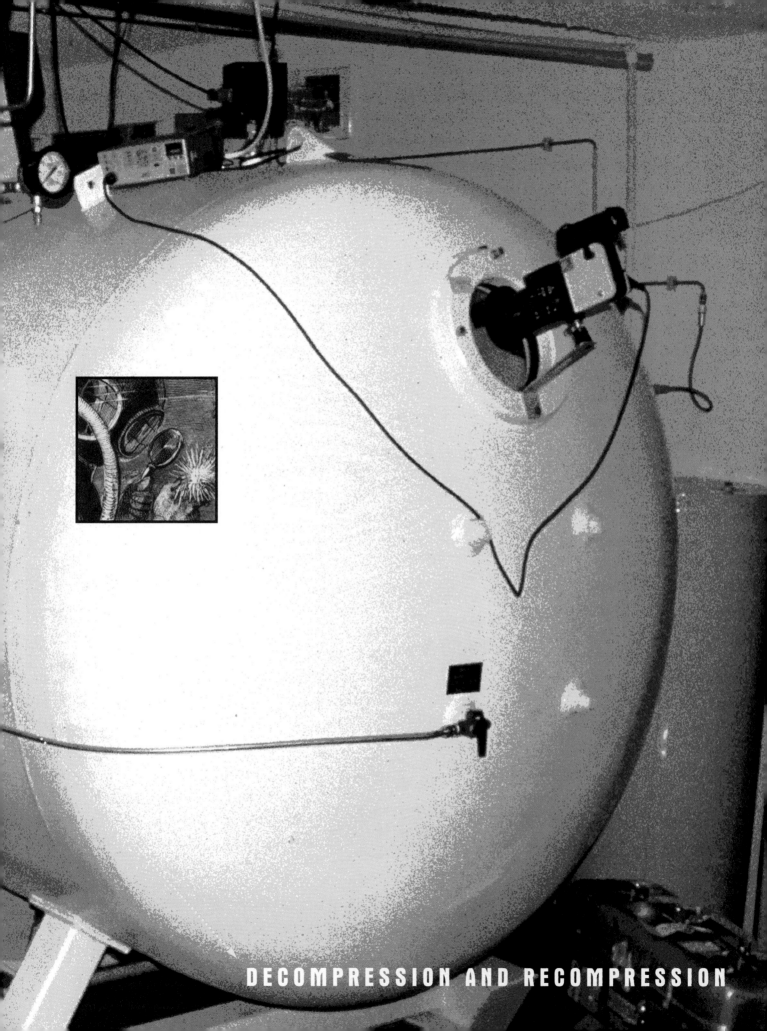

CHAPTER FIVE

DECOMPRESSION AND RECOMPRESSION

The study of decompression effects is a fascinating aspect of diving. The complexity of the physics and physiology involved, however, makes exact answers difficult to find. As a result, after over 100 years of research and evolution, there are different theories and tables around the world, many of which apply to different and highly specific circumstances. It is important to understand the background for some of the prevailing theories so that appropriate techniques can be used for your diving situation.

LEARNING OBJECTIVES

By the end of this chapter, you will be able to:

1 Correctly define the decompression and recompression terms presented in **bold letters.**

2 Define and briefly explain theoretic tissue (or compartment) half-times.

3 Briefly explain why NAUI uses the modified US Navy Dive Tables.

4 Meet the dive table calculation objectives listed in this section.

5 Briefly explain the proper dive table procedures for:
   - Cold or strenuous dives
   - Ascent rate variations
   - Surface interval of less than 10 minutes
   - Multilevel diving
   - Omitted decompression
   - Flying after diving

6 State the NAUI policy regarding Nitrox (mixed-gas) diving.

7 State two primary advantages of using a dive computer.

8 List several uses and names for hyperbaric chambers, and state at least two hazards associated with their use.

9 Define altitude diving, and list at least four procedural differences between diving at altitude and sea level.

DECOMPRESSION THEORIES

As you extend your diving range to foreign countries, you may meet other divers using unfamiliar tables. Supporting each of these tables is a different decompression theory, each based on research. Most of these theories began with the work of Hill and Bert in 1870 as well as with Haldane (in England) in 1908.

The Haldane Theory

Decompression sickness (DCS) is a serious bodily affliction caused by the formation of nitrogen bubbles in the body, which results from too rapid a reduction of pressure. This problem affects not only divers but also construction workers in bridge piers and tunnels. These laborers typically work in pressurized chambers known as **caissons**. One type of DCS also is known as **caisson's disease**, or **the bends**, because those stricken by the disease tend to walk with a stoop (when they can still walk).

When you dive, gases dissolved in the tissues in your body tend toward equilibrium with the surrounding gases. At the surface, all of your tissues are at equilibrium (i.e., as much gas is going in as going out), so the tissues have no net gain or loss of gas. When diving, however, much more gas enters the tissues than leaves, producing a net increase in the amount of gas in those tissues. This continues until the tissues are once again at equilibrium with their surroundings or you reduce the ambient pressure or surface, whichever comes first.

Haldane observed that animal subjects that were saturated at depths shallower than appoximately 33 feet of sea water (fsw), or 2 atmospheres absolute (ata), could be brought directly to the surface without showing signs of "the bends." This observation implied that tissues at equilibrium at 33 fsw could surface without incident. Surfacing from 33 fsw is a total pressure reduction of 50%. Extrapolating from this information, Haldane reasoned that tissues could always withstand a total pressure reduction of 50%, whether from 33 feet to the surface, or from 99 feet to 33 feet. This is the famous **Haldane ratio** of 2:1 pressure reduction. Later research proved that this ratio was too liberal, however, and it has since been modified to approximate 1.58:1 (Figs. 5-1 and 5-2).

The human body is not comprised of just one type of tissue. The heart, brain, muscles, bones, blood, and fatty tissues are different types of body tissue. Each behaves differently under pressure, taking up and giving off gases at different rates, but all tend toward reaching equilibrium with the ambient pressure. Rather than model the body directly, such as by measuring the gas uptake of human muscle and other specific tissues, a broad range of theoretic tissues or "compartments" was established to span the types of body tissues. These terms will be used interchangeably in this text.

The speed with which one of these compartments absorbs, or eliminates, gases is defined by its **half-time**. A compartment's half-time is the

Fig. 5-1. Summary of Haldane's ratio. As long as the calculated pressure in any tissue was no more than twice the pressure at the next dive depth, the diver could be allowed to proceed to the next dive step.

33 Feet	=	66 FSWA	
↑		↑	= 2:1
99 Feet	=	132 FSWA	

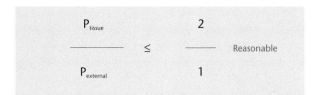

$$\frac{P_{tissue}}{P_{external}} \leq \frac{2}{1} \quad \text{Reasonable}$$

Fig. 5-2. Haldane's observation of a 2:1 surfacing ratio applied to a change of depths without surfacing. If this theory was reasonable, a change of depth from 99 fsw to 33 fsw should also be safe.

time required for that compartment to absorb or eliminate one half of the pressure difference between what it started with and the ambient pressure that it is exposed to. After the first half-time, 50% of the gas would be gone and 50% would remain. After the second half-time, 50% of the remaining gas would be gone, for a total of 75% gone. After the third half-time, 87.5% of the excess gas would have left the tissue. After six half-times, over 98% of the excess gas would be gone, which is close enough to 100% for normal purposes.

Haldane and his co-workers used tissue half-times, called "compartments," of 5, 10, 20, 40, and 75 minutes to model the human body. During the course of a dive, pressures in the various tissues were calculated. If the absolute pressure in any tissue exceeded that at 66 fswa, the diver would not be allowed to surface directly. For each diving depth, the maximum length of time before stops were required was calculated (Figs. 5-3 and 5-4).

Haldane also proposed a method of **stage decompression**, where the diver would ascend to the shallowest stop possible without exceeding

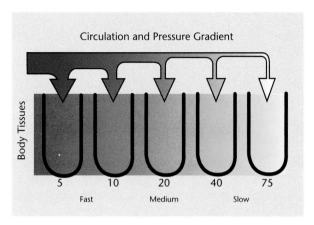

Fig. 5-3. A half-time is the length of time it takes a specific tissue to become 50% saturated with nitrogen. Fast tissues, such as brain and heart tissue, saturate rapidly; while slow tissue, such as bones, saturates slowly. Times for each type of tissue have been established and form the basis for modern decompression theory.

the 2:1 ratio. A diver would remain at that stop until enough gas left the body tissues so that he or she could ascend safely to the next 10 fsw stop or safely surface.

Tables based on these principles were produced for the Royal Navy. They also formed the basis for further work by other researchers.

US Theory

The US Navy used the Haldane Royal Navy tables until their own were developed in 1937 by the US Navy Experimental Diving Unit in Washington, DC. The first major difference between

Fig. 5-4. Uptake and outgassing in an exponential tissue. After six half-times of gas uptake, the tissue is 98.44% saturated at the external pressure. Similarly, after six half-times of outgassing, the tissue is very nearly saturated at the surface pressure, and the tissue has lost its memory of the dive.

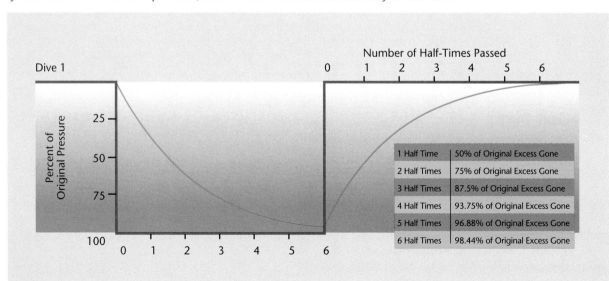

1 Half Time	50% of Original Excess Gone
2 Half Times	75% of Original Excess Gone
3 Half Times	87.5% of Original Excess Gone
4 Half Times	93.75% of Original Excess Gone
5 Half Times	96.88% of Original Excess Gone
6 Half Times	98.44% of Original Excess Gone

the two sets of tables was the use of different sur-facing ratios for the different tissues. Second, it also was decided that only the inert portion of the gas was important from a decompression view-point, because the oxygen portion was metabo-lized during pressure reduction. The third modifi-cation was the inclusion of longer half-time tissues in the model. By 1965, the US Navy decompres-sion model evolved through research and use (Figs. 5-5 through 5-8).

While the total pressure surfacing ratio is based on the total tissue pressure, the nitrogen pressure surfacing ratio is only concerned with the tissue nitrogen pressure. When breathing air, the nitro-gen ratio is 0.79 times the total ratio (i.e., the gas fraction of nitrogen). It is easy to figure out the maximum allowable tissue nitrogen pressure sim-ply by multiplying the nitrogen ratio by the 33 fswa surface pressure (Table 5-1).

The **M-value system** was developed in the model to address the concept of decreasing supersaturation ratios. Quite simply, the M-value is the maximum allowable nitrogen pressure in a specific tissue of the model. The nitrogen pressure surfacing ratio when breathing air is 0.79 times the total ratio, as used by Haldane. The surfacing M-value is determined by multiplying the nitrogen pressure surfacing ratio by the pressure at the sur-face (i.e., 33 fswa) (Table 5-2). Therefore, when div-ing to 60 feet (where the nitrogen pressure is 73.5 fswa), the 5-, 10-, and 20-minute tissues cannot exceed their maximums regardless of how long you stay down. The 40-minute tissue will reach its limit after 64.5 minutes. Rounding this value to the nearest 5 or 10 minutes produces the 60 minutes at 60 feet US Navy **No-Decompression Limit** (NDL). The 40-minute tissue is said to "control" this dive to 60 feet, because that tissue forces the

TABLE 5.1 SUMMARY OF THE HALDANE-ROYAL NAVY DECOMPRESSION MODEL	
TISSUE HALF-TIME	SURFACING RATIO
5 Minutes	2:1
10 Minutes	2:1
20 Minutes	2:1
40 Minutes	2:1
75 Minutes	2:1

end of the dive. The 40-minute tissue controls sin-gle dives using the US Navy tables for depths between 43 and 74 feet (Figs. 5-9 and 5-10).

The US Navy also made a major addition to the Haldane model with the concept of **repetitive div-ing**. Working surface-supply divers stay on the work site until the job is finished. The decompres-sion tables are their only limits, because their air supply is virtually unlimited. Only with the inven-tion of scuba in 1943 did the scuba diver, who bounced up and down to change tanks, become important. The Haldane tables gave a diver no credit for any time spent on the surface, but in the US Navy model, the diver is assigned to a letter group based on the pressure at surfacing in the 120-minute tissue. This group is based on 2 fsw per letter. So, a group-A diver has between 33 and 35 fswa total pressure, or 26.00 to 27.65 fswa nitro-gen pressure, in his or her 120-minute tissue. While the diver remains on the surface, the nitro-gen leaves the body, placing the diver in a reduced-letter group. On returning to the water, that new letter group is used to determine the residual nitrogen time (RNT) at the dive depth. RNT is based on the amount of nitrogen in the 120-minute tissue, and it is measured in minutes. RNT is considered to be time already spent at the repetitive dive depth (Fig. 5-11).

Fig. 5-5. Uptake of gas in Royal Navy model on a dive to 100 feet. The five-minute tissue is effectively saturat-ed at the dive depth after 30 minutes, six half-times. The 75-minute tissue, however, has barely added gas after 30 minutes, and will take a total of 75 minutes to just reach 50 feet. Eventually, all tissues will saturate, but this will take 7½ hours, much longer than a normal dive.

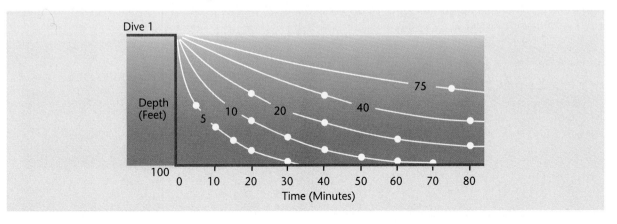

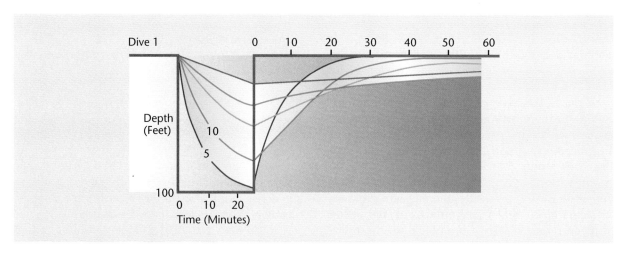

Fig. 5-6. Tissue pressures on a 25-minute dive to 100 feet according to the Royal Navy decompression mode. The first 25 minutes of the dive are not difficult to calculate. However, upon surfacing after 25 minutes, tissue tracking becomes complex, as each tissue has a different level of pressure on ascent, and outgasses according to its own half-time. It is unrealistic to keep these equations in your head, so tables summarizing them are produced.

British Theory

The Royal Navy theory also is a descendant of the earlier Haldane–Royal Navy tables. The Royal Navy tables use more conservative surfacing ratios than their US counterparts, thus providing less time at depth. They also provide an extremely conservative repetitive-dive procedure, because all repetitive dives are combined and worked as single dives regardless of surface intervals.

The Royal Navy tables were in use by the British Sub-Aqua Club (BSAC) as recently as 1972. Divers using the Royal Navy tables had to add bottom times or repetitive dives made within 12 hours of a dive to 30 feet or more. The total combined dive time and the deepest depth reached in either dive were used in the tables to determine the diver's decompression requirements. Once the diver had spent 60 minutes at 60 feet, he or she could not return to that depth without stage decompression until 12 hours had passed.

The 1980 BSAC *Decompression Table Workbook* uses the BSAC/Royal Navy Physiological Laboratory (RNPL) tables. These tables are based on a more recent theory than the Royal Navy tables, and they allow more time at depth than those tables and less time than the US Navy tables. A technique also has been introduced to allow some surface-interval credit for second dives, although divers with more than two dives per day must still use the "multiple-dive rule" of adding all bottom times and using the deepest dive depth. The BSAC/RNPL tables have been produced with very easy-to-remember decompression stop times. Unlike the US Navy tables, where the first stop over the NDL varies from 2 to 10 minutes at 10 feet depending on the dive depth, the first stop over the limit is always 5 minutes at 5 meters for dives shallower than 20 meters and always "5 at 5" and "5 at 10" for deeper dives in the RNPL tables.

Fig. 5-7. U.S. Navy modifications to Royal Navy theory. The U.S. Navy believed that longer half-times should be represented in the decompression model, so they added the 120-minute tissue. The 75-minute tissue was shifted to an 80-minute tissue.

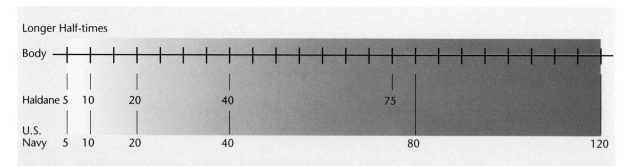

TABLE 5.2 SUMMARY OF THE 1965 WORKMAN - U.S. NAVY DECOMPRESSION MODEL			
TISSUE HALF-TIME	TOTAL PRESSURE SURFACING RATIO	NITROGEN PRESSURE SURFACING RATIO	SURFACING M-VALUE
5 minutes	4:1	3.15:1	104 FSWA
10 minutes	3.4:1	2.67:1	88 FSWA
20 minutes	2.75:1	2.18:1	72 FSWA
40 minutes	2.22:1	1.76:1	58 FSWA
80 minutes	2:1	1.58:1	52 FSWA
120 minutes	1.96:1	1.55:1	51 FSWA

Swiss Theory

The Haldane theory also provides the origin for the Swiss theory, as developed at the Laboratory of Hyperbaric Physiology at the University of Zurich. Swiss theory uses 16 tissues, with half-times of 2.65 to 635.00 minutes, to determine NDLs for single and repetitive dives as well as decompression requirements for longer dives. Unlike Haldane theory and its British and American descendants, Swiss theory extends to cover altitude diving. The M-values, or maximum surfacing nitrogen pressures, are no longer constant; rather, they are mathematic functions of atmospheric pressure. This further complicates an already complex situation, but tables and computers can be produced that are valid at reduced atmospheric pressures.

Canadian Theory

The Canadian tables published by the Defence and Civil Institute of Environmental Medicine **(DCIEM)** are not derived from the work of Haldane. None of these theories is an exact representation of the physics and physiology of the human body in decompression. Instead, they are a fitting of mathematic equations to a time–depth history and a symptom-free result. Haldanian equations use parallel tissues, each taking up and giving off gas from the ambient environment without regard to neighboring tissues. The DCIEM theory employs a set of serial tissues. The first tissue takes up and gives off gas from the environment, and the second and succeeding tissues take up and give off gas from the preceding tissue only and not from the ambient gas supply.

This serial model has been designed to produce results that are conservative compared with those of the US Navy tables, and tables produced from this theory are applicable to sport-diving situations. These tables were validated using Doppler measurements to detect subclinical decompression stress or "silent bubbles." The resulting tables should provide the best margin of safety based on human experiment.

The DSAT Theory

In 1987, Diving Science and Technology Corporation (DSAT) introduced a decompression model

$$\frac{P_{tissue}}{P_{external}} - \frac{2}{1} \qquad \frac{P_{TN}}{P_{external}} - \frac{1.58}{1}$$

Fig. 5-8. US Navy modifications to Royal Navy theory.

using the 60-minute compartment as the basis for repetitive-diving control. This model considers compartments of as long as 480 minutes. DSAT suggests that this is appropriate for recreational diving as opposed to the longer half-time tissue adopted for commercial and military diving operations.

The number of repetitive groups for dive tables developed were increased by DSAT to reduce the RNT penalties. Also, NDLs of less than the US Navy limits were incorporated into the DSAT tables as a safety factor. The net effect of the DSAT tables is less no-decompression time for the first dive, but longer bottom times for repetitive dives. Shorter surface intervals are required between dives. The DSAT tables have been tested and proven to be successful.

Dive Tables

Despite the numerous dive tables that are available throughout the world today, NAUI still recommends use of the US Navy Dive Tables, although others are approved for use if they are more conservative. More information and data are available for the US Navy tables than for any other tables in existence. It is strongly recommended, however, that limits below the US Navy NDL be considered when using the US Navy tables, and that a 3-minute precautionary stop at a depth of 15 feet be performed at the end of all dives below 60 feet in depth and for all repetitive dives. The stop time does not count as either bottom time or surface interval time (SIT). For the purposes of this discussion, the no-stop limit for a given depth will be those identified on the NAUI Dive Tables. For example, your NDL for 60 feet is 55 minutes (i.e., group I) rather than 60 minutes (i.e., group J). The maximum rate of descent is 75 ft/min, and the maximum rate of ascent is 60 ft/min. However, the US Navy is about to release new dive tables. NAUI has adopted the new ascent rate of 30 ft/min, and the depth of decompression stops should be at the level of the diver's mouth (Figs. 5-12 and 5-13).

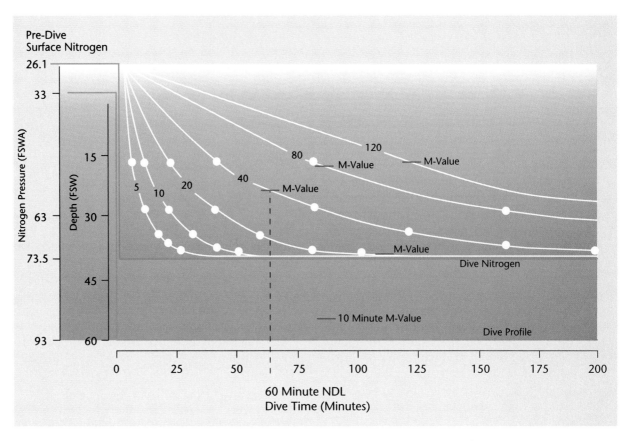

Fig. 5-9. When diving to 60 feet, where the nitrogen pressure is 73.5 FSWA, the 5- and 10-minute tissues cannot exceed their maximums, 104 and 88 FSWA respectively, regardless of how long you stay down. The 40-minute tissue will reach its limit after 60 minutes, producing the 60 minutes at 60 feet USN No-Decompression Limit (NDL). The 40-minute tissues are said to control this dive to 60 feet, since that tissue forced the end of the dive. The 40-minute tissue controls single dives using the U.S. Navy tables for depths between 31 and 60 feet.

Fig. 5-10. U.S. Navy no-decompression limits. When the U.S. Navy model is applied to normal diving depths, time limits for dives without decompression stops are produced. Breaking the table up into ten foot increments produces discrete steps rather than a smooth continuous function.

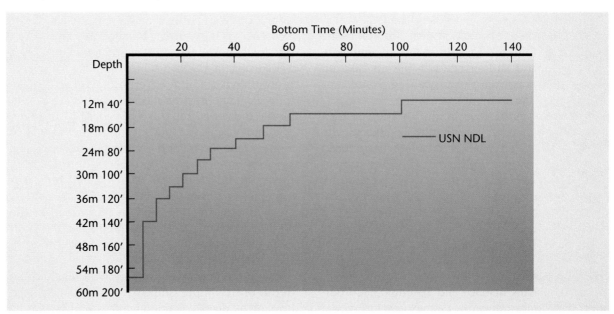

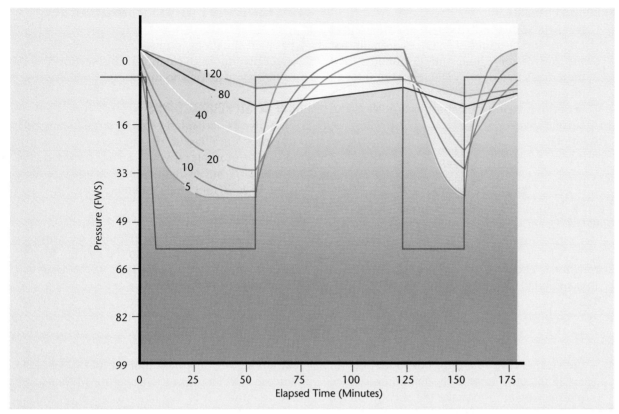

Fig. 5-11. U.S. Navy tissues on a safe repetitive dive. A second dive can be made safely for dive times shorter than the no-decompression limits by taking residual nitrogen into consideration during dive planning calculations.

As a NAUI advanced diver, you should be able to:

1. Determine the correct repetitive group designation for any single or repetitive dive schedule that is possible with the NAUI Dive Tables.

2. Correctly calculate the adjusted maximum dive time (AMDT) for a repetitive dive. For example, calculate that the AMDT for a group-E diver planning a dive to a depth of 70 feet is 19 minutes.

3. Correctly calculate the minimum surface interval that is required to make a repetitive dive of a given duration that does not exceed the maximum time limit. For example, find that the minimum surface interval required before a group-

Fig. 5-12. NAUI Dive Tables and Dive Time calculator.

H diver may make a 30-minute dive to a depth of 60 feet is 2 minutes and 24 seconds.

4. Correctly calculate the maximum depth allowable for a repetitive dive of a given duration. For example, determine that a group-F diver who wants to make a 20-minute dive may not exceed a depth of 50 feet.

Fig. 5-13. Consult the tables before each dive.

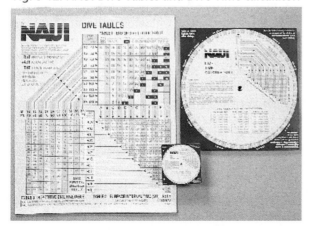

Sample Problems

1. A NAUI advanced diver dives to 99 feet (30 m) for 20 minutes, surfaces, remains at the surface for 1 hour and 25 minutes, and then dives to a depth of 50 feet (15 m) for 35 minutes (Fig. 5-14). What is the diver's repetitive-group designation following the second dive?

Solution:

$$\frac{99 \text{ ft}}{20 \text{ min}} = \text{group F.}$$

SIT of 1:25 = group E.

RNT for group E to 50 ft = 38 min + actual dive time (ADT) of 35 min = total nitrogen time (TNT) of 73 min

$$= \frac{50 \text{ ft}}{73 \text{ min}} = \text{group J.}$$

2. What is the AMDT for the second dive in question #1?

Solution:

AMDT for group E to 50 ft = 42 min.

3. If the diver in question #1 wanted to make the second dive to a depth of 70 feet (21 m) for 25 minutes, what is the minimum surface interval required to make the second dive a no-decompression dive?

Solution:

70 ft for at least 25 min requires group D.

SIT to attain group D from group F = 1:30.

4. If the diver in question #1 wanted to make the second dive 1 hour after the first dive, what is the maximum depth allowable with a no-required-stop dive time of 30 minutes?

Solution:

Group F with 1:00 SIT = group E.

First AMDT for group E equal to or exceeding 30 min is 50 ft.

If you had any difficulty working these sample problems, please refer to The NAUI Textbook for a review of NAUI Dive Table procedures.

Fig. 5-14. Question #1 Profile.

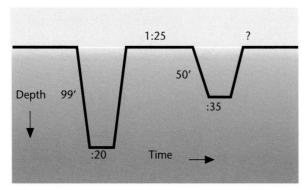

SPECIAL DIVE TABLE PROCEDURES

Certain situations require special procedures for correct dive-table calculations. This section identifies those situations and their proper procedures.

Cold or Strenuous Dives

If a dive is particularly cold or strenuous, *use the next greater bottom time* to determine your repetitive group. For example, if you are cold during a dive to 90 feet (27 m) for 20 minutes, consider the dive schedule as 90 feet for 25 minutes.

Ascent Rate Variations

Any delays in ascent during a no-decompression dive are simply added to the bottom time of the dive in minutes. Precautionary stop time can be considered part of the dive time to add a margin of safety, but this is not required. NAUI considers dive time to be from the time that you descend until the time that you surface from that dive. When using the dive tables, ascent times that are slower than 60 ft/min are of little benefit compared with a precautionary stop. When using a dive computer, it is essential to follow the ascent time that computer requires.

Surface Interval of Less than 10 Minutes

If the time between dives is less than 10 minutes, the two dives are considered to be a single dive with a schedule consisting of the deepest depth of either dive and the combined dive times of the two. The surface interval is ignored. An example would be a dive to 60 feet for 30 minutes followed by one to 50 feet (15 m) for 25 minutes. The dive schedule for these dives is 60 feet for 55 minutes (Fig. 5-15).

Multilevel Diving

The US Navy Dive Tables are based on the concept of spending the entire dive time at a single depth, but recreational divers seldom remain at a constant depth while diving. In this case, the US Navy tables charge you with more nitrogen than you actually absorb when diving at multiple levels. Procedures have been developed to manually calculate **multilevel dives** (i.e., a dive with varying depths) using the US Navy tables. Use of these techniques is not recommended, however, because they are complicated and errors easily made. Those who wish to avoid the "maximum-time-at-maximum-depth" penalty when diving at varying depths are encouraged to consider the use of a dive computer that continuously calculates the exact depth and the time spent there, thus allowing longer bottom times without decompression stops (Fig. 5-16).

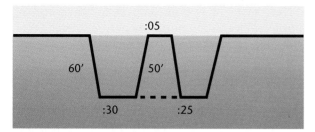

Fig. 5-15. Less than ten minutes SIT.

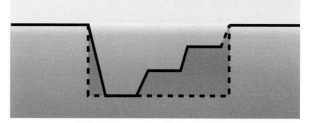

Fig. 5-16. Penalty time for a square-wave dive.

Omitted Decompression

The US Navy procedure for omitted decompression, which involves recompressing the diver in water, has been updated based on the conclusions reached by noted physicians and physiologists. The US Navy procedure specifies decompression at depths of 40, 30, 20, and 10 feet, with 1 minute between stops. This procedure has been replaced with the following: divers who have missed decompression stops are to remain out of the water, rest, breathe 100% oxygen if adequate supplies exist to handle an emergency as well, drink fluids, be monitored for signs and symptoms of DCS and be transported to a hyperbaric facility if symptoms of the bends are suspected. No exposure to altitude should be allowed for 24 hours.

The rationale for the new procedure is that bubbles form in the circulatory system very quickly on surfacing. In addition, there are air supply and thermal considerations. In-water recompression breathing air does not eliminate bubbles after they have formed, and DCS actually can result or be aggravated by in-water recompression. Breathing oxygen on the surface is more beneficial than the in-water procedure on air.

A diver who has omitted his or her required decompression should refrain from further diving for at least 24 hours. This rule holds even if no symptoms of DCS are evident.

Flying After Diving

Reducing ambient pressure to below that of sea level by ascending in an aircraft after diving can produce DCS. The following procedures are to be followed when you plan to travel by aircraft after diving:

1. The altitude of an unpressurized aircraft in which you are flying should not exceed 8000 feet, which is equivalent to the cabin pressure of a commercial airliner.
2. Wait at least 12 hours following no-decompression diving before flying. (Safety stops are to be not considered decompression for this procedure.)
3. Wait at least 24 hours before flying following any dive with required decompression.
4. Shorter, deeper dives rather than long, shallow dives are preferred when flying is planned. Short, deep dives are limited by the "fast" tissue half times. These tissues also outgas quickly, so your residual nitrogen is less when you fly than it would be for "slow" tissues that outgas slowly.

Dive Computer Theory

Dive computers differ from most traditional dive tables in that they can track multilevel dives rather than the square-wave profile the tables require. Most sport dives are multilevel, and significant increases in available underwater time can be obtained by using a computer. Dive computers use either a table-based or a model-based program. There are computers based on the US Navy tables, the Spencer No-D limits, the Swiss model, the Reduced Gradient Bubble model, and others. This wide variety of dive computers on the market can give a large range of decompression data for similar dive profiles. It is up to the individual diver to decide which is best for his or her purposes. The actual design and features of dive computers is covered in the Equipment section.

Nitrox Diving

The no-stop limits for various depths can be extended by using a gas mixture containing a higher-than-normal percentage of oxygen and a lower percentage of nitrogen. Because less nitrogen is breathed, less nitrogen is absorbed. Such diving is referred to as **Nitrox**, **oxygen-enriched air**, or **enriched-air nitrox diving**, and it is common in science and the military. During the late 1980s and early 1990s, divers engaged in "technical diving" began to use nitrox on a regular basis. Special tables, tank-filling equipment, and training are required for Nitrox diving.

The NAUI recognizes Nitrox diving as a specialty course. Divers should seek such training before using any such mixture (Table 5-3).

TABLE 5.3 COMPARISON OF DEPTH LIMITS FOR MAX. PO$_2$			
GAS	%N$_2$	%O$_2$	MAX DEPTH
Air	79	21	220'
Nitrox 1	68	32	130'
Nitrox 2	64	32	110'

Additional Dive Table Problems

1. Two hours after surfacing from a cold dive of 30 minutes to a depth of 80 feet (24 m), you plan a dive to 70 feet (Fig. 5-17). What is your maximum bottom time with no required decompression?
   Solution:

   $$\frac{80\ \text{ft}}{30\ \text{min}} = 80\ \text{ft}/35\ \text{min for a cold dive} = \text{group H.}$$

   2:00 SIT = group E.

   AMDT for group E at 70 ft = 19 min.

2. You spend the first 10 minutes of your first dive for the day at 110 feet (33 m), then another 20 minutes at 50 feet (15 m) (Fig. 5-18). What is your total ascent time from the 50-foot level and your repetitive-group designation at the end of the dive?
   Solution:

   110 ft/30 min = group J.

   Ascent time = 7 min of decompression + 110 s ascending = 9 min.

3. Your first dive is to 70 feet (21 m) for 28 minutes, followed by a surface interval of 1 hour and 30 minutes. Your second dive is to 50 feet for 35 minutes, followed by a surface interval of 9 minutes. Your third dive is to 45 feet for 35 minutes (Fig. 5-19). What is your repetitive-group designation after the third dive?
   Solution:

   $$\frac{70\ \text{ft}}{28\ \text{min}} = \text{group F.}$$

   SIT of 1:30 = group D.

   TNT for 50 ft = RNT of 29 min + ADT of 70 min (combine second and third dives, because SIT was less than 10 minutes) = 99 min = 50 ft/100 min = group L.

Note that this is a decompression dive and is shown for illustration purposes only.

4. As a group-D diver, you plan a dive to 75 feet (23 m). According to the procedures presented in this section, how many minutes may you spend on the bottom (not just underwater) during this dive? For this question, use a descent rate of 75 ft/min when determining the maximum time that you can spend on the bottom without exceeding the AMDT (Fig. 5-20).
   Solution:

Your descent should take 75 seconds (descent rate, 75 ft/min), and your ascent should take 75 seconds (maximum ascent rate, 60 ft/min). The precautionary decompression stop time is considered to be "neutral" time and is not counted. The AMDT for group D at 80 feet it 17 minutes. Subtracting the descent and ascent times leaves a maximum of 14.30 minutes that may be spent on the bottom during this dive. This is hardly worth the effort, so a longer surface interval or a shallower dive should be considered. This example illustrates the need to plan your dives. If you actually spent 17 minutes on the bottom (including the descent time), a decompression stop would be required rather than precautionary.

Aids to Decompression

A variety of equipment is available that helps you to make decisions about decompression. None of these devices, however, can make those decisions for you. You decide how deep to dive and how long to remain at depth. These two considerations are the most important in avoiding DCS. Although the devices mentioned can provide good advice, it is still your decision to avoid pushing the limits that will help you to prevent DCS.

Fig. 5-17. Question #1 Profile.

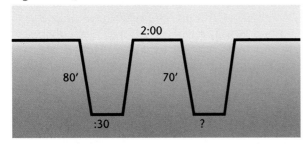

Fig. 5-18. Question #2 Profile.

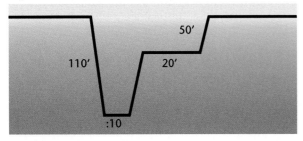

Fig. 5-19. Question #3 Profile.

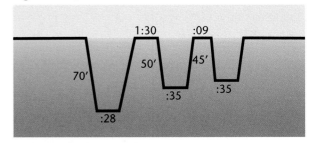

Fig. 5-20. Question #4 Profile.

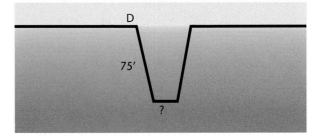

The most common aid to decompression, the dive tables, already has been discussed. US Navy tables are available in a variety of formats on plastic cards that you carry on your dive (Fig. 5-21).

Aside from tables, additional equipment is available for use in decompression calculations. Capillary depth gauges, diaphragm depth gauges, oil-filled depth gauges, analog watches, digital watches, analog bottom timers, digital bottom timers, and dive computers can be purchased at your local dive shop. These items are discussed in the equipment chapter.

HYPERBARIC CHAMBERS

The treatment for serious diving problems such as DCS or air embolism is recompression. This is carried out in a hyperbaric chamber.

The Sport Diver

Chambers are not often covered in detail during entry-level scuba courses, and divers usually have no firsthand contact with them until treatment is needed. As a diver, familiarity with chambers may alleviate any fears associated with them and better prepare you to deal with circumstances that might befall either you or divers you know.

One type of diver needing such treatment consists of those with an "undeserved" hit. This is the statistically significant group of individuals who do everything "by the book" and still suffer DCS or air embolism. There will always be a small, unpredictable incidence because of individual variations and undetectable abnormalities. This is the risk that all divers assume.

The "over-the-limits" diver falls into a second group, or those of "deserved" hits. These are divers who have taken their diving activities beyond the limits of their tables or computer. One example is diver who takes up deep, repetitive diving without adequate guidance. Another is the egotistic diver who, because of experience, thinks that the "odds can be beaten" and liberalizes or experiments with diving activities. Those using dive computers without knowing their limitations also are subject to decompression problems.

Another type of treated diver can be classified as "inadequately trained." In this group are the totally untrained divers who use scuba with no instruction. Unfortunately, these divers usually require treatment for air embolism secondary to breath-holding on ascent. Another example is the novice diver who knows enough to go diving but not to monitor depth–time parameters and avoid DCS. Whether

Fig. 5-21. A NAUI Instructor can demonstrate the use of the dive time calculator.

this lack of knowledge results from total ignorance or the inadequate development of good habits is irrelevant. Training must establish a general knowledge of what decompression is, internalize the importance of following decompression guidelines, and ingrain good habits that will optimize safety.

The following sections present an overview of chambers. They will familiarize you with some common vocabulary and start you on an exploration of what is available for treating sport-diver injuries.

General Characteristics

Hyperbaric chambers are pressure vessels. They contain a volume of gas that can be held at a pressure different from the ambient pressure. Chambers usually are cylindric in shape, with hemispheric ends. Some chambers that are used in commercial diving are completely spheric. These shapes allow hull strength to be achieved via the efficient use of structural material.

Certain characteristics are used for describing chambers. To relate and compare one chamber with another, diameter measurements are commonly used. The 54 inch–diameter chamber is often found in diving communities. It is a relatively small, economic chamber that is capable of treating persons with an inside tender and of switching personnel during the treatment if necessary. The 96-inch chamber may be found in large medical facilities, where its large size allows many patients to be treated simultaneously. A 26-inch chamber also may be found in medical facilities, where its small size allows one patient to be treated in a cost-effective manner.

In addition to using diameter denotations, chambers also are described by their rated working pressure, which is usually expressed in pounds per square inch (p.s.i.) or ata. Most chambers for treating divers are rated to a working pressure or 6 ata, or 165 fsw. Many chambers used for medical treatment are rated for 3 ata, or 66 fsw. These can be very useful for treating the more common type of DCS; most treatment of DCS as well as AGE is conducted at 60 fsw.

In addition, chambers can be characterized by the number of compartments and locks that they possess. **Locks** are doorways or access openings that are pressure sealed when closed. **Compartments** are spaces that can be pressurized independent of each other and of the ambient pressure. Compartments are separate enclosures sharing a common lock between them, and they are properly called "chambers" or "locks." A chamber with two compartments therefore might be called a multi- or a double-lock chamber (Fig. 5-22) with inner and outer doors and inner and outer chambers. If it is capable of containing more than one individual in the inner chamber, it could also be termed a multiplace, multilock chamber. Some chambers have small compartments for passing supplies in and out; these compartments are termed "medical locks." The doors (i.e., locks) on medical locks commonly open outward and therefore must be "dogged" closed. The doors (i.e., locks) of the large-occupancy chambers commonly open inward so that increased internal pressure works to seal the door closed.

Any given chamber will have a number of **penetrators**, or sealed holes through which various tubes or wires penetrate into the inside space. During chamber design and fabrication, penetrators will be incorporated to meet the needs of the chamber's anticipated uses. To increase and decrease the pressure within the chamber, penetrators with valve systems input gas supplies, and similar valved pipes are used to exhaust gases from the chamber. These pipes constitute the plumbing of the chamber.

Communications are established between the inside and outside of the chamber by wires introduced through a penetrator. Lighting and electrical cables also may penetrate the chamber hull. Monitoring devices may penetrate the hull to sense internal atmospheric conditions or detect changes in the status of occupants. Medical patients in small chambers may need drugs, fluids, or breathing assistance that is provided to them via special penetrators specifically designed for these purposes.

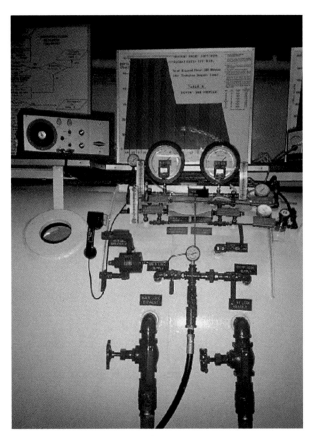

Fig. 5-22. A double-lock hyperbaric chamber with controls.

Compressors and Gas Sources

To pressurize chambers, compressors or sources of already compressed gas are needed. Backup systems (either compressors or gas cylinders) also must be present in case of a primary-source failure.

The pressures required for chambers are relatively low, but volumes of the gas involved are usually quite high. A typical 54-inch chamber's inner lock is some 8 feet long (the chamber is approximately 12 feet in overall length) and has a volume of approximately 120 cubic feet. High-volume, low-pressure air compressors are less expensive than high-pressure air compressors and are commonly used for chambers unless a high-pressure compressor is already present for other reasons. Just as with the compressors for scuba cylinders, chamber compressors must use special lubricating oils, and air intakes must be guaranteed clean, pure air. Proper maintenance is very important.

Cylinder banks of compressed air can be used as backup gas sources. Cylinder banks of compressed oxygen are used as sources of oxygen breathing gas in larger air-pressurized chambers. Liquid oxygen sources are commonly used to supply oxygen gas for hospitals and are the primary source of oxygen for many hyperbaric chambers.

Special gas supplies such as nitrogen, helium, and nitrogen-oxygen or helium-oxygen mixtures find special application in the commercial diving industry. These special gases usually are stored in compressed-gas cylinders and may be available for use in chambers if needed.

Chamber Types and Their Uses

A variety of chambers are available in the marketplace. Choices should be made based on the intended use and cost-effectiveness. In hyperbaric medical facilities, the number of patients that must be treated at one time usually determines the size of the chamber.

For the recreational diving community, pressure needs, size (i.e., room for inside tender and patients), and simplicity (i.e., getting the job done at minimal cost) are determining factors in chamber size. Because of infrequent use and little or no monetary reimbursement for treatments, chambers solely dedicated to treating recreational divers usually lose money, or break even at best, even with volunteer help or local governmental support. Ideally, the recreational diver would be treated at a large medical or commercial facility if one is close by; however, the unpredictability and long treatment schedules for injured divers can wreak havoc with routine, scheduled operations.

The "bent" recreational diver is not a welcome sight for anyone, including the diver. If the diver presents himself for treatment as soon as the symptoms occur, outcome is usually good. Treatment personnel receive a lot of gratification from knowing they have returned an individual to a happy, productive life. Prompt treatment is directly related to the efficiency in attaining lasting resolution. Unfortunately, this is not always the outcome. Divers should know what type of recompression facility is available to them in their diving area, how to contact that facility for consultation, and how to get there quickly for treatment.

Monoplace Single Lock

Small acrylic plastic, one-person, one-lock chambers can be found at some medical centers. Their normal use is for hyperbaric medical therapy of various conditions such as gas gangrene. They use an environment of 100% oxygen that is pressured to less than 3 ata. These chambers can treat less severe cases of DCS. They are not preferred for life-threatening DCS or air embolism, however, because of their pressure limitations (see the previous section). Often, these chambers are used for follow-up treatment of DCS in a fashion similar to their use in medical therapy.

Small steel chambers that are rated at higher pressures (i.e., 6 ata or higher) have been used to transport victims under pressure using a total air environment. To be useful, they must be capable of "mating" with the treatment facility's lock so that the victim can be transferred under pressure into the treatment chamber. Conceptually, such chambers are a holding vessel that is used to inhibit deterioration of the victim before reaching a treatment facility. Once locked into such a chamber, however, victims cannot receive hands-on care. A transport chamber that allows space for an inside tender is a better choice if available. During transport, victims continue to breathe air and therefore continue to onload nitrogen, thus compounding their decompression obligations. Severely ill divers who are being transported generally will benefit more from hands-on care and surface oxygen administration than they will from being in these small chambers.

Lightweight portable chambers such as the SOS Hyperlite, sometimes called "hyperbaric stretchers," are set up to pressurize a patient and provide oxygen therapy during transit. These chambers are small enough to pass through the main chamber hatch, where the patient is then removed under treatment pressure (Fig. 5-23).

Multiplace Double Lock

Large chambers with space for many people and both inner (i.e., occupant) and outer (i.e., passageway) compartments/locks can be found at larger hyperbaric medicine facilities. These are used in the medical therapy for various conditions. Commonly, such chambers are pressurized with air at lesser pressures (i.e., approximately 2.4 ata). Patients typically wear oxygen masks or hoods that provide 100% oxygen and dump their exhaled gases outside the chamber. Tenders in these chambers usually breathe the chamber air. Treatment of DCS victims in follow-up therapy would be similar to the medical therapy usage at such facilities (Fig. 5-24).

As mentioned previously, the 54-inch, multiplace double-lock chamber is used in some locations as the treatment chamber for diving injuries. It is often subsidized by government and/or dive operations, staffed by on-call volunteers, and is mainly a public-service operation in need of support and income. Some larger facilities have these chambers as a backup for their larger chambers.

Both small and large "livable" chambers are used in the commercial diving industry to provide surface decompression and/or habitat spaces for working divers and recompression for injured divers. If available, such facilities could also be

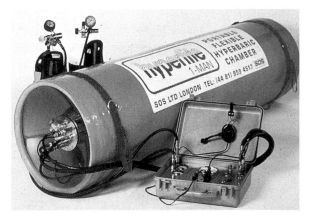

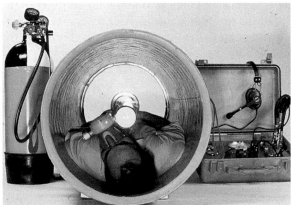

Fig. 5-23. Hyperlite portable chamber used in many areas of the world.

used for the treatment of sport-diver injuries; however, most commercial companies do not treat recreational divers (Fig. 5-25).

Divers seeking information about chamber facilities should be aware of the ever-changing status of their availability. Directories of chamber locations exist, but for a variety of reasons, a listed chamber may not be available for the treatment of divers at a given time. The Divers Alert Network is only a phone call away and can serve as an excellent source of information to assist with diving emergencies that require recompression.

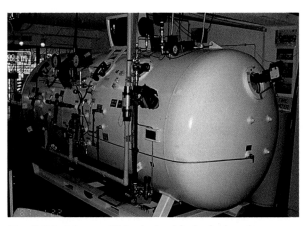

Fig. 5-24. A large, 60-inch double-lock chamber.

Chamber Operations & Safety Concerns

At any chamber, there are several tasks during a treatment. The number of actual personnel involved may vary from a few to several, but the tasks fall into recognizable categories (Figs. 5-26 and 5-27).

Operations Personnel

Supervisor. The supervisor controls the entire chamber operation, including the monitoring of compressed gas sources, integrity of all equipment, chamber pressure and gases, and the status of the operating personnel and treatment subject. The supervisor must be ready to intervene immediately during the normal course of treatment if necessary.

Timekeeper. Treatment schedules are based on depth and time, just as in a dive. To ensure proper treatment, the timing must be controlled. To document the treatment, any activities affecting the subject or any change in the subject's condition must be logged into the time record. Because inside tenders are "diving," their depth and time profiles also must be logged. The timekeeper logs all relevant events and times, and he or she keeps the treatment schedule "on time." Commonly, the timekeeper also is responsible for communications with personnel and the subjects inside the chamber.

Operator. This operator monitors and controls the chamber pressure. The chamber must be vented through with fresh gas periodically (i.e., "venting the chamber") as dictated by the chamber schedule. This is the chamber operator's job.

Tender. Scuba-diving patients can be very ill people. Proper monitoring and care often must be conducted with "hands-on" contact, and the inside tender is the "hands-on" person taking care of the recompression subject. This individual needs to have experience in acute care and is often a paramedic or a nurse. The tender is under pressure

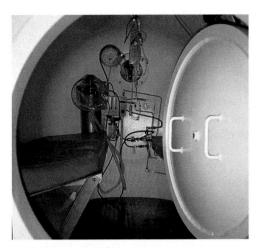

Fig. 5-25. Inside a double-lock chamber.

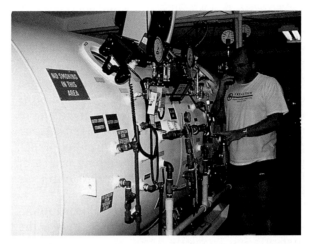

Fig. 5-26. Outside chamber operator.

with the subject and is "diving." On long recompression treatments, the tender has the potential of becoming a treatment subject as well if his or her own decompression obligations are not met. Chambers with multiple locks allow the switching of tenders to enhance both tender safety and subject care.

Physician consultant. In remote sites on commercial diving operations, recompression treatments are often run by established company guidelines, and a physician consultation is not ordinarily needed. Things do not always go as anticipated, however, and when the standard protocols fail to yield good results, diving medical officers (i.e., physicians) are brought in to direct modifications of the treatment schedules or to "lock in" and assume the monitoring and acute care of the subject. In the commercial diving industry, diving is well controlled and monitored; DCS usually is detected early and treated immediately.

Were the same true of the recreational diving industry, DCS would be rare and treatment outcomes better. Because of the variables involved with the recreational diver, consultation with a physician is very desirable. This physician should be versed in the diagnosis and treatment of diving-accident injuries and should have access to other consultants when necessary. Because of poor diving habits and delays in seeking or obtaining treatment, scuba diving–accident victims can end up with protracted courses of treatment and the need for long-term therapy and rehabilitation. Early physician involvement can sometimes improve outcomes.

Operational Procedures

In the United States, treatment schedules for DCS and air embolism are standardized in the US Navy format, so the operational procedures for most chamber facilities are similar. An initial

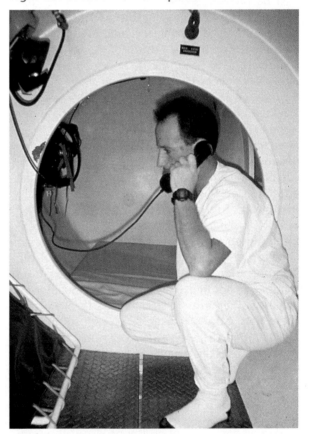

Fig. 5-27. The inside chamber tender can assist the patient and communicate with the outside tenders.

assessment of the victim is made to establish the severity of the problem at that point in time. If the condition is not life threatening, a more-thorough history and examination is conducted before placing the victim in the chamber. A nonlife-threatening recompression treatment schedule usually will be run at a pressure of 60 fsw using alternating oxygen and air-breathing periods. Typical treatments last between 5 hours to days. Treatments may go even longer, however, and can reach days of saturation in the commercial diving industry.

Specific Safety Concerns

Before beginning any treatment schedule, safety concerns must be addressed. These include fire, toxins, and patient condition.

Fire. Fire is a potential hazard because of the use of pure oxygen, particularly at the increased pressures involved. If the total chamber environment is oxygen, as in monoplace medical chambers, the problem is most significant. If an air-filled multiplace chamber with oxygen-breathing masks or hoods incorporating "overboard dumps" is involved, the problem is still a concern.

Chambers can be equipped with fire suppression systems to dowse fires, but prevention is the first priority. To create a fire, three ingredients must be present: a burnable material, an oxygen-like supporter of combustion, and an ignition source. To reduce the risk of chamber fire, as many of these elements as possible are controlled. Chambers, gas equipment, and anything that enters the chamber is kept "oxygen clean" (i.e., all greases, oils, and so on are eliminated). Combustibles are minimized within the chamber by paying special attention to clothing and supplies. Sources of ignition are eliminated by keeping electronic devices and electrical circuits either outside of the chamber or completely sealed. Lighting is through portholes or fiber-optic cables where possible. All who enter the chamber are inspected for potential hazards. In chambers where oxygen-breathing equipment is used, overboard dumps are incorporated to direct exhaled gas out of the chamber, thereby removing excess oxygen from chamber. In addition, oxygen analyzers monitor for oxygen spillage into the chamber. In chambers where pure oxygen is used to pressurize and run the chamber, the elements of combustibles and ignition sources are the only controllable factors.

Toxins. The pressurized gases that chamber occupants breathe sometimes can be "toxic." For example, oxygen at increased pressures can cause seizures. Individuals usually can tolerate 100% oxygen at pressures of 60 fsw or less if they are resting, but any physical exertion increases the likelihood of a seizure, as does an increase in body temperature, carbon dioxide buildup, and mental agitation. The dosage of oxygen required is controlled by the total chamber pressure and the subject's time on oxygen. Seizure-sensitive individuals may not tolerate the usual protocols, and such instances must be dealt with accordingly.

A buildup of carbon dioxide in the chamber from the occupant's exhaled gases can cause from very minor symptoms to death, depending on the levels. To eliminate the problem of carbon dioxide buildup problem, the chamber is "vented" periodically. To accomplish this, fresh gas is blown into the chamber from the compressor or cylinder bank at the same time as the chamber gas is exhausted to the outside. These gas flows must be matched, or an overall pressure change within the chamber will occur. Venting is done periodically for short intervals based on a schedule that is calculated for the individual chamber and its number of occupants. In addition to cleaning the chamber of carbon dioxide, venting also helps to control other occupant waste gases as well as humidity, thereby assuring overall comfort for those inside.

Carbon monoxide and other gas contamination can be a rare problem in chambers, just as in scuba air. This problem can be prevented by good compressor maintenance and inspections. Air intakes should be inspected before each run to ensure that chemicals, solvents, paints, lubricants, and so on have not been used or placed near the intake. Compressed cylinder gas purchased from outside sources should be at least smelled and tested for oxygen concentration before use.

Patient Condition. One of the major concerns during any recompression treatment is the safety and welfare of the subject being treated. Even an individual with mild DCS can become disoriented, fearful, panicky, or manifest combative behavior inside the chamber. Chamber personnel are aware of such possibilities and make every effort to inform, forewarn, and comfort individuals under their care. Progression (i.e., worsening) of a patient's symptoms during treatment is a negative sign, and treatment schedules often must be modified to control the situation. Similarly, regression of symptoms during attempted reductions in chamber pressure may necessitate schedule extensions or a different schedule.

As mentioned previously, oxygen can cause seizures. Should a seizure occur, the tender must remove the subject's oxygen mask and prevent injury. Oxygen seizures usually are brief and require no specific treatment other than removal of the oxygen. The inside tender is very important in severe diving-accident cases, and he or she is the most sensitive monitor of subject status and the means of treating or controlling changing conditions inside the chamber.

Chamber Operator and Physician Needs

As a patient's friend or as a patient yourself, you can do a great deal to help the chamber personnel and physician. The first and most significant step is to plan for safe dives, including accident-management plans for evacuation to the nearest recompression facility. Log your dives, and know your options for emergency treatment.

Second, seek aid when you even think some-one (including *you*) has DCS or air embolism. Do not attempt to treat DCS by returning to the water. In-water recompression treatment using air is extremely dangerous, and it is not recommended. In-water treatment using special equipment, special gas supplies, and special expertise has been done; however, it is used only as a last resort even by those trained and prepared to do so in remote dive operations. As a sport diver, you must seek chamber treatment. Breathing oxygen on the scene and during transport to a chamber is your first aid of choice. (Please refer to other chapters for the diagnosis of DCS and air embolism.)

Third, cooperate with chamber personnel by doing what is asked of you, and be honest in all answers to their questions. Do not let your ego or image get in the way of good diagnosis and treatment. If you made one error, do not compile the problem with rationalization or denial. Be helpful to yourself by letting others help you.

Finally, understand and have compassion for the chamber personnel and consultants. These people are trying to be helpful, are often volunteers, and have stresses and tasks associated with their function that you may have little or no perception of during the course of treatment itself (Fig. 5-28).

A Chamber Experience

If you have the opportunity to take a "chamber ride," do so. There is nothing that will impress you more than being inside a chamber during pressurization, venting, and ascent. Many chamber crews who are active in treating divers will organize orientation sessions for interested groups. Although individual chambers differ, there are elements that most experiences will have in common.

One is noise. Chambers are noisy. Most are steel "bells" that reverberate when struck by dropped objects and general activities. Gases rush in through small orifices during pressurization and venting, and unless muffled, the noise can be too loud to talk over. In addition, as the gas density increases with the increasing pressure, voices become altered and sometimes difficult to understand.

Other obvious sensations occur from the rapid change in temperature and humidity with pressure changes. During pressurization, the chamber warms and feels stuffy. During ascent, the chamber cools and "clouds" of humidity can form.

If you are in a chamber for very long, the confinement and realization of your loss of control over what is happening can affect you. If you are in for treatment, however, these feelings will be outweighed by those of the concern and humanity that will surround the whole "caring" experience.

A chamber ride is not a treatment. It will, however, yield an idea of what treatment would be like.

Summary

Divers need chambers, which come in various shapes and sizes and often serve routine functions unrelated to treating the victim of a sport-diving accident. They are complex systems that require expertise to run and maintain. You should be prepared to seek one out whenever you even think the need exists. Leave your ego and image behind when you seek such aid.

ALTITUDE DIVING

Ⓦhile you may believe that you will never dive at altitudes above sea level, the potential for underwater experiences using scuba at altitude is great. As access increases, we all may be able to travel to moderate- or higher-altitude dive sites. A high-altitude dive may be defined as any that is conducted at an altitude of greater than 1000 feet. At present, many high-altitude freshwater lakes, ponds, mine shafts, caverns, caves, and rivers are regularly dived by recreational scuba divers.

As an advanced scuba diver, you should know how to dive at altitudes beyond sea level. Further, your safety and enjoyment depend on your ability to use the dive tables correctly under such circumstances. Make sure that you are trained for altitude diving before you use the information included here.

Perhaps the most significant differences that you will encounter at higher altitudes are the variances in buoyancy control, in the use and types of dive tables, and in your depth-gauge readings. In addition, you should be aware of the special techniques and potential hazards that are involved at higher altitudes. This section provides information for use in diving at sites above sea level.

Fig. 5-28. Large hospital hyperbaric facilities are often well staffed and equipped.

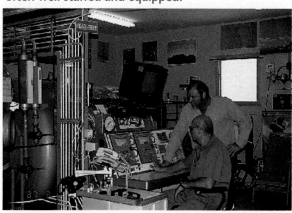

Differences at Higher Altitudes

What are the primary differences you will face when participating in altitude diving, and how can you safely deal with them? All altitude diving is done at least 1000 feet above sea level, and it differs from ocean diving in two important ways:

1. Freshwater (almost all altitude diving is in freshwater) is less dense than seawater.
2. Atmospheric pressure at altitude is less than at sea level.

As you have learned already, the lower density of freshwater results in your being less buoyant and thus requiring less weight on your weight belt. Also, the lower density of freshwater causes your depth gauge to read differently than in seawater. The reduced atmospheric pressure at altitude adds to the variance in depth-gauge readings from those taken at sea level. Finally, and most importantly, the lower atmospheric pressure at higher altitudes radically increases your susceptibility to DCS if you do not follow special altitude dive tables.

The second part of the question deals with how to avoid the potential problems associated with diving at higher altitudes. Obviously, you should decrease the amount of weight that you use to establish neutral buoyancy in water. Additionally, to avoid problems associated with potential DCS, you should adjust your depth gauges to compensate for the increased altitude so that they will display the actual diving depth. Some dive computers automatically compensate for altitude diving, although they may not necessarily account for diving on the first day of arrival at altitude. Before using your comuter, check the manual to see how it treats this situation.

Because you are effectively heavier when equipped with normal, open-water equipment at altitude and in fresh water than when diving in seawater, weight must be removed if true neutral buoyancy is to be achieved. Typically, you will need to remove 2.5% of the normal total seawater weight of your body plus all equipment, which is usually from 3 to 8 pounds. If you dive without a wet suit or weight belt in the ocean, you will need to add air to your buoyancy compensator for altitude diving. For example, if you weigh 150 pounds and have 50 pounds of equipment on when diving at sea level in saltwater, you will need to remove 5 pounds from your weight belt to approximate neutral buoyancy in freshwater.

Procedures for Altitude Diving

The procedures for altitude diving obviously vary from those used for diving in seawater and at elevations below 1000 feet. These differences in diving practice, however, are not as difficult to master as you might imagine, and with proper training and equipment, any qualified open-water scuba diver can enjoy scuba diving at altitude. Table 5-4 summarizes the necessary procedures for use by saltwater divers when diving at altitude.

Having made these changes in preparation for your dive, it is important that you clearly understand the effects of reduced atmospheric pressure at altitude. Table 5-5 includes information regarding the changes in atmospheric pressure at altitudes from sea level to 15,000 feet, tabulated in increments of 1000 feet. You should be aware that the closed-cell neoprene of your wet suit will expand as the suit is taken to higher altitude, thus making it more buoyant. This buoyancy increase is small, but it may be noticeable.

It should be clear at this point that all altitude dives must be calculated formally, especially when diving at higher altitudes. In no circumstance should you "guess," even if the dive is planned to be relatively short and shallow. Another reason to

TABLE 5.4 SUMMARY OF PROCEDURES FOR DIVING AT ALTITUDE

PROCEDURAL CHANGE	RULE
1. Weight belt adjustment	Remove 2 1/2% of total weight of diver and ocean gear from weight belt (3 to 8 lbs.)
2. Flying after an ocean dive	Wait 24 hours before flying following dives that do not exceed time limits and even longer following any dives requiring decompression.
3. Diving on same day as arrival at altitude	Treat as a repetitive dive. Adopt repetitive dive group letter G on arrival for elevations up to 10,000 feet.
4. Decompression	• If dive is not too deep, use capillary depth gauge readings directly with the U.S. Navy Dive Tables to determine allowable bottom time. Use readings directly for 60 ft/min ascent rate and depths of any decompression stops. • If dive is deep or if capillary guarge is not available, use any other depth gauge and: — determine equivalent ocean depth, ascent rate and depth of any decompression stops from the altitude dive tables. — apply the equivalent ocean depth to the U.S. Navy Dive Tables to obtain allowable bottom time, and decompress accordingly.
5. Depth gauge correction	• For capillary gauges, if above 3,000 feet, subtract 3% of reading per 1,000 feet of elevation.

be especially careful in dive planning and execution at higher altitudes is that most dive sites are located a great distance from hyperbaric facilities. If an accident occurs, you might not be able to reach a recompression chamber in a reasonable amount of time.

Among the precautions you should take when diving at altitude are:

1. If you recently made an ocean dive, you should wait at sea level for at least 12 hours before ascending to altitude. As in the "flying after diving" procedures that you learned in your initial open-water courses, you must be aware of the potential problem of bends resulting from the lower atmospheric pressure at altitude or the lower cabin pressure in the airplane transporting you to the altitude-diving site.

2. You should consider yourself to be in a repetitive-dive situation, even though you have not made a dive, when you first reach any higher-altitude dive site. This circumstance will require you to assume that you are in a higher group-letter designation depending on the altitude to which you have arrived. This is because of the nitrogen accumulation in your body resulting from the altitude change, which will require several hours to normalize (Table 5-6).

3. You should never use unmodified standard dive tables (e.g., NAUI, US Navy, or others) when diving at altitude. Further, you must have the information to modify the tables correctly so that you can accurately determine your allowable bottom time and ascent rate for the altitude at which you dive. All standard tables are based on "seawater at sea level" calculations, and altitude dives are vastly different from the conditions on which the standard dive tables are based.

The following information must be obtained to use dive tables at higher altitudes:

1. The equivalent ocean depth of your dive.
2. The allowable ascent rate of your dive.
3. The depth of any (potential) decompression stops that you may need to make.

A capillary depth gauge can be used on shallow- to medium-depth dives. Capillary depth-gauge readings actually are greater than the true depth, and they can be used without correction to determine your allowable bottom time and decompression stops. In addition, you can use the ascent rate that is indicated by the capillary-depth gauge at any altitude and in freshwater. For example, at any altitude, a capillary depth-gauge reading of 40 feet may be interpreted as 40 feet on no-decompression time available on the first dive. Further, you may then read the gauge directly for any indicated decompression stops; if a 10-foot stop is required, you may correctly stop at the capillary depth-gauge reading of 10 feet to accomplish the necessary stop.

Should you choose to use an oil-filled depth gauge, a rather complex procedure is required to reduce the ascent rate, both actual and gauge indicated, to less than 60 ft/min. Table 5-7 yields the equivalent freshwater ascent rates at altitude for the ocean rate of 60 ft/min. If you use a dive computer, it must be suitable for the altitude where you will dive. Be sure to use your backup devices if using a computer.

Table 5-8 shows the theoretic depth at altitude for the actual diving depth in freshwater. This illustrates the tables developed by ER Cross for calculation purposes when diving at altitude. These calculations are based on US Navy tables and must be used with them for accuracy and safety. Decompression stops must be modi-

TABLE 5.5 ATMOSPHERIC PRESSURE VS. ALTITUDE	
ALTITUDE, FEET	ATMOSPHERIC PRESSURE PSIA
Sea Level	14.70
1,000	14.17
2,000	13.66
3,000	13.17
4,000	12.69
5,000	12.23
6,000	11.78
7,000	11.34
8,000	10.92
9,000	10.51
10,000	10.11
11,000	9.722
12,000	9.349
13,000	8.987
14,000	8.636
15,000	8.297

TABLE 5.6 REPETITIVE DIVE GROUP ON ARRIVAL AT ALTITUDE FROM SEA LEVEL	
ELEVATION, FEET	GROUP LETTER ON ARRIVAL
1,000	B
2,000	B
3,000	C
4,000	D
5,000	D
6,000	E
7,000	E
8,000	F
9,000	F
10,000	G
11,000	G
12,000	G
13,000	H
14,000	H
15,000	I

TABLE 5.7 MODIFIED FRESH WATER ASCENT RATES EQUIVALENT TO AN OCEAN RATE OF 60 FT./MIN.

ALTITUDE, FEET	PROPER ACTUAL (NOT INDICATED) ASCENT RATE, FEET PER MINUTE
0	61.6
1,000	59.4
2,000	57.2
3,000	55.2
4,000	53.2
5,000	51.2
6,000	49.4
7,000	47.5
8,000	45.8
9,000	44.0
10,000	42.4
11,000	40.7
12,000	39.2
13,000	37.7
14,000	36.2

TABLE 5.9 MODIFIED FRESH WATER DECOMPRESSION STOPS CORRESPONDING TO STANDARD OCEAN STOP DEPTHS

ALTITUDE, FEET	PROPER ACTUAL DEPTH OF INDICATED OCEAN STOP, FT.		
	STAND. 10 FT. STOP	20 FT. STOP	30 FT. STOP
0	10.3	20.6	30.8
2,000	9.6	19.1	28.7
4,000	8.9	17.7	26.6
6,000	8.2	16.5	24.7
8,000	7.6	15.3	22.9
10,000	7.1	14.1	21.2
12,000	6.5	13.1	19.6
14,000	6.0	12.1	18.1

fied for freshwater and altitude. Table 5-9 provides the information that allows you to calculate the proper decompression stop depths that correctly correspond to the standard ocean stop depths.

Typically, you will need your depth gauge primarily for determining decompression information; however, some altitude dive tables require actual depth information. Should you use such tables, you must determine the actual depth, which will require depth-gauge correction.

How do various gauges differ from true depth in their readings when used underwater? When using the capillary depth gauge to determine true depth, you simply subtract 3% of the actual reading per 1000 feet of elevation at the dive site. This correction is not needed at 1000 feet, but it is accurate for use at sites located above 3000 feet. For all other types of conventional depth gauges, but not dive computers, you should add 1 foot per 1000 feet of elevation, then add 3% of the gauge reading. While this procedure has a small inherent error, it is useful for all routine altitude-diving calculations. To assist you in calculating true (i.e., actual) depths when diving in freshwater at high altitudes, use Tables 5-10 (corrections for noncapillary gauges) and 5-11.

TABLE 5.8 THEORETICAL DEPTH AT ALTITUDE FOR GIVEN ACTUAL DIVING DEPTH IN FRESH WATER

ACTUAL DEPTH	THEORETICAL DEPTH AT VARIOUS ALTITUDES (IN FEET)									
	1000	2000	3000	4000	5000	6000	7000	8000	9000	10000
0	0	0	0	0	0	0	0	0	0	0
10	10	11	11	12	12	12	13	13	14	15
20	21	21	22	23	24	25	26	27	28	29
30	31	32	33	35	36	37	39	40	42	44
40	41	43	45	46	48	50	52	54	56	58
50	52	54	56	58	60	62	65	67	70	73
60	62	64	67	69	72	75	78	81	84	87
70	72	75	78	81	84	87	91	94	98	102
80	83	86	89	92	96	100	103	108	112	116
90	93	97	100	104	108	112	116	121	126	131
100	103	107	111	116	120	124	129	134	140	145
110	114	118	122	127	132	137	142	148	153	160
120	124	129	134	139	144	149	155	161	167	174
130	135	140	145	150	156	162	168	175	181	189
140	145	150	156	162	168	174	181	188	195	203

TABLE 5.10 CORRECTION FOR BOURDON AND BEL-LOWS DEPTH GAUGES	
ALTITUDE, FEET	CORRECTION TO ADD TO GAUGE READING, FEET
Sea level	0
1,000	1.2
2,000	2.4
3,000	3.5
4,000	4.6
5,000	5.7
6,000	6.7
7,000	7.8
8,000	8.7
9,000	9.7
10,000	10.6
11,000	11.5
12,000	12.3

True depth is obtained by increasing the depth as corrected by this table by a further 3%.

TABLE 5.11 CAPILLARY GAUGE CORRECTIONS	
ALTITUDE, FEET	FACTOR TO MULTIPLY GAUGE READING TO DETERMINE ACTUAL, FRESH WATER DEPTH, FEET
Sea level	1.026
1,000	0.989
2,000	0.953
3,000	0.919
4,000	0.885
5,000	0.853
6,000	0.822
7,000	0.791
8,000	0.762
9,000	0.733
10,000	0.705
11,000	0.678
12,000	0.652

SUMMARY

Special care is required when diving at higher altitudes in freshwater. You should always observe the explicit altitude limits that are imposed by the tables included in this chapter and not "guess" at any information regarding an altitude dive.

Diving at higher altitudes can be a challenging and rewarding experience—if you follow the guidelines. When contemplating such dives, you should always contact the instructors or dive businesses located in the area of the planned dive to determine local rules and suitable sites.

SUGGESTED READINGS

- Buhlman AA, Michel GP: *Decompression: decompression sickness*, Springer-Verlag, 1984.
- Lewbel GS: *The decompression workbook: a simplified guide to understanding decompression problems*, Pisces Books, 1984.
- Loyst K: *Dive computers: a consumer's guide to history, theory, and performance*, Watersport Publishing, 1991.
- Mount T, Gilliam B: *Mixed gas diving*, Watersport Publishing, 1993.
- Naval Medical Research Institute: *An evaluation of recompression treatment tables used throughout the world by government and industry*, Naval Medical Research Institute.
- NOAA Diving Manual: *Diving for science and technology*, US Department of Commerce, National Oceanic and Atmospheric Administration, 1991.
- Wienke BR: *Basic decompression theory and application*, Best Publishing.

CHAPTER SIX

DIVING TECHNIQUES

Diving is among the most enjoyable of the many adventure sports; however, accidents do occur. This chapter aims to reduce the chances of one happening to you. If you and your buddy are adequately trained and prepared, you will have a lifetime of enjoyable diving ahead of you, because the few accidents that do occur usually are preventable.

The major cause of diving fatalities is panic, and there is always an excellent alternative to a panicked response. All you must do is put it into action. This chapter focuses on eliminating as many of the contributing factors to accidents as possible.

LEARNING OBJECTIVES

By the end of this chapter, you will be able to:

① **Correctly define the terms presented in bold letters.**

② **List and explain three factors to consider in dive planning.**

③ **List and explain the proper procedures for a buddy check.**

④ **List some equipment modifications that can be made to improve efficiency.**

⑤ **Explain why overweighting is dangerous.**

⑥ **List and explain five options for emergency ascents, including the advantages and disadvantages of each.**

DIVE PLANNING

There is little room in diving for impetuosity. Our sport demands care, attention to detail, and advance planning.

Long-Term Planning

Long-term planning begins as soon as you decide to make a dive. You make a commitment in terms of purchasing a spot on a commercial dive boat, make a date with your dive buddy for a shore dive, or perhaps purchase your plane tickets for a diving vacation. Now is the time to begin listing all of the things that you will want to accomplish before the dive. You will want to consider with whom as well as with what, when, where, and how you will dive (Fig. 6-1).

You should choose your dive buddy carefully. This choice may make the difference between having fun or not having fun, or in achieving your purpose. Advanced planning also will include check-

Fig. 6-1. NAUI dive tables, dive roster, and dive planning slate.

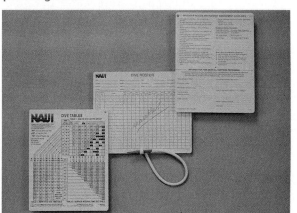

ing all of your diving equipment. Repairs will take some time, so you must plan ahead.

Time of the year is important wherever you plan to dive, because conditions will vary with the season. Locales with no variation in dive conditions year-round are very rare. Your purpose in diving will facilitate this choice. Lobster hunters dive during lobster season, and photographers want good water visibility. Shore divers must be more wary of winter conditions than boat divers will.

Time of month can be significant as well. A full or new moon means the tides will be more extreme, and the resulting spring tides may or may not be significant depending on local conditions. You may prefer to choose a one-quarter or three-quarter moon; this is the time of the neap tide when tidal changes are less dramatic.

Time of day is also important. Dive boats usually leave right on schedule. If you are not aboard at departure time, you will probably miss that dive. Plan enough lead time to drive to the dock, park your car, and unload your gear. This often consumes quite a bit of time. Always check the departure time, because it actually may be the night before the dive itself.

Once you arrive at a dive site, you must evaluate the water conditions. Many divers use the acronym **SEABAG** to assist them in planning. The SEA portion is usually conducted before suiting up. S stands for site and includes things such as parking, access, entries and exits, depth, currents, and water visibility. E stands for emergency, when emergency procedures and plans are discussed. A stands for activities. Each of these are discussed later (Fig. 6-2).

Shore diving requires careful consideration of the tide. High tide brings clean water into shore, but it also increases the size of the breaking waves. High tide may allow easier access to the water at a rocky shore or easier skimming over entangling aquatic plants just beneath the surface. Low tide invariably brings lowered visibility, smaller surf, and a more difficult rocky-shore entry. The perfect time is the slack tide between the tidal changes.

Wind is often less in the morning. Increased wind chop on the surface of the water adds to the discomfort level of any dive, which is why many divers prefer to get an early start. Less wind translates into calmer water on the surface.

Departure time may not always be your decision. If you are sharing a commercial dive boat with other divers, the choice most likely will be made for you. The intended dive location is important, but it is not always possible for the boat to reach this site safely and comfortably. You

Fig. 6-2. It is important to make a careful assessment of the dive site.

will be in the hands of the captain, crew, and divemaster on board. They will be cognizant of your safety, comfort, and interests when they choose alternatives to a stated destination.

A shore dive puts the responsibility squarely on your shoulders and those of your dive buddy. Many factors will influence your choice of site, including:

1. Purpose for the dive (e.g., photography, search and recovery, game collecting).
2. Access to the dive site (e.g., parking, distance away, type of neighborhood).
3. Rocky or sandy shore.
4. Ease of entry and exit.
5. Underwater terrain.
6. Presence of longshore currents.
7. Length of kick to the desired dive spot.
8. Depth contours and dropoffs.
9. Exposure to undesirable water conditions.
10. Skill level necessary to make the dive.

The means of transport to the dive location will depend on the length of time available, expense involved, location of the chosen site, purpose of your dive, and many other factors. You may be fortunate enough to be able to choose between a commercial dive boat, live-aboard dive boat, private boats of varying sizes, a ferry, and of course, your own legs.

Short-Term Planning

Final preparations will go more smoothly if you leave enough time to accomplish all of the necessary tasks comfortably. As the time for your planned day of diving approaches, you will pack your gear in the reverse order that you will use it. Pack early enough to avoid last-minute rushing. It is a great help to make your own personal checklist and include such items as light chargers, cameras, dive computers, sleeping bags, and so on. Packing with the aid of such a list will prevent your forgetting any vital piece of equipment. Anything that will reduce stress at any point helps in the overall safety and fun of diving.

If you are packing for a plane trip, protect any gauges that are sensitive to pressure changes. Do not allow them to go unprotected into an unpressurized luggage compartment; either carry them aboard or place them in an airtight box. Dive computers will not be damaged by pressure changes as long as they are turned off while airborne. Some computers automatically adjust for altitude and will not be damaged by a pressurized aircraft cabin.

Check the latest weather report, and telephone any available source for additional information. Lifeguards, surf reports, marine forecasts, harbors, dive boats, fishing boats and stores, and waterfront establishments (e.g., restaurants, stores, hotels) are good sources.

Make certain that you and your dive buddy are mentally and physically in good condition for diving. Also make certain that you have information on emergency services in case of any accident. Your knowledge of the process for notifying rescue and emergency personnel, either by telephone or radio, could save a life. In addition, do not forget important items like food, drinks, dry clothes, and carts, which are not ordinarily found on a checklist.

Once you have arrived at the destination, there are many tasks to perform before you dive. A dive from the shore necessitates choosing a vantage point and assessing the diving conditions. Watch the water long enough to determine the size, shape, and duration of the wave sets and lulls. Attempt to ascertain any longshore currents by observing floating objects, persons on the surface, the presence of aquatic plants on the surface, and any other visible signs of water movement. Look for rip currents by noticing foam, "dirty" water, silt, or disturbances in breaking waves. Plan your entry and exit away from any rip current (see the Environment chapter).

Assess the probable visibility by noting the color and clarity of the water. Ascertain the best direction for your dive and the probable distance to the chosen spot.

Choose your entry and exit site as well as at least one alternate in case current, wind, injury, or some unexpected situation eliminates your first choice. Talk with the lifeguard, other divers, surfers, and/or swimmers about the existing conditions.

Make certain that this dive is well within the your skill level and that of your buddy. Do not consider any dive that requires greater strength and conditioning than either of you possess. If one of you feels apprehensive, change to your alternate location or cancel the dive for that day.

Diving from a boat will free you from some of the aforementioned tasks. The captain and/or divemaster will choose your dive location based on many factors, but primarily with safety in mind. It remains your responsibility, however, to ensure your own personal safety. Again, it is not prudent to jump into the water without ascertaining the factors affecting your decision whether to dive.

Be aware of the anticipated depth of the dive area, and judge for yourself if this depth exceeds your personal limits. You should not dive beyond the depth limits of your training.

Look at the water to determine the presence of any current. The boat will usually align itself bow to stern in a current, but depending on wind conditions and the shape of the boat, this may not always be the case. Look at the stern to see if a small wake exists. Aquatic plants on the surface of the water indicate little or no current. If a current is present, request that a current line be deployed.

Notice the size of the ocean swell, because this will indicate the amount of surge and the depth to which this surge will exist. Determine if this factor will affect your plans. Large waves and surge can cause seasickness and make both entries and exits hazardous.

Ascertain any presence of wind and its accompanying surface chop. Decide if this affects your plans. Also, remember the accompanying boat swing produced by the wind, and consider how this will alter your exit plans.

The **dive plan** is an essential part of all safe and fun dives. Whether you are diving from a boat or the beach, once you and your partner have decided to make the dive, you will want to consult with one another on several key factors. The intended depth and duration of the dive are essential along with contingency factors already discussed. The direction of the dive (begin upcurrent), and the type of compass course to be followed also should be considered.

Each buddy must ascertain the air consumption rate of the other. Plan your turnaround time based on the consumption of the diver with the higher

rate. It will be more fun, easier, and often safer to return to the boat or beach underwater and avoid a long surface kick.

The Buddy Check

You have spent a great deal of time and energy formulating your dive plan. If at all possible, do not deviate from it. A cardinal rule never to be broken consists of a thorough **buddy check** (Fig. 6-3). This is fundamental, whether your buddy is a stranger or an old friend. The items of a good buddy check often are followed by using the term SEABAG, mentioned previously. Again, the SEA portion is usually done before suiting up, while the BAG section is the actual buddy check. BAG stands for buoyancy, air, and "gear and go."

The buoyancy portion of this check consists of:
1. Familiarization with your buddy's weight-belt release.
2. Proficiency in the inflation, both orally and power assisted, of your buddy's buoyancy compensator (BC).
3. Familiarization with BC straps, clips, closures, buckles, releases, and valves.

The air portion consists of:
1. Working pressure and existing pressure of your buddy's air cylinder, and discussion of the turn-around pressure and back-on-surface pressure plan.

Fig. 6-3. A complete buddy check is conducted prior to entering the water.

2. Presence, absence, and location of your buddy's safe second stage or alternate air source.
3. Presence and/or use of a reserve valve.
4. Procedure to follow in any out-of-air emergency.

"Gear and Go" consists of checking that you have all of your other equipment.

Once the buddy check has been completed, inform the lifeguard or divemaster that you are entering the water, the direction that you intend to take, and the intended time of your return. The lifeguard or divemaster also should be notified when you are safely back.

Additional Concerns

Recreational diving is a very enjoyable activity. It is potentially dangerous, however, for a diver with any of the following conditions:

1. Under the influence of alcohol, "street" drugs, and some prescribed drugs.
2. A chest or head cold.
3. An ear or sinus infection.
4. Fatigue.
5. Extreme fear.
6. Depression.
7. Poor physical condition.
8. Smoking.
9. Asthma.
10. The dive is beyond his or her physical, emotional, or educational limits.

Remember that it is better to cancel a dive than to rationalize or hide a potential problem.

COMMUNICATIONS

The more advanced that your diving skills become and the more time you spend underwater, the more sophisticated your **underwater communication** skills need to be. The most fundamental of these skills relies on hand signals. Take the time to become proficient at hand signaling, and you will increase your fun and enjoyment of diving (Fig. 6-4). You and your buddy may enjoy developing your own special signals as well. Many divers use signals for indicating various forms of marine life.

You use a different set of signals when you communicate by feel rather than sight. These **tactile signals** are used during line work or when in physical contact with your buddy. You may be using a buddy line when in low visibility, a search-and-recovery exercise, holding hands, or simply touching. The number of times that the signal is repeated holds the key to its meaning, as follows:

Stop = one pull, squeeze, tap

OK, proceed = two pulls, squeezes, taps

Fig. 6-4. Hand signals should be reviewed prior to the dive.

Surface, up = four pulls, squeezes, taps

Come here, help = five pulls, squeezes, taps

Note that three pulls is omitted as a signal. The purpose of this is to create a space between ordinary signals and more urgent messages.

There are times when you will need to communicate or receive communications audibly. Some commercial dive boats use an underwater recall system that sounds like a siren. It is used in case of emergency or when repositioning the boat. This sound requires that you surface immediately (at the appropriate rate and with the appropriate safety stop) for further instructions. The divemaster or crew will tell you whether to hold your present position or return to the boat.

If there is no recall system, apply the same rules as in the tactile system. For example, one sharp handclap or rap with a knife against your cylinder translates to stop, two indicates go, and so forth.

Your BC should have a whistle attached for use on the surface; however, do not blow it unless you are in distress. A whistle can be heard much more clearly than your voice, and the lifeguard or divemaster on duty will respond when it is blown (Fig. 6-5). Just as with tactile signals, five blasts on your whistle means to come quickly, or help! The whistle can be difficult to use with very cold hands and lips.

Written communication allows a more complex exchange of information. An underwater slate and pencil can fully convey messages that are too complicated for hand signals. A slate in your BC pocket ensures your ability to make yourself understood.

Flags are employed when other types of signaling are impractical (Figs. 6-6 and 6-7). Boats use three different types of flags:

1. Red/White: This is considered to be the sport-diver flag. It is recognized internationally and indicates there are divers in the area and stay clear for a 100-foot radius.

Fig. 6-5. A whistle can be heard a long distance in an emergency.

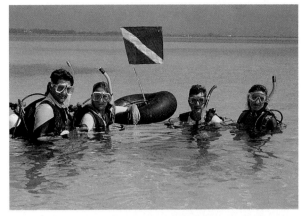

Fig. 6-6. A dive flag can be mounted on a surface float and towed to the dive site.

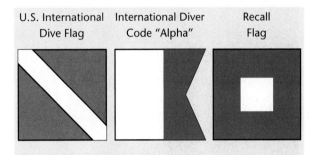

U.S. International Dive Flag	International Diver Code "Alpha"	Recall Flag

Fig. 6-7. Dive flags.

2. Blue/White: This is an international code flag. It indicates that a diving operation is underway and to stay clear.

3. Blue/White (Square): This is an international code flag. It is used as a diver recall.

Divers who leave the immediate vicinity of their boat and those who dive from the shore are vulnerable to injury by boat traffic. Under these conditions, use a diver flag and float. Stay within a 100-foot radius of your flag.

Voice communication has long been possible underwater. You may actually speak underwater, either through your regulator or not, but most divers are not easily understood. Good vocal communications require an air space around your mouth. Commercial divers are able to speak with surface personnel through use of full-face mask or helmet systems. These are expensive and cumbersome, but there have been recent developments enabling sport divers to speak and be understood underwater.

Several manufacturers offer devices that fit over the regulator second stage, either outfitted with a small electronic speaker or providing the communication via cables. Each buddy must wear one to achieve two-way communications.

An apparatus also is currently available that allows a diver to be heard by several others in close proximity. Speech is transmitted through a small microphone to an external speaker, which usually is attached to a diver's cylinder.

Another development in this field permits two-way conversation between the surface and divers underwater via cable. Wireless systems that permit diver-to-diver communications also are now available; transmitters and receivers are attached to the mask strap.

EQUIPMENT CONSIDERATIONS

Some simple equipment modifications can improve efficiency. A clip on your console can be snapped to your BC to keep your instruments free from entanglement. Specially designed holders are available to secure your extra second stage in the center of your chest, where it will be readily accessible yet out of the way (Fig. 6-8). A lanyard or short length of line will secure your dive tables to your BC and prevent their accidental loss. You can reduce the likelihood of entanglement if you secure knives, lights (in a holster), and other instruments by locating them on the inside of your arms or legs, in pockets of your suit, or on your BC waist strap. Never hang any piece of equipment (including cameras) around your neck, and anything dangling from your wrist is an invitation for entanglement.

Fig. 6-8. The console can be clipped to the BC to avoid dragging on the bottom, and the octopus second stage is attached in the "golden triangle" area of the diver's body.

Knives should be in good condition and capable of severing a monofilament line. Mask-strap ends may be turned inward or taped in place. Avoid hanging easily opened spring clips on your BC or weight belt, because they can unintentionally become clipped to lines. Do not attach anything to your weight belt that is also attached to something else, which could prevent jettisoning of your weights in an emergency.

Most octopus regulators come complete with a longer hose than that of the primary second stage. If you intend to pass your primary second stage to your buddy in case of an out-of-air emergency, switch the longer hose to your primary second stage and use the shorter on your octopus rig. You also will find that this shorter hose makes it easier to manage the octopus rig when not in use.

Divers usually do not have immediate access to medical attention. Carry a first-aid kit, and possibly oxygen, and be prepared to render first-aid assistance (Fig. 6-9).

As discussed earlier, predive planning includes the inspection of equipment before diving as well as checking its operation before entering the water. Uncomfortable incidents have been precipitated by as simple an oversight as a missing snorkel purge valve or badly deteriorated fin strap. Before entering the water, verify the operation of both your primary and secondary second stages, BC inflator valve, submersible pressure gauge, reserve valve (if present), and compass.

BUOYANCY CONTROL

Buoyancy control is the mark of a skilled diver. The ability to achieve neutral, positive, or negative buoyancy at will is essential to enjoyable diving. Under most conditions, a diver endeavors to be neutrally buoyant throughout the dive. A number of factors affect your buoyancy, and while some are personal, others depend on your equipment. To achieve skill in buoyancy control, you must learn to control these factors (Fig. 6-10).

The percentage of muscle, bone, and fat in your body are personal factors affecting buoyancy. Individuals with a large percentage of muscle and/or with large, dense bones are often negatively buoyant. Those with a greater percentage of fat are often positively buoyant. Be aware of changes during any periods of weight gain or loss.

Fig. 6-9. Emergency oxygen kit in a waterproof case.

The amount of air in your lungs also greatly affects your buoyancy. With practice, you will become skilled in controlling your vertical movement by changing this volume of air. By making long exhalations, you can retain less air, thereby slowing your rate of ascent or assisting in your initial descent. Conversely, taking deeper breaths will slow a too-rapid descent by making you more buoyant. The difference between a full and an empty lung can change your buoyancy by as much as 8 pounds depending on your lung capacity.

Other factors controlling buoyancy relate to your equipment and objects that you carry. Several items of equipment make you positively boyant. These include your exposure suit, some BCs (because of air trapped in the foam padding and between the inner bag and cover), and some cylinders (usually aluminum but also some steel) when empty or nearly so. The amount of positive buoyancy from an exposure suit changes with depth because of the compression of the air or neoprene. You must determine individually the amount of weight that is required to neutralize this positive buoyancy in water. Your guiding principle, however, should be to use the minimum amount of weight that will provide neutral buoyancy at 15 feet of depth with an empty BC and a nearly empty cylinder. This ensures your ability to execute a precautionary safety stop at 15 feet at the end of a dive without risking premature surfacing. Take the time, perhaps at the end of your next dive, to make the necessary determinations.

The most common method of carrying the required weights is on a weight belt with standard webbing filled with lead shot or with pockets. Whichever you choose, some basic principles apply. The belt should have a quick-release buckle, and the majority of the weight should be equally divided. Attach one or two weights just in front of your hips. Your cylinder constitutes a significant weight at your back, and better vertical and horizontal balance is achieved by placing weights in front of the hips.

The addition of **ankle weights** may be appropriate with dry suits. These weights add a small amount of weight to each ankle; however, ankle weights also can add significantly to the comfort of wet-suit and other divers, especially those using light, floating plastic fins. Ankle weights also keep your feet submerged for more effective snorkeling.

Some systems employ weights that are integrated with the backpack and BC. These systems either eliminate the necessity for a separate weight belt or allow the amount of weight on the belt to be reduced. Use of such a unit involves

Fig. 6-10. Diver showing proper trim and neutral buoyancy.

several important considerations. You should be trained in its use and maintenance. You and your buddy must be thoroughly familiar with the weight-release location and method of operation. Also, the weights may require maintenance, because salt buildup and corrosion can reduce the efficiency with which the weights can be jettisoned from some systems.

The weight of the entire unit (i.e., cylinder, BC, and weights) usually exceeds 50 pounds. Some people may find this excessive.

Loss of Buoyancy

Diving with excessive ballast is dangerous. These added pounds demand extra energy to move you and your equipment from one point to another either above or underwater, more air is needed in your BC to achieve neutral buoyancy, and extra energy is needed to push the over-inflated BC through the water. Many modern BCs can provide as much as 45 pounds of lift; however, they should not be used to compensate for overweighting.

Overweighting adds to your stress in any event requiring extra effort (e.g., long surface kick, increased currents, wind, buddy needing assistance, and so on). Additionally, if the BC malfunctions or fails to hold air, an overweighted diver may be in a life-threatening situation. If the diver is unable to control his or her descent and is too heavy to ascend, the weight belt must be ditched. A rapid ascent can be slowed by assuming a horizontal flare position to create drag, and this should be practiced under an instructor's supervision.

Excess Positive Buoyancy

If the weight belt is ditched or the power inflator on the BC sticks open, rapid positive buoyancy will be evident. Many divers wearing dry suits or thick wet suits can wear more than 30 pounds of weight. A BC can be filled to maximum capacity within a matter of a few seconds, producing more than 50 pounds of lift. Loss of a weight belt at depth is not uncommon, and a sudden increase in buoyancy should trigger immediate emptying of the BC and checking of the weight belt (see the emergency ascents discussion that follows). If your weight belt comes off underwater, you should immediately kick down and grasp it. To replace a weight belt, lie face down, hold the buckle in the left hand, place it on the left hip, and roll with your left side down and right side up until the belt wraps around your body. Supporting the weights on your back makes it easier to secure the strap in the buckle.

If the power inflator sticks open, the low-pressure quick disconnect should be disconnected immediately. Air also should be vented from the BC immediately via the oral-inflator mechanism or the dump valve if present. If this is not possible, your positive buoyant ascent will be rapid. The diver must exhale and flare out horizontally to slow the ascent (see buoyant ascent discussion that follows). The best prevention of an uncontrolled BC inflation is proper preventive maintenance of the inflator mechanism.

Items carried such as cameras, tools, and game bags can add significantly to your negative buoyancy and create drag. Be certain that you are able to support these items. Also, be aware that releasing such items will require immediate adjustments in your buoyancy.

The best policy to follow is that of frequent adjustments in your buoyancy. This will ensure that you are always neutrally buoyant.

THE BUDDY SYSTEM

The buddy system increases the fun of diving. It also can deter accidents by assuring assistance when it is needed (e.g., during predive equipment checks, entrapments/entanglements, out-of-air emergencies, medical emergencies).

Buddy diving usually occurs in pairs or in multiples of two. For this system to work, the divers must be committed to its principles and willing to expend the necessary effort. Ideally, buddies position themselves shoulder to shoulder, and they retain the same position relative to each other during the entire dive. If it is necessary to proceed in single file, the leader must stop as soon as possible and wait for the follower to catch up. In pairs of unequal experience or differing interests, it is important that both individuals have an opportunity to make dive-plan decisions, determine the pace, and have equal freedom to cancel the dive. Being a dependent diver is unsafe.

Threesomes are the most difficult buddy system to execute safely, and they have been implicated in fatal diving accidents. Divers in such an arrangement can become complacent about their responsibility. Also, often before the dive ends, one diver is alone. In a threesome, try to maintain the same position relative to your buddies, and never change to a twosome or a single during the dive.

If separated from your buddy, look around in a complete circle, look up, ascend a few feet, and repeat the search, watching for bubbles. If you do not locate your buddy within 1 minute, began an ascent while continuing to circle. Your buddy should be performing the same search procedure, and you should surface within a short distance of each other. If you reach the surface and your buddy is not there, look for his or her air bubbles breaking the surface. Swim over to those bubbles and then follow them down to rejoin your buddy. Never continue your dive alone.

EMERGENCY ASCENTS

When faced with any problem, stop, think, and then act. Problems such as the loss of a mask or a fin can be solved underwater and not result in an emergency ascent.

An **emergency ascent** is one in which the diver ascends directly to the surface to avoid a life-threatening circumstance such as a medical condition, some mechanical problem, or an environmental threat. The most frequent reason for an emergency ascent among recreational divers is an out-of-air emergency. This usually is preventable by adequate dive planning and instrument monitoring. A skilled, competent, and advanced diver will consciously decide to eliminate this excessive risk by never allowing it to happen.

The out-of-air diver has gone through the last few increasingly restrictive breaths, and he or she has arrived at the no-air point after exhaling and attempting to inhale. Remind yourself firmly that no matter how it feels, there is air in your lungs and that the amount of air is sufficient to start the emergency ascent procedure.

Several choices face the out-of-air diver. All involve preplanning, conscious thought, avoiding panic, and a practiced skill. The skills learned in your entry-level scuba class require continuing practice for you to retain proficiency. Practice and overlearning of the skills necessary to conduct emergency out-of-air ascents safely are important factors in avoiding panic. These skills should be practiced under the supervision of an instructor.

Now, however, you must decide whether to surface by yourself (i.e., **independent ascent**) or contact your buddy for assistance (i.e., **dependent ascent**).

Independent Ascents

There are some circumstances under which the independent method of ascent is preferred. For example, if you are unsure of your buddy's ability or willingness to render assistance, the surface is closer than your buddy is to you, the water is fairly shallow (i.e., 40 ft or less), or if you have a redundant scuba system.

Redundant System Ascent

A **redundant system** ascent requires a second, independent source of air. The redundant system often consists of a small cylinder and extra regulator. The redundant system may provide enough air to make an emergency ascent, and it may be the safest way to deal with an out-of-air emergency. One common unit consists of a cylinder containing 15 to 40 cubic feet of air that is attached to the primary cylinder. Disadvantages include the cumbersome surface weight of the system, increased resistance underwater, and cost as well as maintenance considerations.

In an out-of-air situation, the diver switches second stages or offers it to the out-of-air buddy. He or she then looks toward the surface, extends a hand overhead, uses the BC inflator valve to vent excess air, and breathes normally while swimming directly to the surface at a normal ascent rate.

Redundant systems are common among divers in highly technical specialties such as cave, ice, deep, and wreck diving. These specialties all require additional training.

A very small redundant scuba system that holds approximately 1 to 2 cubic feet of air also is available. While very compact, it may not contain enough air to accomplish a slow ascent and safety stop during an emergency (Fig. 6-11).

Emergency Swimming Ascent

The out-of-air diver knows that air is in his or her lungs. During ascent from relatively shallow depths, that volume of air will increase, and that

Fig. 6-11. A completely self-contained redundant scuba system can also be used for emergency ascents.

air most likely is sufficient for the time that it will take to reach the surface. The diver retains the second stage in the mouth, looks toward the surface, extends a hand overhead, uses the BC valve to exhaust excess air, and swims directly to the surface as close to the normal rate of ascent as possible while exhaling gently all the way (Fig. 6-12). Because scuba delivers air at the ambient pressure, additional air may become available to an out-of-air diver as the ambient pressure decreases during ascent. Attempts to inhale should be made, because additional air may be available. These attempts also may help to open the smallest of airways within the lungs, thus preventing lung overexpansion injuries. With training, a relaxed diver can execute the **emergency swimming ascent** from surprising depths. A neutrally buoyant diver becomes buoyant on ascending a short distance, thereby reducing the required effort to swim to the surface; indeed, keeping the rate of ascent slow enough is the more common problem. Finally, exhalation should not be forced.

In a desperate situation, where the diver feels that he or she will not make it to the surface, the weight belt should be dropped. This will then become a positive buoyant ascent, which is described later.

Buoyancy Compensator Breathing

Air contained in your BC is breathable provided that you have not activated a carbon dioxide cartridge. With proper training, you could find this to

Fig. 6-12. An emergency swimming ascent may be the best choice in shallow water.

be a viable way of obtaining emergency air. To access this air, you first must clear any water from the inflator hose. Blow into the inflator mouthpiece while rolling from a facedown position away from the inflator hose and over to your back. Look toward the surface, extend a hand overhead, and exhale into and inhale from the mouthpiece while holding the valve open. Breathe continuously, allowing any excess air to escape from your mouth or nose as you swim to the surface at the normal rate of ascent.

This method must be practiced under carefully controlled conditions before being added to your repertoire of emergency procedures. One risk from this type of ascent is inhaling bacteria that may be present in the BC. Before practicing this technique, it is imperative to clean thoroughly the interior of your BC, because certain types of bacteria can cause lung infections.

Buoyant Ascent

A diver may elect to execute a **buoyant ascent** by removing the weight belt or retaining expanding air in the BC (Fig. 6-13). Because controlling the rate of ascent is very difficult, a buoyant ascent is considerably more risky and should be used

only if you cannot swim to the surface. You may elect to start a buoyant ascent at the bottom or change an emergency swimming ascent to a buoyant ascent on the way up. Once the weights are discarded, the diver arches backward into a belly-up position, extends the arms and legs horizontally (i.e., spread-eagled), and continues to exhale gently to the surface. This technique is known as **flaring**. Remember, expanding air from your regulator and cylinder may become available to breathe as the water pressure is reduced.

A skilled diver will practice assuming the buoyant-ascent position, because it also is useful in circumstances other than out-of-air emergencies. Examples are the accidental loss of weights, a jammed inflator or exhaust, or overinflated BCs or dry suits. An excellent way to practice this technique is to surface dive in snorkeling equipment without a weight belt and practice flaring on ascent. Even in a full wet suit, the ascent rate is remarkably comfortable.

Dependent Ascents

Dependent emergency ascents require a buddy who is trained, willing to assist, in the immediate vicinity, and who has enough air for two divers. Procedures should be discussed with your buddy and rehearsed frequently while on dry land until your response to an out-of-air sign is fast, automatic, and elicits little or no anxiety in you or your buddy.

Alternate Air Source

The **alternate air source** has evolved into the preferred means for resolving an out-of-air situa-

Fig. 6-13. If the weight belt is ditched, it should be removed and held out to the side before releasing it.

tion. The alternate air source may take several forms, all of which provide an extra second stage so that each diver has a source of air. The "octopus" is an extra second stage regulator with a second, normally longer hose for the out-of-air diver's use. Another type of alternate air source is a combination regulator and BC inflator mechanism. Many divers prefer this type, because it eliminates one extra hose on the scuba regulator.

The method of air sharing depends on the type of alternate air source that is available. With the octopus configuration, the donor gives the out-of-air diver the octopus regulator. After the out-of-air diver receives the second stage from the buddy and has established breathing control, the divers hold firmly to each other on the forearms, look to the surface, and ascend at a normal rate while breathing normally and controlling buoyancy. Eye contact should be maintained during such an ascent (Fig. 6-14).

With an integrated regulator mounted on the BC, the methods are somewhat different. The hose generally is too short to allow its passage to a distressed diver. In this case, the donor gives the primary regulator from his mouth to the out-of-air diver and puts the integrated regulator into his or her own mouth to breathe.

Because of the duplicate second stage, this ascent can be the most reliable of the dependent methods. Procedures must be clear and discussed between buddies before diving, however. For instance, which second stage will be passed to the out-of-air buddy? Also, where will the extra second stage be located? The fastest response time has been found to be with passing the second stage from the mouth of the donor, and this may be of some psychologic advantage to the recipient. It is highly recommended that the extra second stage be mounted in the center of the chest for easy accessibility by both the donor and recipient. The mounting mechanism must be secure enough to hold the second stage with absolute reliability yet release quickly enough for the minimum response time. Of course, whichever second stage goes to the recipient will be the one with the longer hose.

Another factor to consider is that if one diver is out of air, the companion diver also may be getting low on air. With two divers sharing the same air supply, the demand for air from that system is doubled. The natural stress and anxiety associated with the incident also will probably increase the respiratory demand in both divers. So, the remaining air supply in the donor's cylinder may be depleted quite quickly.

As you can see, there is no standardization of technique for shared-air, alternate air–source

Fig. 6-14. An octopus assisted ascent, with arms linked, and air venting from BCs.

breathing. There is continual experimentation with new procedures and equipment. This skill should be practiced occasionally with your dive buddy, and certainly whenever you dive with someone new.

Buddy Breathing

If an alternate air source is not available, it may be necessary for the divers to share a single regulator. **Buddy breathing** is the most complex of the shared air–ascent methods. The out-of-air diver faces the buddy and signals that he or she is out of air, and the donor takes a deep breath and then passes the second stage to the recipient, who takes two breaths. The divers then alternate, each taking two breaths apiece. Each diver must slowly exhale when the regulator is out of the mouth. Both individuals keep one hand on the second stage and firmly hold their buddy with the other. As soon as the breathing cycle is stable (usually within a few breaths), the ascent should begin. Because both hands are in use, maintaining buoyancy control is more difficult. The ascent must be executed slowly and carefully. Good eye contact will assist in reassuring the person needing air and will reduce anxiety.

To retain the skill of buddy breathing, constant practice is both necessary and highly recommended. Frequent practice sessions will add confidence and increase the chance of a successful outcome in a real emergency.

Determination of which method of ascent to use is affected by many factors. The best method for any given situation depends on the individual circumstances. A controlled emergency swimming ascent is appropriate for shallow water, while an air-sharing ascent is preferred for deeper depths.

While the safety of these procedures can be enhanced significantly by planning and practice, avoiding out-of-air emergencies altogether is preferable. Whenever a diver rapidly ascends to the surface, there is an added risk of pulmonary barotrauma and decompression sickness, and further diving must be curtailed. The diver should remain on the surface and watch for any signs and symptoms of these maladies.

Disease Risks Associated with Sharing Mouthpieces

Recently, there has been some discussion about the potential risks of disease transmission through sharing scuba regulators. Specifically, the human immunodeficiency virus (HIV), which is responsible for the acquired immunodeficiency syndrome (or AIDS), and hepatitis B and C are particularly worrisome.

It has not been shown that HIV can be transmitted via saliva. There is a possibility, however, that blood could be in the saliva because of gum irritation or cuts in the mouth. HIV does not survive outside of living tissue, and it is easily destroyed by heat and chlorine. Also, it would be greatly diluted in water.

Hepatitis viruses can be transmitted in both blood and saliva. They also are more resistant than HIV to drying and dilution in water.

It is not possible to estimate precisely the likelihood of contracting disease through sharing a scuba mouthpiece underwater. Most experts feel that the transfer of HIV by sharing a regulator is highly unlikely. The chances of contracting hepatitis, however, may be greater. If you have any questions regarding this matter, ask your physician.

REFRESHER TRAINING

Scuba diving requires the development of very specific skills that are unlike those normally encountered in everyday life. Constant reinforcement is required. Most experts agree that monthly dives are necessary to maintain diving skills at their highest level. Even a few month's leave from diving can degrade your skills, and this should be followed by a personal review of the key subjects (e.g., medical aspects, dive-table calculations emergency and rescue procedures), a pool practice session, and a dive in highly controlled conditions.

A lapse in excess of 1 year may indicate the need for more formal refresher training. Contact a NAUI instructor to evaluate your status. Possible recommendations may include classroom review and testing, followed by one or more refresher dives for a return to your previous skill level. Another way to refresh your skills may be to enroll in the next-higher class level or pertinent specialty class to renew and augment what you already know.

SUMMARY

Ⓨour training as a diver does not end with the advanced diver course. A variety of skills and techniques are used in specialized areas of diving, such as cave, wreck, ice, and deep diving. Some essential techniques that you will use as an independent diver (i.e., not under direct supervision) have been discussed in this chapter. You are encouraged to seek additional training for diving situations that you are not familiar with or trained in.

SUGGESTED READINGS

- Barsky S, Long D, Stinton B: *Dry suit diving: a guide to diving dry*, Watersport Publishing.
- Blount S: *Treasure hunting with a metal detector in, around, and under water*, Pisces Books.
- Keatts HC: *Guide to shipwreck diving: New York and New Jersey*, Pisces Books.
- Lang ML, Egstrom G: *Proceedings of Biomechanics of Safe Ascents Workshop*, American Academy of Underwater Sciences, 1989.
- Lippmann JL: *Deeper into diving*.
- Somers L: *Tethered scuba diving*, Michigan Sea Grant College Program, 1987.

CHAPTER SEVEN

NAVIGATION FOR DIVERS

o *navigate* means to control a course through the use of calculations regarding position and direction. To a diver, it means controlling a course while diving so that you always know where you are in relation to a given point, such as an exit site.

Navigation has many applications for divers. The skill can be used to locate or relocate a dive site, conduct a dive pattern or environmental surveys, and search for lost objects. All divers need a variety of navigational skills, because even the best underwater visibility simply is not sufficient to permit navigating by vision alone.

LEARNING OBJECTIVES

By the end of this chapter, you will be able to:

1. Briefly describe the navigational terms that appear in **bold letters**.
2. List at least eight items of equipment for diving navigation.
3. List at least five ways to measure distance for diving navigation.
4. List at least six aids to natural navigation.
5. Briefly describe how to take a "fix" on a position by using natural aids to navigation and compass bearings.
6. Briefly describe the theory of compass operation.
7. List the basic types, features, selection criteria, and procedures for care of a diving compass.
8. Briefly describe how to determine and prevent compass deviation.
9. Briefly describe how to cope with underwater obstacles and water movement (i.e., currents).

The process of underwater navigation relies heavily on references to surface positions. Navigational markers, landmarks, latitude and longitude, navigational radio transmissions, charts, and so on are all useful references for the diving navigator. This chapter will help you become familiar with these resources.

There are four basic items of information that are required for navigation: direction, depth, distance, and time. When these components are known and applied to a reference, you can determine your location, which is what navigating is all about.

NAVIGATIONAL EQUIPMENT FOR DIVERS

For most recreational-diving purposes, the diving compass, watch, and depth gauge are the simplest available navigational devices. The compass is used to maintain a **heading** (i.e., a course followed or to be followed); a heading may change from time to time. Progress is timed with the watch, and the depth is noted.

Diving Compasses

There are two basic types of diver compasses: **direct reading**, and **indirect reading**. Various models of each type are available (Figs. 7-1 and 7-2). A compass card direct-reading compass reads 0° to 360° in a clockwise direction on a circular compass card. It has no **bezel**, however, which is a rotating collar on a diving compass that is equipped with alignment marks to indicate a course that is to be followed. In contrast, a needle direct-reading compass has a north-seeking needle and numbers on a rotating bezel. Bezels read 0° to 360° in a clockwise direction. Other compasses have a north-seeking disc called a **compass card**. Diving compasses also need to be equipped with a **lubber line** (i.e., a reference line that is aligned with the user to obtain and follow a course or bearing).

An indirect-reading compass has fixed degree markings on the compass body that read from 0° to 360° in a counterclockwise direction. This type also has a rotatable bezel containing only **index marks** that temporarily indicate a heading or **bearing**. This type was designed to combine the advantages of both direct-reading compass types. Other desirable features of a diving compass include a low profile, luminous dial, dampening of the compass needle, and the ability to operate accurately even when slightly tilted from a level position.

Use of Diving Compasses

There are two basic uses for a compass: to establish a bearing to be followed for movement in a certain direction, or to determine a bearing to an object. Let us determine how to perform each of these functions with each type of compass.

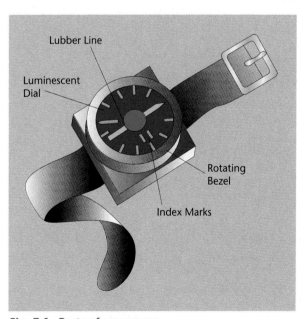

Fig. 7-1. **Parts of a compass.**

150°

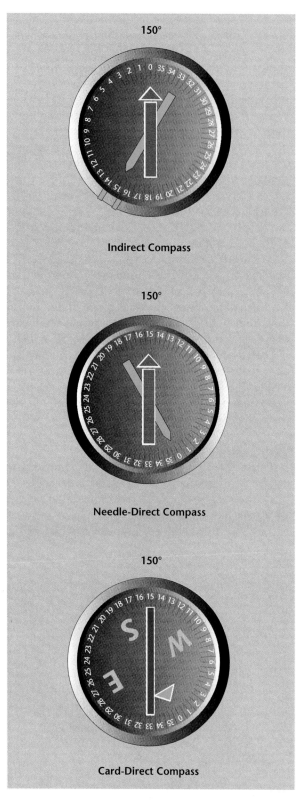

Indirect Compass

150°

Needle-Direct Compass

150°

Card-Direct Compass

Fig. 7-2. Direct- and indirect-reading compasses.

Establishing Direction

To establish direction with a needle direct-reading compass, align the desired direction on the bezel with the lubber line. Rotate the entire compass until the needle points to north, or 0°. The lubber line then indicates the direction of travel.

With the card direct-reading compass, rotate the compass until the desired direction is beneath the lubber line. The lubber line then indicates the desired direction. In this case, there is nothing to set, and the course heading is indicated under the lubber line.

A needle-direct compass has an advantage over the card-direct compass, because the desired bearing is located physically at the point of the lubber line and does not need to be remembered. With a card-direct compass, the bearing needs to be mentally recalled or written on a slate.

To establish direction with an indirect-reading compass, simply set the index marks of the bezel to the desired bearing and rotate the compass until the index marks bracket the needle. The lubber line will then indicate the proper direction.

Establishing Bearing

The advantages of both types of direct-reading compasses are combined within the indirect-reading compass. With this type, the selected bearing does not need to be remembered, and the needle points directly to the actual course heading.

To determine the bearing to an object with a needle direct-reading compass, point the lubber line toward the object and rotate the bezel until 0° is aligned with the needle. The bearing at the point of the lubber line is the bearing to the object.

Determining a bearing with a card direct-reading compass also involves aiming the lubber line toward an object. The reading on the card at the point of the lubber line is the bearing to the object.

To establish the bearing to an object with an indirect-reading compass, simply point the lubber line toward the object. The bearing to the object will be indicated by the compass needle. The bearing can be set by simply aligning the index marks with the needle.

Other Navigational Equipment

The accuracy of any type of diving compass is improved with use of a **compass board**. This is a board on which the compass is mounted and that extends the length of the lubber line.

Another type of compass that is useful for surface navigation by divers is the **hand-bearing compass**. This is a special compass that is designed to take accurate bearings. It is primarily useful for dive-site relocation.

A **maneuvering board** can be useful when precise navigation is required, as in underwater mapping. The diver plots direction and distance on the board, and he or she can then use the board to determine bearing to the point of origin at any time.

An underwater timer or dive watch also is a useful piece of navigational equipment. When time and speed are known, distance can be calculated. Alternatively, when time and distance are known, speed can be determined.

Measured lines are frequently used by diving navigators, especially when distances must be measured exactly. These lines usually are marked at regular intervals, and they are stored on a reel for ease of use and to prevent tangling.

Underwater navigation is similar to celestial navigation, because in both, you must consider depth, which is the equivalent of altitude for an aviator. Therefore, underwater navigation requires use of a depth gauge.

Finally, diving navigation can be enhanced by the use of **charts**, which are the aquatic equivalent of a map. A chart depicts the coast and offshore bottom depths. It also will include other features, such as islands, shipwrecks, and submerged objects (Fig. 7-3).

Measuring Distance

To navigate accurately, divers must be able to measure distance reasonably well underwater. Measuring distance may be accomplished in several ways, ranging from rough approximations to extremely precise measurements (Fig. 7-4).

Approximations of distance can be achieved with cylinder pressure readings at a constant depth. If a dive team uses 500 p.s.i. of air while swimming in a given direction, the return distance will be approximately the same for 500 p.s.i. of air provided that depth, swimming speed, and water movement remain constant.

Fig. 7-3. A nautical chart and other navigational tools.

Fig. 7-4. **Diver reel and line for measuring distances and marking locations.**

Kick cycles also can be used to approximate distance. The cycle of a kick is defined as one complete kick of both legs, and it usually is counted when one leg reaches the top of the kicking motion. A diver must know the distance that is traveled with each kick cycle when he or she is swimming at normal speed. This can be determined by counting the number of kick cycles that are required to swim a known distance, then dividing the distance by that number. For example, if 30 kick cycles are required to swim 100 feet, the distance covered with each kick cycle is approximately 3.3 feet (Fig. 7-5).

Time and speed can be used to measure distance as well. You should know how many seconds are required to swim a given distance under water at a constant depth and easily maintained speed. This information can be used in conjunction with a time measurement to determine a dis-

Fig. 7-5. **A wide flutter kick is used to measure kick cycles.**

tance covered. If 80 seconds are required to swim 100 feet, the following formula will determine your swimming speed:

$$D/T = S$$

where D is distance, T is time, and S is speed. Or, in this case:

$$100 \text{ ft}/80 \text{ s} = 1.25 \text{ ft/s}$$

When speed and time are known, distance also may be calculated. For example, if you swim for 140 seconds at normal speed, the distance may be determined with the following formula:

$$D = ST$$

Or, in this case:

$$D = 1.25 \text{ft/s} \times 140 \text{ s} = 175 \text{ ft}$$

When visibility is limited, the situation requires starting and stopping, or very accurate measurements of distance are required, arm spans may be used. The exact length of the span of the arms, measured with the arms extended in line with rather than perpendicular to the body, is needed. The arm span will be approximately equal to your height. You can then measure distance underwater by extending one arm backward and placing the fingertips on the bottom, extending the other arm forward in the direction of travel, moving forward while pivoting on the fingertips of the extended hand while keeping that hand stationary, then bringing the trailing hand forward, and so on. Distance then can be measured by multiplying the length of the arm span by the number of spans that were required.

Yet another means for measuring distance underwater is with a measured line. One end of the line is secured to a stationary object or held by your dive buddy while you unreel the line and swim the distance to be measured. Do not use a line that stretches, however, or your measurements will be inaccurate.

MEANS OF NAVIGATION

Y̆ou may navigate by using natural aids, instruments for reference, or both in combination. When your location is confirmed with visual checkpoints, you are navigating by **pilotage**. When your location is an estimation based on distance and direction, you are navigating by **dead reckoning**. Divers frequently use both pilotage and dead reckoning for underwater navigation.

Natural Navigation

There are many navigational aids in the underwater environment. A diver can estimate his or her approximate location reasonably well by means of natural aids. One is **sand ripples** on the bottom, which usually parallel the shore and are steepest on the shoreside (Fig. 7-6). Others include sun and shadows, direction of water movement, orientation of certain stationary marine life (e.g., sea fans, kelp), bottom contour and depth, formations, and underwater landmarks (e.g., a wreck). Surge is stronger in shallow water near the shore or around pinnacles, and it decreases in deeper water.

Another key to natural navigation is use of a **dive pattern**, which is the total course or dive path to be followed on a dive. The pattern may be square, rectangular, or some other shape (Fig. 7-7). The configuration of the pattern is not as important as the dive buddies agreeing on it before diving and adhering to the general pattern during the dive. A dive pattern with square corners is the easiest to perform; a a circular pattern is the most difficult and is not recommended (Fig. 7-8).

Fig. 7-6. Using natural aids for navigation.

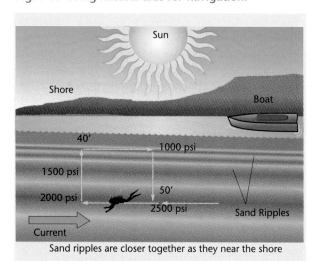

Sand ripples are closer together as they near the shore

Fig. 7-7. Typical dive patterns.

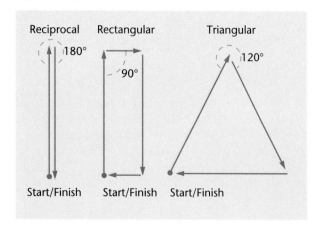

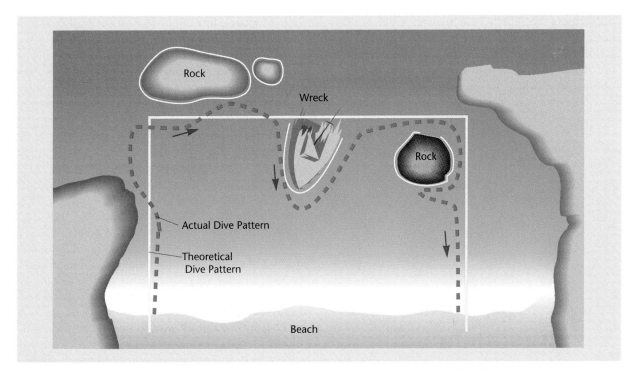

Fig. 7-8. For increased accuracy in natural navigation, follow a general course while diving.

When **natural aids** are used in conjunction with a dive pattern, reasonably accurate navigation is possible. Imagine a dive with a square dive pattern where you begin diving at the anchor of a boat, parallel to shore, at a depth of 50 feet and with the sun on your right. With 2500 p.s.i. of air in your tank on reaching the bottom, you and your buddy move slowly but steadily for 500 p.s.i. parallel to the sand ripples on the bottom. You then agree to make a 90° turn toward shallower water on the right and are aided by the sand ripples on the bottom. With the sun in your face, you move into 40 feet of water during the next 500 p.s.i., then agree to make another 90° turn to the right. Again, you parallel the sand ripples on the bottom, and the sun is now on your left. After another 500 p.s.i., you and your buddy agree to your final right turn. The sun is now to your back, and you are swimming perpendicular to the sand ripples. As you approach a tank pressure of approximately 500 p.s.i. and a depth of 50 feet, the anchorline of the boat comes into view and you begin your ascent (see Fig. 7-6).

Strict adherence to a dive pattern is not essential for effective navigation. Temporary deviations from a heading to investigate points of interest are acceptable if the general direction and some pace of forward progress are maintained or if the distance is measured.

Another form of natural navigation identifies a position at the surface. A given position can be determined from observations of terrestrial objects. When the direction and distance to two or more land-based objects are known, the resulting position is called a **fix**. Direction is established by natural means through the selection of objects that align with one another, such as a phone pole that is in line with the edge of a house. Two such sets of in-line objects result in a very precise fix. The angle between the two directions should be as great as possible, but they should not be in a straight line (i.e., < 180°). Notes and simple drawings of a fix should be made (Fig. 7-9).

Compass Navigation

A compass provides a navigational reference even when natural aids are not available. The magnetic needle of a compass aligns itself with the Earth's magnetic poles. **Magnetic north** is a

Fig. 7-9. Two sets of in-line objects establish a "fix."

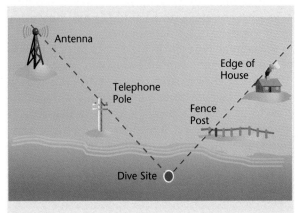

point near the North Pole toward which a magnetic needle points. **True north** is a geographic location referring to the Earth's axis rather than to the magnetic poles; it not the same as magnetic north (Fig. 7-10).

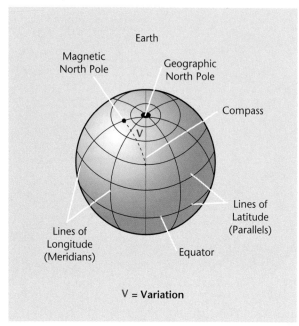

Earth

Magnetic
North Pole

Geographic
North Pole

Compass

V

Lines of
Latitude
(Parallels)

Lines of
Longitude
(Meridians)

Equator

V = Variation

Fig. 7-10. Earth with true and magnetic north and variation.

Compass **variation** is the local difference in degrees between true and magnetic north. Fortunately, diving navigation involves relative direction rather than true direction, so the effects of any variation do not pose problems for divers.

Compass **deviation** occurs when the needle is attracted by nearby metal or some magnetic source, such as another compass. Deviation can cause errors in compass readings for divers, so you must be aware of its effects and prevent any deviation. Usually, a metal object needs to be within 3 feet of a compass to cause a deviation. This can be tested with your own diving equipment by placing your diving compass on a floor, noting the needle reading, and then moving your other equipment past the compass and seeing if any deviation occurs and, if so, at what distance.

A popular type of diving compass is the indirect-needle type, with index markers on a rotating bezel. This section explains how to use this type of compass; manufacturer's instructions will explain how to use other types. No matter which type of compass you select, however, there are procedures for its use and care with which you need to be familiar.

To set a heading with your compass, point the lubber line of the compass in the desired direc-

tion of travel, and align the index marks so that they bracket the compass needle. To follow a heading, simply keep the lubber line aligned with your body and the compass needle between the index marks.

Keeping the compass aligned with the centerline of your body is very important. If the compass is worn on the wrist, good alignment can be obtained by fully extending your arm without the compass and then grasping the elbow joint of the extended arm with the middle finger of the arm with the compass (Fig. 7-11). An even more accurate way to align the compass is to hold it in both hands and extended in front of the diver.

A console-mounted compass can be aligned by holding the console in both hands with the elbows tucked against your sides. This method is not as accurate as the two other positions described, however (Fig. 7-12).

The most accurate way to use a compass is to mount it on a compass board, which is held in both hands and extended in front of the diver. The extended lubber line on the compass board increases the accuracy of the compass.

When following a heading, you should sight across a compass rather than looking down on the instrument. As you look across the compass, select an object ahead of you that is directly in line with the course you wish to follow. You then can make your way to the object without having to watch the compass continuously. When the object is attained, use the compass to select another object on the heading to be followed. Simply repeat this procedure for as long as you desire to follow the heading.

Your compass can assist you in conducting very precise dive patterns. You can perform a square pattern by swimming the first leg on a

Fig. 7-11. Navigating with a wrist-mounted compass.

Fig. 7-12. Navigating with a console-mounted compass.

heading of 0°, the second on a heading of 90°, the third on a heading of 180°, and the fourth on a heading of 270°. An out-and-back pattern is referred to as a **reciprocal course**, which is always 180° opposite that of an initial heading. For example, if you swam away from a boat on a heading of 10°, your reciprocal course for returning to the boat would be 190°.

A compass also can be used for surface navigation to fix a position when in-line objects are not available. Compass bearings to various terrestrial objects can assist you when relocating a dive site, although this type of fix is not as precise as that using two or more sets of aligned objects. Position relocation from a boat using a hand-bearing compass also can be quite accurate.

Care of your diving compass is required to keep it functioning properly. This instrument should not be dropped, shocked, or abused. Leaving a compass in the sun for prolonged periods can cause the liquid inside to expand, and a leak can result. The instrument should be rinsed after use, because sand and grit can jam the bezel. The bezel should turn freely but still hold a setting. Do not place or store your compass near magnetic items or magnetic fields.

Combining Navigational Techniques

Both natural navigation and compass position-fixing techniques are used to locate a dive site. If swimming from shore, you may travel along a course indicated by a set of in-line objects (such a course is called a **range**) or along a reciprocal course indicated by a compass bearing from an object on shore. This heading is maintained until the course intersects another line of direction that fixes the desired position.

A compass heading is selected and set before descent. This heading frequently uses the shore-line as a reference. Therefore, you will know if you are swimming toward or away from shore once you are on the bottom.

On reaching the bottom, landmarks are noted to indicate your point of departure, especially if you intend returning to that point at the end of the dive. Other natural aids to navigation are noted as well.

Turn yourself to align your centerline with the initial bearing of the compass, take a sighting on a distant object along the course you wish to follow, and then move in that direction. Distance is estimated and your heading changed as is appropriate to maintain your planned dive pattern. Natural aids to navigation (e.g., depth, shadows, water movement, and so on) are noted all along the way. Frequently referring to your compass and depth gauge allow you to navigate more accurately than by using natural aids only.

You should take pride in returning to your exact starting point at the end of a dive without surfacing. Your combined navigational skills have made your dive easier and more enjoyable. Not only that, but if anything of note is discovered on a dive, you are confident that you can relocate it because of good navigational techniques that you employed throughout the dive. At times, it is easier to find a small reef or wreck by following a bearing from a known point on a larger reef than it is to try descending directly onto the smaller site.

NAVIGATIONAL PROBLEMS

Two problems that you undoubtedly will encounter in underwater navigation are obstacles and currents. An obstacle will interrupt your dive pattern or measuring of distance. A current will affect your speed when swimming with or against the water movement, and it also will cause **leeway**, which is side-slippage in the direction of a current when you are swimming across it. The error that leeway produces can seriously affect a dive pattern and even a heading.

An obstacle can be circumnavigated by modifying your dive pattern. By swimming perpendicular to your intended course while measuring the distance from that course until you are clear of the obstacle, you then can swim past the obstacle and in a reciprocal course back to the original, intended line. This is one situation where effective distance measuring, such as kick cycles, is very useful.

There are several ways to handle the effects of leeway underwater. First, navigate close to the bottom, where water movement is at a minimum. Next, navigate from object to object along a heading. If visibility is poor or no objects are available for visual reference, angle yourself in the direction of the current to compensate for the leeway. Practice and experience will enable you to make reasonable estimations of how much to compensate for side-slippage in a current (Fig. 7-13).

It is possible to measure the strength of a current and to calculate complex vectors to navigate accurately in currents. One method used to measure a current is to measure the time that is required for a floating object to travel a known distance. For example, if you measure the time in minutes for an object to travel 55 yards and multiply that result by 32, this gives the time for an object to travel one mile. If the measured time was 2 minutes:

$$2 \text{ min} \times 32 = 64 \text{ min}$$

$$64 \text{ min} \times 1 \text{ h}/60 \text{ min} = 1.06 \text{ h}$$

$$1 \text{ mile}/1.06 \text{ h} = 0.94 \text{ mph}$$

Another method is to measure the time for an object to travel 100 feet. This distance traveled in 1 minute equals 6000 feet traveled in 1 hour, or approximately 1 knot (i.e., 1 nautical mile per hour). To reach a fixed object while swimming across a current, you must know the speed of the diver and of the current. If these two speeds are the same, the ratio of the two is 1:1. If the diver is twice as fast as the current, the ratio is 2:1. For example, if the diver swims at 1 mph, he or or she travels one-quarter miles in a period of 15 minutes. If the diver swims perpendicular to a current that also is traveling at 1 mph, he or she must start swimming upcurrent one-quarter mile of the desired destination.

Fig. 7-13. Compensating for leeway.

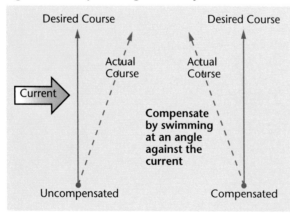

USING CHARTS

Charts can be useful in diving navigation. They contain information on depths, formations, wrecks, bottom composition, landmarks, bearings, distances, and more. Because divers typically cover very small distances in relation to those on charts, corrections for variation are required when using them. These coastal "maps" may not allow divers to navigate as accurately as they desire.

Charts establish position and measure distance by means of **latitude** and **longitude**. You are probably familiar with the grid-like lines extending around a globe horizontally at the equator and vertically from the poles. Latitude is the angular distance in degrees north or south of the equator, while longitude is the angular distance in degrees east or west of Greenwich, England. A line of longitude is also referred to as a **meridian**. Such lines of latitude and longitude appear on charts, and they are used to establish position as well as to provide an accurate scale for distances.

Proper interpretation and use of charts requires training. Such training is readily available through Power Squadron and other boating courses. These courses are inexpensive and recommended, because the navigational techniques that you will learn are applicable to diving navigation.

ADVANCED UNDERWATER NAVIGATIONAL EQUIPMENT

Among the most sophisticated equipment for underwater navigation are acoustic beacons and receivers. These are small, battery-operated devices that transmit and receive a high-frequency signal when activated. A diver who is equipped with a receiver determines the direction of the beacon by slowly rotating in the water until the receiver produces an audible tone in a headset. A compass bearing (i.e., the angular direction to an object expressed in terms of compass degrees from the north, such as a bearing of 207°) is then noted, and the diver swims toward the beacon until it is visually located. Scientists or commercial divers often mark expensive instruments or structures underwater with these types of "pingers" to relocate them.

SUMMARY

Ⓓiving navigation is more than just taking a bearing and swimming. Advanced divers know how to organize and execute a dive while knowing their approximate location at all times by using natural and compass navigational aids. A compass is one of the diver's most valuable tools, and it is important to learn its correct use. This chapter has described some of the features and methods of using a compass underwater. Only by continued practice while diving, however, will most divers become competent and proficient navigators.

SUGGESTED READINGS

- Blount S: *Treasure hunting with a metal detector in, around, and underwater*, Pisces Books.
- Keatts HC: *Guide to shipwreck diving: New York and New Jersey*, Pisces Books.
- Lippmann JL: *Deeper into diving*.

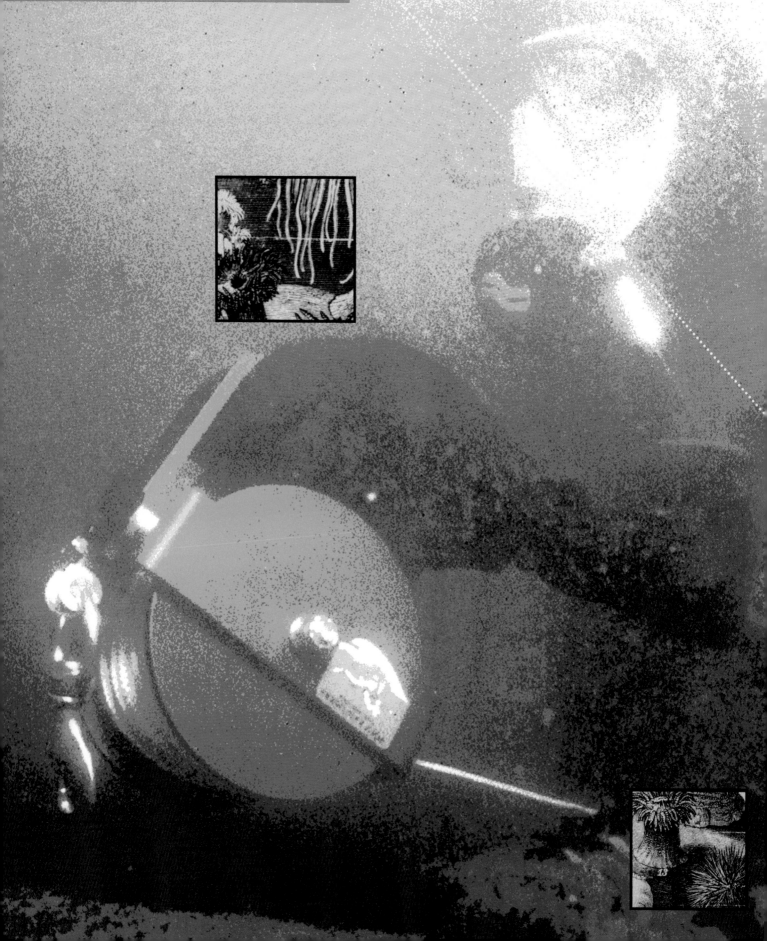

CHAPTER EIGHT

LIMITED VISIBILITY DIVING

ost recreational divers prefer diving in clear water; however, there are times when diving in lower visibility can be equally challenging and enjoyable. Further, you may have a specific diving interest in mind that usually is pursued in low-visibility water. Popular types of low-visibility diving are night diving, cavern and/or cave diving, and hunting for artifacts. Night diving is covered in the following chapter; this chapter discusses some of the many other types of reduced-visibility diving as well as procedures for comfortably enjoying this unique and challenging environment.

LEARNING OBJECTIVES

By the end of this chapter, you will be able to:

1. Define the terms presented in **bold letters.**
2. State six causes of low visibility.
3. Explain the use of a buddy line.
4. Explain the proper techniques for use of a dive light.
5. Explain four methods to orient yourself in limited visibility.

WHAT IS LIMITED VISIBILITY?

What is **limited-visibility diving**? Underwater visibility is considered to be limited when you cannot see another diver at a distance of 10 feet or less in a horizontal direction.

WHY DIVE IN LIMITED VISIBILITY?

Why would you ever want to dive in water with a horizontal visual limit of less than 10 feet? There are so many reasons why that only a small number will be mentioned here. Among the reasonable answers are:

- The only water in the area is of limited visibility.
- To explore wrecks located in such water.
- To earn the NAUI limited-visibility specialty rating.
- To search for lost objects.
- To explore a previously undived site.
- Artifact hunting.
- To locate clearer water at greater depths.
- To examine marine life (which may be abundant in such water).

Many other reasons also are equally valid. Whatever your personal requirements, make sure that you have had adequate advanced training before diving in any limited-visibility setting.

FACTORS DETERMINING WATER VISIBILITY

Pure water is transparent, but pure water does not occur in many places. The range of underwater visibility is controlled primarily by particles that are suspended in the water. Other factors affecting visibility include darkness (i.e., night) or extreme overcast during daylight hours, overhead environments that limit the available light (e.g., cavern zones, caves, the interior of sunken wrecks), silt or debris being stirred up (many times by the divers themselves), plankton blooms, suspended silt, mud, chemicals, or polluted water. In the case of diver-induced low-visibility conditions, simply being trained in antisilting swimming techniques can mean clearer water and thus more enjoyable clear-water diving.

Other causes of turbid water relate to the weather conditions. During the rainy season in many areas, rivers and streams can transport large quantities of sediment-laden water into lakes and oceans. Water visibility can be drastically reduced following intense rainstorms. During the dry season in such areas, clearer water can be expected because of the lack of runoff.

The type of bottom sediment that is present also is an important factor influencing water visibility. Coarse-grained sand is dense and quickly settles down to the bottom when disturbed. Fine-grained sediments such as silts and clays, however, can be kicked up by divers' fins and create clouds that are able to reduce visibility to zero in a short time. In these habitats, divers must practice good buoyancy control and swim off the bottom to avoid stirring up sediment.

You should choose dive sites that lie upcurrent from the entry points of streams and rivers. Obviously, diving on calm days or nights will enhance your chances of finding clearer water. Your best potential visibility will occur around reef areas away from the shore. You should avoid cove or bay areas, which usually have lower visibility. Further, the lee shore of islands usually is clearer, as are dropoffs and rocky shoreline areas. Periods of tidal change should be avoided, because the radical movement of the water at such times may create more suspended matter, resulting in lower visibility.

Thermocline interface areas sometimes may be multilayered; in other words, you may find layers of clearer water sandwiched between more turbid layers. During the spring and fall months, temperate-zone lakes and quarries are **isothermal**, which means they are the same temperature from the surface down. Suspended sediments are carried throughout the water column by natural wind-induced circulation, and this means that visibility is essentially the same regardless of depth. As the surface waters warm, however, a thermal stratification develops. There is a narrow zone of rapid temperature change with less sediment influx. The upper layer of water may have very limited visibility, but the colder, deep water will be clear. It is not uncommon to have a visibility of 3 feet at the surface and 20 feet below the thermocline.

Tannin is a brownish-orange chemical that is released by trees lining the banks of springs and waterways in Florida and other southern US states. Tannin-stained freshwater is sometimes low in suspended particulate matter. Thus, even though visibility is low, a light may dramatically increase your visibility under such conditions.

In the ocean, **plankton** (i.e., small, freefloating plants and animals) can remain suspended in the water column for long periods of time. The quantity of plankton depends on the season, amount of sunlight, nutrients, water movement, and thermal structure. A plankton bloom commonly occurs in the spring and summer months, and it can turn the water a soupy-green color, limiting visibility. Prolific blooms of some plankton are called **red tides**, which are not actually related to the tides. During a red tide, the water can turn a reddish-brown color and virtually eliminate all light below the plankton layer.

TECHNIQUES FOR LOW-VISIBILITY DIVING

Many of the specific techniques for low-visibility diving also are appropriate in normal, open-water dives. Among the most important factors to consider are visibility, navigation or direction of your swim, and careful dive planning. Divers generally will enjoy all types of diving more if they consistently avoid stirring up the silt and sediments that form the substrate of almost all open-water dive sites. Even in very low-visibility water, it is still important, both for safety and enjoyment, to minimize the addition of visibility-limiting substances to the water. Therefore, do not make things worse than they already are by using poor diving techniques that churn up the bottom and reduce visibility even further. Your body trim while swimming near the bottom is very important; ideally, you should be swimming with your head slightly down and your feet slightly up from the horizontal. A bent-knee, cave-diving kick can be used to avoid disturbing the bottom (Fig. 8-1).

Buddy Diving

The most obvious concern in limited-visibility diving is **diver separation**. The major increase in risk from low-visibility diving is the reduction in your ability to communicate and interact with your buddy underwater. You can, however, compensate for this reduced ability and thus lessen the increased risk. Remaining within touching distance of your buddy is a necessary skill to be mastered. Staying in sight of your buddy, frequent visual buddy referencing, and in very low-visibility conditions, actual contact with your buddy also are important considerations.

In addition, it is important to recognize that stress and personal task loading increase as the water visibility decreases. You should plan shorter durations and less mobile, shorter-distance swims for your low-visibility dives. In addition, it is a good idea to monitor your instruments and direction more frequently than you would while in clearer water. If you swim slower than usual, these increased tasks can be accomplished in a timely manner and you can enjoy your dive more.

Diver separation can be stressful to some individuals. If you become separated from your buddy despite your slower, more-regulated pace, you should stop swimming, breathe normally, relax, and listen. You might hear bubbles nearby. Further, visibility can be much improved a few feet off the bottom, so carefully rise upward a few feet off the bottom and, circling slowly, scan the area. Look for your buddy, bubbles, or a silt trail that might indicate a diver's presence. Search for no more than 1 minute and then surface, continuing to circle slowly once there. If your buddy does the same, once you are together on the surface you can briefly discuss the cause for your underwater separation, make plans to avoid a reoccurrence, and resume your dive.

Buddy Lines

When water conditions produce visibility that is near or at zero, you should consider using a **buddy line**. This is a 4- to 6-foot length of 3/8-inch synthetic braided or three-strand twisted line with hand loops at each end (Fig. 8-2). Floating line is preferred, because it reduces the possibility of

Fig. 8-1. A bent-knee "cave diving" kick is used to avoid stirring up a silty bottom.

Fig. 8-2. A buddy line assures contact in very low visibility (shown in clear water here for detail).

snagging on objects at the bottom. Alternatively, the buddy line can have loops of surgical tubing on each end that fit over the wrist; this way, the hands are free for other tasks. You also may hold hands if you prefer. This will enable buddies to remain in direct contact and signal each other by a prearranged series of tugs or hand squeezes if you are holding hands.

The buddy line introduces an additional potential risk for entanglement, and appropriate precautions must be taken to avoid any underwater difficulties. Practice using the buddy line when in clear water, because this will greatly enhance your success when using the line in actual low-visibility conditions. Finally, the use of buddy lines in confined underwater spaces is unwise. This increases the danger of entanglement or of the line becoming ensnared with a fixed object.

Tether Lines

When a current is present and visibility is near zero, you should consider the use of a **tether** or lifeline. Diving under such conditions is a very advanced situation, however, and should only be attempted by those who are properly trained. The tether is a line from the diver to the surface that should be placed on the body beneath all scuba equipment. A harness is commonly worn by the diver for this purpose. The line is secured by a locking carabiner or a bowline knot that will not slip.

Use of tether techniques requires a fully dressed safety diver at the surface as well as a number of other prearranged safety procedures and line signals. Only one diver is in the water at a time. In most instances, the tethered divers are in increased jeopardy of line entanglement. Consequently, knives must be carried in easily accessible positions in the divers' equipment configuration; chest- or arm-mounted knives are recommended.

Diving Lights

As you descend, light is absorbed by the water, which causes the diving environment to become darker. If particulate matter is not too great, you may choose to use a dive light. In water with a high concentration of suspended particles, your light may be reflected to the point that it becomes of little or no use. For maximum effect, you should hold the dive light to the side and above the object that you are attempting to see, because this will minimize the scatter problem that is caused by the intervening, suspended materials (Fig. 8-3).

Use of diving lights implies courtesy, so never aim your light directly at your buddy's face. (Light signals are covered in the Night Diving chapter of this book.) Always aim your light at any hand signals that you give and not at your buddy. Also, do not give nonilluminated signals. Using one or more backup lights is advisable under low-visibility conditions; should your primary light fail in open water, you can continue the dive with your backup. If a light is necessary and all lights fail, you and your buddy should surface and terminate the dive.

Orientation

As you enter turbid water, you lose the surface references of light and the pull of gravity and, thus, your spatial reference. This sensation can be

Fig. 8-3. Lights can be used in limited visibility, such as when diving around wrecks, even in the daytime.

pleasurable if you are in total control of the situation. Because of light changes, you may experience brief tunnel vision or vertigo; however, you can control both potential problems by remaining vertical and grasping an object (e.g., anchor line, rock, and so on). Should either problem persist, you can surface, using your depth gauge, watch, and slightly positive buoyancy to make a safe and controlled ascent. Buddies should stay close together, because the visual reference of a buddy can lessen the impact of any potential disorientation problems.

During your first dives in low-visibility water, you should dive in a known area or with a buddy who has been in that area before. This will minimize the natural tendency to be anxious under new conditions, and it will enable you to practice and rehearse all necessary techniques before you enter the low-visibility underwater conditions. This is valuable, because your task loading will be increased (i.e., you must keep close track of your rate of descent, depth, and location of your buddy).

It is always a good idea to use the anchor line or a drop line for a controlled descent and ascent (Fig 8-4). Under conditions of near-zero visibility and moderate current, the buddy team using a buddy line also may choose to use an underwater

Fig. 8-4. An anchor line can be used for descent in low visibility conditions.

reel so that a continuous line may be run throughout the dive from the anchor or dropline point of attachment. Control is assured, but you must be vigilant to avoid line entanglements as you increase the number of lines being used. In some areas, permanent lines are available for divers to follow and should be used in open-water areas when provided.

Horizontal control can be maintained by use of a reel, line, and depth gauge, or by use of a depth gauge and compass (Figs. 8-5 and 8-6). As in flying, you must trust your compass and follow its directions in low visibility. How you "feel" under these conditions is not an accurate method for determining your direction. To enjoy diving in very low-visibility conditions, you must be a competent underwater navigator.

Several methods can be used to ensure proper direction referencing. These include:

1. Reel and line (if trained and practiced in these skills before attempting to use them in actual low-visibility conditions).
2. Time your trip out, and follow a timed reciprocal course on your return.
3. Reference objects or bottom slope, reversing the sides that they appear on for the return trip.
4. Be aware of depth changes and current direction.
5. Use the direction of surface light (if available).
6. Remember that ripples on the bottom usually occur parallel to the shore.

As stated previously, avoid silt on the bottom, especially in freshwater or under no-current conditions. The use of protective gloves (to avoid being cut by objects you do not see) as well as exposure suits is important during low-visibility diving. In zero-visibility conditions, holding one

Fig. 8-5. A reel can be used to mark locations in limited visibility.

hand well out in front of the mask may protect it from breaking in the event that you accidentally run into an unseen, stationary object. The other hand may be placed beneath you as you swim in a slow, neutrally buoyant, fins-off-the-bottom fashion. The dive knife should be arm- or chest-mounted to ensure easy access if you inadvertently become entangled in a submerged line or rope. A smaller dive knife is recommended for use in low-visibility; this will enable you to mount it on the arm or chest and thus increase your access to it in case of a line entanglement in such conditions.

Fig. 8-6. Diver with a reel showing a cave-diving kick.

SUMMARY

Diving in limited-visibility water can be an exciting and challenging addition to your diving repertoire. Activities that are frequently pursued in conditions of lower visibility include the location of submerged objects, hunting and collecting, searching for artifacts, and river dives. As you improve your limited-visibility diving skills, your ability in clearer water will also be enhanced by the increased awareness and antisilt techniques that you develop. Further, you will broaden your diving potential by developing the ability to dive in more diverse sites. Finally, you will be a more skilled and more competent diver under all possible diving conditions.

SUGGESTED READINGS

- Barsky S: *Diving in high risk environments*, Dive Rescue International, Inc., 1993.
- Blount S: *Treasure hunting with a metal detector in, around, and underwater*, Pisces Books.
- Keatts HC: *Guide to shipwreck diving: New York and New Jersey*, Pisces Books.
- Lang ML, Egstrom G: *Proceedings of biomechanics of safe ascents workshop*, American Academy of Underwater Sciences, 1989.
- Lippmann JL: *Deeper into diving.*
- Somers L: *Tethered scuba diving*, Michigan Sea Grant College Program, 1987.

CHAPTER NINE

NIGHT DIVING

Diving is a collection of amazing experiences. Your first open-water dive, the first eel that you see, and the thrill of a wreck dive (even if it was only a 1958 Chevy at the bottom of the local quarry) all occupy a special place in your memories. If you have never made a night dive, you have some wonderful memories ahead. There are a variety of different creatures that appear at night, and the behavior of many animals also changes in the darkness.

LEARNING OBJECTIVES

By the end of this chapter, you will be able to:

① **Define the words shown in bold letters.**
② **Explain why colors are more vibrant under the illumination of a dive light.**
③ **List all items, aside from normal basic diving equipment, that are essential to night diving.**
④ **Discuss the different available types of dive lights and batteries.**
⑤ **Explain the maintenance procedures for dive lights.**
⑥ **Demonstrate the three main signals that are used with dive lights.**

THE REWARDS

Why dive at night? For excitement, for the sight of lobster crawling around in the open, for phosphorescence bursting off the tips of your swim fins, for the gentle stroking of giant parrotfish or sleeping sunfish, or for a once-in-a-lifetime dive with millions of mating squid. Freshwater divers often see more pike, walleye, and muskies at night. Many types of eel and octopus also swim freely at night, whereas they usually stay hidden in crevices during the day. You dive at night for fun and adventure.

Night diving has a way of focusing your attention and making the things that you encounter more interesting and more colorful. Using a light source that is undiluted by the filtering effect of the water makes those colors more vibrant than you have ever seen them in the day. You will also encounter creatures that you have never seen on day dives, and you will find the timid, daylight creatures amazingly approachable in their nocturnal stage.

Indeed, while it may seem that your range of vision will be limited at night, you will find that the reward is a newfound appreciation in the microcosm. Small coral polyps often open up at night. You will find that your air may last longer as you limit your attention to a small and interesting section of reef or bottom, as opposed to hurrying by oblivious to some of the most fascinating sights. Even the most mundane dive sites seem to undergo a transformation after the sun goes down.

THE PREPARATIONS

Rewards have their way of demanding tribute before they can be collected. Pay your dues by becoming completely comfortable with your skills and equipment in the water before making a night dive.

Dive the area in daylight first, and choose one with easy entry, calm and shallow water, and prominent landmarks. Remember that orientation and judging of distance are difficult at night. If possible, arrive before dark to reorient yourself and prepare your equipment for the dive.

KEEPING TRACK OF WHERE YOU ARE

A compass is a must for night diving. Even more helpful is a daytime orientation at the spot to key in on specific underwater landmarks. For shore dives, consider using two **range lights**, set up in a line, to show you the path back to your exit point after surfacing. These can be two lanterns on the beach or a similar alignment of battery-powered lights. Do not have the misfortune of using a porch or street light for a return reference only to have it turn off before you get back to shore! A surface float can be lighted by placing a chemical glow stick in a plastic milk container; for boat diving, chemical glow sticks can be placed on the anchor line for reference. It is a good idea to have someone on shore when beach diving, and it is essential to have someone in the boat while night diving from a vessel (Fig. 9-1).

THE THREE-HAND COMPLEX

Clearly, human beings have been given too few hands for them to night dive efficiently. How do you adjust your buoyancy compensator while simultaneously holding your light, reading your

Fig. 9-1. Lining up shore lights to form a "range" is an excellent means to help divers find the exit point.

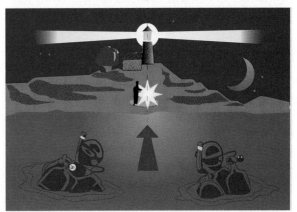

depth gauge, and carrying your camera? For your first few night dives, try to limit extraneous equipment, and use gear with which you are familiar. Your first experience is truly not the place to try out a new mask or buoyancy compensator.

The answer to the "extra hand" dilemma is buddy co-operation. You hold the light while your partner reads the depth gauge and maintains the reference ascent rate. Your buddy holds the light while you make camera adjustments, and one of you holds the bag while the other lucky one puts in lobster!

EQUIPMENT

As night diving has become more popular, manufacturers have improved equipment to make this activity easier. Many gauges now glow in the dark, making them easy to read even without direct light. You should carry a knife for diving at night, and whistles may be need for signaling divers on the surface.

Dive Lights

Night divers use a minimum of two lights per diver. Small minilights are a great backup in case a primary light fails, because they allow a check of gauges during ascent to get you back to the surface. A powerful, primary underwater light will brighten the way and make a night dive more enjoyable. Get the brightest light that you can afford. Your enjoyment of night diving is directly tied to how comfortable you are and how much you can see. While relative "foot candle" ratings are useful for comparing different models, the best demonstration is turning the light on in a darkened room. Check the pattern on a wall. If it is too wide, the light will not reach very far underwater; it it is too narrow, it may not light a reasonable area during, for example, your search for lobster. Also remember that water causes significant attenuation (i.e., loss) of the light. Most dive lights may only reach approximately 20 unless the water is extremely clear. Powerful cave-diving lights, however, can project much farther.

A waterproof light is required for each diver on a night dive. There are a number of different available types of lights and batteries, all of which suit different purposes (Fig. 9-2).

A **travel dive light** should be compact and lightweight. If you spend a lot of time in remote locations away from power or if your budget is bare, a light that uses regular, disposable batteries is

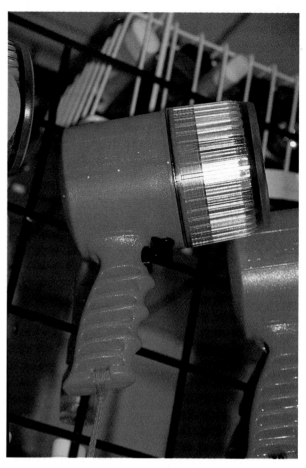

Fig. 9-2. Dive lights are available in a variety of types and sizes.

appropriate. Several flashlight-size models are available that weigh less than 1 pound. They will not have the intensity or beam angle of a larger light, but their advantage is in their compact size. Many divers use a compact travel light as their sole light for night diving.

A **primary dive light** is somewhat larger than a travel dive light, and it will have greater power and a larger beam angle than smaller, compact lights. They also are heavier and require more batteries. A typical hand-held dive light weighs approximately 5 pounds on land. A large cave-diver's light often will have a separate battery pack that is connected to the light by a cable; these can weigh as much as 10 pounds.

A stretchable or adjustable lanyard should be attached to your dive light to prevent its loss. The stretchable or adjustable feature is important so that your hand can pull free if light becomes caught. Some lights float, and others sink. The ideal light would have slight positive buoyant and float with the beam pointing up. This would make it easier to recover if lost.

Battery Selection

There are several different options for powering a dive light. The two main types of batteries are both disposable and rechargeable. **Disposable** battery lights have a lower initial cost, require limited maintenance, and do not require electric outlets for charging. They are ideal for traveling and occasional use. Most compact dive lights use either size AA or C batteries.

There are two types of **rechargeable batteries**: gel-cell and ni-cad. **Gel-cell** batteries have a burn time of approximately 2 hours and recharge in approximately 15 minutes. They require a periodic recharge-maintenance program even when not in use.

Ni-cad (i.e., nickel-cadmium) batteries commonly are used in rechargeable dive lights. Small ni-cad AA or C cells can be used in a compact dive light. Larger dive lights have internal ni-cad battery packs that must be charged according to the manufacturer's instructions. Follow these manufacturer rules on charging cycles carefully, because some lights can be damaged by overcharging or charging too fast. These batteries accept many recharges and have a burn time of from 1 to 2 hours. Wattage output is relatively constant throughout the burn time but then drops sharply.

Over the long run, the most cost-effective dive light is a rechargeable system. Batteries are expensive, and you will find that the rechargeable light quickly becomes a good investment. Rechargeable lights also are more environmentally acceptable. You may want to pick up several extra battery packs, however, to sustain you on vacations when night dives come in multiples.

Dive-Light Maintenance

The primary cause of a flooded light is an improperly seated O-ring. You should take extra precaution to seal the light in a well-illuminated area. Preferably, do it before you dress to dive. Check and carefully clean the O-ring, and apply a light film of silicone grease to it. Be sure that all wires or foreign matter are clear of the sealing surface. Carefully screw down the lens, or snap the sealing latches evenly. Examine the look of the light to assure that everything seems to be even, flush, and properly positioned. If you can see the O-ring, it should appear as a solid black line.

If a light is flooded with either salt- or freshwater, it often can be salvaged. Open the light, pour out the water, and liberally flush the light with freshwater. If the batteries are disposable, remove and discard them. Allow all pieces to dry, or use a hair blowdryer to speed drying. Look for the source of the flooding, such as switches, O-rings, or cracks in the material. Replace the O-rings or repair the case as needed. Reassemble the light and test for leaks.

Avoid banging the light unnecessarily, especially when it is turned on. Banging tends to make the bulb filaments fail. Use a rubber strap to retain the light on your wrist, because you occasionally may need to have your hands free to deal with an equipment problem.

Ni-cad batteries may need to be recharged many times to reach their full capacity. Following extended storage, the battery pack must be recharged to full capacity. If the batteries are discharged to the same point many times in a row, they will develop a memory, which reduces the light's burn time. This memory can be erased by running the battery down to a yellow glow and then recharging it.

Chemical Glow Sticks

Another essential piece of equipment is a **chemical light stick** (i.e., cyalume) or a small, single-battery marker light that is attached to your gauge console or cylinder valve. This will make it easy for you and your buddy to keep track of one another (Fig. 9-3), and they also can be used as a backup for signaling if the primary light fails.

The light-stick tube contains two separate chemicals. When the tube is bent, thin glass inside breaks and allows the chemicals to mix, which produces a glow that can last several hours. They are available in a variety of sizes and colors, which can be useful for identifying different groups of divers or dive leaders.

Strobe Lights

Strobe lights (i.e., compact, high-intensity, flashing lights) are available for emergency signal-

Fig. 9-3. Chemical light sticks come in assorted colors and sizes.

ing at the surface. They can be seen for miles and are more likely to attract the attention of people on the shore. They also are small enough to be carried in a buoyancy-compensator pocket.

Surface Lights

In addition to dive lights, you will need other lights for above-water use. These include lights to use in dive preparations as well as surface lights to mark the entry/exit location. It is a good idea to use regular flashlights for above-water use. This conserves the batteries and bulbs in your dive lights, and some dive lights will overheat unless cooled by immersion in water. It probably also would be wise for your flashlights to be waterproof in case they fall in the water.

Lights to mark the entry/exit point can be anything from a lantern to a flasher. The main idea is for these lights to be distinctive so that they will not be readily confused with others in the dive area. Be careful to avoid using lights that might resemble navigational aids, especially flashing red, green, or white lights. Amber or yellow are good alternatives. Strobe lights can be used on the group leader, on the anchor line, or near a beach exit point for their easy identification. For shore diving, the surface float can be marked with a chemical glow stick inside a plastic milk bottle.

THE NIGHT DIVE

If possible, pick a calm, familiar, shallow spot for your first night dive. Avoid the presence of kelp, big surf, and wave-washed rocks at night, and stick to open-water areas. Boat dives to shallow or protected reefs are excellent. It is a good idea to limit the dive area to a reasonable boundary. You will have checked the area earlier in the day, and your gear is now ready. Take a moment to go over the dive plan with your partner. Set up your return lights, don your gear, and do a last-minute check in a lighted area. Finally, activate your "chem light" or personal marker light before entering the water.

When entering the water from shore, lay down and swim in the shallow water, remaining close to your buddy. This will prevent you from falling or being knocked down. Take bearings on the point where you wish to exit before submerging so that you can navigate during the dive to finish near your exit point. If you have a long surface swim and conditions allow, you might want to keep your light switched off to conserve batteries.

Check with your buddy once you reach the diving area, and test your lights before descending

together. You may experience disorientation or vertigo from lack of a point of reference during the descent. Shining your light on your bubbles or using a descent line helps to prevent this. Once on the bottom, be alert for surge and current lest you be swept into unseen obstructions. Move slowly and stay together, looking not only from side to side but up and down as well. Do not shine your light into your buddy's eyes but rather on his or her chest or the ocean bottom if you are near it. Agree on an attention-gaining signal, such as rapid wiggling of the light, covering and uncovering the light, or line pulls. A buddy line also may be used. You will notice that it is helpful to hover just above the bottom to prevent the sand or silt from clouding the water; some divers in special environments prefer to adjust themselves to slight negative buoyancy on the bottom to avoid floating unaware toward the surface.

Lights permit us to communicate more easily at night, both underwater and on the surface. Shine your light on your own hand to communicate with hand signals. To signal with the light, the following signs are universally used:
1. *OK* is expressed by circling with your light.
2. *Distress* is expressed by a rapid up-and-down movement of your light.
3. *Attention* is conveyed by a back-and-forth, side-to-side motion of your light (Fig. 9-4).

If you should become separated from your buddy, stop, turn slowly, and look for your buddy's light or bubbles. Locating your buddy's light will be easier if you shine yours away from the direction you are searching, or ir you press your light against your chest. If you do not locate your buddy after 1 minute, surface. Your buddy should do the same. Leave your light on after reaching the surface, however; when your buddy is sighted, signal by making a large "O" for "OK" in the air with your light. Your buddy should return the signal. Descend again after getting back together and checking your reference points.

During ascent, shine the light on your bubbles and gauges to judge the rate of ascent. Keep one hand over your head as protection against surface obstructions. If you have navigated correctly, you should be near your exit point on surfacing at the end of the dive. Changing into dry, warm clothes after the dive is essential.

You should agree to terminate the dive when one of the following occurs:
- Failure of either diver's primary light source if no backup is available
- Either diver's air pressure reaches 500 psi (in standard cylinders)
- Either diver is excessively cold

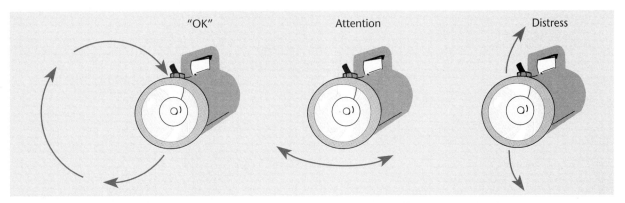

"OK"   Attention   Distress

Fig. 9-4. Light signals used for night diving.

- The divers are separated and cannot find each other underwater
- The planned end of the dive has arrived
  Potential hazards that are associated with night diving include:
- Disorientation
- Claustrophobia
- Entanglement
- Boat traffic
- Silt, which causes backscatter in light
- Contacting hazardous creatures
- Being startled by fast-swimming creatures such as seals and sea lions

When diving from a vessel, it is best to anchor as close to the dive site as possible, preferably in a sandy, flat area that is adjacent to the reef. The anchor or descent line should be lighted at middepth and the bottom for diver reference. The vessel should never be left unattended. If a current is present, a floating trail line with a light marker should be deployed. A distinct surface light also should be placed at a high point on the vessel for easy reference by divers at the surface.

Fig. 9-5. Night diving can offer unique photographic possibilities.

SUMMARY

Ⓝight diving is exciting, fun, and adventurous, and can offer unique photographic possibilities (Fig. 9-5). There is a great deal to see and experience in the dark, mysterious waters of the sea at night. To enjoy night diving to its fullest, you should know the area, your buddy, and your gear well. You will find that night diving can be rewarding and will increase your confidence in your diving ability. Give nocturnal bubbling a try.

SUGGESTED READINGS

- Bohler T: *Night diving,* NAUI.
- Lang ML, Egstrom G: *Proceedings of Biomechanics of Safe Ascents Workshop,* American Academy of Underwater Sciences, 1989.
- Lippmann JL: *Deeper into diving.*

CHAPTER TEN

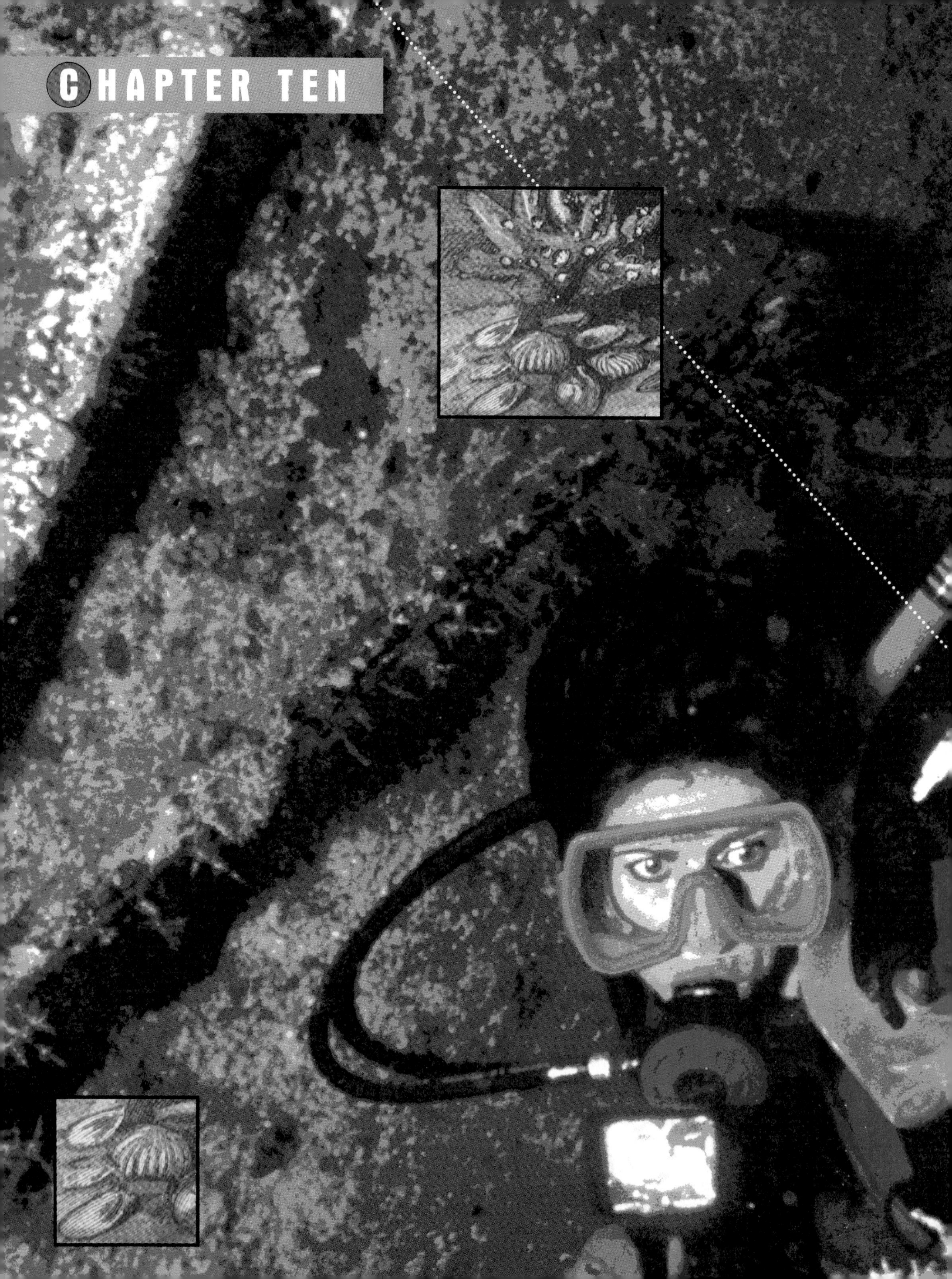

SEARCH AND LIGHT SALVAGE

As a diver, you may be asked to find a lost object underwater and bring it to the surface. You or a friend might lose some item from a boat, and you may want to recover it. As a NAUI advanced scuba diver, you should be able to select and perform an appropriate search pattern to locate and then salvage an object, provided that it weighs less than 100 pounds. Divers should not attempt to retrieve objects that weigh more than 10 pounds without using a lift bag; however, do not use your BC in such a way.

LEARNING OBJECTIVES

By the end of this chapter, you will be able to:

1. Briefly describe the search and salvage terms that appear in **bold letters**.
2. List at least five items of special equipment that are recommended for search and light salvage.
3. Discuss potential risk factors that are associated with search and light salvage.
4. List the three general steps to be followed when searching for an item underwater.
5. Illustrate and describe at least three underwater search patterns, and explain the circumstances under which each should be used.
6. List at least three safety rules for salvage diving.
7. Briefly describe the procedures for salvaging an object using a lift bag.

ORGANIZATION

Most people believe that finding something underwater is not difficult. Locating an object underwater, however, often is equivalent to parachuting into a dense fog on a vast desert and then initiating a search!

Many factors affect the outcome of an underwater search. These include visibility, depth, bottom contour and composition, aquatic vegetation, site accessibility, water movement, information provided to the searchers, and the organization of the searchers. Of these factors, only the organization of those who will be searching can be controlled. Therefore, organization is very important.

The basic rules for organizing an underwater search are:

1. Personal safety is a priority.
2. Define the area to be searched.
3. Assemble the required equipment.
4. Identify any hazards that may be associated with the search.
5. Select and conduct the search pattern that is best suited to the area.
6. Keep track of the areas to be searched.

Personnel

Recreational divers can benefit from a knowledge of underwater search and salvage methods. Careless divers and boaters frequently lose items such as masks, fins, weight belts, sunglasses, and fishing gear. If a dive team can identify the loca-

tion of the lost object and the conditions permit, it may be recovered using systematic search techniques.

Recreational divers must remember that their knowledge and ability is limited by their training, equipment, and experience. Searches should be limited in both their area and depth, and they must exclude adverse conditions such as zero visibility, polluted water, heavy current, the proximity of dams, or an overhead environment.

If several divers are to participate in a search, each should understand exactly what the other members are supposed to do. With this information, a minimum of communication will be required while underwater. A dry-run practice of the chosen search pattern or procedure on land before attempting it underwater can save a great deal of time and confusion when the actual diving begins.

Defining the Search Area

If a diver has deployed a marker float, the area to be searched is well defined. When defining the area to be searched, consider dividing a large area into smaller ones. For keeping track of the areas that have been searched, consider the ways in which this can be accomplished. A number of surface markers or marker buoys probably will be required.

It is important to gather as many facts as possible. Your chances of success are much better if the search area and lost object are well defined. Find out exactly what was lost, how it was lost, where and when it was lost, what the water conditions are like, and what the bottom topography and composition are like in the search area.

Equipment

Besides your basic diving gear, special equipment may be needed for search and light-salvage operations. Some of that equipment may include:

1. Surface floats/marker buoys.
2. Anchors and search lines or reels.
3. Dive lights.
4. Compass board.
5. Diver's sled and tow line.
6. Tool kit.
7. Spare-parts kit.
8. First-aid kit.
9. Lift bag.
10. Separate air supply.
11. Ropes and carabiners.
12. Underwater metal detector.

Risk Factors

A prudent diver will understand the potential risks involved with any activity. Naturally, underwater search and recovery dives include all of the risk factors that are associated with routine diving. Because of the specific requirements associated with this type of diving, however, some of these factors become more noteworthy.

Entanglement

The potential of entanglement in fishing nets, fishing lines, or other debris often is increased, because the diver must work near the bottom and often in very limited visibility. If visibility is completely obscured, the diver will need to search by feel. Further, the search line itself presents a potential entanglement hazard. Good line-handling techniques as well as good buddy communications are mandatory.

Physical Injury

Because the diver often is swimming about and feeling for a lost item in very limited visibility, the possibility of an accidental encounter with sharp objects is greatly increased. Divers are encouraged to wear sturdy, protective clothing (including heavy gloves) and to make all movements slowly and systematically.

Diver Separation

Problems associated with limited visibility and the potential for diver separation were discussed in a previous chapter. Special care and technique is required to avoid diver separation when searching in limited visibility. The use of a search line, however, does provide a common connection that reduces the possibility of separation.

Loss of Control in Current

Current complicates any underwater search effort. In such a situation, divers have more difficulty in maintaining position and systematically covering a designated area. Further, the current actually may carry the diver into debris or complicate resolution of an entanglement. Novice divers are well advised to forego search and recovery activities in current.

Loss of Ascent Control

Divers must observe great care when lifting an object by flotation. Because of air expansion in the flotation unit, it may rise rapidly to the surface. Divers must not "ride" a fast moving object to the surface at rates exceeding those of a normal ascent.

Whenever an object is being hoisted or floated to the surface, all divers must take exceptional care to remain clear of that object. During ascent, air expansion in the flotation unit can cause rapid acceleration. If the flotation unit or object strikes a diver, the diver could be injured. Of greater concern, however, is the possibility of the object being floated (or lifted) to the surface breaking away from its attachment point and falling back to the bottom. A falling object could strike a diver, causing serious injury or even death.

Risk–Benefit Assessment

All search and recovery operations should include a risk–benefit analysis. Is the risk that is associated with searching for or recovering an object justifiable in terms of the benefits that will be derived from finding and recovering that object? For the average recreational diver, looking for a lost mask at the local dive site under normal diving conditions generally is a justifiable task that, if properly done, involves minimal risk. Searching for a pair of sunglasses dropped from a pleasure boat in a dirty harbor where the water may be polluted, however, places the diver at an unacceptable level of risk. Sunglasses are not worth contracting a disease, but unfortunately, many divers do not consider potential health hazards associated with rivers and harbors in such places. Risk–benefit assessment requires that the diver examine the environment, circumstances, worth of the object, skill, equipment availability, personal training, previous experience, and many other factors.

Laws and Regulations

Even though a vessel is sunken, abandoned, a derelict, or aground, both it and its cargo belong to the owners of that vessel. In most cases, it may be the property of an insurance company. Salvagers must obtain permission to salvage the vessel, and they must adhere to any relevant laws and governmental regulations. In some situations, major consideration must be given to the potential for environmental impact. Keep in mind that many objects are protected under various laws that are intended to preserve items of historical significance. Whatever is salvaged must be documented with an admiralty court; state, federal, and foreign governments also may have claims whenever the object or vessel falls within their jurisdiction.

Search Procedures

One capable person needs to be in charge of a search operation, and everyone involved must agree to follow the instructions of the search leader. First, establish depth and time limits for the search and salvage operations. Next, discuss and agree on emergency procedures for accidents that may occur. Then, select and practice the search pattern that is most likely to be used underwater.

Be prepared to mark the location of the object once it has been located. An item can quickly become lost after it has been found if its location is not marked. A diver-deployed buoy can be attached to the item underwater and released to float to the surface.

Everything possible must be done to avoid disturbing the bottom and stirring up silt. Do not wade around in the water, and avoid treading water in a vertical position near the bottom. Use slight positive buoyancy to ascend rather than swimming upward from the bottom. Also, avoid contact with the bottom as much as possible. Slight positive buoyancy that requires you to swim with your fins slightly above a horizontal plane is desirable.

SEARCH PATTERNS

Before any search and salvage operation, a search pattern must be selected. When making this decision, you should consider the number of searchers who are available, their training and experience, available equipment, water and bottom conditions, and the above-water conditions.

An **underwater search** usually is conducted by swimming a definite pattern. The two fundamental types of search patterns are straight line and circular; all accepted search patterns are simply variations of these two basic themes. Different patterns lend themselves better to one type of search than to others depending on the type of bottom, depth, obstructions, and the base of operations. Several search patterns are described here, and an imaginative combination of two or more of these basic patterns usually will prove effective in almost any instance.

All search patterns involve measuring distance. This can be accomplished by using measured lines, counting kick cycles, swimming for a measured time, or counting arm spans when visibility is limited. A **kick cycle** is defined as one complete kick of both legs, and it usually is counted when one leg reaches the top of the kicking motion. Kick cycles can be calibrated by swimming along a measured length of line and counting the number of full kick cycles that are required to cover that distance. For example, if 25 kick cycles are used to cover a distance of 100 feet, then each kick cycle covers a distance of 4 feet. Alternatively, one can measure the time that it takes to swim a known

distance along a line to get an idea of distance covered over time. Skill in the areas of navigation and distance measuring are prerequisites for attempting any underwater search.

When swimming any line-controlled pattern such as the semicircular and circular search, it is necessary that the line remain taut at all times. This means that the diver controlling the line will place a slight strain on it, and may even need to angle his or her body to maintain this strain. These patterns should not be attempted with a line that is longer than 50 feet, because the effectiveness of this pattern depends on maintaining a taut line. A slack line causes an erratic pattern.

In addition, recreational divers work as buddy teams, unlike public-safety dive teams who often deploy single, tethered divers. On semicircular, circular, and other taut-line arc searches, the inside diver (i.e., the diver closest to the pivot point) controls the line distance and tautness. The buddy swims on the outside of the arc, handles the reel, and maintains a fixed distance from the inside diver.

The Contour Search

When the probable depth and approximate location of an object lost offshore are known, a **contour search** can be very effective (Fig. 10-1). In a contour search, the contour of the bottom along a shoreline is followed at a constant depth. This method is not a true "pattern"; rather, it is a search technique.

The search is initiated approximately 100 feet down the shore from the estimated location and at a depth slightly greater than that estimated. You then follow the contour of the bottom, which means that you maintain a constant depth, until you are

Fig. 10-1. Contour search pattern.

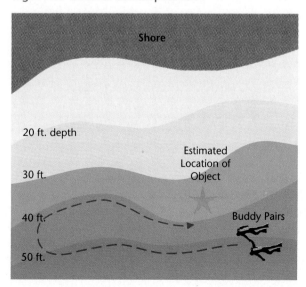

approximately 100 feet up the shore from the object's estimated location. At this point, you turn at a right angle toward shore, to a shallower depth. The distance that you move toward shore as well as the new depth will be determined by the visibility. You then turn parallel to shore again at the new depth and swim parallel to your first course in the reverse direction. The distance between sweeps will be determined by visibility and the size of the object. With low visibility or small objects, the distance between sweeps will be closer together. Successive sweeps at shallower depths are conducted until you either find the object or conclude that it is not in the area being searched.

Compass-Controlled Patterns

Fairly precise patterns can be maintained by using a compass and counting kicks. Both parallel and box patterns may be used. Such patterns are especially useful when searching for a medium- to large-sized object in moderate to good visibility.

The **parallel search** is conducted by swimming on a fixed compass heading for a given distance. The distance is maintained by counting kick cycles or time. At the end of the swim line, the divers turn 90° to the line of search, swim a short distance (which is visibility dependent), and then turn 90° to parallel the previous line on a reciprocal compass heading. This procedure is repeated numerous times, and fairly large areas can be covered with it quickly (Fig. 10-2).

Another compass-controlled search pattern is the **expanding box** (or **square**) search pattern (Fig. 10-3). In this pattern, the dive team swims on a predetermined course for a short distance from the starting point using the kick count or swim time as a control. The divers then turn 90°

Fig. 10-2. Parallel search pattern.

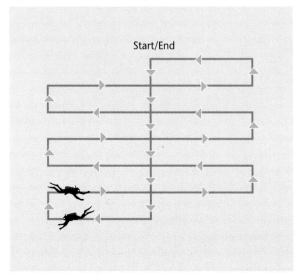

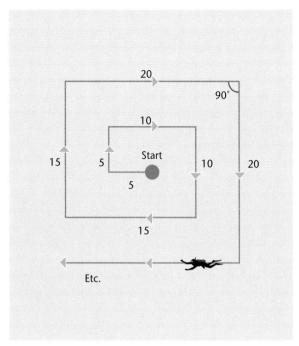

Fig. 10-3. Expanding box search pattern.

and swim a slightly longer distance. This procedure is repeated to provide an expanding, box-shaped pattern (or a straight-sided spiral). The degree of expansion on each side is controlled by the visibility.

Circular Search

The **circular search** is popular because of its simplicity and effectiveness in many situations. It is most useful when there are no underwater obstructions in the area being searched and visibility is reasonably good (Fig. 10-4).

One end of a line is secured firmly in the center of the area to be searched, and this line serves as a hub. One member of a buddy team remains at the anchored end while the other holds onto the line, keeping it taut while he or she swims circular sweeps to search for the lost object. The diver at the anchored end can face one direction and will then know when a complete circle has been completed. After each complete circle, the diver at the anchor gives a line pull signal to the searching diver, who then lets out more line and repeats the sweeps in everwidening circles until the object is located or the circles become too large for effective use of the line. The anchored end can then be moved in a predetermined direction, and the search can be repeated. Areas being searched should overlap each other somewhat to ensure that the entire area is covered.

Another method that can be used to keep the divers together is using an anchor, stake, or weighted object as a central pivot point. The

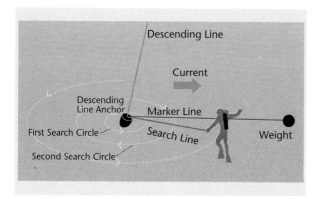

Fig. 10-4. Divers performing circular search pattern with a line.

divers swim a given distance from the pivot point and make a circular sweep completely around it. The search line must remain taut throughout the sweep. If the object is not located, a length of line is played out (the actual length depending on the visibility), and a second complete circular sweep is made. Subsequent sweeps of increasingly larger circles may be made.

In limited visibility, it may be necessary to lay a reference line. Each time the circling divers encounter the reference line, they expand the pattern by an appropriate distance. If visibility is extremely poor, the diver may have to sweep the bottom gently with his or her free hand, using an arc motion to feel for the object. In such situations, it is preferable to have the inside diver perform the search and the outside diver hold the reel and swim above the search diver and slightly outside; this is to monitor movement and bubbles. On a silty bottom, the outside diver often commands a reasonably good view of the search diver using this technique, which is somewhat inefficient but does maintain the buddy system.

Semicircular Search

A variation of the circular sweep is the **semicircular search**, which is used from a shoreline, pier, or jetty that form the extremes for a semicircle. In this technique, a line is anchored in the center of the search area and along the straight edge. The line may extend from shore or be anchored at the bottom. Searching is conducted in the same manner as a circular sweep, except you reverse direction at the end of each semicircular sweep (Fig. 10-5).

In addition to its use from shore, a version of the semicircular search is useful when searching for objects that have fallen overboard from an anchored boat. A boat at anchor swings in an arc on the anchor, especially when there is wind. Any object falling into the water at a certain position relative to the boat will probably not be where

you think it is because of this lateral movement of the vessel. A line that is attached to the anchor can be used to sweep back and forth in the area transversed by the boat, increasing your chances of success by employing an appropriate, methodic searching method.

Straight-Line Search Patterns

The majority of search patterns are based on straight lines, and these patterns are very adaptable to a variety of conditions and situations. Straight-line searches can be conducted in several ways:

1. A compass or a compass board may be used to navigate along straight lines to search an area methodically.
2. A line can be strung in a straight line along the bottom, used as a reference for a straight-line search, and then repositioned to allow methodic searching.
3. A grid of rope or PVC pipe can be spread out on the bottom.
4. A planing board or diver's sled can be towed along a straight-line course by a boat.
5. A number of geometric shapes can be used, including square, rectangular, square spiral, or jackstay.

Using a compass to conduct a search pattern is not easy. There may be no landmarks on a featureless bottom, and at times you may even believe that you are going in the wrong direction. You may not be able to navigate with the compass and search effectively at the same time. One member of a buddy team should be responsible for navigation and swimming a search pattern. The other member should maintain buddy contact and con-

Fig. 10-5. Semicircular search pattern.

tinuously, thoroughly scan the surrounding area for the object being sought. More accurate patterns can be achieved with a compass board than with a compass on its own.

Use of a **planing board** (i.e., sea sled) or a tow bar behind a boat is reserved for when a large object (e.g., a wreck) is being sought and the search area is very large. Hazards are associated with use of a planing board, such as entanglement, rapid ascents, and bumping into submerged objects. Use of a sea sled is discouraged unless you have training and supervised experience in using one.

A **grid search** is useful when looking for small objects in a well-defined area. The grid is constructed of rope or PVC pipe, and it is spread out on the bottom. In this way, a very minute search can be conducted. If the bottom is soft and the lost object small, sifting the mud or sand square by square may be necessary to recover the item.

Jackstay Search

The **jackstay search** is used to cover a relatively large area on a flat bottom. A base line is established on one edge of the search area, and a movable line is laid perpendicular (often by compass) to the base line. Remember that there are many variations of the jackstay search pattern. A second line that parallels the baseline is placed at the opposite edge of the search area. Using the movable guide line, divers can search an area systematically (by feel, if necessary) (Fig. 10-6).

This type of search is conducted by having two buddy teams swim parallel to a guideline but in opposite directions. The inside diver of each team maintains gentle contact with the guideline. In poor visibility, the other diver may maintain contact with the guide diver by holding onto the diver's harness or a separate, short buddy line. Using their free hands, the divers sweep the bottom and feel for the object. When each team reaches the base or edge line, they signal the other team by using two distinct line pulls. If the other team has reached the other perimeter (or edge of the search area), they return those two pulls. The line is then moved a predetermined distance, which depends on the visibility and search-precision requirements. Search-precision requirements relate to the size and value of an object. The guideline would be moved in smaller increments if you were searching for a diamond ring than it would if you were searching for an outboard motor. The teams now swim in the opposite direction, and the procedure is repeated until the entire search area has been covered.

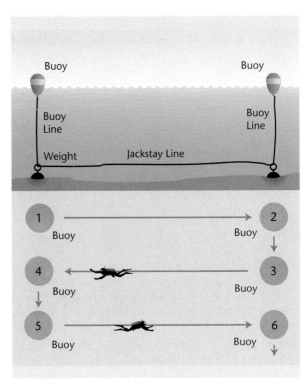

Fig. 10-6. Jackstay search pattern.

Some recommend that this type of search be conducted by two individual divers (instead of by two pairs of divers) moving along the line in opposite directions. Although when using only two divers it is slightly easier for the divers to coordinate and the procedure obviously requires less personnel, it does separate the dive buddies. This violates the buddy-diving protocol that has been established for recreational divers.

A **running jackstay search pattern** is useful for searching small, elongated ponds. This technique requires placement of a line tender on opposite shores. A line is stretched between the tenders and then allowed to sink to the bottom. The search divers (a buddy team) swim along the line and feel the bottom. One diver may be positioned on each side of the line. When the divers reach the opposite shore, the line is moved a predetermined distance by the tenders, and the search is continued in the opposite direction. This procedure is repeated until the designated area has been covered.

LIGHT-SALVAGE PROCEDURES

When the object of your search has been located, the next step is to recover it. This can be as simple as picking it up or as complex as rigging a hoist or lift bag and then raising the object.

In addition to the previously listed gear that is needed for salvage work, you also must be equipped with the specific knowledge and skills for the task. Physics calculations often are required to lift an object from the bottom (see examples in the Physics chapter). The following principles and procedures are important, and they should be studied carefully.

Safety Requirements

The safety requirements for light-salvage operations include:

1. *Knot Tying and Rigging*: You must be able to tie the following knots properly when rigging objects to be lifted: bowline, sheet bend, clove hitch, and a round turn and two half hitches.
2. *Lift Bag Use*: You must be able to estimate the correct size of the lift bag, inflate it using an independent air source, and maintain complete control of the lift bag as it ascends.
3. *Thinking*: You must be able to remain calm, think, analyze, and act to minimize or correct any errors.
4. *Training*: You must have the proper training for the lift that you intend to make.

Types of Lift Bags

A number of commercially made lift bags are available, and these come in a variety of styles, sizes, and shapes for specific uses. For light-weight objects, divers have used a simple, inverted goody bag with a trash-bag plastic liner. An extra buoyancy compensator works nicely for lifting things like weight belts or small anchors. Large steel drums have been used in salvage operations as well.

The most popular type of lift bag is the **open-bottom** style. These lift bags are shaped like a parachute, with a manual dump valve on the top and an opening on the bottom to add and vent air. They have straps and clips (or shackles) for rigging, and they are very versatile. These bags usually roll up into a compact bundle for easy handling underwater. Lift bags are rated by their lifting capacity, and open-bottom lift bags come in sizes ranging from 50 to 12,000 pounds. Large bags are for use by commercial divers, and these must be handled with care.

Pillow bags are totally enclosed lift bags that have overpressure relief valves to vent the expanding air. They often are used for raising sunken boats and for towing, because they can be distributed inside spaces without respect to the orientation of the bag. Once filled, they need not be manually dumped on ascent. Pillow bags come in sizes ranging from 250 to 6000 pounds.

Lift bags can be any number of shapes. **Ocean salvage tubes** are long, cylindric bags that are used for pipe-laying and other construction projects. They also often are used to raise sunken boats by suspending them underneath or along-side like pontoons. They are available in sizes up to 3000 pounds.

Controlling a Lift

The capacity of a lift bag must not exceed by a great deal the weight of an object to be lifted, because air in a lift bag expands during ascent. If a 200-pound lift bag is used to raise a 50-pound object from a depth of 66 feet (20 m), the lift will gain 100 pounds of buoyancy during ascent. This will cause the lift to rise rapidly, and dangerously, out of control. It could even come completely out of the water on reaching the surface, spill its contents, and then drop the lift back down on the divers below. The first important step in light salvage is to match closely the capacity of the lift bag to the weight of the object being lifted.

A lift bag should be inflated with air from an independent cylinder and not from the divers' cylinders. The purpose of this is not to conserve air but to ensure that your regulator and hoses do not become entangled in the lift as it begins to ascend.

If a lift bag is inflated until the object begins to rise, you probably have put too much air into the bag. It takes time to overcome inertia in water. Add air to the lift bag slowly, and test the lift from time to time by raising it from the bottom. Your lifting will tell you how much additional air is required and help to overcome any inertia that the lift may develop.

When the lift begins to ascend, both you and your buddy must clear the area beneath and should ascend with it. One of you should control the dump valve on the lift bag; the other should remain beside and in contact with the object being lifted so that he or she can watch and help control it if necessary. If the lift bag being used is not equipped with a dump valve, a line should be attached to the top of the bag so that it can be pulled to force the air down and out of the bag as required. If a lift rises faster than it should and becomes uncontrollable, release it and swim away. If you release too much air from a lift and it begins to sink, let it go, follow it to the bottom, and start over. Swimming to support a sinking lift is dangerous, because the lift becomes heavier as its volume decreases with increasing depth.

When an object has been lifted to the surface, it can be pushed to the exit point and pulled out. If the object is to be removed from deep water, a line should be secured to it before lifting by the bag so that it will not sink if it falls.

Lift Example: You have offered to recover a sunken outboard motor. It rests in 35 feet of saltwater, weighs 100 pounds on land, and displaces 0.5 feet of water when submerged. You have a lift bag that holds 5 cubic feet of air and an extra 15-cubic-foot cylinder that is available to fill the bag. How much air will you need to add to the lift bag to make the motor neutrally buoyant?

Answer: First, calculate the weight to be lifted underwater. Because the motor displaces 0.5 cubic feet of water, it will be buoyed by the weight of the water that is displaced:

$$0.5 \text{ ft}^3 \times 64 \text{ lbs/ft}^3 = 32 \text{ lbs}$$

$$100 \text{ lbs} - 32 \text{ lbs} = 68 \text{ lbs to be lifted}$$

Next, translate the weight that is to be lifted into an equivalent amount of air:

$$\frac{68 \text{ lbs}}{64 \text{ lbs/ft}^3} = 1.1 \text{ ft}^3 \text{ of air required at depth}$$

Now, if 1.1 cubic feet of air is required at a depth of 35 feet, how much surface air is this? Using Boyle's Law:

$$P_1 V_1 = P_2 V_1$$

where:

$$P_1 = (35 \text{ ft} \times \frac{1 \text{ atm}}{33 \text{ ft}}) + 1 \text{ atm} = 2.1 \text{ ata}$$

$$P_2 = 1 \text{ atm}$$

$$V_1 = 1.1 \text{ ft}_3$$

$$V_2 = X$$

Substituting and solving for X, we find that the 1.1 cubic feet of air at a depth of 35 feet will make the motor neutrally buoyant, and it will have a volume of 2.3 cubic feet of air at the surface. The 15-cubic-foot cylinder will be ideal for the task.

SUMMARY

The capability to search for objects underwater and bring them to the surface is a valuable skill for recreational divers. Simply possessing the basic knowledge and skills presented in this chapter, however, does not qualify an individual to search for bodies, crime evidence, or sunken treasure. Further, these techniques for lifting objects to the surface should be used with great caution and only after completing a course in search and recovery techniques taught by a qualified instructor.

Search and salvage is a specialty area. You are only introduced to the activity in this NAUI advanced class. Search activities that require further training in a specialty course include special zig-zag patterns employing lines, special techniques for searching in swift-flowing rivers and around marina docks, and proper use of a diver's sled. Salvage training includes the use of larger lift bags and drums, winches and block-and-tackle devices, and detailed calculations pertinent to salvage operations. If you need to be involved in search and salvage or simply are interested in this activity, learn what you need to know by completing the NAUI search and recovery specialty course.

SUGGESTED READINGS

- Barsky S: *Diving in high risk environments*, Dive Rescue International, Inc., 1993.
- Blount S: *Treasure hunting with a metal detector in, around, and underwater*, 1987.
- Frederick J: *Diver's guide to river wrecks*, 1982.
- Gentile G: *Advanced wreck diving guide*, 1988.
- Giguere JP: *Make money in diving*, 1981.
- Giguere JP: *Salvage laws for weekend divers*, 1981.
- Larn R, Whistler R: *Commercial diving manual*, 1986.
- Meuninck J: *Diving opportunities for fun and profit*, 1986.
- Potter JS: *The treasure diver's guide*, 1988.
- Rowe AR: *Relics, water, and the kitchen sink*, 1979.
- Tucker WC: *Diver's handbook of underwater calculations*, 1986.

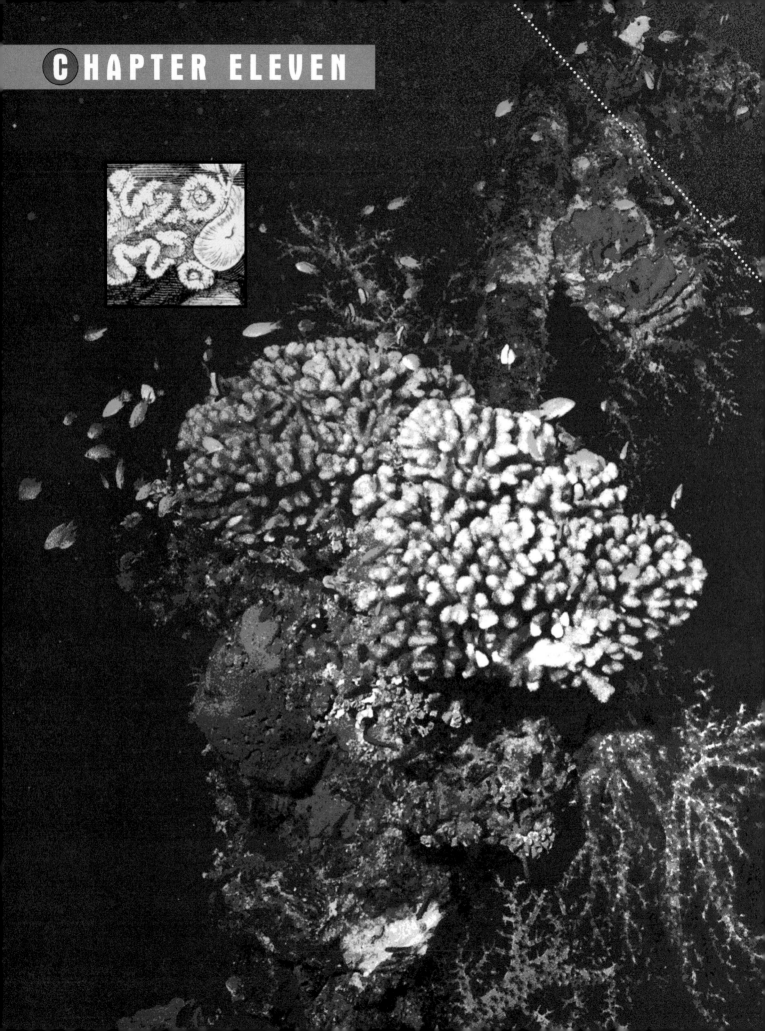

CHAPTER ELEVEN

DEEP DIVING

This chapter introduces some aspects of deeper diving. D*eep diving*, as defined for this NAUI advanced course, is any diving that occurs between 60 and 130 feet. For our purposes, dives below 130 feet almost always are considered to be beyond the scope of recreational diving. Dives below 130 feet almost always require decompression, so we refer to these dives as *technical dives*. Deep dives differ from shallower dives with respect to temperature changes, breathing resistance, reduced light, possible narcosis, additional buoyancy adjustments, and anxiety. A *precautionary stop* is recommended at the end of deep dives, and the term refers to a nonrequired decompression stop (i.e., 3 minutes at 15 feet) that is made as a safety precaution. All deep dives and repetitive dives should incorporate these factors.

LEARNING OBJECTIVES

By the end of this chapter, you will be able to:

① Define the terms shown in **bold letters**.
② List and explain five personal-limitation considerations in deep diving.
③ Describe the steps that are required for planning a deep dive.
④ Describe cylinder, valve, and regulator options for deep diving.
⑤ Discuss gas management procedures for deep diving.
⑥ List and explain four potential hazards in deep diving.

PERSONAL LIMITATIONS

Some of the reasons to dive deep may include exploration, photography, and the identification of marine life. Some people dive deep as an ego challenge. Our egos are the essence of our quest for adventure. A healthy ego gives us confidence, persistence, creativity, and flexibility, and it is vital in our ability to manage stress. Over-confidence (or an unhealthy ego), however, can lead to errors in judgment or diving beyond limitations. It is both exhilarating and satisfying to participate in well-planned, well-executed deep dives. As you read this chapter, you hopefully will analyze your own motivation and ego as well as integrate these common-sense concepts.

How deep is deep? It is difficult to assign a specific depth for all people. A reasonable and prudent depth depends on many factors, including (but not necessarily limited to) the diver, environmental conditions, equipment, and accompanying divers. The following are factors to consider when assessing personal limitations with regard to diving depth. Remember that other factors also may come into play based on individuals, diving conditions, and circumstances.

Emotional Status

Diving is not an activity for a person who is emotionally unstable. Individuals who tend to lose control or panic during a crisis may well find occasion to do so in diving. Although panic and subsequent actions may be life threatening even at very shallow depths, the consequences can be quite dramatic at deeper depths. Recklessness or emotional instability in a diver is a serious liability, both for the individual and his or her companion divers. These traits may be amplified further by the narcotic effects of nitrogen at depth.

Health and Fitness

Persons who are in poor health or physical condition generally are considered to be more susceptible to the emotional and physical stress associated with diving. Both stress and a person's response to stress can be amplified with increased depth. It also has been documented that such individuals are more susceptible to decompression sickness. Persons in poor health should seek the advice of a qualified physician and consider either imposing significant limitations on themselves or foregoing scuba diving all together. Individuals who are in generally poor physical condition but have no serious health problems should embark on a fitness-improvement program under the guidance of a physician or professional health/fitness counselor.

Training

The training program must provide the diver with a comprehensive insight into the physiologic and psychologic factors that are associated with extending the diving depths. The diver must be schooled in personal, dive-companion, and environmental assessment so that he or she may make an informed risk–benefit analysis. Greater emphasis must be placed on dive organization and planning, and trainees must develop high proficiency in the use of dive tables and computers. The diver then must participate in a series of supervised training experiences designed to progressively advance diving skill, demonstrate proper procedure and technique, and solve potential problems that might be encountered on deeper dives. Supervised problem-solving actually should be practiced at depth. For example, a diver previously may have demonstrated adequate skill proficiency in alternate air–source breathing during ascent from a depth of 20 or 30 feet; however, the emotional stress associated with performing this procedure from deeper depths may be significant in some individuals. Ideally, a diver should be capable of providing air to another diver from the maximum depth of training.

Experience

To be a good diver, you must dive regularly. If you intend to extend your diving depth beyond the shallows of a coral reef, you should acquire considerable shallow-water experience first and then work up to the deep depths through a series of progressions. In addition to progressive acquisition of experience, a prudent diver always will do a series of "buildup" dives before making deep dives. For example, many individuals are seasonal divers. At the beginning of each diving season, a prudent diver will begin with shallow, simple dives and progressively work up to deeper, more complicated dives.

Self-Discipline

Diving requires a certain degree of self-discipline, and the deeper the depth, the greater the need for it. One might observe a group of good and experienced deep divers casually preparing for a dive. Their mannerisms may appear to be casual, but each individual should have mentally rehearsed the dive, checked and rechecked their equipment, verified dive-table calculations or planned a computer profile, taken a very close look at their fellow divers, and given proper attention to even the most minor detail.

Underwater these divers will monitor their breathing rate, cylinder pressure, time, depth, position (relative to the ascent line), and a host of other status indicators, all while completing a task. They know through progressively acquired experience when things are going right and wrong. They know their physical, emotional, thermal, depth, distance, and air-supply limits. The deeper the depth, the smaller the margin for error. These divers know when to turn back or abort the dive. Self-discipline is acquired through training, experience, and emotional conditioning.

Environment

The nature of the environment dictates both depth and personal limitations. Thousands of divers casually cruise at 100-foot depths in clear, warm, tropical waters every week wearing only a thin, nonrestrictive dive skin. For an experienced diver, such a dive can be exhilarating and rewarding. For the same diver, however, a dive to the deck of a sunken ship in the dark, icy waters of the Great Lakes while encased in a dry suit could be extremely difficult. When planning deep dives, one must consider wave conditions (producing adverse conditions at decompression or safety stop depth), current, visibility, and water temperature. If the environmental conditions are unsatisfactory or too demanding on the diver, a prudent individual will cancel the dive. Only through a progressive acquisition of environmental experiences will an individual develop the necessary skill and knowledge that is required to make such decisions.

Diving Companion

Solving a problem and safely ascending back to the surface from deep depths can be extremely complicated, especially if you do not have a capable companion. When selecting a companion for a deep dive (or any dive for that matter), first try to select someone who is not going to be a problem. If the diver exhibits evidence of inadequate training, lack of experience, nervousness, overconfidence (i.e., cockiness), carelessness, or other undesirable traits, find another buddy or postpone the dive. Ideally, you should dive with an individual who you know is properly trained, experienced, equipped, and have dived with before.

Equipment

For dives up to but not exceeding 130 feet, conventional recreational scuba-diving equipment generally will be adequate. However, depending on the environment, dive profile, underwater task, and the diver's air consumption, the volume of air in a conventional scuba cylinder may be marginal or even insufficient for safe diving. Divers are encouraged to maintain 15% to 30% of their air supply in reserve for any unexpected or increased air demands that might be associated with ascent (i.e., difficulty locating the ascent line, sharing air with another diver).

Divers also must consider that added thermal protection may be necessary at deeper depths, especially in northern waters. Wet suits compress considerably at depth, both reducing thermal protection and buoyancy. Many cold-water divers now use dry suits for deep dives, even in the summer months.

When diving from a vessel, it is imperative that divers maintain their orientation and return to the surface via the ascent line. Precise compass navigation may be required. Ideally, the ascent line should be marked clearly, especially if more than one descent line is in the area (as found on some popular shipwrecks). For some locations, and especially if the visibility is limited, divers will use a guideline that is dispensed from a small reel. The guideline (e.g., tag line, distance line) is attached to the ascent line and played out as the diver moves away.

Obviously, divers will need instrumentation for determining depth and dive time. The increased popularity of dive computers has greatly simplified deep diving. Complete dependence on these computers, however, also has led to decompression sickness in some divers.

PLANNING A DEEP DIVE

Many factors must be considered when planning to dive deep (Fig. 11-1). Some things to consider include the dive site, environmental conditions, equipment selection, cylinder size and valve, regulators, and other equipment.

Dive Site

If possible, select a dive site that is protected from heavy wave activity and offers good anchorage. Many popular dive sites, especially shipwrecks, have permanent moorings that are placed by diving or governmental organizations. If diving from shore, select a site where the planned dive depth is readily accessible within a short swimming distance.

Environmental Conditions

One environmental condition to consider is the bottom topography, that is, depth, steepness of walls, and presence of caverns. Also, underwater visibility should be such that divers can move freely around the bottom (or shipwreck) and easily locate the ascent line at the end of the dive. Water temperature must be anticipated so that the correct exposure suit can be worn.

Sea and weather conditions are not always ideal, and divers may encounter high waves and limited visibility. Anchoring a vessel, diver deployment, descent, underwater navigation, ascent, decompression, and diver retrieval must be adjusted accordingly. In some situations, it may be wise to cancel the dive and return under more favorable conditions.

Equipment Selection

The water temperature may be colder at deep depths, and a neoprene wet suit will compress, which reduces both its thermal protection and buoyancy. Compensation for significant buoyancy changes will be necessary. It is mandatory that each diver be equipped with a dive timer and depth gauge (or dive computer). Because emergency ascents are more complicated and riskier from deeper depths, availability of an alternate air source is even more important than it is in shallower dives. Many deep divers prefer to use an independent scuba or a dual valve/regulator scuba for complete self-sufficiency. The small, portable, combined cylinder-and-regulator units may not provide sufficient air for ascent from deeper depths.

For dives in the range of 60 to 130 feet, primary equipment should be upgraded to include:

1. A scuba cylinder with minimum capacity of 80 cubic feet.

Fig. 11-1. Deep wreck diving requires good dive planning.

2. A primary cylinder equipped with a "Y" or "H" valve. A secondary scuba cylinder or *pony bottle*, which is a small (approximately 15 ft) cylinder with its own regulator, may be used instead of the special valve configuration. A separate pony bottle can be mounted to the primary cylinder as a totally redundant, alternate air source.

3. Two regulators for the primary gas source. One may be used on secondary scuba. One regulator is to be fitted with a 40-inch (1 m) hose and the other with a hose of at least 60 inches (1.5 m).

Scuba Cylinder

Cylinders for scuba diving are available in volumes ranging from approximately 60 to 190 cubic feet. Smaller auxiliary or "pony" cylinders range from 11 to 40 cubic feet. The standard aluminum cylinder, which is commonly used by recreational divers, is less popular among deep and technical divers because of its volume, buoyancy, and size characteristics. In selecting a scuba cylinder, a diver must consider:

1. Maximum intended diving depth and duration (i.e., required gas volume).
2. Environmental protection garments (i.e., buoyancy characteristics).
3. Ballast requirements.
4. Diver's stature (e.g., long cylinders on short divers are awkward).
5. Maximum weight of the cylinder or cylinder assembly that the diver can handle.

A diver who intends initially to dive in the range of 60 to 130 feet and later advance to deep air and technical diving will be served better by a 95- to 120-cubic-foot cylinder. A prudent diver, however, will select the cylinder to satisfy both present and future diving needs.

Cylinder Valve

A diver using a single scuba cylinder in shallow water will find the standard "K" valve to be adequate. Valves with integrated low-pressure warning mechanisms have declined in popularity. A prudent diver will seriously consider selecting a "K" valve from one of the modular valve systems. These modular systems enable the diver to change valve configurations if necessary. A modular valve system may be expanded as follows (see photographs in the Equipment and Technical Diving chapters):

1. Basic "K" Valve: Single cylinder use in less than 60 fsw.
2. Basic "K" Valve with "H" Valve Adapter: Converts the single "K" valve to a dual outlet for primary and backup regulators. This valve is for a single cylinder to be used in depths of 60 to 130 fsw. Either regulator may be independently isolated if a malfunction occurs.
3. Two Basic "K" Valves with Crossbar: Expand two single cylinders to a dual-cylinder scuba with two regulator outlets (i.e., primary and backup) for advanced technical diving.
4. Two Basic "K" Valves with an Isolation Crossbar: Expand two single cylinders to a dual-cylinder scuba with ability to isolate either cylinder for advanced technical diving.

It also should be noted that several manufacturers supply a "Y" valve to facilitate use of dual regulators on a single cylinder. Either regulator may be independently isolated in the event of a malfunction; however, the "Y" valve cannot be expanded to a dual-cylinder configuration.

Traditionally, the American scuba industry has used a standard scuba yoke connector (i.e., CGA850 or CGA855 connection). The yoke system, however, is limited technically to 3000 psig under Compressed Gas Association guidelines. For higher pressures, the DIN447 300-bar connector has become the standard fitting. The **DIN connector** features a "trapped" O-ring configuration that virtually eliminates the potential problem of blown O-rings, which has occasionally occurred with yoke fittings (see the Equipment chapter).

Today, most deep and technical divers use the more dependable DIN valve for both high- and low-pressure cylinders. Most regulators are now available with either yoke or DIN connectors. Several manufacturers have designed DIN cylinder valves with insert adapters that also allow for the use of conventional yoke regulators.

Regulator

Generally, any well-maintained recreational diving regulator should suffice for shallow-water recreational diving. If you intend to extend your diving activities into the realm of deep diving, however, you are encouraged to select a proven, high-performance regulator. The US Navy periodically evaluates scuba regulators and publishes test results. These results as well as those completed by other agencies often are published in recreational and technical diving publications.

Your first concern is performance. Will the regulator deliver a sufficient volume of gas with minimal breathing effort under high workloads at the anticipated maximum dive depth? Remember that your gas-flow requirements can more than quadruple in a high-stress situation. If applicable, will the regulator perform adequately in cold water, or will it ice (resulting in freeflow) under conditions of high demand?

Next, consider reliability. Does the regulator have a proven record of reliable performance within your intended application parameters? A reliable equipment dealer and other divers should be able to assist you in identifying both desirable and undesirable regulators. Avoid regulators with a history of malfunction and that require continuous repair. Also, what safety features are incorporated into the regulator design?

Regulator maintainability is another important consideration. Some regulators require complex and expensive maintenance procedures; others are very simple to maintain. Because regulators used for deep diving must always operate at the highest level of performance, maintainability becomes an important consideration.

A regulator must be physically comfortable as well. Weight and design characteristics are very important in reducing jaw fatigue.

Finally, a regulator must be compatible with your scuba system. Obvious compatibility requirements include things such as DIN connectors. Less obvious considerations include the physical size of the first stage relative to present and future valve and manifold configurations.

Other Equipment

A second category of equipment also is necessary for deep diving: safety-support equipment. Standard equipment, including a first-aid kit, oxygen, backboard, communication equipment (e.g., VHF or CB radio, phone), and transportation equipment should be available at the dive site. In addition, there should be stable and designated decompression stops, additional air supply, and a surface-support station.

A **decompression bar** may be deployed from a boat for divers to hold while performing safety stops. In any body of water with surface wave motion, decompression on an anchor line is not recommended. A wave passing overhead at a 15-foot stop can change your depth by the height of the wave. A much safer situation exists when a weighted line or decompression bar is suspended from midship. This ensures your depth relative to the surface, eliminates anchor-line jerking, and provides a stable, designated decompression stop. Extra full cylinders with attached regulators can be connected to this bar for use by divers who might be very low on air. Alternatively, one or more 20- to 25-foot hoses from a cylinder on the boat can be hung overboard and attached to the decompression bar. Divers should be well versed in gas management and self-discipline, however, and generally should not require extra gas to be hung at the decompression station.

The surface station normally will be a boat that is equipped with all emergency equipment and personnel listed earlier. In addition, however, the station also could be a dock, pier, or even the shore if it is very close to a dropoff. How close is very close? The answer is how long a distance can you (or do you want to) tow your dive buddy in case of an emergency.

Personnel

Your next step is to select **personnel**, which consists of your dive buddy and support personnel. When you are selecting a buddy, look for someone with equal or greater experience. It also is a good idea to have made a few shallow dives with this person to ensure good communication and compatibility. You and your buddy will need to make a mutual commitment to personal preparedness. You should be well rested, well nourished, have consumed no alcohol for 24 hours before diving, and precheck your equipment and procedures. A minimum of 20 dives in shallower water of the same type and location should be completed before venturing deeper. You should have a reason for diving deeper rather than just "to do it."

Deep diving involves greater risk, including increased exposure to decompression sickness, and it also means a longer way to the surface in case of emergency. Because of the possibility of impaired mental and physical function resulting from the effects of nitrogen narcosis, it is recommended to have support personnel (i.e., a divemaster or dive guide) present (Fig. 11-2).

If applicable, the divemaster has overall responsibility for the entire dive, including:

1. Final confirmation of the dive site with safe, acceptable conditions (i.e., depth, currents, visibility, weather).
2. Supervision and direction of divers and support staff.
3. Inspection of the divers' equipment and the safety equipment.
4. Determination and recording of profiles.
5. Development and implementation of emergency procedures and accident management if necessary.

The divemaster generally stays at the surface and supervises all aspects of the diving activity. The **dive guide**, who is sometimes referred to as an underwater tour guide, generally is a person who is familiar with dive sites. Responsibilities of the dive guide include:

1. Supervision of divers during entry, descent, stabilization (which includes establishing neutral buoyancy), the excursion, ascent, precautionary safety stops, and exiting the water.
2. Navigation and identification of special points of interest.
3. Recognition of and assistance with any problems that the divers might encounter.

The dive guide goes in the water with the divers. At many Caribbean destinations, the roles of the divemaster and dive guide are fulfilled by the same individual.

Deep diving requires a great deal of expertise. Participating in organized diving activities with trained professionals will increase the enjoyment of your dive (Fig. 11-3).

Fig. 11-2. Surface-support personnel and safety equipment are helpful for deeper diving.

Fig. 11-3. Diver descending down a deep wall.

Dive Profile

Planning your **dive profile** should involve more thinking than just choosing a time and depth. Some guidelines are:

1. Plan the dive not to exceed the Maximum No-Decompression Dive Time limits of the NAUI Dive Tables. These time limits are more conservative than the US Navy limits. If you are using a dive computer, you may be able to make a multilevel dive that is longer than the square-wave time limits.

2. Make sure the dive profile is realistically tailored to the underwater terrain and depth.

3. Select a profile that is feasible considering the air supply and consumption rate for both you and your buddy.

4. Take an underwater slate with you that has your primary and contingency profiles written out.

5. Dive your plan.

6. Do the deepest part of your dive first, and move progressively shallower as the dive progresses.

7. Allow both time and sufficient air to make a slow, controlled ascent with safety stops. A good practice is to plan your turnaround and return to your ascent point at one half of your starting cylinder pressure plus 300 psi.

8. Perform a safety stop at a depth of 15 feet for at least 3 minutes at the end of every dive.

9. If you and your buddy are not using identical models of dive computers, the dive must follow the more conservative of the two.

GAS MANAGEMENT

D ivers must be able to estimate how long their air supply will last at a given depth. Air consumption may be expressed in terms of pressure or psig per minute. Many divers prefer to use this method, because they feel it is easier to relate to pressure as the air supply commonly is related to pressure rather than to volume. The use of pressure values, however, can be somewhat misleading. For example, which diver has more air, one with 2200 psi in a steel 70-cubic-foot cylinder or one with 2200 psi in an aluminum 80-cubic-foot cylinder? In reality, the diver with the steel "70" has approximately 64 cubic feet of air, whereas the diver with the aluminum "80" has only 57 cubic feet. So, if you use cylinders of different size, you must determine your air consumption for each cylinder independently.

For example, assume that a diver swimming at a depth of 33 feet (i.e., 2 ata) for 20 minutes uses 1500 psig of air from an aluminum "80." By dividing 1500 psig by 20 minutes, we find that the diver has consumed 75 psig/min. We now logically can calculate the surface equivalent air consumption. If the diver consumed a given amount of air at 33 feet (2 ata), how much air would that diver consume at the surface (i.e., 1 ata) at the same breathing rate? The diver would consume 50% as much, or 37.5 psi/min. By determining your air consumption in "psig" at a fixed depth using a given cylinder size, you can compute the estimated consumption at the surface and other depths.

Using the surface air-consumption rate, you may compute your air consumption for a given depth. For example, a diver has a surface air consumption rate of 35 psig/min. Now, assume that the same diver, using the same scuba cylinder, wishes to determine the air consumption for an 80-foot dive. By multiplying 35 psig/minute by the absolute pressure at a depth of 80 feet (i.e., 3.42 ata), the estimated air consumption at 80 feet is determined to be 120 psig/min. Assuming that 2500 psig of air is available (excluding the 500 psig reserve) and that all air is consumed at depth, the air supply would be satisfactory for approximately 21 minutes.

EMERGENCY PROCEDURES

Because of the increased risks in deep diving, a fine-tuned emergency procedure is necessary; after all, your life may depend on it. By doing your deep dives through organized courses, PRO-Facility outings, or NAUI DREAM Resorts, you will be supported by highly trained professionals and a fine-tuned emergency procedure. Here is what to look for:

1. Trained professional staff who are currently certified divemasters and/or instructors with current dive rescue, cardiopulmonary resuscitation, and diving first-aid training.
2. Rescue equipment, including an oxygen kit, first-aid kit, backboard, and blanket.
3. Communication equipment, which may include a UHF radio, CB radio, or telephones to alert medical support if necessary.
4. Information and an access plan for evacuating a victim to the nearest hospital and/or hyperbaric chamber.
5. Transportation by boat and/or vehicle for evacuation.
6. Contact the Diver's Alert Network (DAN) for assistance in emergency evacuation and hyperbaric treatment.

Remember, good accident management is no accident. It takes a serious amount of training, experience, and dedication to produce competent, efficient emergency procedures. Your piece of mind is worth a few extra dollars added to the cost of your outing to dive with professionals.

If you are diving on your own, you must prepare your own emergency plan using the guidelines presented here. You must decide to what detail you will provide for yourselves and what kind of local assistance can be obtained. Any training that you can obtain in the areas of oxygen administration, first aid, and diver rescue will be beneficial.

POTENTIAL HAZARDS

When, for various reasons, things do not go according to plan during a deep dive, you must be prepared to deal with any problems that may occur. Some potential problems are listed here, along with suggestions for dealing with them:

1. *Emergency Decompression*: If the no-decompression limits are unintentionally exceeded, you must make whatever decompression stops are required.
2. *Omitted Decompression*: The US Navy procedure for omitted decompression, which involves recom-

pressing the diver in the water, is no longer a viable option. In-water decompression has been eliminated as an acceptable procedure based on recommendations by noted physicians and physiologists. If the required decompression is missed, you should remain out of the water, rest, breathe 100% oxygen, drink fluids, and be alert for signs and symptoms of decompression sickness. If the bends are suspected, proceed at once to the nearest medical facility for examination and possible transport to a hyperbaric facility. The DAN should be contacted at (919) 684-8111 by the attending physician. In-water decompression does not eliminate bubbles once they have formed, and it can make the situation much worse than it would otherwise be. A "bent" diver requires medical attention and recompression in a controlled, air environment.
3. *Rapid Ascent Rate*: If your rate of ascent is too fast and you are able to arrest it at a depth of greater than 20 feet, simply pause for the estimated length of time that it should have taken you to reach that depth if you had been ascending at the proper rate. If an uncontrolled ascent takes you all the way to the surface from a depth of greater than 30 feet, you should get out of the water, breathe pure oxygen, and watch for signs of decompression sickness.
4. *Cold or Strenuous Dives*: If a dive is cold and strenuous, use the next-greater depth and bottom time schedules. If a dive is particularly cold or strenuous, use the next-longer bottom time schedule.
5. *Instrumentation Failure*: If your instrumentation providing information about your decompression status fails, you should ascend to a depth shallower than 30 feet and then perform precautionary decompression that is appropriate for your best estimate of your decompression status. Your buddy's instruments may help you to estimate this status. If to the best of your recollection you are well within the no-decompression limits, a simple precautionary stop may suffice. If, however, you are uncertain about your decompression requirements, extended decompression is recommended. After surfacing, diving activities should be terminated for the day.
6. *Separation from Buddy*: Deep diving requires close visual contact between buddies. If you become separated, you should strive to regain contact with your buddy as soon as possible. Look for exhaust bubbles for approximately 1 minute, then begin to ascend while scanning the water around you. You will have to perform your safety stop because of the deep dive. If

your buddy does not meet you on the surface, you must decide whether to descend again and search. Do not jeopardize your personal safety if insufficient time remains to dive again to the depth in the area you were separated. Diver rescue from great depths also may be particularly challenging.

EFFECTS OF INCREASED PRESSURE

The obvious effects of increased pressure are that increased exposure to a higher ppN_2 can cause decompression sickness and narcosis (covered in detail in the Diving Physiology chapter). The risk of decompression sickness will be minimized greatly by staying above 80 feet and planning your dives conservatively to remain well within the no-decompression limits. Bounce dives, which are successive, relatively short up-and-down dives, are discouraged, because they apparently favor bubble formation.

Other effects of increased pressure include increased breathing resistance, anxiety, and the potential for ear equalization problems. More subtle, but nonetheless important, minimizing factors include common-sense things like getting a good night's sleep, eating a good breakfast, and drinking plenty of nonalcoholic fluids.

INSUFFICIENT EXPERIENCE

Insufficient experience is a major factor in diver-distress situations for deep diving. Whether the insufficient experience results from not having mastered basic skills or infrequent diving activities, this problem manifests itself in overweighting, lack of buoyancy control, lack of equipment familiarity, improper use of dive tables or computers, and unsafe diving practices. These most common hazards can be minimized by your participation in ongoing continuing-education programs and organized diving activities.

INCREASED STRESS

There is an increased amount of stress on divers during deep dives, and this can result in both mental and perceptual narrowing. These situations create taskloading, which may include some combination of the following:

1. Potential lack of familiarity with the dive environment, dive buddy, and/or diving equipment.
2. If using tables, there is a more critical time and depth limit.
3. Effects of narcosis.
4. Less available light.
5. Extra tasks such as photography.
6. Anxiety about air consumption.
7. Unexpected currents or changing weather.
8. Use of more sophisticated equipment.
9. Greater buoyancy fluctuation.

This taskloading can be minimized with proper planning and participation in a comprehensive deep-diving course that intentionally and gradually exposes you to greater depths, more refined procedures, and increased taskloads. Another related hazard that results from a combination of taskloading, and possibly some narcosis, is lower levels of diver awareness.

THE DEEP DIVE

Once the dive has been planned, the equipment assembled, and the briefing completed, the actual dive may begin. Each dive site and dive may be somewhat unique, so it is difficult to prepare a precise diving procedure that can be applied to all dives. General procedures that apply to any dive, however, are discussed here.

Assemble and Check Equipment

All equipment should be laid out and checked before donning any diving suits. The dive support station is assembled, and if any equipment is missing or malfunctioning, corrections must be made. In some cases, a diver may be disqualified from the dive because of equipment problems or lack of a sufficient air supply.

Suit Up

Suiting up should be delayed until the briefing has been completed and all equipment readied. Divers should avoid long surface exposures in suits and equipment. Divers should coordinate suiting up and donning scuba so that all divers can enter the water at one time. A complete buddy check also is conducted.

Final Briefing

Just before the divers enter the water, the lead diver or supervisor will repeat the key points of the dive plan, including air pressure, depth and time limits, and will visually check each diver. This final briefing should take less than 1 minute.

Dive Support Station

Some divers will combine the surface float, descent–ascent line, bottom weight, emergency air-supply system, and stop weights into a single unit—the dive support station—to facilitate equipment management and deployment. For example, when making a deep dive from shore in a quarry or lake, the descent–ascent line (stored by stuffing it into a rope bag) and bottom weight may be secured to the surface float. The emergency air supply system and stop weights are secured to the float with a separate 15-foot line. The entire unit is pushed to the dive site by a diver swimming on the surface. The bottom weight is lowered, and the line is made taut to the surface float. Once the descent–ascent line system is secure, the emergency air-supply system is lowered to a depth of 15 feet. Advanced deep divers configure their diving equipment and plan their dive so that all necessary breathing gas (including emergency gas) is carried by the diver. The diver will designate 20% to 33% as emergency gas. The scuba will have a dual manifold with redundant regulators and isolation capability.

Deployment

Ideally, the station will have been positioned by a surface swimmer. Buddy teams will enter the water quickly and proceed to the descent line. If the dive support station is used and not previously positioned, the first team will position the station. If conditions are satisfactory, more than one buddy team may descend concurrently. If visibility is poor or the surface conditions rough, two-person buddy teams may deploy in a staggered fashion to avoid confusion and crowding during entry and descent.

Descent and Buoyancy Control

Once the divers are on the descent line, they should begin descent immediately, especially if there is wave activity or current at the surface. Hold on to the line and descend feet first. The feet-first position is much better for equalizing pressure, establishing orientation, maintaining control, and reducing diver stress. One hand remains on the line, and the other is used for buoyancy-unit operation and equalization. Conditions permitting, many divers will pause briefly at 15 to 30 feet and perform a quick buddy check as well as verify equipment operation and security. Descent can be controlled by holding the descent line in your hand, locking it in your arm at the elbow, or wrapping your lower leg around it. Ideally, buddies should remain together throughout descent, facing each other on opposite sides of the line. Slow the descent as you approach the bottom, and adjust to neutral buoyancy. If the bottom is silty, avoid contacting it.

On the Bottom

Approach the bottom cautiously, and do not stir up the silt. If the boat's anchor line is used for descent, the first team should check and, if necessary, reposition the anchor. If operating from a large vessel, a crew member often will check and secure the anchor.

If the visibility is poor, you may need to use a reel to assure your return to the ascent line. It is especially important to maintain visual or physical buddy contact throughout the dive. In limited visibility, stay within touching distance or use a buddy line. Stay well above silty bottoms, maintain neutral buoyancy, and avoid kicking in a position that allows your fins to fan the bottom. If you become separated on a deep dive, it may be difficult or dangerous to surface, reunite, and continue the dive. In this case, the dive may well be over.

Use natural features or an object such as a shipwreck to maintain orientation, or use a reel. Relying on compass navigation to return to your ascent line in limited visibility generally is unwise. If the water is clear, however, you have more navigational latitude.

Establish a relaxed breathing pattern, and avoid exertion if possible. If you overexert yourself or become "stressed" at depth, your air supply can be consumed quite rapidly. Further, some regulators, and especially those in a poor state of repair, may exhibit breathing resistance under high breathing demand at depth, because cylinder pressure is reduced. This can give the impression of a depleted air supply. If you begin breathing heavily, you should stop, check your cylinder pressure, and relax. If you cannot bring your breathing under control, signal your buddy that you wish to ascend and terminate the dive.

Cylinder pressure must be monitored throughout the dive. Remember that you will consume approximately twice as much air per minute at 100 feet as you do at 30 feet. This same air supply will last only one half as long, and the frequency of monitoring your pressure gauge must be increased accordingly, especially near the end of the dive. Thus, the diver with the highest rate of air consumption controls the dive. Some dive computers calculate air consumption and display the number of minutes of air time remaining at your current rate of consumption rate. This is a valuable asset, especially for a novice deep diver. Some divers will move to the furthest planned distance from the ascent line immediately upon reaching the bottom and then slowly work their way back to the line.

Ascent

Ascend as a buddy team, facing each other with one hand on the ascent line. Discharge air from the buoyancy compensator (and/or dry suit) as needed, and remain neutrally buoyant throughout the ascent. Some divers use slight positive buoyancy and do not even kick as they ascend the line. Maintain an ascent rate not exceeding 30 ft/min, and slow this rate in the last 60 feet of your ascent. Use your dive time/depth gauge or dive computer to monitor the ascent rate. Remember, at a rate of 30 ft/min, it takes 20 seconds to ascend 10 feet. Keep in mind that a proper ascent is a controlled ascent, and ascent control depends directly on a diver's skill at buoyancy control.

Safety or Decompression Stop

Recreational divers are instructed to avoid exceeding no-decompression limits for the maximum depth of the dive. During ascent from any dive, divers are encouraged to make a safety stop at 15 feet for no less than 3 minutes. This is essen-tial when ascending from a no-decompression deep dive (Fig. 11-4).

Exit and Postdive Activity

On completion of the safety stop, divers should ascend slowly to the surface. Remember that it should take at least 30 seconds to ascend from the stop (a depth only 3 feet deeper than the average pool). Persons returning from a deep dive should not be required to manually retrieve the anchor or descent–ascent line bottom weight. Do not run, exercise strenuously, or take a hot shower for several hours after the deep dive. Do not ascend to altitude for 12 hours, or 24 hours following a mandatory- or emergency-decompression dive. In most cases of decompression sickness, symptoms manifest in less than 2 hours following the dive. Divers should remain with other divers for at least a 2-hour period, and they should monitor themselves for any unusual symptoms that might suggest decompression sickness for 24 hours. Finally, enter the dive information in your log book.

Fig. 11-4. Decompression station with extra cylinder and regulator hanging down on a line.

Fig. 11-5. Deep diving requires training, experience, and self-sufficiency.

SUMMARY

Deep diving is an activity that requires training, experience, and knowledge of the increased potential hazards that are involved with diving to deeper depths (Fig. 11-5). Advanced information and training in the areas of decompression, dive planning, equipment requirements, and emergency procedures is required. Deep diving can be exciting and rewarding, but it should only be considered after successfully completing the proper training and certification.

SUGGESTED READINGS

- Barsky S: *Diving in high risk environments,* Dive Rescue International, Inc., 1993.
- Barsky S, Long D, Stinton B: *Dry suit diving: a guide to diving dry,* Watersport Publishing, 1992.
- Blount S: *Treasure hunting with a metal detector in, around, and underwater,* 1987.
- Frederick J: *Diver's guide to river wrecks,* 1982.
- Gentile G: *Advanced wreck diving guide,* 1988.
- Gilliam B, von Maier R: *Deep diving: an advanced guide to physiology, procedures, and systems,* Watersport Publishing, 1992.
- Lang M, Egstrom G: Biomechanics of safe ascents. *Proc Am Acad Underwater Sci,* 1990.
- Lang M, Vann R: Repetitive Diving. *Proc Am Acad Underwater Sci,* 1992.
- Mount T, Gilliam B: *Mixed gas diving: the ultimate challenge for technical diving,* Watersport Publishing, 1993.
- Potter JS: *The treasure diver's guide,* 1988.
- Tucker WC: *Diver's handbook of underwater calculations,* 1986.

CHAPTER TWELVE

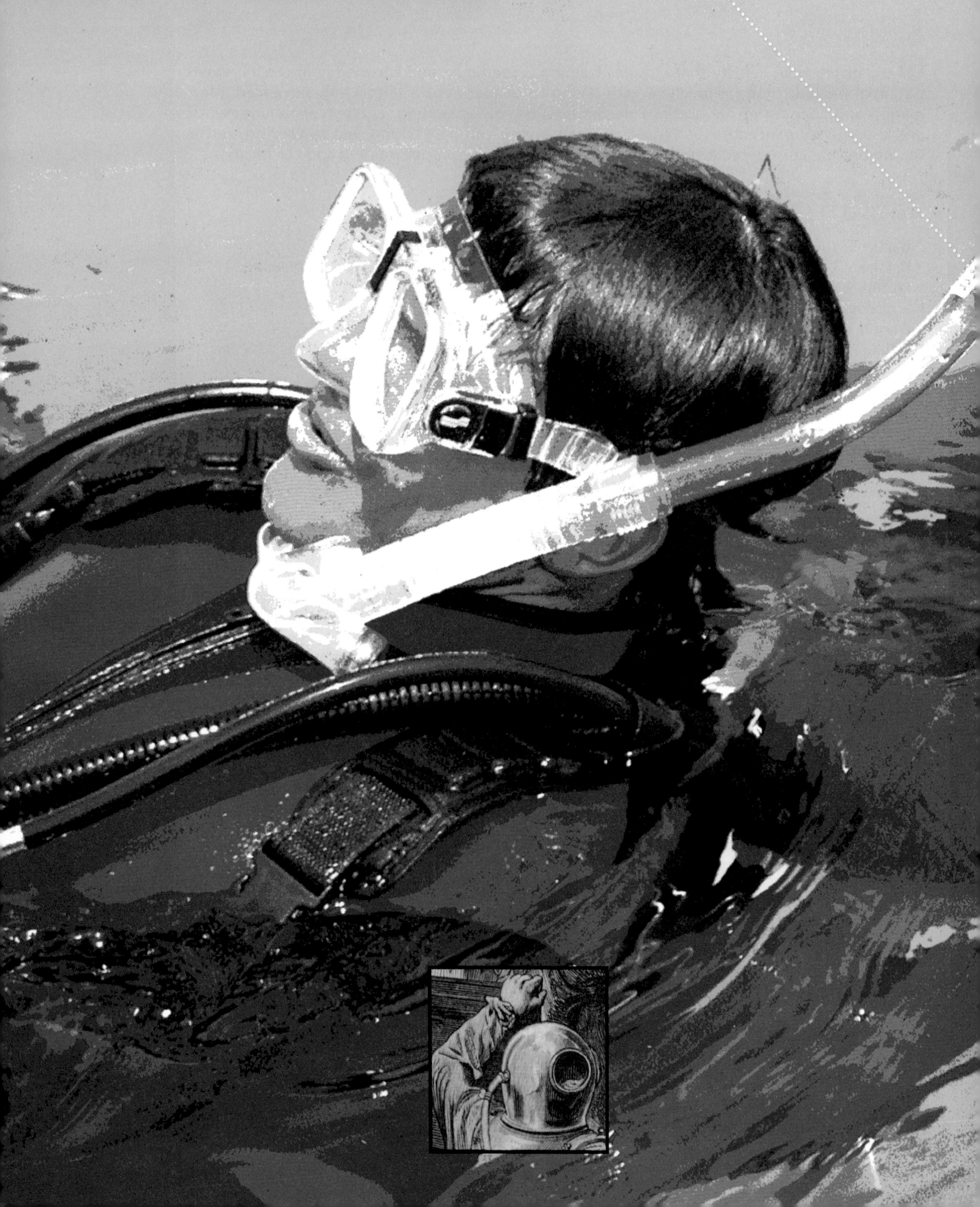

DIVER RESCUE

Thus far in your diving education, you have learned to bring an unconscious diver to the surface and to administer in-water artificial respiration. You have been encouraged to acquire the skills of first aid and cardiopulmonary resuscitation (CPR), and you have learned the basics of first aid for various diving maladies and injuries. You must know and be able to do more, however, to respond to and manage diving accidents. This chapter increases your knowledge of rescue and accident management techniques, but you will need to complete the NAUI Dive Rescue Techniques course to develop all of the skills and knowledge that are needed for a diving emergency.

LEARNING OBJECTIVES

By the end of this chapter, you will be able to:

1 Define the terms shown in **bold letters.**

2 List five signs that indicate a diver is on the verge of panic.

3 List and explain the six steps in rescue preparation.

4 Explain the technique for recovering a submerged victim.

5 List and explain the 10 steps in accident management.

RESCUE TECHNIQUES

A **rescue** is the prompt act of removing a person from imminent danger. A rescue begins when danger to an individual is recognized, and it ends when that person has been freed from the situation. As the term is applied to diving, a rescue usually ends when the victim has been removed from the water. At that point, first aid and accident management begin.

Problem Detection

The ability to identify a dangerous situation as early as possible is invaluable. The seconds saved by early detection of a problem can save a life. Whether you are in the water, aboard a boat, or on shore, be alert for signs of distress.

When you are under the water, the following signs may indicate an imminent rescue situation:

1. Shallow, rapid breathing (i.e., a continuous bubble trail).
2. Upright position with pumping knee action and "dog-paddling" hand and arm movements.
3. Quick, jerky, fumbling movements.
4. Wide, fright-filled eyes.
5. Mouthpiece abandonment.
6. Bolting for the surface.
7. No signs of breathing.
8. Attention focused on one object only.
9. No response to signals.
10. Choking.

If you are observing divers who are at the surface, watch for the following signs:

1. Treading high in the water with no air in the buoyancy compensator (BC).
2. Abandonment of mask and mouthpiece.
3. Lack of response to signals or verbal communications.
4. Chin barely above the water while the diver is gasping.

5. Continuous overfilling of the BC.
6. Choking and coughing.
7. A diver who is facedown with no signs of breathing.

An interesting note is that divers who are in distress at the surface seldom call out or signal for assistance.

Rescue Preparation

You cannot simply jump in the water and go to the aid of a distressed diver when you recognize a dangerous situation. The better prepared you are to effect a rescue, the greater your chances of success. Rescue skills must be practiced if you expect them to succeed when needed. The following methods of preparation should be considered carefully:

1. Complete the NAUI Dive Rescue Techniques training.
2. Don enough equipment to be able to rescue a diver. The minimum recommended equipment consists of mask, fins, and if a thick exposure suit is worn, a weight belt so that you can descend if necessary.
3. Take some flotation with you that can be extended to the person in distress (Fig. 12-1). A BC, life preserver, surface float, or even a cooler chest are good examples of items that you can carry.

Fig. 12-1. A surface float is a good place for a tired diver to rest.

4. Instruct nearby divers, if they are trained and practiced, to don scuba gear and follow you on the rescue attempt. If the diver should sink and you are not able to reach him or her, the scuba divers behind you could reach the individual quickly.

5. Instruct nearby observers to point continuously toward the distressed diver's location, which will help guide you to him or her.

6. Instruct a nearby observer to stand by to summon medical assistance if needed and to make ready the emergency equipment.

7. Monitor the condition of the rescuer, victim, and environment throughout the entire rescue.

Entry and Approach

Enter the water in a way that allows you to maintain visual contact with the victim. Swim with your head above the surface so that you can keep the victim in sight. Using your arms to swim may make it easier to keep your head up. Swim quickly but not as fast as you can; otherwise, you may experience a severe oxygen debt just about the time you need to assist the person in distress. Pace yourself and conserve energy for the actual rescue.

As you approach the diver in distress, quickly assess the situation. Your goal is to make the diver buoyant. If you can get the victim to establish buoyancy, that is the best action. Use verbal commands. If the victim is panicky, however, cooperation is unlikely, and the next best course of action is to extend flotation to the person in distress. If this cannot be done, position yourself behind the victim and establish buoyancy. This can be accomplished by inflating the diver's BC or ditching his or her weight belt. As a last resort, make yourself buoyant and make contact with the victim (Fig. 12-2).

If it appears that a diver is on the verge of exhaustion and is not buoyant, do not delay in your approach. If you are trained, make contact as soon as possible and establish positive buoyancy. While maintaining your personal safety, do everything possible to prevent the diver from losing consciousness and sinking.

If the diver does sink before you arrive, swim to the spot where the person disappeared from view and then surface dive straight down and try to reach the diver. If you are unsuccessful, surface, look for others to assist you, call for assistance, and try again. Without wasting time, try to take a "fix" on your exact location while you are catching your breath between dives. Remember to stay calm and care for you own personal safety.

Fig. 12-2. One method of towing a tired diver is by the cylinder valve.

Assists

If you go to the aid of a diver in distress and are successful in making the diver buoyant, your work will be much easier. Typical problems are divers with too much weight on or who either fail to inflate the BC or have a malfunction. In such cases, only two additional steps are involved:

1. Get the diver to rest, breathe deeply, and recover. Do not insist that the diver breathe through a snorkel or regulator until overcoming the respiratory distress.

2. Assist the diver to shore or the boat. If necessary, use the transport techniques that you learned in your previous diver-training courses. Maintain eye contact with the person you are assisting, and reassure him or her periodically.

Recovering a Submerged Victim

The paramount concern for an unconscious, underwater, nonbreathing diver is to get that individual to the surface. Establish buoyancy on the diver by removing the weight belt or slightly inflating the BC if necessary. Use the do-si-do position to control the diver on the ascent. It is not necessary to tilt the victim's head back, because the risk of pulmonary barotrauma is minimal for an unconscious diver. Expanding air will escape from an unconscious person regardless of the head position; it is only difficult to get air into a person who is unconscious (Figs. 12-3 and 12-4).

In-Water Artificial Respiration

Get the diver buoyant and in a horizontal position at the surface, and then call for help. If the person is wearing a wet suit and his or her weight belt has been discarded, additional buoyancy may not be required at this point. Avoid excessive inflation of the victim's BC, because this often interferes with your efforts to ventilate the distressed diver. Make sure that you are buoyant as well. If you are wearing a weight belt, it can be discarded at the first opportunity after the victim is at the surface and buoyant; however, some rescuers prefer to retain their own weight belt to aid in swimming.

Remove the diver's mask. Your mask should be retained for better vision in wind or seas and in case you need to dive down to recover equipment or a diver who might have slipped from your hold. Open the diver's airway and then look, listen, and feel for breathing. Often, this action is all that is required to allow a person to breathe on his or her own. If the person is not breathing, turn the head toward you and drain any water from the mouth. Look and feel to make sure that the mouth and throat are clear, and then begin artificial respiration, which consists of two full breaths initially

and then one breath every 5 seconds. Some rescuers prefer a cycle of two breaths every 10 seconds, which facilitates faster transport of the diver.

Do everything possible to keep water from entering the diver's mouth and nose. Position your back toward any surface chop, and use mouth-to-nose rather than mouth-to-mouth ventilations if the water is not calm. Cover the diver's mouth and nose if a wave passes over him or her.

In-water artificial respiration is very demanding. You will approach exhaustion in a very few minutes unless you make yourself buoyant and remain as low in the water as possible. Pace yourself if you have a long distance to cover. In addition, rotate the diver's head slightly toward you, and tread higher in the water only during inflations. Lower yourself back into the water and rest as much as possible between breaths.

Resuscitation

Resuscitation is the combination of external cardiac compressions and artificial respiration. CPR cannot be performed in the water. If you suspect cardiac arrest, transport the diver to the shore or boat as quickly as possible while continuing ventilations, then remove the diver from the water and place him or her on a firm surface and commence CPR.

Fig. 12-3. A do-si-do position is excellent for controlling the ascent of an unconscious diver.

Fig. 12-4. The do-si-do position allows the rescuer to give artificial respiration to an unconscious diver.

Oxygen administration also may be required. If trained personnel and equipment are available, this should be started as soon as possible.

Equipment Removal

If the distance to the shore or boat is only a few yards, do not concern yourself with equipment removal until you are in contact with the bottom or the boat. If you must transport the diver a considerable distance while performing artificial respiration, the following suggestions should be kept in mind:

1. Weight belts and the distressed diver's mask are removed first.
2. If you are wearing a scuba tank, it should be removed as soon as possible, because it pulls down and back when you administer in-water artificial respiration.
3. Removal of the victim's scuba unit is affected by several factors. Is it the only source of buoyancy? How far do you need to transport the victim? How easy is it to get the unit off, and can you do it alone without interrupting ventilations? Unclip and remove the BC in small steps between ventilations.
4. Your fins should be removed only when you can stand in shallow water or are in contact with a boat (Fig. 12-5).

Removing the Victim from the Water

One of the most difficult aspects of diver rescue is getting an unconscious, nonbreathing victim out of the water with minimal interruption of artificial respiration. Techniques are as numerous as the sit-

uations. Different procedures are needed for shallow and sloping beaches, surf exits, deep-water shore exits, piers and wharves, and boats (Figs. 12-6 and 12-7). You will learn various exit methods in your NAUI Dive Rescue Techniques course. For now, you should consider how you could accomplish this for the situations in which you dive.

Fig. 12-6. Simulated unconscious diver being hauled onto a boat.

Fig. 12-5. The BC and cylinder may have to be removed from an unconscious diver for transport or hauling onto a boat or the shore.

Fig. 12-7. Simulated unconscious diver being hauled out of the surf by two rescuers, one under each arm, with their arms locked behind the victim's back.

ACCIDENT MANAGEMENT

After an unconscious, nonbreathing diver has been removed from the water, initiate first-aid procedures. If you are the most qualified person to handle the situation, manage the accident.

Accident management involves a plan. A partial listing of possible tasks that must be assigned for an Emergency Action Plan to be successful includes:

1. Assign someone to summon medical assistance. Be sure that person gives information on how they can be reached if additional information is needed. They should report when aid is summoned. One person should stand by the phone or radio in the event of a call for additional information, and the Diver's Alert Network may need to be contacted if hyperbaric treatment is indicated.
2. An accounting must be made for all divers who are involved in the diving activities. Divers must be recalled and a roll call taken.
3. Locate the victim's buddy as soon as possible. If he or she cannot be found, a search must be conducted immediately in the area where the first victim was recovered.
4. Control the group and any observers.
5. Station someone to meet and direct emergency medical personnel traveling to the scene.
6. Assign someone to keep a time log of all activities and events.
7. Assign someone to locate the victim's identification and any medical history or medical alert information.
8. Monitor the victim continuously, even if he or she regains consciousness and indicates a feeling of well being.
9. Assign someone to prepare a list of all witnesses to the accident. This list should include names, addresses, and phone numbers.
10. Secure the victim's equipment. Do not test the gear. Turn off the air, but do not remove the regulator from the tank. Rinse the equipment with freshwater and hold it for release to the proper authorities.

As you can see, there are many things to manage during a diving accident. Many of these tasks should be assigned before the dive begins, and if you are administering first aid, the task of accident management is even more difficult. Try to identify trained and qualified individuals who can be tasked with administering first aid to the victim while you or someone else who is trained manages the situation.

SUMMARY

By now, you should be acutely aware that additional training is essential to effectively rescue a diver, administer first aid, manage the accident, and coordinate evacuation of the victim. Only the fundamentals of these topics have been addressed in this chapter. Get the recommended training so that you will be prepared. Know what to do, how to do it, and decide in advance that you will act if an accident occurs.

SUGGESTED READINGS

- Auerbach P: *A medical guide to hazardous marine life.*
- Bennett P, Moon R: *Diving accident management.* In *Proceedings of the 41st UHMS Workshop.*
- Daughery C: *Field guide for the dive medic,* National Association of Dive Medical Technicians, 1983.
- Diver's Alert Network: *1992 report on diving accidents and fatalities.*
- Diver's Alert Network: *Underwater diving accident manual.*
- Edmonds C: *Dangerous marine creatures.*
- Lippmann J: *Deeper into diving.*
- Lippmann J: *Oxygen first aid for divers.*
- Lippmann J, Bugg S: *DAN emergency handbook.*
- Work K: *MedDive.*

CHAPTER THIRTEEN

TECHNICAL DIVING

In recent years, a new term, **technical diving**, has emerged to describe a type of diving that generally is considered to be beyond the limits of traditional sport diving. While traditional sport diving refers to no-stop scuba dives on air up to a depth of 130 fsw, technical diving can be defined as advanced sport diving that often encompasses greater depths and exposure times than traditional sport-diving limits allow, and it often involves diving in an overhead environment.

LEARNING OBJECTIVES

By the end of this chapter, you will be able to:

1 **Correctly define the terms presented in bold letters.**

2 **State the differences between traditional sport diving and technical diving.**

3 **Discuss the different types of gas mixtures that technical divers use.**

4 **State the advantages and disadvantages of enriched-air Nitrox.**

5 **Discuss the types of equipment that technical divers use.**

Technical divers use methods and equipment that have been borrowed from commercial and military applications, such as mixed gases, rebreather units, and custom decompression tables. It allows divers to explore a wide range of underwater environments and perform tasks that are beyond the scope of traditional sport diving.

Technical diving requires a great amount of training, preparation, and equipment. Many of these divers are "pushing the limits" of diving; however, most are very conservative within the operational parameters of technical diving. Without proper training, this type of diving activity carries an increased risk of injury.

DEEP AIR DIVING

Deep air diving is practiced by many technical divers up to a depth of approximately 200 fsw. Candidates for this type of training must demonstrate good diving techniques and comfort in the

Fig. 13-1. Technical divers often perform lengthy decompression stops.

100- to 130-fsw range. This type of diving generally is taught through diving to progressively greater depths, with increasing requirements for trainees to demonstrate dive planning, equipment handling, and decompression scheduling. Technical divers are trained to recognize and understand their personal limitations (Fig. 13-1).

ENRICHED-AIR NITROX

Today, many divers are seeking the advantages of using alternative **breathing-gas mixtures**. Mixed-gased technology is evolving to improve both the safety and performance of divers by optimizing a diver's breathing gas during dives or various portions of a dive. Gases such as air, Nitrox, Trimix, Heliox, and oxygen are often used, and it is not uncommon for a technical diver to use several different gas mixtures during a dive.

Various mixtures of nitrogen and oxygen are used for dives up to a depth of 130 fsw. The term **Nitrox** initially was used to denote a mixture of nitrogen and oxygen (Fig. 13-2). Later, the term **enriched-air Nitrox** (EAN or EANx) evolved in recognition of the gas-blending process. EAN 32, also known as NOAA Nitrox I, is a gas mixture that consists of 32% oxygen and 68% nitrogen. Another popular mixture, known as EAN 36, consists of 36%

Fig. 13-2. A dedicated cylinder properly marked for use with nitrox gas.

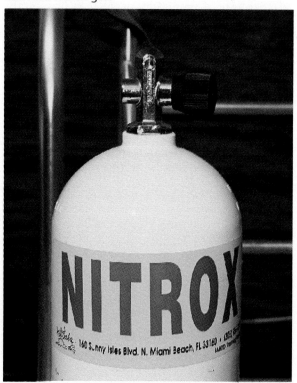

oxygen and the balance in nitrogen; it has a depth limit of 110 fsw. Custom EAN mixes are used to depths up to 170 fsw. The strategy in using Nitrox is to reduce the nitrogen concentration in the diver, which is the source of decompression problems, and replace it with oxygen, much of which is consumed metabolically. No-stop times can be greatly increased, and decompression times can be reduced using Nitrox gas (Table 13-1).

Special techniques must be used when mixing breathing-grade oxygen and oil-free compressed air. One method involves injecting a specific volume of oxygen into a compressor intake, where it combines with atmospheric air before compression. Another more common procedure, called the **partial pressure–blending method**, involves adding a predetermined amount of oxygen into a bank of storage cylinders or a scuba cylinder and then topping off the cylinder with oil-free compressed air. All blending-system components and cylinders must be properly cleaned and designated for oxygen service. The EANx is analyzed for its oxygen content by the blending technician and again by the diver who purchases the gas (Figs. 13-3 and 13-4).

Some potential risk factors are associated with breathing Nitrox. Central nervous system **oxygen toxicity** can result from even relatively short exposures to increased partial pressures of oxygen. Factors associated with this include the percentage of oxygen in the mixture, dive depth, and duration of exposure. The National Oceanic and Atmospheric Administration (NOAA) has established time-exposure limits that are based on the partial pressure of oxygen in the breathing gas. Partial pressure of oxygen cannot exceed 1.6 ata, and this can be breathed only for a certain amount of time. Total diving time is limited in any 24-hour period. Moderate exertion, thermal stress, or lengthy dives require that the maximum allowable partial pressure of oxygen be reduced.

The transition from sport compressed-air diving to EANx is quite simple for the traditional sport diver. Training in Nitrox diving is becoming increasingly popular and is widely available. Divers using EANx with conventional open-circuit scuba use the same diving skills, techniques, and procedures as do compressed-air scuba divers. They must have additional training in physics, physiology, decompression and EANx table use, however, and use a dedicated EANx cylinder that is filled at a participating dealer.

Fig. 13-3. Nitrox gas must be analyzed for oxygen concentration.

Fig. 13-4. Using an oxygen analyzer.

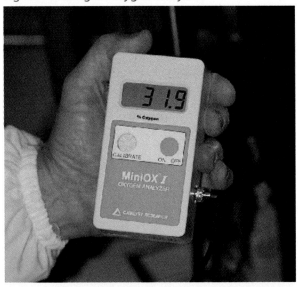

TABLE 13.1 COMPARISON OF NO-DECOMPRESSION LIMITS FOR AIR (U.S. NAVY) AND NOAA NITROX I (68% N_2, 32% O_2).		
DEPTH (fsw)	AIR NO-DECOMPRESSION LIMITS (min)	NITROX I NO-DECOMPRESSION LIMITS (min)
50	100	200
60	60	100
70	50	60
80	40	50
90	30	40
100	25	30
110	20	25
120	15	25
130	10	20

Advanced training in Nitrox deals with using custom EANx blends, diving to greater depths, and decompression diving. Training is gradually intensified to develop and reinforce a more comprehensive understanding of mixed-gas diving, physics, physiology, stress prevention and management, equipment selection and use, dive planning, and gas management.

TRIMIX DIVING

For diving at greater depths (generally beyond approximately 190 feet) where air or Nitrox are either not safe or practical, other gas mixtures are used. **Trimix** gas consists of a mixture of two inert gases and oxygen. Helium, nitrogen, and oxygen commonly are used by technical divers. The individual gas concentrations are predetermined, based on the planned depth and specific environmental considerations of the specific dive. Adding helium to the breathing mixture can significantly counteract the narcotic effects of nitrogen. Technical divers can develop gas mixtures with specific Equivalent Narcosis Depths (END) by using a formula that considers the percentage of nitrogen in the mixture as well as the depth of the dive. For example, a diver breathing a Trimix containing 14% oxygen, 50% helium, and 36% nitrogen at a depth of 300 fsw would have an END of 119 fsw.

A typical Trimix dive to 250 fsw for 30 minutes might use a bottom mix of 17% oxygen, 50% helium, and the balance in nitrogen for the deepest, working portion of the dive. The oxygen concentration is below the 21% concentration found in air to avoid oxygen toxicity problems at depth. The 50% helium replaces a large portion of the nitrogen that is found in air and creates an equivalent narcosis depth of 85 fsw on air. During the decompression phase of the dive, a Nitrox mixture typically would be breathed, finishing with either pure oxygen from 20 fsw to the surface or EAN 80 from 30 feet to the surface. Because of the considerable decompression obligation, a person on a dive such as this might consume as much as 200 to 400 cubic feet of gas (see the Physics chapter discussions of Dalton's Law and Mixing).

Obviously, special dive tables must be used in accordance with the percentages of nitrogen and helium in the mixture. Several types of custom dive tables are used by technical divers, and some even use computer programs to plan mixed-gas dives.

EQUIPMENT

Most technical divers use conventional open-circuit scuba equipment that is specially configured. The highly precise gas switching that was described earlier requires detailed planning, multiple cylinders with special manifolds, and high-performance regulators with custom-length hoses, and it may require specialized equipment such as full-face masks with communications, programmable decompression computers, reels, and decompression lines. Diver propulsion vehicles are sometimes used because of the distance traveled as well as the weight and bulkiness of the equipment being worn (Figs. 13-5 through 13-7).

Technical divers use highly redundant systems on extreme dives. Technical diving in caves also requires that equipment be streamlined for safety and protection of the delicate cave formations. Many of the cylinders can be staged before the dive, but redundancy often requires that the diver wear as many as four large cylinders. A typical configuration might consist of two 104-cubic-foot cylinders with a crossover manifold and two regulators, which contain the bottom mix, and a pair of side tanks that contain the decompression gases Nitrox and oxygen, each with their own regulators secured to the diver's harness.

Fig. 13-5. Technical diver with multiple cylinders, manifold valves, and long-hose regulators.

Fig. 13-6. Diver rigging oxygen for decompression.

Fig. 13-7. Diver propulsion vehicles can be used for long underwater excursions.

Technical divers are looking forward to the continued development of **closed-circuit technology**, which will eliminate the need to carry so many cylinders. A fully redundant, closed-circuit **rebreather**, which recirculates exhaled gases that have been "scrubbed" of carbon dioxide, could potentially offer a 12-hour supply of gas. This will certainly change the way that many technical divers go about their avocation.

Additional important equipment for technical diving are lights, reels, harnesses, gas-analysis devices, dry suits, lift bags, and cameras. High-intensity lights with separate battery packs are carried on deep, wreck, and cave dives. Strong and reliable guideline reels are required equipment for cave dives and also are used by some wreck-penetration divers. Double-tank harnesses and custom buoyancy compensators are the norm, and double buoyancy compensators often are used for redundancy in case the primary unit fails. Some technical divers invest in their own equipment for gas mixing and analysis, including compressors, boosters, cylinders, and regulators. Most, however, support professional dive shops that have made a considerable investment in the proper equipment. Custom decompression tables are available on software for personal computers. For thermal protection on long dives in cold water, dry suits are used. In addition, some divers use special gases like argon for suit inflation (Figs. 13-8 and 13-9).

Having a recompression chamber on site usually is not feasible for most diving operations. While its potential value is not disputed, its cost usually is the factor in determining presence of a chamber. For many of the exploratory dives to the frontier, a recompression chamber on site is a major comfort to the participants.

TRAINING

Extensive training and practice are the keys to technical diving. Recreational divers who are interested in pursuing technical diving should be very experienced and comfortable in the water. It is difficult to place an exact number of dives required before one should consider technical diving, because this would vary widely with individuals. As a minimum, however, an advanced certification with considerable diving in a variety of habitats should be considered.

Many training courses are available in Nitrox, mixed-gas, deep-diving, cave-diving, and gas-blending techniques. Technical divers view depth as a relative term and not an absolute number that applies to everyone. Deep dives are worked up to progressively, assuring the proper comfort level and competence that are required before progressing any deeper. Technical divers stress the importance of independence and self-sufficiency in the individual diver. Dive training for caverns and caves stresses equipment-handling and gas-management techniques. Those who are involved with this type of diving must clearly recognize the risks of decompression sickness, entrapment, disorientation, and separation from a buddy.

Detailed planning and preparation are the keys to technical diving operations. To conduct these dives properly, one can incur significant expense. In addition to the cost of training and the equipment discussed, the cost of the gas also can be considerable. Technical divers have invested many thousands of dollars in their equipment and training.

Fig. 13-8. Hi-intensity lights with battery packs are useful in many situations.

Fig. 13-9. Diver using an isolation manifold.

SUMMARY

Undoubtedly, technical diving will continue to grow in popularity as new equipment technologies and frontiers are discovered. More widely available training programs probably will develop as well. Thousands of divers have been trained in the use of enriched-air Nitrox, and advanced scuba divers can progress easily to the EANx diver specialty course offered by many NAUI instructors.

Technical diving emphasizes responsibility, detailed dive planning and preparation, self-sufficiency, and a knowledge of personal limitations. This may prove to be a whole new field that recreational divers might consider if they have the proper background and training.

SUGGESTED READINGS

- Barsky S: *Diving in high risk environments*, Dive Rescue International, Inc., 1993.
- Barsky S, Long D, Stinton B: *Dry suit diving: a guide to diving dry*, Watersport Publishing.
- Gentile G: *Advanced wreck diving guide*, 1988.
- Gilliam B, von Maier R: *Deep diving: an advanced guide to physiology, procedures, and systems*, Watersport Publishing, 1993.
- Lang M, Egstrom G: Biomechanics of safe ascents. *Proc Am Acad Underwater Sci*, 1990.
- Lang M, Vann G: *Repetitive diving.* Proc Am Acad Underwater Sci, 1991.
- Mount T, Gilliam B: *Mixed gas diving: the ultimate challenge for technical diving*, Watersport Publishing, 1993.
- Somers L: *Technical diving*, Unpublished manuscript.

CHAPTER FOURTEEN

QUEST 7

BOAT DIVING

Boats are an integral part of diving. In pursuing this activity, you will likely encounter every type and size of dive boat, from a tiny inflatable all the way to a luxurious live-aboard. All dive boats have certain elements in common, however, and also some basic differences. Techniques that are used to dive from different boats can vary as well.

LEARNING OBJECTIVES

By the end of this chapter, you will be able to:

1. Define the terms presented in **bold letters.**
2. Discuss the advantages and features of inflatable boats.
3. List the three different types of keels for inflatable boats.
4. Discuss the different types of open skiffs.
5. List the steps to prepare for and dive on a charter dive boat.

You can dive from almost any boat, but some are better than others. What do you look for in a dive boat? Basically, all share four elements: deck space, stability, convenient boarding and exiting, and power. Diving is an equipment-intensive sport, and all that gear must go somewhere. Further, people need room to set up cylinders and suit up. An inflatable or runabout with the equipment neatly arranged can be better than a cabin cruiser if the larger boat lacks sufficient deck space. Diving activities also require a stable platform. Too much rock and roll is detrimental to cylinders and equipment as well as to people. Finally, it takes a strong engine to effectively move any heavily loaded vessel. This does not necessarily require top speed; rather, it requires power. Dive boats can be considered to be the "pickup trucks" of the boating world.

This chapter examines the different types of dive boats, and it discusses the techniques that are appropriate to each. There is a bit of overlap, so to avoid repetition, procedures that are common to all boats are covered in the final section on charter boats. Techniques that are unique to a certain type of dive boat are covered in the specific section for that type.

INFLATABLES

Inflatable boats should not be confused with rubber rafts. Today's inflatables are high-performance boats, and they are as rugged as any comparably sized hard-hull craft. They are easily stored in limited spaces, transportable in small vehicles, and require less fuel than hard-hull boats of the same size. Divers today have a wide (and sometimes confusing) choice of inflatable boats, and all at very competitive prices (Fig. 14-1).

What should a diver look for in an inflatable boat? First, some sort of hard floor and a keel are necessary. Soft, fabric-floored boats are intended primarily as dinghies or tenders, and they will not stand up to the abuse of diving. They also accept only small engines, which would be hard-pressed to move the extra weight of diving equipment.

If required by law, the capacity plate usually is mounted on the transom. The plate contains information on the maximum weight, number of passengers, and maximum horsepower engine allowed. Rated capacity should be cut by 40% to 50% when divers are involved. If a boat is rated for eight passengers, it will accommodate four to five divers with equipment. An inflatable should be at least 11 feet long to accommodate two divers. Boats from 11 to approximately 14 feet are easily transportable and can be carried and assembled by two people; they usually are best for offshore runs to local reefs, up to approximately 5 miles from shore.

Inflatables of 15 to 16 feet belong in the next category. These boats usually are stored on trailers and are permanently set up. They will accommodate up to six divers and are appropriate for open water runs of up to 15 miles (if they are properly equipped for going offshore). Anything larger than 16 feet generally is considered too big for most sport-diving purposes.

Originally, all inflatable boats were made of nylon impregnated with **neoprene** and **hypalon**. This required a lot of hand labor during assembly. Recently, manufacturers have changed over to plastics for lower cost, greater durability, and more automated assembly methods.

There are three types of keels for inflatable dive boats: inflatable keels, wooden keels, and fiberglass hulls. **Inflatable keels** are light, easy to transport, and easy to set up. They are the least likely to get damaged when running over rocks or obstructions; however, they tend to bounce more in swells and wind chop, resulting in a harsher ride. **Wooden keels** impart a firmer shape to the bottom material, allowing the boat to cut through chop more effectively and turn with less skidding. They require more care and assembly, however,

Fig. 14-1. Inflatable boats are very popular for diving.

and make the boat more difficult to transport assembled. In addition, such boats are heavier than those with inflatable keels.

The third type of boat has a **fiberglass hull** that is mated to inflatable tubes. They are called RIBs, or **Rigid Inflatable Boats**. These offer the best performance and smoothest ride, but they sacrifice two of the primary advantages to an inflatable boat: compact storage, and light weight. Why would someone buy one of these instead of a comparable-sized, hard-hull boat that costs less? In a word, performance. The lighter weight of RIBs as opposed to that of comparable rigid vessels as well as their improved stiffness result in more speed. They can use greater-horsepower engines than other inflatables, and they can use it more effectively. They can be more economic to operate by achieving good performance with less power. In addition, their inflatable tubes make them more stable than conventional boats and virtually unsinkable.

Regardless of which type of inflatable that you choose, look for the maximum deck space. Avoid boats with intricate consoles, seats, and remote steering that sacrifice storage capacity. Remember, all that diving gear must go somewhere, and this is an important factor to consider in any type of boat for serious divers. If this will be used primarily as a dive boat, some creature comforts may need to traded for more deck space.

Diving procedures for inflatables are primarily the same as for any small boat. Be sure to fly appropriate signals such as a red-and-white dive flag and a blue-and-white international alpha pennant. These are required when diving off any boat, regardless of its size. Also, because space is at a premium, cylinders, regulators, and backpacks should be assembled before leaving the dock. Everything on deck probably will get wet, so divers should wear wet suits and boots for the trip. Anything that must remain dry (e.g., wallets, fishing licenses, lunch) should be packed in a waterproof container.

Trim is important in any boat, because it can affect the balance, handling, and seaworthiness of a small craft. Arrange your passengers and cargo to balance the vessel fore and aft as well as port and starboard. The key is to get the boat onto a plane, where the vessel levels out and skims over the water rather than pushes against it. If the total weight approaches the engine's capacity, the craft might not plane until some passengers move forward temporarily. Thus, crew members can serve as movable ballast.

On arrival at the dive site, cylinders should be put overboard and attached to a line. This will open a lot of deck space for your final suiting up.

The regulator should be attached to the cylinder valve and the air turned on. Jacket buoyancy compensators can be partially inflated to keep the scuba unit on the surface. A major advantage of an inflatable board is its stability; more than one person at a time will be able to move around. Enter the water with a backward roll or slip-in, then don the scuba units in the water. Remember to check the anchor on your initial descent. Failure to do so could result in a long swim if the boat slips anchor while you are underwater.

When returning to the boat after the dive, remove the scuba unit in the water and attach it to the line. In a strong current, hook the cylinder to the line first, then take it off and pull yourself back to the boat. Bringing the cylinders back on board and securing them for the trip home should be the last thing done before the anchor is pulled.

OPEN SKIFFS

Boats that are designed for fishing often make the best dive boats. Those designed for touring or water-skiing often have reduced space and stability. Most skiffs are made of **fiberglass**, many with foam sandwiched between the layers to provide buoyancy. Hull design will determine the boat's riding characteristics. Flat or cathedral hulls generally are very seaworthy but have a harsher ride because of bounce in short-interval chop. Deep vee hulls cut through the waves more smoothly but can be less stable at anchor. Also, because of their higher profile, these skiffs may be harder to board unless a platform or ladder is used (Fig. 14-2).

Welded aluminum boats with deep vee hulls are rapidly gaining acceptance because of their lower cost. Weight must be arranged carefully in these boats to keep the bow down, especially during high winds. Any metal boat also requires protective measures against electrolysis.

The most popular sizes for open skiffs range from 16 to 21 feet, although both smaller and larger ones are available. More room generally is available than in an inflatable, but skiffs also ride wetter. Therefore, it is best to suit up before leaving the dock.

Diving procedures are almost identical to those for inflatables, but in some larger skiffs, it may not be necessary to don cylinders in the water. Many divers prefer to remove their scuba units, however, along with their weight belts, before climbing back on board. The outboard motor often can be an effective stepladder for climbing back into the boat, but a better choice is a sturdy ladder with flat rungs that extend into the water.

Fig. 14-2. Open skiffs can be specially outfitted for diving.

The engine usually should be shut off before anybody enters the water; however, currents, sea conditions, or lack of an anchorage occassionally make it necessary to drop off divers while the boat is moving. This is called **liveboating**, and it should not be attempted without considerable training under supervision. Divers should be ready to exit as soon as the skipper announces arrival at the site. The engine is placed in neutral, and on command, the divers execute a backward roll. They should immediately swim clear of the boat to allow the skipper to move out of the area. Before returning on board, swim well clear of any shallow reefs or obstructions, because boarding will take longer than the entry did. The boat is vulnerable to running aground while drifting without power, so do not approach the boat until the skipper informs you that the engine is in neutral. Remove your scuba unit, hand it to someone on the boat, and then climb aboard quickly as soon as you are given the order. This is a special procedure that requires considerable practice and experienced boat handlers.

RUNABOUTS, CABIN CRUISERS, AND LARGER YACHTS

Runabouts come in a wide variety of layouts and sizes, from 20 footers with rudimentary cabins to 28 footers, which is near the largest size that can be trailered. Trailer boats are limited by beam (i.e., width) rather than by length on US interstate highways. As with skiffs, boats that are designed for fishing generally make the best dive boats. For ease in boarding, there should be no rail around the rear portion of the deck. On larger boats with inboard engines, a step-through gate is desirable. Many runabouts are powered by automobile

engines that are converted for marine use with an outdrive (referred to as an *inboard-outboard*). Because of their seaworthiness and greater fuel capacity, the effective range of these boats extends to over 50 miles. They are dry riding, allowing divers to travel fully clothed and in comfort both to and from the dive site.

The owner will have many important decisions to make regarding deck space versus creature comforts. A bewildering array of options is available that can quickly deplete a budget; however, some are essential for a dive boat. These include a VHF radio, a good fathometer (i.e., depth-measuring device) to find reefs, and a swim step to make it easier to get back on board. Also highly recommended are strakes, which are horizontal ribs that run along the hull, to deflect spray and make the ride smoother. Another desirable accessory is a LORAN navigation uni, or a GPS (i.e., Global Positioning System) unit, which uses electronic coordinates to help you return to favorite dive spots without long fathometer runs.

Although there is more room to move about on this sort of boat, the deck has a tendency to "shrink" when it is time to dive. It might be necessary to dress in shifts. Even on boats of this size, it usually helps to put cylinders overboard before the divers suit up.

Choices in the category of **cabin cruisers**, large yachts, and sailboats are so varied, and their dive procedures so similar to those of charter boats, that diving from them is covered in the next section. Because of difficulties in maneuvering and anchoring larger vessels, actual diving from these boats often is done from tenders or skiffs. This is especially true of sailing craft (Fig. 14-3).

Fig. 14-3. Cabin cruisers offer somewhat more luxury for diving.

CHARTER BOATS AND LIVE-ABOARDS

Charter boats and live-aboards can range from converted fishing boats barely longer than runabouts all the way to luxurious yachts of over 100 feet. Diving procedures, however, are essentially the same for all. Over the years, a code of "dive-boat etiquette" has been developed by skippers, instructors, and crew. It is based on courtesy and respect for others. Regardless of the size of a vessel, the key to effective boat diving is cooperation. If you know the basic rules, you will feel at home on any boat anywhere, from California's Channel Islands to the Red Sea (Fig. 14-4).

Before the Trip

Pack your dive bag the day before the trip, and work with a checklist to make sure that nothing is missed. Do not wait until the evening before the trip to pack in case you discover that something is broken or missing. Remember to bring spare straps, O-rings, dive log, certification card, and fishing license. Make sure your equipment is marked to avoid confusing it with someone else's.

On Board the Boat

On board the boat, anything left on deck probably will get wet, so all nondiving gear should be stored below, either in the galley or the bunkroom. Many skippers will allow wet suits to be worn in the galley but no hard gear. In the bunkrooms, everything should remain dry. Check with the crew as to specific procedures on your boat.

Fig. 14-5. Charter dive boats can be very crowded so it is important to have your equipment well organized.

If seasickness strikes, try to go up on deck and "feed the fishes" to the lee, or the downwind side of the boat. Getting sick indoors is considered a serious breach of boat etiquette. The head (i.e., marine toilet) also is not designed for this purpose.

When it is time to suit up for diving, work with your buddy and help each other. Stake out your own area on deck, centered around your dive bag. Always work out of your bag, removing items only as you need them, and returning them to the bag immediately after the dive (Fig. 14-5).

Never leave a cylinder standing unattended. If it is not secured in a rack, it should be lying down.

Fig. 14-4. Live-aboard dive boats are usually large and offer many amenities.

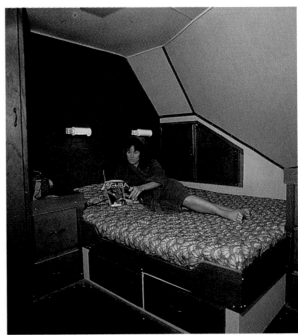

Fig. 14-6. Charter boat cylinders neatly stowed in racks.

Never walk around on a rolling deck while wearing fins. To avoid holding up other people at the exit gate, finish all preparation and buddy checks before heading toward it. Fins should be the last things to go on, and this is done just before entering the water (Fig. 14-6).

Entry

One of the hardest concepts for some divers to grasp regarding entry is that a boat at anchor is a moving platform. Many live-aboards have high profiles and are extremely sensitive to the wind. At anchor, they will swing in a very predictable arc. If you jump off at the wrong time, the boat can swing right over you. Many skippers will put out a swing buoy at each end of the boat's arc for use as a reference. Use the port exit while the boat is swinging to starboard, and vice versa. After the dive, wait near one of the buoys and let the boat come to you. Sometimes the skipper will set a stern anchor to eliminate swinging.

After jumping in and waiting for your buddy, swim together away from the exit area so that the next divers can follow closely behind. It usually is a good idea to descend along the anchor line, but be sure to stay approximately one arm's length away from the line at all times. As the boat bounces on the waves, the line will become slack and then tighten again. If you are too close, it could hook around your cylinder valve or other equipment and give you quite a jerk.

In the Water

Some boats have an emergency underwater recall system that sounds like a police siren. If you hear it during a dive, surface immediately, ascending at the recommended rate, and look toward the boat for a signal to stay clear or come aboard. There may be other types of recall systems as well, such as banging on metal underwater or starting the engine. Listen carefully to the predive briefing for this information.

If there is a current, begin your dive upcurrent. In case you are swept beyond the boat on return, look for the **current line**. This is a long line with a float at the end, trailing behind the boat. Swim for this line instead of the boat and then pull yourself back hand-over-hand, either facedown or on your back. To avoid bunching up the line in front of you and becoming entangled, bring the pulling hand well past your waist before letting go.

Return

When reboarding the boat, watch the movement of the swim step or ladder as it bounces in the swells. Time your climb when the ladder or step is at its lowest point. This not only saves effort, it will prevent you from being hit by the ladder when it comes down. Once on the swim step, remain on your hands and knees. If you sit on the step and the boat pitches or rolls, you will flop on your back, out of control. Be ready to hand your camera, game, or speargun to the crew member at the ladder. Make sure the speargun is unloaded. Depending on the boat and divemasters in charge, you might be asked to remove your fins and weightbelt before boarding (Figs. 14-7 and 14-8).

Immediately after the last dive of the day, store all equipment in your gear bag. When showering, save some water for divers coming after you by making it a "Navy shower." Get wet and then turn off the water while you lather up, because hot, fresh water is always in short supply. After you have soaped yourself up, rinse off quickly.

Fig. 14-7. Some boat ladders require the removal of fins before boarding.

Fig. 14-8. A crew member is usually present at the swim step to assist with gear and boarding.

SUMMARY

D iving from a boat opens a world of opportunities for divers. Several types of boats are available for diving, and each has its own advantages and disadvantages. Be sure to obtain the proper training and experience with boats before you attempt to operate one. The suggestions outlined here will help make your boating experiences more enjoyable.

SUGGESTED READINGS

- Barsky S: *Boat diving*, Best Publishing, in press.
- Fagan B: *Cruising guide to California's Channel Islands*, 1983.
- Rinehart LT: *The Captain's LORAN book. Florida east and west coast including Alabama, Mississippi, Texas*, 1988.
- US Coast Guard Auxiliary: *Boating skills and seamanship*, ed 10.

CHAPTER FIFTEEN

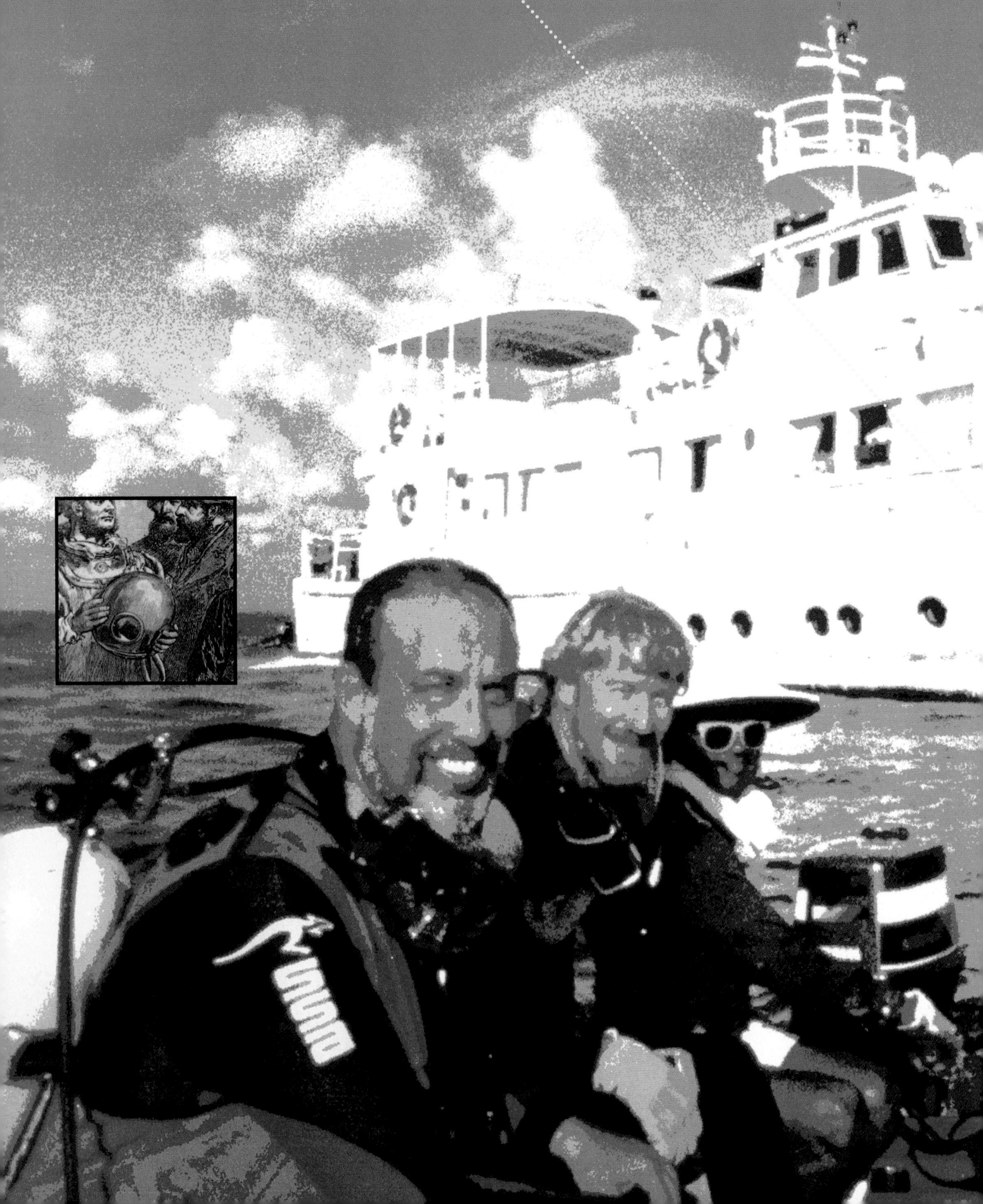

TROPICAL PRINCESS

6FT

BOATING AND SEAMANSHIP

Boat diving has many advantages. First, you can access locations that generally are not diveable from shore. Second, boat diving usually provides access to areas of better visibility as well as to those richer in aquatic life.

Knowledge of boats and how to operate them can be important skills for a diver. Whether you own a boat, aspire to own one, or plan to dive from boats, the following information will give you a basic understanding about them.

LEARNING OBJECTIVES

By the end of this chapter, you will be able to:

1. Define the terms presented in **bold letters.**
2. Discuss the responsibilities of operating a boat.
3. Discuss six terms of basic ship handling.
   List three important rules of the road.
4. List five criteria for the safe anchoring of a boat.
5. List five common knots that are used in boating.

No one chapter can inform you of everything that you need to know to be a good diving boater. The information presented here is intended primarily for small, personally owned, power-driven boats. For more in-depth information or further programs and courses, contact the US Coast Guard, US Coast Guard Auxiliary, US Coast Guard Power Squadron, and professional maritime academies.

RESPONSIBILITIES

Can you operate a boat? Do you need to be a licensed captain? If you own your own boat, can you let your diving friends help pay for expenses?

In most states, there are no "drivers licenses" that are required to operate your own boat, provided that the board is not for hire. You most likely will be required to pay special fees, however, such as those that are required for boat registration.

Being a good dive buddy is an excellent prerequisite to being able to operate a boat properly. If you perform impeccable dive planning procedures as well as equipment, safety, and predive checks, you are well on your way to becoming a responsible boat operator. Boating requires organization and attention to detail similar to diving.

Aside from being a good dive buddy, you now have a **responsibility** to every person, both diver and nondiver, on your boat to operate that boat properly. You also have a responsibility to other boats around you and to any swimmers, snorkelers, surfers, sailboarders, and jet skiers in the area. You must obey any rules and regulations, and you must use common sense, much like when operating a vehicle.

Responsibility means that your boat is properly equipped. Just as certain equipment is necessary for diving, specific safety equipment is required for your vessel. A personal dive boat most likely will fall into one of two classifications of motor boats: under 12 m (approximately 38 ft), or under 20 m (approximately 65 ft). The US Coast Guard requires specific lighting, bells or whistles, and emergency equipment such as fire extinguishers and life jackets (diving buoyancy compensators do not qualify).

You do not need to be a licensed captain to operate your privately owned recreational boat. If you receive compensation from passengers, however, you must have a licensed boat operator on board at all times or be one yourself. Although the rules on this now are more realistic, "compensation" can mean money, sharing fuel expenses, launching or trailer parking fees, supplying food and refreshments, buying meals, and under some circumstances, gifts. When you fall into the category of having a licensed captain aboard, your boat most likely will be reclassified, be required to undergo other inspections, and need to carry additional equipment.

Common nautical terms are described in Table 15-1.

BASIC SHIP HANDLING

To operate and steer your boat, you must have an understanding of six basic forces that act on your boat. These forces react differently during various speeds and conditions. The following overview and definitions of these forces will help you to become a more competent shiphandler. These six basic forces affect your boat when going ahead or astern and fast or slow, and these forces must be accounted for when casting off from a dock, docking the

TABLE 15.1   NAUTICAL TERMS

Left	Right
Port	Starboard
Red	Green
Odd*	Even*

*Numbers on channel buoys.

Remembering is easy. All the larger words are on the same side, and the smaller words are on the other side.

Bow - forward section of the boat	
Stern - rear section of the boat	
Port - left side (facing the bow)	
Amidship - middle of the boat	
Forward - toward the bow of the boat	
Aft - toward the stern of the boat	
Galley - kitchen	
Head - bathrooms	

boat, leaving and approaching harbors and piers, or meeting and passing other boats.

Propeller Thrust

Your boat moves forward through the water because of **propeller thrust**. This thrust occurs because the pitch of the propeller creates a low-pressure area in front of the propeller and a high-pressure area behind it. The boat will move foward toward the low-pressure area.

Rudder Force

Rudder force involves the direction of the boat. When you turn the rudder to one side, a high-pressure area is created on the leading-edge side of the rudder and a low-pressure area develops on the trailing-edge side. The stern of the vessel will swing (or turn) toward the low-pressure side. This is why the stern will swing to the opposite side from which you turn the rudder.

Side Force

Side force is the direction that your boat moves in relation to the direction of the spin (or rotation) of your propeller. If you have a right-handed propeller (i.e., facing from the stern to the bow), your propeller turns clockwise and the stern of the boat will swing to the right when idling forward and to port on backing. Visualize that as the propeller turns, the tips of the propeller blades "walk" along the bottom. Side force is much more pronounced at slower speeds.

Pivot Point

The **pivot point** on your boat (i.e., where it turns) varies with speed and how the boat is loaded. On most, the pivot point is one third of the distance back from the bow when the boat is moving forward.

Bank Cushion

Bank cushion can be seen when passing close to or near another boat or seawall; the bow of your vessel will be pushed away. When moving ahead, water is funneled back along a narrow channel, which causes the bow to be pushed out or away. The opposite happens in reverse, where the stern is pushed away.

Bank or Bottom Suction

As your vessel moves forward, water is pulled (or sucked) from ahead of the propeller and discharged astern. When you move into shallow water (e.g., a harbor or reef), a **bottom suction** effect is caused, and the stern of the boat will sink lower into the water.

THE RULES OF THE ROAD

The three worst emergencies that might occur while at sea are:
1. Collision with another vessel.
2. Sinking, which usually is caused by the first emergency.
3. Fire, which usually is caused by the second emergency.

This section examines ways to prevent a collision with another boat.

Similar to our freeway systems, there are specific **waterway rules** governing when and where boats are allowed to maneuver. The international collision prevention regulations (abbreviated as COLREGS) apply to offshore waters and the high seas. Rules for inland waters also are modeled on these regulations, which are designed to prevent "risk of collision." You will find it extremely difficult to convince the US Coast Guard or a judge that "risk of collision" did not exist when two vessels have collided. Ironic as it may seem, most collisions occur during daylight hours and in open seas with unlimited visibility. You should have a proper lookout, travel at a safe speed, warn a vessel that may not see you, and avoid hampering another vessel's progress.

Before any discussion of the basic rules of the road, you must understand the buoy system to ensure that you enter and exit harbors both safely and correctly. When coming in from sea to the harbor, the red channel buoys are kept to your right (i.e., starboard) side. The three R's will help you to remember: red, right, returning (Fig. 15-1).

Who has the **right of way**? Sailboats generally are assumed to have right of way over power-driven vessels, and for the most part, this is true. There are power-driven boats, however, that do have preference over sailing vessels because of the nature of their work or other circumstances.

Simple Collision Avoidance

To avoid a collision, use the following rules:
1. *Head-on Boats*: When meeting another boat head on (i.e., bow to bow), both boats should alter course to starboard (i.e., right) if possible.
2. *Crossing*: When crossing, the vessel ahead of you and on your starboard side has the right of way. You are the "give way" vessel and must slow or turn to starboard and pass behind. The "stand on" vessel should maintain course and speed.
3. *Overtaking or Passing*: Any boat that is being overtaken or passed from astern is called the "stand on" vessel. If your power boat is being overtaken by a sailboat, you are the "stand on" vessel and have the right of way. The "stand on" vessel

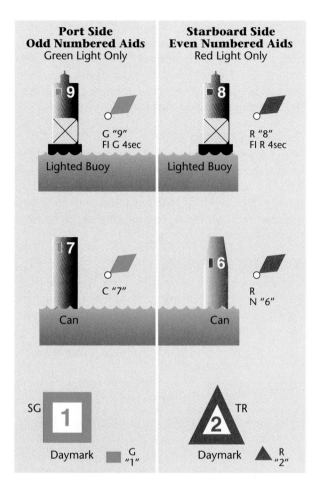

Port Side
Odd Numbered Aids
Green Light Only

9
Lighted Buoy

G "9"
Fl G 4sec

7
Can

C "7"

SG 1
Daymark

G "1"

Starboard Side
Even Numbered Aids
Red Light Only

8
Lighted Buoy

R "8"
Fl R 4sec

6
Can

R
N "6"

TR 2
Daymark

R "2"

Fig. 15-1. A standard system of buoys provides valuable information to boat operators.

is obligated to maintain course and speed. You must give way to any vessel that you are overtaking until all danger or risk of collision is past.

4. *Day Shapes and Signal Lights*: Who should you watch out for and keep well clear of? As mentioned earlier, certain boats are given the right of way because of the nature of their work. Such vessels will display day shapes during daylight hours and signal lights at night. There is a chain of consideration or privilege, or "pecking order," for who is first, second, third, and so on (Fig. 15-2). You must stay well clear of those above you in this chain of command. Dive boats will fall into categories two and six.

Chain of Command

Which boats fall where in the chain of command, and what day shapes and signal lights will they display? Memory phrases for the signal lights can assist you in remembering them. Day shapes and signal lights are displayed on the mast.

Not Under Command

The night signal is two all-round, red-over-red lights in a vertical line where they are best seen.

FIGURE 15.2

Rules of Good Seamanship*
Don't fail to comply with the rules or precautions governed by good seamanship or special circumstances.

General Prudential Rule*
If all else fails, the rules may be broken in order to avoid immediate danger.

CAUTION: Stay well clear of lights you don't understand.
*Now combined in "Responsibility" rule.

Steering and Sailing Rules
1. Risk of collision exists if another vessel's compass bearing doesn't change or changes very little relative to you.
2. To avoid collision: Avoid crossing ahead.
   —take early and positive action
   —make obvious course and speed changes
   —slow, stop or reverse if necessary
3. **If in doubt**: Between crossing and head-on, assume head-on; or between crossing and overtaking, assume overtaking and act accordingly.

In Restricted Visibilty (Fog, Rain or Snow)
1. Proceed at a safe speed.
2. If you hear a fog signal head, slow to minimum speed or stop. Then proceed with caution unless you've determined that risk of collision does not exist.
3. If you take avoiding action base on radar:
   —take early action; avoid course changes to:
   • port for a vessel ahead except when overtaking, or
   • toward vessels abeam or abaft your abeam.

RIGHT OF WAY

stand on vessel*	maintain	course speed
give way vessel		keep well clear

*Shall take action if give way vessel does not take timely, sufficient and appropriate action to avoid collision.

If you are: vessel below line, give way

1. Meeting head on: pass port to port.

2. Crossing: <u>Starboard vessel</u> has right of way over port vessel.

3. Overtaken from more than 22.5° abaft the beam Overtaking (includes sail overtaking power)

4. sailing: <u>Starboard tack</u> in same <u>Leeward</u>
   port tack   tack   windward

5. • not under command
   • restricted in maneuverability
   • constrained by draft (international only)
   • fishing
   • sailing
   • power driven
   give way to vessel above you on this list

6. In narrow channels <u>vessels restricted to channel</u>
   vessels under 20 meters, or fishing or sailing

Fig. 15-2. Boaters should know the rules of the road and right of way rules when operating a vessel.

Memory phrase: "Red over red. Should've stayed in bed." The day shape is two black balls in a vertical line.

These vessels normally are broken down in some capacity. They often have steering or engine difficulties, and they cannot maneuver easily.

Restricted In Maneuverability

The night signal is all-round, red-white-red lights in a line. Memory phrase: "Restricted with reason." The day shape is a ball-diamond-ball shaped sequence.

These vessels cannot maneuver easily because of the nature of their work. They include dive boats or underwater operations (e.g., laying cable or pipe), aircraft carriers (e.g., launching or landing only), mine sweepers, and buoy tenders.

If a tug boat is pulling a tow, it will display a day shape and two or three white signal lights. This will occur, however, only if it is maneuvering with difficulty or the tow is greater than 200 m (650 ft) astern.

Deep-Drafted Vessels

The night signal is three all-round red lights in a vertical line. "Rudder rubbing rocks" is the memory phrase.

It is unlikely that you will encounter a supertanker displaying a black cylinder day shape (optional) or three red lights. If you do encounter one, you will quickly understand its right of way because of its enormous size. Deep-drafted vessels that display day shapes and signal lights can barely maneuver in the confines of a narrow channel because of their size and draft.

Fishing Vessels

While stationary and fishing, fishing vessels show an all-round, red-over-white light. "Red-over-white, fishing at night" is the memory phrase.

A boat with nets out behind it is considered to be a fishing vessel. A boat with nets dragging behind or alongside also is considered to be a fishing vessel. Such vessels are occupationally restricted, and they will display a basket (if under 20 m, or approximately 65 ft) for a day shape. A fishing vessel at night will display red-over-white signal lights; trawlers will display green-over-white lights plus a series of special signals when in inland waters. A sport fishing boat that is trolling (i.e., lines behind the boat) is not occupational, shows no day shape or signal lights for fishing, and therefore deserves no preference other than common-sense courtesy in the right-of-way pecking order.

Sailboats

The light signal for sailboats is all-round red-over-green. "Red-over-green, sailboats are seen" is the memory phrase. Different light patterns and locations are required for sailboats of various lengths.

Sailboats do not always have the right of way over a power-driven boat. A sailboat has the right of way over such a vessel only if it is solely under sail. If the sailboat is motoring, it should display the cone-down day shape. The sailboat using its engine is now considered to be a power boat, and it is treated accordingly. Determining the right of way also must include the possibility of encountering offshore traffic lanes and restricted-visibility considerations.

Power-Driven Vessels

Recreational boaters and sailboaters constitute the greatest number of other boaters that you will encounter. Unless you are being overtaken (i.e., passed from behind), you must stay well clear and give the right of way to anyone higher than you in the pecking order.

Sound and Fog Signals

Many commercial vessels communicate their intentions (e.g., turning port, starboard, backing down) by radio. Some vessels still use internationally recognized sound signals (Fig. 15-3).

Fig. 15-3. Sound signals are also used under various types of restricted visibility.

FIGURE 15.3	
International Sound Signals Legend	
Whistle	
Prolonged blast four to six seconds	—
Short blast one second	•
Bell	B
Gong	G
Rapid ringing of bell five seconds	BBBBB
Rapid ringing of gong five seconds	GGGGG
Clear ring of bell five times	▲▲▲▲▲
Restricted Visibility, Every Minute	
Under 100 meters	
Anchored	BBBBB
Aground	▲▲▲▲▲BBBBB▲▲▲▲▲
Over 100 meters	
Anchored	
Bow	BBBBB
Stern	GGGGG
Anchored	
Bow	▲▲▲▲▲BBBBB▲▲▲▲▲
Stern	GGGGG
Restricted Visibility, Every Two Minutes	
Power vessel underway	—
Power vessel underway but not making way	— —
Limited or restricted in maneuverability	— ••
Good Visibility	
Turning starboard	•
Turning port	••
Backing down	•••
Danger	•••••
Approaching a bend where visibility is obscured or Backing out of a slip, overtaking, narrow channel	—
May I go starboard	— — •
May I go port	— — ••
Yes	— • — •

Flags and Signals

What should you display during day and night dives? The day shapes and lights are required for vessels over 12 m (38 ft) in length. Dive vessels, however, are specifically mandated to display signals regardless of size unless they have received a certificate of alternative compliance or exemption from the US Coast Guard.

The rule states that a rigid replica of the international code "A" flag not less than 1 m in height is to be displayed. Measures shall be taken to ensure its all-round visibility.

The international code flag "A" is blue and white; it is not the scuba diver's red flag with a white diagonal stripe that is familiar to recreational divers and boaters. The international meaning of this blue-and-white code flag, as found in the international code of signals, is "Diver Down, Keep Clear." A rigid replica of the code flag "A" is authorized for use aboard small vessels (i.e., 12 m) that may not be able to carry or display all of the required day shapes and light signals for vessels engaged in underwater operations. The other flag is not authorized by the rules. The flag must be 1 m in height, and "rigid replica" means a wooden or metal reproduction or flag that does not bend or flap and would remain visible even without a breeze. "All-round visibility" means it can be seen from anywhere. A flag painted on your boat does not meet the above criteria; it also should be lighted.

Many states, however, require that beach divers and boaters use the recreational diver's red-with-white-stripe flag. Therefore, you should check your individual state's regulations. You may be required to fly both the code "A" and the red-with-white-stripe flags.

For night boat diving, the same rules apply. The red-over-white-over-red signal light is used in conjunction with the anchor light. If you anchor without signal lights, make sure that you:
1. Hoist your "divers down" flags.
2. Illuminate the flags.
3. Show a spotlight in the direction of the divers.

ANCHORING AND PREPARING FOR A DIVE

round tackle is a broad term that includes all of the gear used in anchoring. Regardless of the size of your boat, general procedures and criteria are required to safely anchor it. These are:
1. Water depth and bottom characteristics.
2. Effects of wind and current.
3. Locations of established channels and harbor entrances.

4. Existing traffic patterns.
5. Submarine cables and pipelines.

Properly "dropping the hook" is done by slowly lowering the anchor until it reaches bottom and letting out sufficient anchor line to achieve the proper **scope**, which is the ratio between depth and the amount of line that is deployed. After it seems to be set, slowly pull on the anchor by backing the engine to assure this.

The three main reasons that anchors do not hold are:
1. It was dropped incorrectly, causing the anchor, chain, and line to tangle.
2. Not enough scope. It is recommended that you have a minimum scope (i.e., length of line) of seven times the depth of the water for ideal conditions, and a minimum of seven to nine times the depth of the water for rough weather. The anchor and chain should lay on the bottom and pull parallel to it.
3. Using the wrong anchor. For the majority of recreational boats used for diving, the light-weight Danforth anchor is the most widely used and effective (Fig. 15-4).

The best way to anchor a boat for diving is to be able to tie off to a mooring buoy, which preserves the environment and saves both time and energy. Unfortunately, mooring buoys are not always available, and the procedures for **anchoring** a dive boat are:
1. Slow down before you reach the dive site. If other boats are in the area, they may have divers already in the water. If boating near shore, remember that shore divers may not have a float and flag.
2. Look for bubbles before "dropping the hook" to ensure that it does not land on and injure a diver. This is less likely if you let it out slowly.
3. Try to anchor in sand whenever possible. Whenever coral is touched by an anchor, hands, or fins, it is damaged. Preservation and conservation are important. It is highly recommended you have an anchor-line buoy or float. In the event that a diver gets downcurrent and is in need of assistance, you will be able to tie off the anchor line to the float. This is faster, leaves a reference for other divers, marks the anchor, and saves precious time when recalling all of the divers and pulling the anchor. Note, however, that this procedure and whatever recall system will be used must be explained to all of the divers.
4. Hoist your divers-down flags, then put out a trail or current line. A trail line is usually a minimum of 50 feet in length. A float with another divers-down flag on the trail line also is very useful.

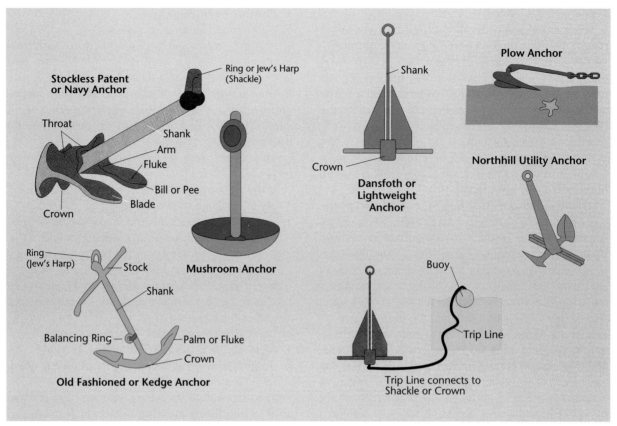

Fig. 15-4. Types of anchors and their parts.

5. Prepare your divers-down line, if used, at mid-ship. The anchor line also can be used for descending and ascending by divers.

6. Many boats deploy a precautionary decompression line with extra scuba cylinders and regulators at a depth of 15 feet, encouraging divers to make a recommended safety stop.

KNOTS

Perhaps the most mystifying of all nautical skills is tying knots. Of the over 2000 kinds that are known, you can comfortably and safely get by with nine basic knots. The ability to know which knot to tie for the proper application is an important and admired skill. Your knot-tying abilities are useful above as well as below the water. The following explanations describe these nine types of knots as well as when and where to use them.

Only practice will make you proficient at tying knots. Because many of these knots are used under the water as well as above, it is a good idea for you and your buddy to practice tying these knots underwater while wearing your diving gloves (Fig. 15-5).

Also, note that when you cut a line, it tends to

come unraveled. This problem can be solved by **whipping**, which is twine that is wrapped around the end of a line, keeping it from unraveling.

Figure-Eight Knot

The figure-eight knot is used to prevent a line from unlaying or running through a block. This type of knot will not jam.

Bowline

The bowline knot makes a temporary eye in a line. It might be used as a temporary substitute for an eye splice in mooring line, and it is one of the strongest, practical, and most useful of knots that you will use.

Square Knot (Reef Knot)

The square knot is a quick way to join two ends. It is secure only if the two lines are the same size and the knot is pressing against something, such as the rolled part of a reefed sail. A square knot may "capsize" and come apart under strain if it is not supported.

Becket Bend (Sheet Bend)

The Becket bend is used to join two ends when the knot must stand alone in "midair." This knot will work with lines of different sizes.

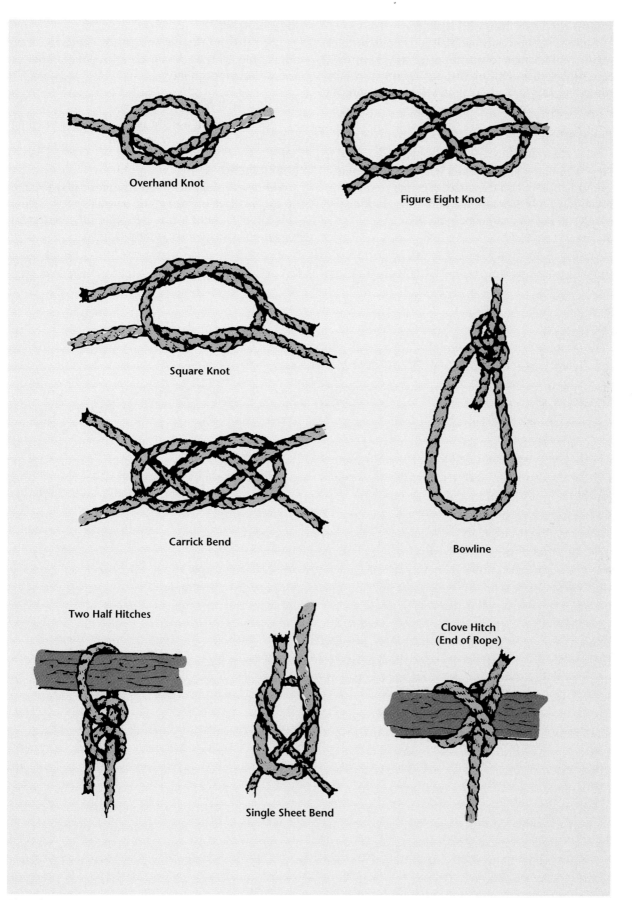

Fig. 15-5. Knots

Round Turn and Two Half Hitches

The round turn and two half hitches is a quick way to make fast to anything of any shape. It remains secure with or without strain from any direction. This knot also can jam, however, and can be difficult to untie.

Clove Hitch

The clove hitch is quick to make and will not jam. It remains secure when it is made around a cylindric object and the strain remains steady, but it can loosen if the standing part goes slack or the strain comes from varying directions.

Rolling Hitch

The rolling hitch is quick, secure, and adjustable. This knot can be slid along a spar or line without loosening.

Bowline on a Bight

The bowline on a bight is handy if you need an eye but the ends are not available.

Sheepshank

The sheepshank is used (theoretically) to take up excess slack or strengthen a weak spot in a line. This knot will hold if it is very carefully made and the strain is absolutely steady.

SUMMARY

Ⓦithin the marine industry, there are many boat captains; however, only a select few stand out as "captains among captains." Your goal is to become known as a "diving boater among diving boaters." The information presented here is only an introduction to small-boat handling and seamanship. It is intended to introduce you to the very basics. Hopefully, you will take the challenge and continue your diving and boating education through more programs and courses.

SUGGESTED READINGS

- Barsky S: *Boat diving*, Best Publishing, in press.
- Fagan B: *Cruising guide to California's Channel Islands*, 1983.
- Rinehart LT: *The Captain's LORAN book. Florida east and west coast including Alabama, Mississippi, Texas*, 1988.
- US Coast Guard Auxiliary: *Boating skills and seamanship*, ed 10.

CHAPTER SIXTEEN

CONSERVATION

Divers generally are conservation minded, and they understand the importance of maintaining a clean, unspoiled underwater environment. The underwater environment is a complex system, involving a wide variety of physical, chemical, and biological factors that work together to keep things in balance. Divers are visitors to this community, and we must take the responsibility to see that this environment is not altered drastically.

Conservation is defined as managing human usage of the waters so that they may yield the greatest sustainable benefit to present and future generations. For conservation to occur, knowledge, commitment, and action are required, and we can take action to help preserve the world under water.

LEARNING OBJECTIVES

By the end of this chapter, you will be able to:

1. Correctly define the conservation terms presented in **bold letters**.
2. Define marine pollution and describe the common types.
3. State at least three actions that a diver can take to preserve the underwater environment.
4. List four direct, negative effects that divers can have on the environment.

MAN'S EFFECTS ON THE ENVIRONMENT

Man can have many **direct effects** on the environment. Disposal of toxic chemicals, sewage effluent, and trash can be both unsightly and harmful to aquatic life. If we dump pollutants into the waters, organisms that live there will either die, become poisonous to eat, or move away. Items that have caused particular problems include plastic six-pack rings, which can snare birds, and plastic bags, which turtles can mistake for their jellyfish prey. These items have been documented to cause death in many species. Dropping anchors on coral reefs also causes severe damage, which kills corals and leads to the reefs losing their beauty. In areas of heavy diver activity, it is better to install permanent moorings for boats (Figs. 16-1 through 16-3).

MARINE POLLUTION

What is **marine pollution**? It is defined as substances or energy that are introduced by man into the marine environment, resulting in deleterious effects or harm to living resources, hazards to human health, or hindrance of marine activities like fishing. Common substances include things like pesticides, plastic, oil, and toxic wastes. It is estimated that approximately 70,000 chemical compounds are in daily use today, and thousands of new compounds are synthesized every year.

A **pollutant** can be a man-made or natural substance. Man-made pollutants include such things as marine litter, pesticides, hydrocarbons, and paints. A **contaminant** is a naturally occurring sub-

Fig. 16-1. Anchoring in sand helps to prevent damage to coral reefs.

Fig. 16-2. Permanent moorings have been installed at many popular dive sites.

Fig. 16-3. Many dive boats can use the permanent moorings.

stance that is found in concentrations above the natural background level for the area or particular organism. Contaminants include sediments, nutrients, organic matter, microorganisms, trace metals, and radioactivity.

Pollution can enter the ocean from a variety of sources. Point-source pollution is emitted from a discrete source like a sewage outfall. Nonpoint-source pollution comes from sources like runoff from storms, ground-water seeps, offshore oil spills, dredge-spoil disposal, offshore dumping of sewage, and industrial wastes.

One of the problems with marine pollution is how to measure and quantify it. Many of the techniques that are used to measure compounds have just recently been developed, so there is not sufficient background data on the natural levels of contaminants for comparison.

Many pollutants are introduced into estuaries, which are the wetland areas where freshwater and saltwater mix. Estuaries are some of the most productive habitats on Earth. Pollutants can be transferred through the complex food webs that exist here, and they can be exported outside of the estuaries to the open ocean by currents and fish who use the estuary as a breeding ground.

A major problem associated with marine pollution is called **bioaccumulation**. This is where marine organisms concentrate pollutants in their tissues through uptake by filtering water, feeding, or passive absorption. **Biomagnification** is where bioaccumulation is passed up through the food chain through various trophic levels, with the concentration of the compound increasing in each level. This is why the top organisms in the food chain (e.g., fish) tend to have the highest concentrations of pollutants.

It may take decades for some pollutants to accumulate and deleterious effects on the environment to show. These effects also may be difficult to quantify, and they may be somewhat subjective. Certain compounds can selectively target different groups of animals or plants depending on the habitat and natural history of the organism.

Laboratory bioassays are experiments that are designed to expose organisms to various concentrations of pollutants under controlled conditions. They usually measure lethal effects on the organism or different life stages of an organism, such as the egg, larvae, or adult. These experiments are used to develop water-quality standards for acceptable limits to be allowed in nature.

DIVERS' EFFECTS ON THE ENVIRONMENT

Divers in particular can have many direct effects on the environment. In diving, a good conservation ethic is to "leave it better than you found it." This might include picking up trash on the beach or underwater. Nondestructive diving minimizes a diver's impact on the environment by practicing good buoyancy control; not allowing fins, gauges, bags, and so on to contact the bottom; not touching the bottom or organisms; and demonstrating care for the aquatic world. Do not touch coral polyps, because this may cause them to die.

It is also not environmentally sound to hand feed fish; this can make them dependent on humans for their food. It also can tend to make them "tame," which alters their natural behavior and may put them at increased risk of being speared. In addition, there is the risk of being bitten while hand-feeding animals. Remember, these are wild animals that can (and should be!) unpredictable.

It is best to resist shell collecting as well. Empty shells provide homes for some creatures that cannot build their own. If we take large amounts of any organism from the waters, those organisms will become more difficult for others to find in the future. The best policy is to look but not touch.

When photographing underwater, do not move animals around to compose a "better" photograph. This might be harmful to them, such as by exposing them to potential predators after removing

Fig. 16-4. Spearfishing should be conducted with respect for all laws and regulations.

Fig. 16-5. Spearfishers take pride in their sport. Many also practice a conservation ethic.

them from a cryptic habitat or by removing them from their food source. Another practice to be discouraged is turning over rocks. This destroys habitat and exposes animals to predation.

Spearfishers and game collectors should set good examples by taking only enough game for a meal. Filling your freezer, giving game away, or helping someone else to get their limit are not consistent with conservation. When the limit on something is 10, it does not mean you should strive to take 10. It means that under no circumstances should you ever take more than 10. It is fine to take less if less meets your immediate needs. Have respect for local laws and regulations (Figs. 16-4 through 16-7).

Fig. 16-6. Collecting can be very exciting and rewarding.

There are many sources of reading material to increase your education in conservation. These include diving publications, newspapers, books, and magazines. Obtain solid information to form opinions that will better inform and influence others. These materials are available at libraries, marine laboratories, and public aquariums. Other options include enrolling in college or university courses and attending seminars such as the NAUI International Conference on Underwater Education or conservation group meetings.

Fig. 16-7. Marine parks are excellent places to dive as they often have strict rules regarding the protection of the marine life and environment.

SUMMARY

Ⓐ commitment to preserve the underwater world is an individual matter. You must decide for yourself that you will do your part to protect the diving environment. Once you have decided, you can take action to educate others. Action is commitment put to work. There are many local and national groups that are committed to protecting the environment, and if one is not in your area, you might consider starting your own.

SUGGESTED READINGS

- Allaby M: *Dictionary of the environment*, New York University Press, 1983.
- Daiber FC: *Conservation of tidal marshes*, Van Nostrand Reinhold Company, 1986.
- Dasmann RF: *Environmental conservation*, Wiley Publishing, 1968.
- National Wildlife Federation: *Conservation directory*, 1988.
- Soule ME, Wilcox, BA: *Conservation biology*, Sinauer Associates Publishers, 1980.
- Vernberg WB, Calabrese A, Thurberg FP, Vernberg FJ: *Marine pollution: functional responses*, Academic Press, 1979.

Glossary

Absolute pressure: the total pressure, including atmospheric and hydrostatic pressures, exerted at any point.

Absolute zero: the lowest temperature that could possibly be reached (-459 degrees F or -273 degrees C).

Absorption: the taking up of nitrogen in tissues.

Air embolism: a lung overexpansion injury characterized by blockage of an artery by a bubble of air.

Algae: non-flowering aquatic plants.

Alternobaric vertigo: vertigo produced after a sudden release of pressure in an ear during an ascent.

Alveolus: microscopic air sac in the lungs.

Ambient pressure: the pressure of the fluid surrounding an object.

Amonton's Law: "For any gas at a constant volume, the pressure of the gas will vary directly with the absolute temperature."

Analog depth gauge: an instrument with hands that point to numbers as a direct result of mechanical force.

Angle of attack: the angle between a diver's longitudinal axis and his or her trim.

Anoxia: low tissue oxygen levels.

Anxiety: fear or apprehension that one experiences in the face of real or imagined danger.

Archimedes Principle: "Any object wholly or partly immersed in a fluid is buoyed up by a force equal to the weight of the fluid displaced by the object."

Asphyxia: suffocation occurring from a blockage of the windpipe. Drowning is a special case of asphyxia.

Backrush: the return flow of water from waves rushing onto a shore. Sometimes mistakenly referred to as "undertow."

Balanced valve: a valve that controls pressure in such a way that the pressure does not affect the force needed to open and close the valve.

Barotrauma: physical damage to the body as a direct result of pressure changes.

Bearing: the angular direction to an object expressed in terms of compass degrees from north, e.g., a bearing of 270 degrees.

Benthic: pertaining to life found in or at the bottom of the oceans.

Bends: see *Decompression sickness.*

Bezel: a rotating ring on a compass or watch that can be set as a reference.

Bloom: a condition of poor visibility resulting from overpopulation of algae or plankton.

Bottom timer: a device that automatically records a diver's bottom time.

Bourdon movement gauge: an instrument that uses a curved metal tube as a pressure detector.

Boyle's Law: "For any gas at a constant temperature, the volume will vary inversely with the absolute pressure while the density will vary directly with the absolute pressure."

Bradycardia: slowing of the heart rate caused by cold water contact on the face and body.

Bronchi: air passage vessels in the chest.

Buoyancy: the upward force exerted on an immersed or floating body by a fluid.

Burst disk: a thin metal disk found in all valves as a safety feature and designed to rupture and relieve excessive pressure in a cylinder.

Capillaries: tiny blood vessels that join arteries to veins in the body.

Capillary depth gauge: an instrument that indicates depth via the compression of air in a transparent tube.

Carotid arteries: the principal arteries supplying blood to the brain.

Carotid sinus: a small dilation in the carotid artery in the neck.

Ceiling: a depth indicated by a dive computer above which one may not safely ascend.

Charles' Law: "For any gas at a constant pressure, the volume of the gas will vary directly with the absolute temperature."

Chart: the equivalent of a map for bodies of water and adjacent coastlines.

Closed-circuit scuba: a system in which all exhaled breath is recirculated within the system and rebreathed.

Collapsing breakers: a type of surf forming from medium swells breaking over a very steep bottom. The waves break over their lower halves with very little splash or foaming.

Compass card: a magnetized disk within a compass that rotates to indicate a northerly direction.

Conduction: the transmission of heat by direct material contact.

Conservation: management of human use of the waters so that they may yield the greatest sustainable benefit to present and future generations. Preserving, guarding, or protecting natural resources.

Console: a housing for two or more diving instruments.

Convection: the transmission of heat by the movement of heated fluids.

Coriolis effect: deflection of winds and currents caused by the Earth's rotation.

Cramp: a muscle spasm producing pain and temporary disability.

Cyanosis: a bluish discoloration of the skin from insufficient oxygenation of the blood.

Cylinder: a vessel that holds matter under pressure.

Cylinder pressure gauge: an instrument used to measure air pressure in a cylinder above water.

Dalton's Law: "The total pressure exerted by a mixture of gases is equal to the sum of the pressure that would be exerted by each of the gases if it alone were present and occupied the volume."

Dead reckoning: navigation by means of estimating distance and direction.

Decompression sickness: a serious bodily affliction caused by nitrogen bubble formation in the body and too rapid a reduction of pressure.

Deep air diving: practiced by technical divers to depths up to 200 feet.

Dehydration: abnormal loss of fluid from the body.

Density: the quantity of a substance per unit volume.

Deviation: error induced in a compass needle reading by the effect of nearby metal or a magnetic source.

Dew point: the temperature to which air must be cooled, at a constant pressure, to become saturated with water and below which condensation occurs.

Diaphragm depth gauge: an instrument that uses the movement of a metal diaphragm in conjunction with mechanical linkage to indicate depth.

Diffusion: the scattering of light. Also the movement of molecules in a liquid or gas from a region of high concentration to a region of lower concentration.

Digital depth gauge: an instrument that uses a pressure transducer, electronics, and a battery to display depth in a digital form.

Diuretics: substances that increase the output of urine by the kidneys.

Dive computer: an instrument that continuously calculates time and depth and provides a digital display of a diver's decompression status.

Dive pattern: the total course or dive path followed during a dive.

Diving reflex: physiological changes, most notably slowing of the heart, produced by water in contact with the face.

Downstream valve: a valve that opens in the direction of gas flow.

Drag: the force of resistance to movement.

Drowning: death caused by aspiration of fluid.

Dry suit: a variable volume exposure suit worn in cold water.

Dump valve: a manually operated exhaust valve for a buoyancy compensator that allows air to be quickly expelled.

Ebb tide: an outgoing tide.

Ecology: the study of living organisms in their environments.

Edema: swelling caused by excessive amounts of fluid in the tissues.

Elimination: the release of nitrogen from tissues.

Embolus: obstruction in the circulatory system.

Emphysema: a swelling or inflation caused by the presence of air or other gas in body tissues.

Energy: the capacity to do work.

Enriched air nitrox (EAN or EANx): a breathing gas consisting of a mixture of nitrogen and oxygen other than that found in air.

Epiglottis: a thin plate of cartilage that folds over and protects the windpipe when swallowing.

Epilimnion: the warmer layer of water above a thermocline.

Equilibrium: a state of balance between opposing pressures.

Euphoria: a feeling of elation and well-being.

Feeder zone: a region in the surf zone that feeds water to a rip current.

Fetch: the time and distance over which wind blows in the process of generating waves.

Fix: the position resulting from known distances and directions to two or more land-based objects.

Flood tide: an incoming tide.

Fluid: a state in which matter, either gaseous or liquid, is capable of flowing.

Food chain: the transfer of energy along a chain of animals in the marine community.

Frenzel maneuver: a method of equalizing pressure in the middle ear.

FSW: Feet Salt Water.

Gas tension: the partial pressure of a gas in a liquid.

Gauge pressure: pressure in excess of atmospheric pressure or that which uses atmospheric pressure as a zero reference.

Gay-Lussac's Law: see *Charles' Law.*

General gas law: a combination of Boyle's and Charles' Laws used to predict the behavior of a given quantity of gas when changes may be expected in any or all of the variables.

Haldanian theory: a theory by John S. Haldane, a British physiologist. His theory of gas absorption and elimination by body tissues forms the basis for decompression tables.

Half-times: the rate of absorption or elimination of gas in tissues at an exponential rate. A "5 minute" tissue is 50% saturated in 5 minutes, 75% saturated in 10 minutes, etc., until essentially saturated after six half-times.

Halocline: the horizontal interface between waters of different densities, especially between fresh water and salt water.

Heading: a navigational course followed or to be followed.

Heat exhaustion: an illness characterized by fatigue, weakness, and collapse caused by inadequate fluid intake to compensate for loss of fluids from perspiration.

Hemoglobin: a component of red blood cells that combines with oxygen, carbon dioxide, or carbon monoxide.

Henry's Law: "The amount of gas that will dissolve in a liquid at a given temperature is almost directly proportional to the partial pressure of that gas."

Holdfast: a rootlike structure that secures algae to the bottom.

Hookah diving: diving with air supplied via an umbilical hose to the surface.

Hydrostatic test: a pressure expansion test for scuba cylinders.

Humidity: the amount of water vapor in a gaseous atmosphere.

Hypercapnia: undue amount of carbon dioxide in the blood, causing overactivity in the respiratory center.

Hyperthermia: an upward variation of body temperature.

Hypertonic: a solution saltier than blood.

Hyperventilation: breathing excessively fast.

Hypocapnia: lower-than-normal carbon dioxide level in the blood that is caused by hyperventilation.

Hypolimnion: the colder layer of water below a thermocline.

Hypothermia: a downward variation in body temperature.

Hypotonic: a solution less salty than blood.

Hypoventilation: inadequate ventilation of the lungs.

Hypoxia: low tissue oxygen levels.

Inert: a substance that does not normally combine with other substances.

Ingassing: the process of gas dissolving into a liquid.

Inner ear: a system of fluid-filled bony channels in the temporal bone. Marked pressure changes between the middle and inner ear can lead to vertigo and hearing loss.

Inspiratory reserve: the maximum amount of air that can be breathed in after normal inspiration.

Integrated regulator: a scuba regulator that is incorporated into an item of diving equipment, such as a BC low pressure inflator.

Isotherm: a line on a chart linking areas of equal temperature.

J valve: scuba cylinder on/off valve with reserve mechanism.

K valve: scuba cylinder on/off valve.

Kelp: a giant brown algae that reaches heights of nearly 100 feet.

Kick cycle: the time from when a fin kicks downward during a flutter kick until that same fin kicks downward again.

Kinetic theory of gases: the basic explanation of the behavior of gases under all variations of temperature and pressure.

Leeway: side-slippage in the direction of a current when moving across the current.

Littoral: pertaining to the sea shore, such as a littoral current.

Longshore current: a current flowing parallel to the shore in the surf zone that is caused by surf approaching the shore at an angle.

Low pressure inflator: a valve on a buoyancy compensator that controls low pressure air from a scuba regulator and can be manually opened to inflate the BC.

Lubber line: a fixed reference line on a compass.

Magnetic north: a point near the North Pole toward which a magnetic needle points.

Manifold: a high pressure connecting pipe between two or more air cylinders.

Mass: the quotient obtained by dividing the weight of a body by the acceleration caused by gravity.

Matter: the substance of which any physical object is composed.

Maximum depth indicator: an indicator of a mechanical depth gauge that is pushed along by the needle of the gauge and which remains at the maximum reading attained by the instrument.

Mediastinal emphysema: a lung overexpansion injury characterized by air in the middle of the chest.

Middle ear: air-filled space between tympanic membrane and semicircular canals.

Neap tides: those tides with the minimum range between high and low water.

Near drowning: the clinical condition that follows the aspiration of fluid into the lungs.

Necktonic: free-swimming forms of life, including fish, that rely on speed and streamlining for their survival.

Nitrogen narcosis: a dangerous state of stupor produced by the narcotic effect of nitrogen in the body under pressure.

Octopus: an extra second stage attached to a scuba regulator.

Open circuit demand scuba: a system in which compressed air is inhaled upon demand from a self-contained unit and exhausted into the environment.

Orifice: an opening or aperture of a tube, pipe, etc.

Outgassing: gas dissolved in a liquid coming out of solution.

Oxygen toxicity: a serious bodily ailment characterized by convulsions and resulting when oxygen is breathed at increased partial pressures.

Panic: The emotional and volatile human reaction that occurs in the presence of a real or imagined danger; characterized by a total loss of logic and mental control.

Parenteral toxins: toxins delivered by means of a venom apparatus.

Paresthesia and hypesthesia: a feeling of "pins and needles" in the body.

Partial pressure: the pressure exerted by each individual gas within a mixture of gases.

Pascal's Principle: "Pressure in a fluid is transmitted uniformly in all directions."

Peer pressure: the pressure placed by peers on fellow divers.

Phytoplankton: Algae that use sunlight to produce carbohydrates. They represent the basic food source for all life in the oceans.

Pilotage: navigation confirmed with visual check points.

Pilot-valve regulator: a regulator second-stage main valve that is opened and closed using air pressure rather than mechanical leverage.

Planktonic: drifting and floating forms of life carried passively by currents.

Pleura: two layers of thin membrane surrounding the lungs.

Plunging breakers: surf that peaks quickly and breaks suddenly when large swells approach a shore with a moderately steep slope.

Pneumothorax: lung overpressure where gas goes into the pleural cavity.

Pressure gradient: the difference between the tension of a gas in a liquid and the partial pressure of the gas outside the liquid.

Propulsion: the act of driving forward.

Range: a course indicated by a set of in-line objects.

Red tide: an extremely heavy bloom of plankton or algae.

Refraction: the bending of rays of light when they pass from a medium of one density into a medium of a different density.

Residual volume: the amount of air remaining in the lungs after a maximal expiratory effort.

Resuscitation: the combination of external cardiac compressions and artificial respiration.

Reverse thermocline: an abrupt transition from a colder layer of water to a warmer layer of water where the colder layer is shallower than the warmer layer.

Rip current: a strong, narrow current moving away from shore and formed when water in a surf zone is funneled through a narrow gap.

Round window: An opening in the inner ear covered by a thin membrane and to which the small bones of hearing that transfer vibrations from the ear drum are attached. As the round window moves in, a corresponding inner ear window, called the oval window, moves outward.

Saturation: a state existing when the tension of a gas in a liquid reaches a value equal to the partial pressure of the gas outside the liquid.

Scrolling: a feature of a dive computer in which no-decompression limits for various depths are displayed sequentially and repeatedly.

SCUBA: Self-Contained Underwater Breathing Apparatus.

Secondary drowning: delayed death following the aspiration of fluid into the lungs.

Seiches: The oscillation of the surface of a lake or a landlocked sea that is caused by wind blowing over the water.

Seismic waves: giant waves resulting from underwater earthquakes and mistakenly referred to as "tidal waves." Also known as "tsunamis."

Semi-closed scuba: a system in which a portion of the exhaled breath is retained within the system and rebreathed.

Set and drift: The direction and velocity of a current.

Silent bubbles: microscopic bubbles formed within the body as a result of decompression and theorized to contribute to the larger bubbles that cause decompression sickness.

Single-hose regulator: a regulator with a single hose joining the first and second stages.

Sinuses: air-filled cavities in the skull.

Skip breathing: the deliberate reduction of breathing.

Slack water: the period of time existing at high tide during which water movement is at a minimum.

Solid, Liquid, Gas: the three fundamental states of matter.

Specific gravity: The density of a specific substance compared with that of pure water.

Specific heat: The ratio of the amount of heat transferred to raise a unit of mass of a substance one degree to that required to raise a unit mass of pure water one degree.

Spilling breakers: a form of surf where waves break far from shore on a shallowly sloping bottom and continue to break to the beach.

Spring tides: tides with the greatest range between high and low water.

Stage: a pressure-reduction step in a regulator or compressor.

Stipes: strands of kelp.

Strangulation: stoppage of breathing caused by obstruction of the airway.

Stress: a physical and emotional state that evokes effort on the part of an individual to maintain or restore equilibrium.

Subcutaneous emphysema: a lung overexpansion injury characterized by air around the base of the neck.

Submersible pressure gauge: an instrument used to measure cylinder pressure while submerged.

Suffocation: stoppage of breathing for any cause and the resulting asphyxia.

Supersaturated solution: a solution holding more gas than is possible at equilibrium for a particular temperature and pressure.

Surf: breaking waves releasing their energy in shallow water.

Surf beat: the periodic rise and fall in the height of waves and surf caused by the reinforcement or reduction of wave amplitude when two trains of waves approach an area at the same time.

Surface equivalent: the effect that the partial pressure of a gas has on the body at depth in relation to an equivalent amount of gas at sea level, e.g., breathing 1% carbon monoxide at four atmospheres is the surface equivalent of breathing 4% carbon monoxide.

Surface tension: the contractive forces at the surface of a liquid.

Surf zone: that area in which the water within waves is moving forward with the waves in the form of surf.

Surge: the back-and-forth subsurface movement of water caused by waves passing overhead.

Surging breakers: surf formed by small swells approaching a very steep bottom. These waves slide up and down the steep incline with little or no foam production.

Swash: the water on the face of a beach that washes back into the main body of water.

Swells: the low, rounded form in which wave energy is transferred through water.

Tachycardia: excessive rapidity of heartbeat.

Thermocline: a horizontal, abrupt transition from a warmer layer of water to a colder layer of water.

Thoracic squeeze: a lung injury resulting from compression of the lungs when the lungs are only partially filled with air.

Tidal current: movement of water produced by tidal changes.

Tidal volume: the amount of air breathed in and out during normal respiration.

Time to fly: the time before you are allowed to fly that is displayed on a dive computer.

Tinnitus: ringing in the ear.

Toynbee maneuver: a method of equalizing pressure in the middle ear.

Trapdoor effect: the inability to equalize pressure in the middle ear because the opening to the eustachian tube leading to the middle ear is being held closed by ambient pressure.

Trial line: a line with a float at the end extended behind a boat to assist divers in returning to the vessel if they should surface downcurrent. Also called a "current line" or "tag line."

Trim: the control of an assumed position or body attitude.

True north: a geographical location with reference to the Earth's axis rather than the magnetic poles and not the same as magnetic north.

Turbidity: a reduction in underwater visibility caused by suspended sediment.

Two-hose regulator: a regulator with both stages and the exhaust valve in a single housing and with two hoses leading to a mouthpiece.

Tympanic membrane: eardrum.

Unbalanced valve: a valve controlling high pressure in such a way that the pressure affects the force needed to open and close the valve.

Upstream valve: a valve that operates against the direction of gas flow.

Upwelling: the vertical movement of water in a body of water and the subsequent replacement of that water from beneath. Caused by wind blowing the surface water away from shore.

Valve snorkel: the tube extending from the bottom of a scuba cylinder valve designed to prevent foreign matter from entering the valve when the tank is inverted.

Variation: the local difference in degrees between true and magnetic north.

Vertigo: dizziness.

Vestibular system: a series of semi-circular canals within the inner ear that provide a person with orientation and a sense of balance.

Visual inspection: internal and external inspection performed on a scuba cylinder at least once per year.

Vital capacity: Maximum volume of air that can be expired after maximal inhalation.

Wave length: the distance between two successive waves.

Wave period: the time required for two consecutive waves to pass a fixed point.

Waves: forms of energy moving in water and caused by the wind.

Wave sets: see *Surf beat.*

Wave trough: the lowest point of a wave.

Work: the application of force through a distance.

Zooplankton: animal plankton that generally feeds on phytoplankton.

Index

SAC = Surface Air Consumption

25 psI   at   75 ft.
3.5
―――
125
 75
―――
87.5
 90.
  2
―――
1800

New Allumin 3000's
     will blow at 5.000.

5 psi rise for every 1° F

Pressure = Force / Area $\left(P = F / A \right)$

10 psi

3 squin

1 squ in
       30